Expert

SQL Server™ 2005
Integration Services

Expert
SQL Server™ 2005
Integration Services

Brian Knight

Erik Veerman

Wiley Publishing, Inc.

Expert SQL Server™ 2005 Integration Services

Published by
Wiley Publishing, Inc.
10475 Crosspoint Boulevard
Indianapolis, IN 46256
www.wiley.com

ISBN: 978-0-470-13411-5

Manufactured in the United States of America

10 9 8 7 6 5 4 3 2

Library of Congress Cataloging-in-Publication Data is available from the publisher.

About the Authors

Brian Knight (SQL Server MVP, MCSE, MCDBA) of Green Cove Springs, Florida, is the co-founder of SQLServerCentral.com and JumpstartTV.com. He runs the local SQL Server users group in Jacksonville (JSSUG) and was on the Board of Directors of the Professional Association for SQL Server (PASS). He is a contributing columnist for *SQL Server Standard* and also maintains a regular column for the database web site, SQLServerCentral.com, as well as doing regular webcasts at JumpstartTV.com. He has co-authored and authored more than nine SQL Server books, including *Admin911: SQL Server 2000* (McGraw-Hill Companies, 2001), *Professional SQL Server 2000 DTS* (Wiley Publishing, 2000), *Professional SQL Server 2005 Administration* (Wiley Publishing, 2006), and *Professional SQL Server 2005 Integration Services* (Wiley Publishing, 2006). He has spoken at conferences such as PASS, SQL Connections, and TechEd, as well as at many Code Camps. His blog can be found at www.whiteknighttechnology.com. He is an independent consultant at Pragmatic Works and spends most of his time trying to think about how to use the word *onomatopoeia* in everyday sentences.

Erik Veerman (SQL Server MVP, MCT, MCDBA) is a Mentor for Solid Quality Learning focusing on training, mentoring, and architecting solutions on the SQL Server Business Intelligence (BI) platform. His industry recognition includes Microsoft's Worldwide BI Solution of the Year and *SQL Server Magazine*'s Innovator Cup winner. He has designed dozens of BI solutions across a broad business spectrum—telecommunications, marketing, retail, commercial real estate, finance, supply chain, and information technology. His experience with high-volume, multi-terabyte environments and SQL Server 64-bit has enabled clients to scale their Microsoft-based BI solutions for optimal potential. As an expert in OLAP design, ETL processing, and dimensional modeling, he is a presenter, author, and instructor. He led the ETL architecture and design for the first production implementation of SQL Server Integration Services (SSIS) and helped drive the ETL standards and best practices for SSIS on Microsoft's SQL Server 2005 reference initiative (Project REAL). He also co-authored *Professional SQL Server 2005 Integration Services* (Wiley Publishing, 2006). As a resident of Atlanta, Georgia, Erik is a leader of the local Atlanta SQL Server User's Group, a PASS and INETA user group chapter.

Contributing Author

Bayer White is Vice President of Information Technology, at Baywood Technologies (www.baywoodtech.com). He is responsible for architecture, development and implementation for wood procurement and security solutions. Bayer also participates in Software Design Reviews (SDR) for future versions of .NET. He has had the opportunity to contribute to the .NET community, by speaking at several Florida code camps, DevConnections, and for the past three years at Professional Association for SQL Server (PASS). Bayer is the co-founder of MSBICentral (www.msbicentral.com), a web community dedicated to Business Intelligence. Bayer blogs at www.whiteknighttechnology.com and he is also recognized as a community contributor by Microsoft's Connected Framework Team for Windows Workflow Foundation. When Bayer is not writing code and speaking, he enjoys spending time with his wife, Robyn, and two-year-old daughter, Sarah.

Credits

Executive Editor
Robert Elliott

Development Editor
Kevin Shafer

Technical Editor
Grant Dickinson

Contributing Author
Bayer White

Production Editor
Kathryn Duggan

Copy Editor
Travis Henderson

Editorial Manager
Mary Beth Wakefield

Production Manager
Tim Tate

Vice President and Executive Group Publisher
Richard Swadley

Vice President and Executive Publisher
Joseph B. Wikert

Graphics and Production Specialists
Carrie A. Foster
Melanee Prendergast
Alicia B. South

Quality Control Technician
Jessica Kramer

Project Coordinator
Jennifer Theriot

Proofreading and Indexing
Aptara

Anniversary Logo Design
Richard Pacifico

Acknowledgments

First, thanks to my wonderful wife, who has always supported me in everything I've ever done and has been patient with the laptop never being put down. You're the cornerstone of my day-to-day life, keeping me grounded. Thanks to my sons and my unborn child for allowing me to work these many late nights. An expression of huge appreciation goes to Grant Dickinson, who was the Technical Editor for this book. Grant went well above a Tech Editor, though, by providing valuable technical info and great constructive help. Thanks also to the makers of my favorite caffeine product, Mountain Dew, for keeping me awake late at night and early in the morning. Last, but most certainly not least, to Erik Veerman, who was an amazing co-author and took this book to the next level.

—Brian Knight

In many ways, this book represents the intersection of what I enjoy doing and the tool that makes it work. The content represents a culmination of years of ETL architecture, development, and mentoring for countless clients, whose interactions and challenges hopefully bring practicality and real-life exposure to these pages. Thank you to my clients for your (at times) painful data processing requirements!

It's been a great four years working with SSIS, and there's more to come. Thanks to Brian Knight for the book idea and for the tremendous community contribution. Also, much thanks to Grant Dickinson on the SSIS product team for his technical reviews of the chapters, which were thorough and insightful. Thanks to Dave Fackler (a partner in crime for years) and Paul Waters (with an unparalleled passion for BI), who both added value here through content reviews and talked through ideas and experiences.

Finally, and most importantly, thank you to my wife, Amy — there's literally no one like her. And I cannot forget my precious children — Meg, Nate, and Kate. My faith, my family, my job, those are the things (in that order) that bring motivation to life and make an effort like this worth it. Soli Deo Gloria.

—Erik Veerman

Contents

Contents

Contents

Contents

Introduction

Several books have been written about SQL Server Integration Services (SSIS)—in fact, the prequel to this book, *Professional SQL Server 2005 Integration Services* (Indianapolis: Wiley, 2006), is commendable in the detail it provides on the tool. However, although many of the technology books out there are written well and are great reference guides when trying to accomplish something, applying the technology to a solution may not always be straightforward.

Case in point, any power tool you buy at your local hardware store comes with a user manual. However, looking through the index, it is quite apparent that the purpose of the manual is to show off the knobs and buttons of the tool. For example, if it is a power saw, it may describe how to raise and lower the saw blade, and how to angle the arm to cut a 45-degree angle. But nowhere in the documentation will you learn to build a dresser or construct a bed! Clearly, you would not expect this in a manual, especially given that the saw can be used for hundreds (if not thousands) of different purposes.

As you would expect, the case is similar for SSIS. The online documentation and the SSIS books written so far do a great job at describing how to use the FTP task, for example, to pull a file from a remote server, and how to connect to the file to then extract the data into a table. What the documentation and books don't describe, however, is how to connect the dots and apply SSIS for a specific purpose. To be sure, many users of SSIS will be very happy with the online documentation to do some standard one-off tasks here and there. But when it comes to using the tool to build a solution, more information is required.

This book is about application—applying the functionality of SSIS to help you envision, develop, and implement your data processing needs.

Whom This Book Is For

For this book, we will be applying SSIS functionality to several common industry areas, including data warehouse extraction, transformation, and loading (ETL), data integration ETL, and advanced ETL development and administration. Therefore, we have targeted this book at three primary SSIS users:

- ❑ *ETL data architects*
- ❑ *ETL developers*
- ❑ *Database administrators (DBAs) responsible for SSIS*

Many of you reading this book may have the background of other industry ETL tools such as Ab Initio, Informatica, and Ascential. Others of you may be all-too familiar with Data Transformation Services (DTS) as your ETL tool. Some of you may be SQL script experts (such as T-SQL or PL-SQL) and are able to build processing algorithms with scripting inside of a relational engine. If you have this background, then you will be familiar with general ETL concepts already, and this book will be your window into transferring your understanding of data warehouse ETL to SSIS.

If you are new to the world of ETL because of a new initiative in your company, or maybe even a self-imposed desire to get familiar with this skill, then you will learn from this book about the basics of ETL and how SSIS can be applied to the purpose.

What This Book Covers

If you have spent time on Amazon.com browsing the SSIS books, then you may have noticed how long these books can be—especially since they only look at the features. The intention of this book is not to tell you all the properties and show you all the features, but rather how to apply the components of SSIS to ETL tasks.

> *This book answers the question: How do I use SSIS to build an enterprise ETL solution that scales and performs, gracefully handles errors, and gives the administrators the right information to manage and monitor the data processing?*

How This Book Is Structured

To convey how to apply SSIS to various tasks, we've structure this book logically first to give you all the background and foundation information on scripting and data extraction, and then the details of data warehousing ETL, error handling, administration, and data integration, respectively. Given the popularity of DTS, a chapter has also been included on migrating to SSIS, and another chapter on scaling SSIS. Following is a brief description of how this book is structured:

❑ Chapter 1 starts off the book with an introduction to the value proposition that SSIS brings to ETL and integration, and it also includes a refresher walk-through of the SSIS basics.

❑ Chapter 2 focuses on advanced scripting. This chapter is placed up front because understanding when scripting should be used and how to implement scripting will be important in your architecture decisions. Several scenarios are presented that show powerful uses of scripting for more advanced requirements that cannot be designed easily with other out-of-the-box components.

❑ Chapter 3 focuses on data extraction and lineage, a central aspect of ETL (the *E* in ETL). This chapter focuses on designing extractions, including incremental extractions, and tracking data from the source to the destination.

❑ Chapters 4, 5, and 6 are dedicated to data warehousing ETL, primarily because a large portion of new data warehouse efforts are leveraging SSIS for the ETL process, and many existing ETL solutions are being rewritten in SSIS. Chapters 4 and 5 focus on the relational database transformation and loading methods for dimension and fact tables. Chapter 6 is dedicated to the SQL Server 2005 Analysis Services support within SSIS.

❑ Chapter 7 focuses on error and event handling, as well as restartability, which overall will provide you with the capability to design solutions that gracefully can deal with processing errors and ease the execution through restartability.

❑ Chapters 8 and 9 address the best practices for moving between your support and production environments. These chapters also address approaches to management of this process, as well as your package configurations and executions.

❑ Chapter 10 focuses on heterogeneous integration. Chances are you will be pulling from or pushing to non-SQL Server systems or files (such as Oracle, DB2, Sybase, Teradata, and non-ANSI code page files, to name a few). This chapter focuses on what's involved when interacting with these systems.

❑ Chapter 11 addresses how to leverage SSIS features that make your migrated packages better. Some of you are involved in migrating DTS-based ETL to SSIS. Because of the architectural differences in the products, your migration will involve some attention. Chapter 11 goes beyond just getting your packages working in SSIS.

❑ Chapter 12 discusses how to best take advantage of memory, when a relational engine should be used, where SSIS packages should be executed, and what the optimal loading techniques are for your destinations.

What You Need to Use This Book

Since this book is about SQL Server 2005 Integration Services, you will get more out of it if you have the developer edition of SQL Server 2005 installed, including the sample applications and the tools. This book has been written for SQL Server 2005 with SP2 installed (which was released in February 2007). If you do not have a licensed copy of SQL Server 2005, you can download a 120-day trial from the Microsoft download site at `http://download.microsoft.com`.

Conventions

To help you get the most from the text and keep track of what's happening, a number of conventions have been used throughout the book.

Examples that you can download and try out for yourself generally appear like this:

Listing: Example Title

```
This section provides the code for the example.
```

> **Boxes like this one hold important, not-to-be forgotten information that is directly relevant to the surrounding text.**

Tips, hints, tricks, and asides to the current discussion are offset and placed in italics like this.

As for styles in the text:

❑ Important new terms and important words are shown in *italics* when they are introduced.

❑ Keyboard strokes are shown like this: Ctrl+A.

❑ File names, URLs, and code within the text are shown like this: `persistence.properties`.

❑ Code is presented in the following two ways:

```
In code examples, new and important code is highlighted with a gray background.
```

```
The gray highlighting is not used for code that's less important in the pre-
sent context, or has been shown before.
```

Source Code

As you work through the examples in this book, you may choose either to type in all the code manually, or use the source code files that accompany the book. All of the source code used in this book is available for download at `www.wrox.com`. When at the site, simply locate the book's title (either by using the Search box or by using one of the title lists), and click the Download Code link on the book's detail page to obtain all the source code for the book.

Because many books have similar titles, you may find it easiest to search by ISBN; this book's ISBN is 978-0-470-13411-5.

After you have downloaded the code, decompress it with your favorite compression tool. Alternately, you can go to the main Wrox code download page at `www.wrox.com/dynamic/books/download.aspx` to see the code available for this book and all other Wrox books.

Errata

We make every effort to ensure that there are no errors in the text or in the code. However, no one is perfect, and mistakes do occur. If you find an error in one of our books (such as a spelling mistake or faulty piece of code), we would be very grateful for your feedback. By sending in errata, you may save another reader hours of frustration and at the same time you will be helping us provide even higher quality information.

To find the errata page for this book, go to `www.wrox.com` and locate the title using the Search box or one of the title lists. Then, on the book details page, click the Book Errata link. On this page, you can view all errata that has been submitted for this book and posted by Wrox editors. A complete book list including links to each's book's errata is also available at `www.wrox.com/misc-pages/booklist.shtml`.

If you don't spot "your" error on the Book Errata page, go to `www.wrox.com/contact/techsupport .shtml` and complete the form there to send us the error you have found. We'll check the information and, if appropriate, post a message to the book's errata page and fix the problem in subsequent editions of the book.

p2p.wrox.com

For author and peer discussion, join the P2P forums at p2p.wrox.com. The forums are a Web-based system for you to post messages relating to Wrox books and related technologies, and to interact with other readers and technology users. The forums offer a subscription feature to e-mail you topics of interest of your choosing when new posts are made to the forums. Wrox authors, editors, other industry experts, and your fellow readers are present on these forums.

At http://p2p.wrox.com, you will find a number of different forums that will help you not only as you read this book, but also as you develop your own applications. To join the forums, just follow these steps:

1. Go to p2p.wrox.com and click the Register link.

2. Read the terms of use and click Agree.

3. Complete the required information to join, as well as any optional information you wish to provide, and click Submit.

4. You will receive an e-mail message with information describing how to verify your account and complete the joining process.

You can read messages in the forums without joining P2P, but to post your own messages, you must join.

After you join, you can post new messages and respond to messages other users post. You can read messages at any time on the Web. If you would like to have new messages from a particular forum e-mailed to you, click the Subscribe to this Forum icon by the forum name in the forum listing.

For more information about how to use the Wrox P2P, be sure to read the P2P FAQs for answers to questions about how the forum software works, as well as many common questions specific to P2P and Wrox books. To read the FAQs, click the FAQ link on any P2P page.

1

Getting Started

This book is about applications. Specifically, this book is about applying the functionality of SQL Server 2005 Integration Services (SSIS) to help you envision, develop, and implement your data processing needs. The discussions throughout the book spotlight how SSIS can help you accomplish your data integration and processing requirements.

Core to the data processing that SSIS does best is extraction, transformation, and loading (ETL). Over the years, this ETL has taken on a range of different meanings, from the general perspective of moving data from somewhere to somewhere else, to the specific application of data warehousing ETL. In fact, ETL has its roots in business intelligence (BI) and data warehouse processing.

This chapter provides important background information for generalized ETL that DBAs will need, as well as basic data warehousing ETL concepts. In addition, this chapter includes a practical review of SSIS functionality and provides the foundation for building the book's examination of applying the functionality of SSIS to help you accomplish your individual goals in data integration and processing requirements.

Choosing the Right Tool for the Job

If you have any inclination toward home remodeling, chances are you enjoy walking through the tools area of your local home improvement store. Hundreds of different tools have been manufactured that perform a variety of functions and, in some cases, some fairly esoteric uses.

Any novice handyman can attest to the adage that the right tool for the job makes the job easier. The same concept applies when it comes to handling data. There's no doubt that, depending on the right situation, there may be a specific tool to handle such a function. Think about all the different types of data processing needs that you have across your organization:

❑ Data synchronization between systems

❑ Data extraction from ERP systems

❑ Ad hoc reporting

❑ Replication (both homogeneous and heterogeneous)

❑ PDA data synchronization

❑ Legacy system integration

❑ Vendors and partner data files integration

❑ Line of business data

❑ Customer and employee directory synchronization

❑ Data warehouse ETL processing

As you may know, when it comes to data processing, there are a lot of tools out there. Some are created for specific situations (such as folder synchronizing tools), whereas other tools are designed to perform a variety of functions for different situations. So, the traditional question often posed is which tool can best meet the business and logical requirements to perform the tasks needed?

Consider the host of tools found in the ever-evolving Microsoft toolset. You can use Transact SQL (TSQL) to hand-code a load, Host Integration Server to communicate with a heterogeneous data source, BizTalk to orchestrate messages in a transactional manner, or SSIS to load data in batches. Each of these tools plays a role in the data world.

Although there can be overlaps, each tool has a distinct focus and target purpose. When you become comfortable with a technology, there's always the tendency to want to apply that technology beyond its intended "sweet spot" when another tool would be better for the job. You've no doubt heard the phrase "when you're a hammer, everything looks like a nail." For example, C# developers may want to build an application to do something that SSIS could potentially do in an hour of development time. The challenge everyone faces entails time and capacity. There is no way everyone can be an expert across the board. Therefore, developers and administrators alike should be diligent about performing research on tools and technologies that complement each other, based on different situations.

For example, many organizations use BizTalk for a host of purposes beyond the handling of business-to-business communication and process workflow automation. These same organizations may be perplexed as to why BizTalk doesn't scale to meet the needs of the organization's terabyte data warehousing ETL. The easy answer is that the right tool for bulk BI processing is an ETL tool such as SSIS. In fact, as shown in Figure 1-1, SSIS provides an excellent platform for leveraging its high-performance data pipeline.

High performance source and destination providers

Native binary file, for archiving and staging

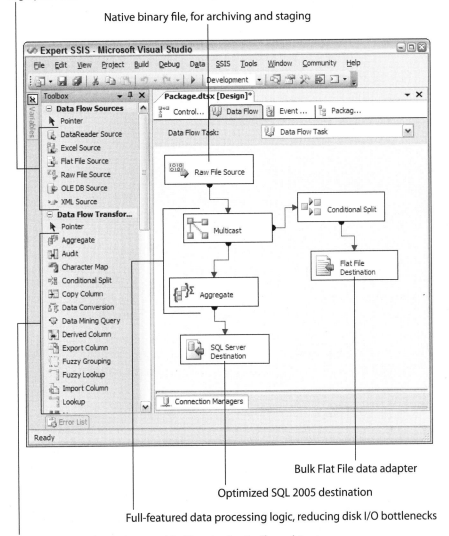

Bulk Flat File data adapter

Optimized SQL 2005 destination

Full-featured data processing logic, reducing disk I/O bottlenecks

In-memory transformations enabled by pipeline buffer architecture

Figure 1-1: SSIS high-performance data pipeline

The process outlined in Figure 1-1 may be simple enough, but essentially what SSIS does is to provide the technology to make the process efficient and scalable, and provide the functionality to handle data errors.

This chapter reviews ETL concepts in more detail, and gets you started with an SSIS example. Before diving into the expert level details found in the ensuing chapters, reminding you about ETL concepts and SSIS features will help solidify the background needed before moving to the details of the SSIS application.

Be Careful About Tool Selection

In some client environments, an ETL tool may be chosen without consideration for the availability of industry skills, support, or even the learning curve. Even though the tool could perform "magic," it usually doesn't come with a pocket magician, just the magic of emptying your corporate wallet. In many cases, thousands of dollars have been spent to purchase an ETL tool that takes too long to master, implement, and support. Beyond the standard functionality questions you should ask about a tool, be sure to also consider the following:

- ❑   Your internal skill sets

- ❑   The trend of industry use of the tool

- ❑   How easy it is to learn

- ❑   The ease of supporting the tool

This book focuses on the three most common categories of SSIS usage:

- ❑   Data warehouse ETL
- ❑   Data integration
- ❑   SSIS administration

Before going any further, it makes sense to consider the purpose and background of each of these types of ETL.

Data Warehousing ETL

Some of you may be well-versed in data warehousing and related ETL concepts, but for those who are not, here is a high-level overview of data warehousing. Data warehousing focuses on *decision support*, or enabling better decision making through organized accessibility of information. As opposed to a *transactional system* such as a point of sale (POS), Human Resources (HR), or customer relationship management (CRM) that is designed to allow rapid transactions to capture information data, a data warehouse is tuned for reporting and analysis. In other words, instead of focusing on the entry of information, data warehousing is focused on the extraction and reporting of information to show trending, summary, and data history.

Databases designed for data warehousing are created in a structure called a *dimensional model*, which involves two types of tables. *Dimension tables* hold informational data or attributes that describe entities. *Fact tables* capture metrics or numeric data that describe quantities, levels, sales, or other statistics. A data warehouse may involve many dimension tables and fact tables. Figure 1-2 shows the relationships between several dimension tables and one fact table in a structure often called a *star schema*.

The focus of this book is not on the design of the dimension tables and fact tables, but rather on getting data into these structures from other repositories. Processing ETL for data warehousing involves *extracting* data from source systems or files, performing *transformation* logic on the data to correlate, cleanse, and consolidate, and then *loading* a data warehouse environment for reporting and analysis (see Figure 1-3).

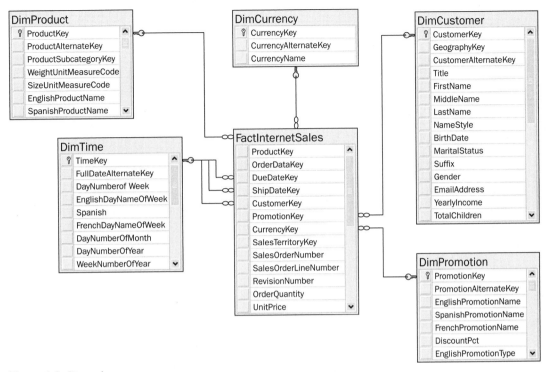

Figure 1-2: Star schema

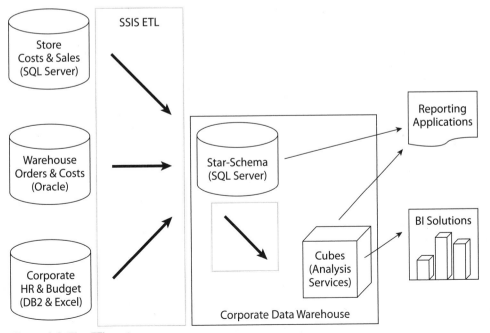

Figure 1-3: The ETL system

For those who are already versed in ETL concepts and practice, you'll know that when it comes to developing a data warehouse ETL system, moving from theory to practice often presents the biggest hurdle. Did you know that ETL typically takes up between 50 and 70 percent of a data warehousing project? That is quite a daunting statistic. What it means is that even though presenting the data is the end goal and the driving force for business, the largest portion of developing a data warehouse is spent not on the presentation and organization of the data, but in the behind-the-scenes processing to get the data ready.

Data Integration

You can also use SSIS to synchronize data between systems, or to replicate data. For example, you may want to create a business-to-business portal site, and you may need the site to interface with the source data on the mainframe. In this case, you may get the data delivered in nightly extracts from the mainframe and load it into your SQL Server table. Another very common ETL task that DBAs face is receiving files from File Transfer Protocol (FTP) servers (or on network shares) that must be processed and loaded into another system. This type of process involves moving files and then processing the data, which may involve de-duping, combining files, cleaning bad data, and so on.

Part of the job of integrating data may include data extraction. *Data extraction* is moving data out of a source, and, although it sounds easy enough, some of the challenges involve extracting only changes and also optimizing the extraction to make it scalable. Chapter 3 provides more information on data extraction for applying SSIS to data sources and extraction techniques.

In addition, if you think you have a perfect data source, think again! Chances are you will be dealing with missing data, mistyped data, NULL values, and just plain dirty data. Refer to Chapters 5 and 7 to learn how to handle real-world data situations. Data quality issues span a range of challenges, and you will need to plan your data cleansing to ensure you can accommodate your final goal of data processing.

SSIS Administration

If you are a DBA responsible for SSIS packages (whether you created them or were given responsibility), then chances are you will have the responsibility of monitoring the package execution and ensuring that the transactions are correctly implemented to keep the database in a consistent state. Some of you will also be responsible for package deployment with a team of people, and securing packages so that only the right people have the ability to access and execute packages.

Although not every environment will be upgrading from SQL Server 2000 DTS, many DBAs do face this situation. DTS adoption was broad because of its ease of use and execution. And now that SSIS is here and proven, you may need to take your packages and move them to SSIS. This is easier said than done, given the architectural changes in the products. Chapter 11 provides more information on DTS migration to help get you there without losing your mind.

Yet another aspect of SSIS is database administration. In fact, in SQL Server 2005, SSIS is also used to help manage your database environment. For example, SQL Server maintenance plans (such as database backups, index defragmentation, database consistency checking, and so on) use SSIS behind the scenes to coordinate the administration operations.

Optimizing and scaling SSIS is another common responsibility for both DBAs and developers alike. Chapter 12 targets scaling SSIS, including ways to optimize destinations and how to take advantage of SSIS functionality to make faster, more scalable packages.

SSIS Review

Many of you have practical, learn-on-the-go experience using SSIS, and are looking to this book to take your knowledge to the next level and to fill in any knowledge gaps. Others of you have a good book knowledge of SSIS and want to extend your skills. And there may be those of you (like us) who like to dive right in, skip the intro books, and go right for the expert material.

To set the stage and provide a common starting point, we will walk you through a package creation that involves many of the SSIS key concepts. It's impossible to wrap all the SSIS functionality into this one example, but you will get a good review of the basic features. If you feel you already know how to use the basic SSIS features comfortably, feel free to skip this section. The ensuing discussions, however, assume that you know some of these basic concepts and will not walk you through these steps again. You should be familiar with some basics such as how to create a solution. This example assumes some SSIS background, so if you need a more fundamental review, see one of the starter SSIS books available such as *Professional SQL Server 2005 Integration Services* (Wiley Publishing, 2006).

In this package creation walk-through, you will start by developing a simple package Data Flow that pulls a limited range of data (by using package variables) from a source and adds some data transformation steps. Since SSIS includes more than just processing data, you will then be working with the control flow and creating complementary tasks and containers with Precedence Constraints to control what happens in what order in this example. The final step is executing the package.

To begin, first start by opening the Business Intelligence Development Studio (BIDS) tool and creating a new SSIS project called ExpertSSIS. Then, rename the default package that is created (Package.dtsx) to Chapter1.dtsx. Confirm that you'd like to rename the package object as well.

Creating a Connection Manager

After creating the package, you can create the first connection manager. Right-click in the Connection Manager pane at the bottom of the package editor and select New OLE DB Connection. On the Configure OLE DB Connection Manager screen, if you do not have an AdventureWorks connection in the Data Connections list, click New. Type **localhost** for the Server Name property, and select AdventureWorks from the Database drop-down box. Click OK to save the connection, and click OK again when you have the localhost.AdventureWorks connection selected. Right-click the newly created localhost.AdventureWorks connection manager and rename it to **AdventureWorks**.

Using the Control Flow

The Control Flow tab is where you perform the package's workflow. For example, you may decide to receive a file through FTP, transform the data within the file, and then archive the file. In that example, you would have three tasks:

- ❑ An FTP Task
- ❑ A Data Flow Task
- ❑ A File System Task

If you need help with the configuration of these tasks, consult one of the starter books such as the *Professional SQL Server 2005 Integration Services* book. Configuration of these tasks is not addressed in this book. Instead, we will concentrate on how to build solutions using the tasks.

In the Control Flow tab of the example package, drag over a single Data Flow Task onto the design pane. This Data Flow Task will perform the transformation of data. Rename the task **Create Product File** by right-clicking the task and choosing Rename.

Select Variables from the SSIS menu, which opens the Variables window. Create three variables in the window:

- ❑ RowCount as an int32 data type
- ❑ StartDate as a datetime data type
- ❑ EndDate as a datetime data type

Create the default value of the StartDate to some date in 2001, and set the default value of the EndDate variable to some date in 2007.

Working in the Data Flow

When you double-click on the Data Flow Task, you are taken to the Data Flow tab. The Data Flow Task streams data from nearly any structured, semi-structured, or non-structured source to nearly any destination. In this case, you will pull data from a SQL Server source, transform the data by using a number of transformation components, and then write the result to a text file. Figure 1-4 shows the Data Flow tab in a package without the components defined yet. Notice that the toolbox contains adapters and transformations that you will be using throughout this book.

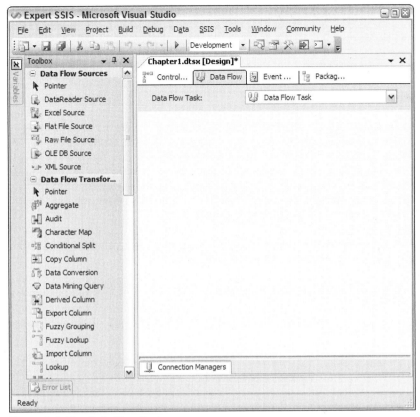

Figure 1-4: The Data Flow Task

Drag over an OLE DB Source from the toolbox. Name the source **Products**. Double-click the source to configure it, as shown in Figure 1-5. Ensure that you're pointing to the AdventureWorks connection manager and then change the Data access mode entry to SQL command. Enter the following command in the SQL command text window:

```
SELECT * FROM Production.Product
WHERE SellStartDate > ? and SellStartDate < ?
```

The query returns all the products that are within a certain date range. The question marks represent parameter values that will be passed in through a variable. Click the Parameters button to map the question marks to the variables you've already created. Each question mark parameter you see in the Set

Query Parameters window is ordinal (see Figure 1-6). So, the first question mark is represented by Parameter0, the second by Parameter1, and so on. Map Parameter0 to User::StartDate and Parameter1 to User::EndDate. Click OK to go back to the Data Flow tab.

Next, drag a Lookup transform onto the design pane. Connect the Product source to the Lookup transform by dragging the green arrow from the source to the transform. Name the Lookup transform **Find Model Name**.

Open (by double-clicking) the Lookup transform to configure it. Point the transform to the AdventureWorks connection manager and to the [Production].[ProductModel] table by using the appropriate drop-down list boxes as shown in Figure 1-7. In the Lookup configuration dialog box, select the Columns tab and you'll see that there are more arrows connecting the input to the lookup columns than you actually need. Right-click each arrow and click Delete until the only one remaining is the arrow that connects ProductModelID on each side, as shown in Figure 1-7. Click Name from the Available Lookup Columns table and then type the Output Alias of **ModelName**.

Finally, click the Configure Error Output button. Change the Error column from Fail Component to Ignore Failure. Click OK twice to exit the transform configuration.

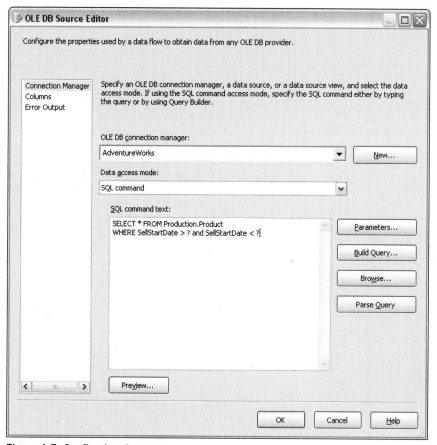

Figure 1-5: Configuring the source

Figure 1-6: Set Query Parameters window

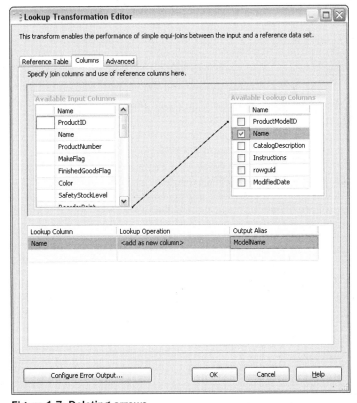

Figure 1-7: Deleting arrows

As a review of the Lookup Transformation Editor, the first tab tells the component where to find the reference (lookup) data. The second tab tells the component which fields it should try to match in the source and reference data sets — the lookup column is the value you want to retrieve. Finally, the error output configuration tells the Lookup what to do with the row in the case of failure.

What this transform does for you now that it is completely configured is try to find the name of the model based on where the `ProductModelID` on the source matches the reference table. If it can't find a match, an error occurs. However, you have configured the transform to ignore the error, and so the `ModelName` column will now contain a `NULL` value if the match is not found. You could have also told the transform to redirect rows where it can't find a match to another output, which would be the red arrow coming out of the transform. At that point, you could have written those rows to a queue, or performed some additional cleanup.

> In some destination table loading (and definitely in data warehouse dimension table loading), if you can't find a matching record in the Lookup, then an "unknown value" needs to be inserted (a `NULL` value in many cases is not acceptable). A more elegant way to do this is through ignoring errors and using a derived column transform to replace `NULL`s with a default value.

Drag a Derived Column transform onto the data flow and connect the output of the Lookup transform to the Derived Column. Name the Derived Column transform **Assign Default Values and Price**. In this scenario, you want to give a special customer discount on products that your company makes (the `MakeFlag` column lets you know if you made the product). There are two ways to perform this conditional assignment:

❑   Use a Conditional Split transformation and then a Derived Column transformation

❑   Use the Derived Column transformation and utilize the SSIS expression language to perform conditional coding

Open the Derived Column Transformation Editor (shown in Figure 1-8) in the data flow to configure the transform. For the first derived column name, you will want to replace the `NULL` values in `ModelName` with the word *Unknown*. You will want this to replace the existing column of `ModelName` by selecting `Replace 'ModelName'` from the Derived Column drop-down box. To solve a business requirement of not having `NULL`s in your warehouse, you can use the conditional operator of a question mark as shown here for the `Expression` column:

```
ISNULL([ModelName]) == TRUE ? "Unknown" : [ModelName]
```

Another entry in the Derived Column Transformation Editor will satisfy requirements for the discounted product price for products that you make. Again, you will want to change the Derived Column drop-down box to `Replace 'ListPrice'`. This time, the conditional logic will be slightly different. You're going to give a 10 percent discount on any product that you make, so you'll read the `MakeFlag` column. If it's set to `true`, then you'll discount. Otherwise, you'll use the existing price in the column. The code will look like this:

```
[MakeFlag] == TRUE ? [ListPrice] * 0.9 : [ListPrice]
```

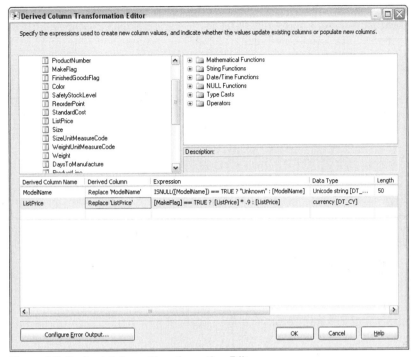

Figure 1-8: Derived Column Transformation Editor

In both of these columns, the `==` TRUE snippet of code is optional, but is useful for full self-documentation of code. If you were to have the statement `ISNULL([ModelName])`, it would essentially mean the same thing as this code. Also note that the columns and variables in the expression language are all case-sensitive.

Your final screen should look like Figure 1-8. Click OK to exit the editor.

Lastly, you want to audit how many rows you are about to write to the flat file. To do this, you can drag the Row Count transform onto the design pane. Connect the transform downstream of the Derived Column transform. Rename the Row Count transform to **Count Inserts** and double-click it to configure the transform.

Set the `VariableName` property in the Component Properties tab to `@intCount`. The variable name is case-sensitive. Because the last row is written through the transform, it is counted and logged to the variable for future use. A typical use for this transform is to count the number of rows transformed and write the result into an audit table.

With the data now transformed, you're ready to write the data to the extract file for use by another party (such as a business partner or another department). Drag over a Flat File Destination and rename it to **Partner Extract**. Double-click the destination to configure it. When the destination opens, click New to create a new connection manager. When the Flat File Format dialog box opens, select Delimited and click OK.

You're now taken to the Flat File Connection Manager Editor (shown in Figure 1-9). Name the connection manager **Partner Extract** and type **C:\ExpertSSIS\partnerextract.txt** for the file name (the directory, of course, must already be created). Select the Column names in the first data row check box.

Figure 1-9: Flat File Connection Manager Editor

Next, go to the Columns page. In this page, make the column delimiter a vertical bar (|) by changing the Column delimiter drop-down box as shown in Figure 1-10.

Click OK to exit the editor and return to the Flat File Destination Editor. Click the Mappings page to confirm the data mappings and then click OK. Each time the data flow is run, the extract file is overwritten.

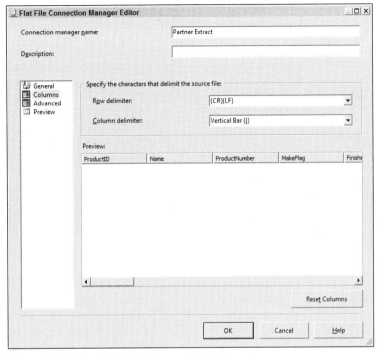

Figure 1-10: Changing the Column delimiter

Precedence Constraints

Precedence constraints are the conductor for your workflow. They dictate which tasks will execute and in what order. Precedence constraints appear as lines in the control flow that connect one or more tasks together. The green arrow represents On Success and means that the second (or downstream) task will only execute if the first (or upstream) task or set of tasks executes successfully. The blue arrow represents On Completion and means that regardless of whether the upstream task completes successfully or fails, the downstream task will execute. This is useful for a clean-up task, for example. The red arrow represents On Failure and means that the downstream task will execute only if the upstream task fails.

You can also place expressions on the precedence constraint. With this functionality, you can put code on the constraint that states that the expressions must be true, and optionally the constraint must be true as well. These are useful if you want to add conditions into your control flow.

Returning to the example application, go to the Control Flow tab and drag over a Script Task onto the design pane. Rename the task to **Stub Code** and drag the green arrow out of the Data Flow Task onto the Script Task. Drag over one more Script Task and call it **Stub Code 2**. Drag the green arrow out of both of the other tasks onto Stub Code 2. These tasks will act only as placeholders for future code. The control flow should now look like Figure 1-11. Currently, Stub Code 2 will execute only after the first two tasks successfully execute.

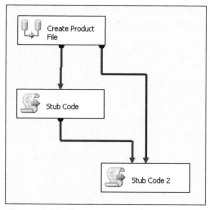

Figure 1-11: Current control flow

Double-click the precedence constraint between the Data Flow Task (named Create Product File) and the Stub Code Script Task. Change the Evaluation operation option to Expression and Constraint. The value should remain Success and the Expression should read `@intCount > 400`, as shown in Figure 1-12. Click the Test button to make sure you have valid syntax. As in the rest of SSIS, variable names are always case-sensitive. This configuration means that the Stub Code Task will execute if and only if *both* the Data Flow Task succeeds and it transforms more than 400 records (read from the Row Count transform in the data flow).

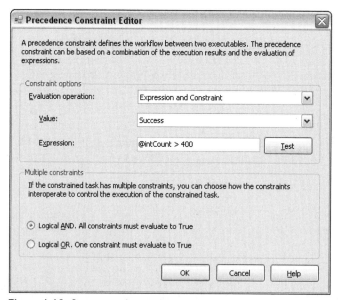

Figure 1-12: Success value and expression

In this configuration, if there are less than 400 rows transformed, Stub Code 2 will never execute, even though there's an On Success precedence constraint between the Data Flow Task and the task. This is because you have a Logical And condition on the Stub Task 2 when multiple constraints are connected into it. This means that both the Data Flow Task *and* the Stub Code Task must successfully execute before the Stub Code 2 Task executes. You may also want the Stub Code 2 Task to execute when either task successfully completes. To do this, you can double-click either of the precedence constraints that connect to Stub Code 2 and change the Multiple constraints option to Logical OR.

Package Execution

Notice that after you change the constraint type, the solid green line turns into a dotted green line as shown in Figure 1-13. At this point, you're ready to execute the package by right-clicking the package in the Solution Explorer and clicking Execute Package. If you transformed less the 400 records, the package will look like Figure 1-13, where the Data Flow and Stub Code 2 executes.

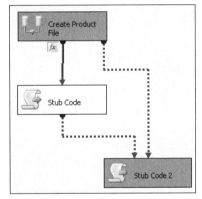

Figure 1-13: Solid line changing to dotted line

One way you can see how many rows transformed is to go to the Data Flow tab before stopping the package. You'll see how many rows transformed through the pipeline (shown in Figure 1-14). You can stop the package by clicking the Stop button (the square blue button on the BIDS toolbar) or by clicking Stop Debugging from the Debug menu. If you have any problems executing the package, you can go to the Progress tab to see the error. After you stop the package, the Progress tab turns into the Execution Results tab, which shows the results of the last package execution.

When you execute a package from the BIDS environment where you can see the results visually, you're executing the package in debug mode. You can also execute the package without debugging by selecting Start Without Debugging from the Debug menu. This performs slightly faster than executing a package from within debug mode, but it's much harder to troubleshoot an issue.

Executing a package outside of debug mode opens a command prompt, as shown in Figure 1-15, and runs the dtexec.exe utility. You can tell the package successfully executed by the DTSER_SUCCESS code at the end of the execution. You can also see how fast each task and container executed after each item completes in the command window, or how fast the entire package executed, which is shown at the bottom of the command line execution output (in the command window).

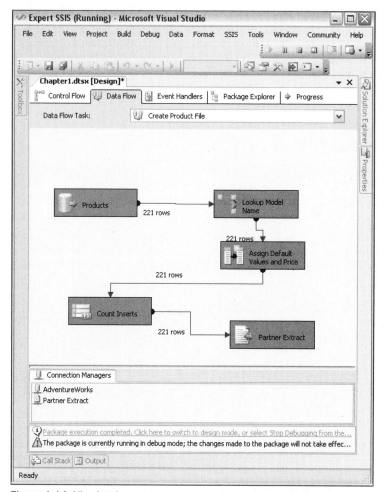

Figure 1-14: Viewing how many rows transformed through the pipeline

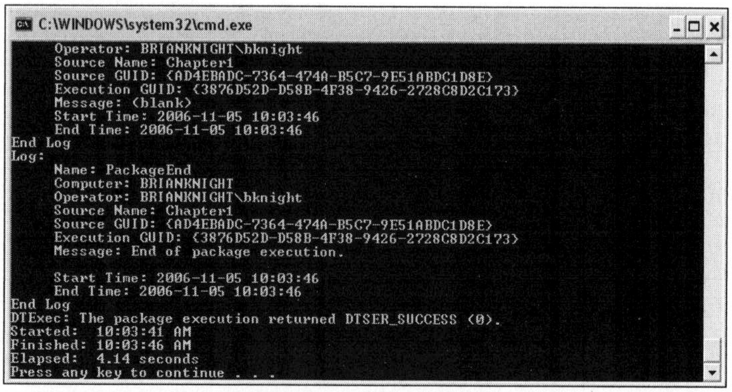

Figure 1-15: Execution of the dtexec.exe utility

Containers

With the package now complete, you could make it more advanced and cleaner by wrapping certain functionalities in containers. *Containers* help you group tasks logically together but also have other functionalities. There are three types of containers that you'll typically need to be concerned with:

- ❑ Sequence
- ❑ ForLoop
- ❑ ForEach Loop

There is actually a fourth type of container called TaskHost, which wraps every task behind the scenes.

The Sequence container group simply groups tasks visually inside a collapsible box, as shown in Figure 1-16. In this figure, Prepare OS and Set Variables will execute sequentially before allowing the Create Product File Task to execute. Sequence containers help you to clean up and abstract the details of your control flow, since you can minimize a container if you don't care about the complexity of what's happening inside the container. Events bubble up to the container, so if a failure occurs in a task, it will fail the parent container by default.

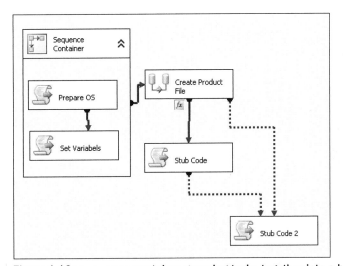

Figure 1-16: Sequence **container grouping tasks together into a box**

Sequence containers aren't just for looks though. You can also isolate transactions to a container so that if a problem occurs in a data task, you can roll back any other data action that had occurred in the container if it's participating in the container transaction. You can also log or create event handlers on anything in the container.

ForLoop containers enable you to do a Do...While loop inside the control flow. Any task inside the ForLoop container will loop continuously until the while condition is no longer met. This comes in handy if you want to continuously loop until a variable is set to TRUE.

One of the most important types of container is the ForEach Loop container. With this container, you specify a collection of items to enumerate through, and then any items inside the container will loop until SSIS enumerates to the end of the collection. Out of the box, you can enumerate through a collection of files in a directory, records in a table, or a list of items that you type. There are other types of enumerators that you can specify, and you can even write your own enumerator.

It's also important to note that after you place a set of tasks inside a container, they can only relate through precedence constraints to other tasks in the container. An individual task inside the container can never relate directly to anything else outside the container. The last thing to point out about containers is that you can embed containers inside containers.

Review Conclusion

Even though this walk-through only highlights the data flow and control flow, you still can see that SSIS is a broad-featured tool capable of a lot of diverse applications.

In the end, it's all about the data — ensuring that the information is handled in the right way to meet your needs. This does not minimize the supporting requirements such as transactions handling, deployment, and execution monitoring, because these are important pieces to building a stable SSIS environment. When you take the primary data processing tasks and add in administration, error handling, scalability, testing, and deployment, the result is like juggling spinning plates. It's no wonder why ETL consumes up to 70 percent of an enterprise data warehouse development effort.

You may know this already: If you can reduce the amount of time it takes to build an ETL solution (including the supporting architecture), then your projects are in a better position for success. This is the value proposition of SSIS — a tool that can integrate all the needed features for a complete ETL system in an architecture that is supportable and extendable. With the right tool and right architecture, more time can be spent on testing the data and presenting the data to the users.

Summary

There are two keys to a successful ETL solution:

❑   Using the right enterprise ETL tool

❑   Employing the right ETL architecture to meet the requirements

First, with SSIS, you'll find the out-of-the-box features provide the depth and breadth of functionality and flexibility needed to create efficient, reliable, and scalable solutions. What's more, the usability and rapid learning curve reduce solution development time. The second ingredient is addressed in the rest of the pages of this book. As a practical guide for SSIS ETL development, you will learn ways to implement your ETL solution requirements from the data to the administration and everything in-between. Putting it all together to get a solution over the goal line requires knowing the big picture and coordinating all the pieces.

Now that we have made the case for SSIS and reviewed some main features, it is time to dig in. In Chapter 2, we will start by considering scripting. Using the Script Task and Script Component in the right ways is central to applying SSIS, and in many of the later chapters, some scripting will be used to handle common situations that cannot be easily applied with other out-of-the-box features.

2

Extending Scripts in SSIS

Whether applying SSIS toward warehouse ETL or data integration, or toward more complicated DBA tasks, the programming extendibility can be a useful and powerful tool to accomplish workflow tasks in the control flow, or data-centric operations in the data flow, that are not easily handled by out-of-the-box components. You can extend SSIS in this way by using a couple of different supported approaches:

❑ Through Custom Tasks, Components, and Enumerators, you are able to compile and register native or managed code, as well as extend the product with reusable components just like the built-in components found in the toolbox.

❑ By using the Script Task or the Script Component, you can write code to accomplish things that are better suited to scripting than what can be accomplished through other components.

Both of these topics are discussed in the *Professional SQL Server 2005 Integration Services* book (Wiley Publishing, 2006). In that book, Chapter 14 discusses writing a custom task or custom component, and Chapter 15 shows how to write a user interface for your component. Scripting is also covered in Chapter 7 of that book, presenting the basics of the Script Task and the Script Component. All those chapters are commendable. It is beyond the scope of this chapter to cover those topics again at that level. However, we felt that more could be said and exemplified about extending your scripting — taking full advantage of scripting in SSIS when it is appropriate.

What is meant here is that there may be specific times when you might want to customize or extend that functionality beyond basic scripting practices. For example, SSIS runs within the .NET Framework, and, therefore, you can use the base .NET libraries in the Global Access Cache (GAC), or you can build your own custom libraries to handle the custom logic that you need. This chapter shows you how to leverage the power of SSIS by explaining how to extend the Script Tasks and the Script Components, including the following:

❑ Working with package variables

❑ Referencing custom libraries

❑ Updating connections in the Script Task

❑ Raising error events

❑ Encryption data in the Script Component

❑ Profiling data in the data flow

Script Tasks and Custom Libraries

Script Tasks are valuable tasks for handling custom functionality because code can be written within the task. But when you want to use the same code over and over again, why rewrite or cut and paste code for each Script Task? A good developer knows that code re-use makes developing code efficient and easier to maintain. That is why it is a good practice to build custom libraries so that they can be used as functional components as well as building blocks within Script Tasks.

> Code reusability is also a great case for writing custom components. However, your code may not be suitable for a custom component because of its unique variability, or perhaps your company policies prevent registering such components on your servers. In these cases, the Script Task is probably the right solution, and with custom libraries, you are still able to consolidate redundant code.

User-Defined Variables

Variables are primarily used as configuration settings within SSIS during runtime. Using variables allows packages to be configured dynamically, rather than having to hard-code settings in the package. There are system variables that are defined by SSIS, and user-defined variables that developers build for their own settings (which a package may use dynamically). Creating user-defined variables and then using them from within Script Task variables is very powerful for dynamic package settings. User-defined variables are created within BIDS and can be tailored to hold many different types of data types.

Let's now walk through the first steps for building a custom script within the Script Task and defining user-defined variables to control how it will function. Start BIDS and create a new project named `UserVariables`, as shown in Figure 2-1.

Double-click the `package.dtsx` package within Solution Explorer. The design view for the package will come up. Now, the important window is the Variables window, so if you do not see it, look on the toolbar and click View ➪ Other Windows ➪ Variables.

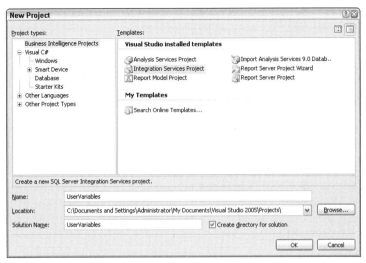

Figure 2-1: Starting a new project

When the Variables window is visible (as shown in Figure 2-2), you will see that there are four columns that show up by default:

❑ **Name** — This column is the name of the variable, and each variable must be unique within its scope.

❑ **Scope** — This column represents where the variable is scoped. You can scope a variable to a package, a container, or a task. If you were to have a variable scoped to a task, no other task would be able to see the variable. When you scope a variable, you cannot change the scope without deleting it and re-creating it.

❑ **Data Type** — This column shows the data type for the variable.

❑ **Value** — This column shows the user-defined initial value for the variable.

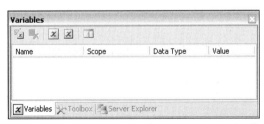

Figure 2-2: Four default columns showing in the Variables window

There is also a toolbar that enables you to add or delete variables, show system or user variables, and view additional columns or attributes about the variables. There are two additional columns you can add if it proves useful to you:

❑ **Namespace** — This generally has very little use. It essentially allows you to qualify a variable with something other than User: or System:.

❑ **Raise Event if Variable Value Changes** — This is set to `false` by default. However, when set to `true`, the `OnVariableValueChanged` event handler will be executed each time the value of this variable is changed.

To create a variable, click the first icon (from the left) on the toolbar. This creates a new variable with default attributes. When you look at the scope of the new variable, you will notice that it has a Package scope. This is because you have not added any tasks or containers.

To create a variable scoped within an example Script Task, go back to the control flow of the package and drag over a Script Task. In the Variables window, with the added Script Task selected, add a new variable. Note that the scope of the new variable is now Script Task.

Let's create a variable that allows a Script Task to be used as a configurable resource for hitting HTTP sites. Change the Name of the new variable to `varHttp`, change the Data Type to String, and clear out the Value so that it will be represented in code as an empty string. Also, create a variable called `varSaveFile` of type String.

Retrieving Variables with Code

To now expand the example, let's use the Script Task to show a variety of ways to read a variable. There are two specific ways that it can be used: the easiest way is the `Variables` object, and the other is the `VariableDispenser` object. The `Variables` object requires less code, but is slightly less efficient and requires more interaction in the GUI. The `VariableDispenser` locks variables for a slightly shorter period of time.

Let's start by double-clicking the Script Task that you created earlier to edit the task. For this example, use the `Variables` object, which requires one additional step in the GUI. The Script Task must know which variables are available to read and which variables are available to read and write. Select Script from the left pane, as shown in Figure 2-3. The `EntryPoint` property is set to `ScriptMain`, which is also the default class that is built and executed when the task is started. The `ReadOnlyVariables` and `ReadWriteVariables` properties let the Script Task know which variables will be passed into the task's code. In this example, `varHttp` has been added as a value to the `ReadOnlyVariables` property. More than one variable can be added by using commas to separate each of the variables entered, if needed.

A common question that we see is what language you will be able to use in the Script Task and Component. Both of these tasks can only use Visual Basic .NET, since the scripting engine in SSIS is built on top of Visual Studio for Applications, which only supports VB. This is illustrated in the `ScriptLanguage` drop-down list box in the Script Task or Component. More languages are likely to come in future major releases of SSIS, but this will require a shift from Visual Studio for Applications or an enhancement to that Visual Studio for Applications platform.

To view the Script Task's code, click on the Design Script button on the Script Task Editor window, found at the bottom of the screen shown in Figure 2-3. Microsoft Visual Studio for Applications opens, as shown in Figure 2-4. Remember that the `ScriptMain` class is automatically set as the `EntryPoint`, and `Main()` is already added to be the first routine to be executed.

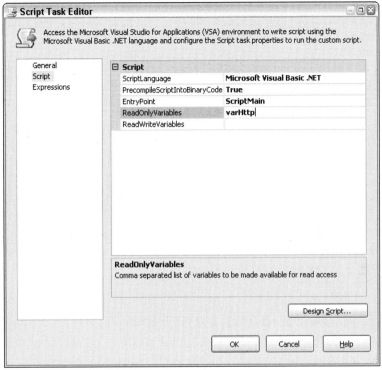

Figure 2-3: Script Task Editor

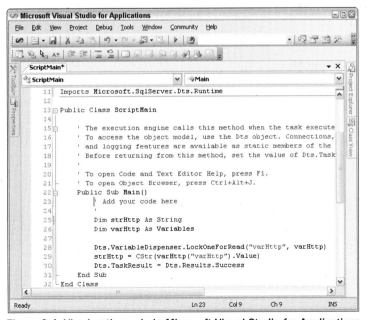

Figure 2-4: Viewing the code in Microsoft Visual Studio for Applications

To access a variable with the `Variables` object, you can use the following code. This code does the same things as shown Figure 2-4 with a slightly easier coding tactic. All this code is doing, though, is simply propagating an SSIS variable to be used as a variable in Visual Basic .NET.

```
Public Sub Main()
    Dim strHTTP As String = Dts.Variables("varHTTP").Value.ToString
    Dts.TaskResult = Dts.Results.Success
End Sub
```

The other option for letting a Script Task know about read-only, user-defined variables is to use the `Dts.VariableDispenser.LockOneForRead` method, as shown in Figure 2-4. This method could be considered a *late-binding approach* because the task is only aware of the variable at runtime, and nothing in the task itself must be configured to make the code aware of the variable. Previously, the variable was set up through the Script Task Editor, which is an *early binding approach*.

If you use the late-binding approach, then a variable collection must be created that will be passed `ByRef` to the `LockOneForRead` method. This will hold the user-defined `varHttp` variable, which was created earlier. Also required is the name of the user-defined variable or key that identifies the item in the collection to be added. At this point, you can retrieve the value of the first item of the collection (indexed by 0), or use the name of the user-defined variable.

Accessing Variables in the Data Flow

Veering from this example slightly is how to access variables from the Script Component in the data flow. This is slightly more complex than accessing variables in the Script Task, but the same concepts apply. When you access a variable from a Script Component, the variable's values are only available to be changed during select periods of the data flow's execution.

The first minor difference to note is that when you list the variables that you want to pass into the component of the data flow, you must not have spaces between each variable name (at least as of SQL Server 2005 SP2). Spaces are forgiven between variables in the Script Task.

The coding syntax also changes slightly in the Script Component. In the Script Component, you'll reference the variable with `Variables.VariableName` as shown in the following code. The `ToString` is not required in the following code and is only used as a good coding practice in order to be very explicit.

```
Public Overrides Sub CreateNewOutputRows()
    Dim strHTTP As String = Variables.varHttp.ToString
    'Some other code here...
End Sub
```

Another distinction is that variables can only be written to in the `PostExecute()` subroutine. This is for performance reasons to keep the variable from being locked constantly as each row goes through the component. The `PostExecute` subroutine is only called after all rows have gone through, and you can write to a variable at that point to show how many rows you transformed.

Building a Custom Assembly

Extending SSIS to use libraries within the .NET Framework is very powerful. Imagine having a corporate encryption algorithm that you must adhere to. Rather than having to rewrite this in SSIS, you could reference the assembly that has already been written from within a Script Task or Component. The ability to access custom functionality provided through assemblies that are either built in-house or proprietary to an organization takes SSIS packages to the next level. Instead of rewriting custom code within a task that may already be encapsulated within an organization's framework, using external assemblies provides an object-oriented approach by promoting code re-use. Code can now reside within an assembly or one location, and then be referenced from multiple tasks.

To create a new assembly, open Visual Studio 2005 and create a new Visual Basic .NET class library, as shown in Figure 2-5. You can also add this project to your existing SSIS solution to keep every dependency organized in the same container. A class library project is the type of the project to use when you need to create assemblies.

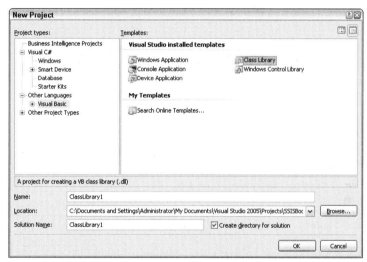

Figure 2-5: Creating a Visual Basic .NET class library

Note that there is no user interface for class library projects like there would be for Windows or web projects. Instead, you will see that a default class is created. For this example, change the class to `HttpFileDownload.vb`, and then combine and add the code from Listing 2-1.

Listing 2-1: Building an Assembly

```
Option Strict On

Imports System.Net

Namespace SSIS.Utilities
    Public Class HttpDownload
        Implements IDisposable
```

(continued)

Listing 2-1: *(continued)*

```vb
        Private webClient As WebClient
        Private m_FileLocation As String
        Public Property FileLocation() As String
            Get
                Return m_FileLocation
            End Get
            Set(ByVal value As String)
                m_FileLocation = value
            End Set
        End Property

        Private m_Url As String
        Public Property WebUrl() As String
            Get
                Return m_Url
            End Get
            Set(ByVal value As String)
                m_Url = value
            End Set
        End Property

        Public Sub New(ByVal HttpFileUrl As String, ByVal PathToDownload As String)
            FileLocation = PathToDownload
            WebUrl = HttpFileUrl
        End Sub

        Public Sub GetFile()
            webClient = New WebClient

            Try
                webClient.DownloadFile(m_Url, m_FileLocation)
            Catch WebEx As WebException
                Throw
            Catch ex As Exception
                Throw
            End Try
        End Sub

        Public Sub Dispose() Implements IDisposable.Dispose
            webClient.Dispose()
            GC.SuppressFinalize(Me)
        End Sub
    End Class
End Namespace
```

The code example in Listing 2-1 shows how to build a simple assembly (in this case, using Visual Basic .NET 2005). This class is going to download a file over HTTP to the calling server. This will later be integrated into a Script Task.

Let's take a quick look at the basic structure of the object. The first thing to notice is `Option Strict On`, which enforces strong typing of objects. *Strong typing* means that object assignments and comparisons must only be set to like objects, therefore reducing memory loss and increasing performance. Next are the two `Import` statements. The `Import` statement enables you to use objects from the .NET Runtime libraries (such as `System.Net`). After you import the object, you won't have to fully qualify the object each time you reference it. The following namespace enables grouping of related classes. If you added an additional class to the namespace `SSIS.Utilities`, then both classes would be represented within that namespace.

The public `HttpDownload` class in Listing 2-1 implements the `IDisposable` interface, which does two things. First, it uses the implemented `Dispose()` method for releasing resources from memory that the custom object utilizes during runtime. In this case, the `WebClient` object is disposed of within the `Dispose()` method.

Within the `Dispose()` method, there is a call to the garbage collector's `SuppressFinalize()` method. The garbage collector reclaims the memory, and by calling its `SuppressFinalize` method and passing in `Me(HttpDownload Class)`, the collector knows that its objects have already been cleaned up through code, and, therefore, there is no reason for the garbage collector to call `Object.Finalize` to destroy its objects.

The `HttpDownload` class also has two properties. These properties can be set externally, or they can be passed into the constructor, when the object is instantiated. The constructor, `New()`, serves as the entry-point where the `HttpFileUrl` and `PathToDownload` parameters are passed in. The `WebClient` object then uses the properties within its `DownloadFile()` method. The `HttpFileUrl` property identifies the URL that a file will be downloaded from and the `PathToDownLoad` property indicates the path where on the local machine the file will be downloaded to.

With the class now created, integrate this into the Script Task, as discussed in the next section. All of the previous code can be downloaded in its compiled and non-compiled format at the Wrox web site (www.wrox.com).

Downloading Files over HTTP

Many sites make files publicly available via the Web, but not via FTP. Files formatted as comma-delimited (as well as many other formats) can be downloaded and then transformed through the Data Flow Task into valuable data. Adding this functionality is simple, especially if you have a developer who has already written the code for you and all you have to do is reference the assembly within an SSIS Script Task. If a developer hasn't provided a class that you can reuse, you'll have to re-create the class code inside the Script Task. Now that you know some of the basics of objects, just follow the next couple of steps and add the code yourself.

In the last section in Listing 2-1, there were two properties added: `FileLocation` (which is the path where the downloaded file will be saved) and `WebUrl` (which serves as the HTTP address that is the Web location from where the file will be downloaded). These properties are set when the object is created.

You can take advantage of the `WebClient` object to add the code that will get files from the Web and download them locally. In Listing 2-1, there was a line of code added that imports the `System.Net` namespace so that the code could have access to the `WebClient` object. The `WebClient` object can send or receive data over the Web by using Uniform Resource Identifiers (URIs), which represent web pages or other resources on the Web.

The method shown in the following code uses the `WebClient` to download a file from a Web site passed in as a parameter, and then stores the file locally within the file system based on the file location parameter, `m_FileLocation`, which is also passed. The `WebException` is thrown if there are any issues such as invalid credentials, or if the site cannot be found from where the file is attempted to be downloaded. An `Exception` object can also be thrown for any other exceptions that are caught. Only that stub code is provided here.

```
Public Sub GetFile()
     webClient = New WebClient

     Try
          webClient.DownloadFile(m_Url, m_FileLocation)
     Catch WebEx As WebException
          Throw
     Catch ex As Exception
          Throw
     End Try
End Sub
```

Adding Assemblies to the GAC

Most .NET development environments allow references to external assemblies. This becomes very useful when you want to reuse the assembly over and over again, versus having to retype the same code. SSIS requires that these custom objects be placed within the Global Assembly Cache (GAC) on the machine that is executing the package to maximize performance of the pipeline and tasks. The GAC is a code cache where assemblies can be placed as a central repository. Even though the framework of SSIS does not provide the choice of placing custom assemblies outside of the GAC, you should be aware that, in most cases, it is better to reference assemblies from a local directory instead from the GAC.

Placing assemblies within the GAC allows them to be referenced by multiple applications on a server. However, it is much easier to manage each application's assemblies within its working directory by giving the developer full control of versioning. When an assembly is referenced from the GAC, each application that references the assembly is affected when the assembly is updated. This might be a nice automated feature at first glance. However, remember that this means applications are being updated without being tested to ensure that the update did not break anything.

To add an assembly to the GAC, it must be given a *strong name*. When an assembly is signed with a strong name, it ensures that the assembly will be unique. An identical or updated assembly cannot be created by another person. This guarantees that the assembly came from the originator and has not been modified by anyone else. The first thing to do when strong-naming an assembly is to create a cryptographic key pair that will be placed in a file.

There are two ways to create a key file:

❑ By using the properties settings of the Visual Studio 2005 project

❑ By manually using the SN utility that comes within the .NET Framework

The SN utility can be found in `C:\Program Files\Microsoft.NET\SDK\v2.0\Bin`. However, you can also select Start ➪ All Programs ➪ Microsoft Visual Studio 2005 ➪ Visual Studio Tools ➪ Visual Studio 2005 Command Prompt. At the command prompt, type **sn –k "C:\MyKeyFile.snk"**. This will build your strong-name key file within the `C:\` root, as shown in Figure 2-6.

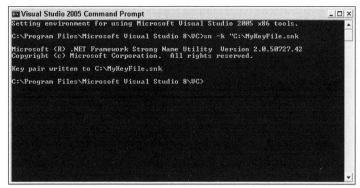

Figure 2-6: Using the command prompt for the SN utility

When signing an assembly with a strong name through the properties of the class library project, a strong-name file must be specified. To do this, select Project ⇨ Properties from the toolbar. When the properties window appears, select the Signing tab, then select the Sign the assembly check box, as shown in Figure 2-7. Choose a strong-name key file by using the drop-down menu and selecting Browse to find the key file created. If the key has not been created using the SN utility, it can be created by selecting New instead of Browse from the drop-down list.

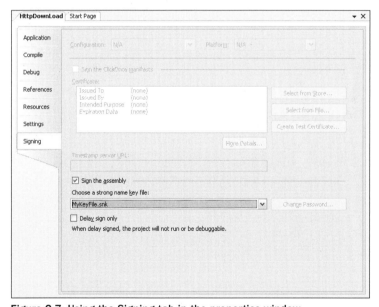

Figure 2-7: Using the Signing tab in the properties window

As shown in Figure 2-8, Visual Studio 2005 makes it even easier to create new keys, as well as providing the option for password-protecting them.

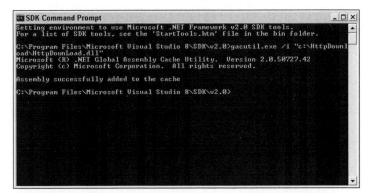

Figure 2-8: Using Visual Studio 2005 to create a strong-name key

In the properties window, select the Compile tab and set the configuration to Active (Release). This optimizes the assembly for production by removing any debugging information. You should never send code to production without having the Release setting set or your code may run significantly slower. The project can now be built by selecting from the toolbar Build ⇨ Build Solution. Take note of the build output path, because it will be needed when the assembly is added to the GAC.

The easiest way to add the assembly to the GAC is by copying the assembly to `C:\WINDOWS\assembly`. However, the Global Assembly Cache Tool (`Gacutil.exe`), which is found in `C:\Program Files\Microsoft.NET\SDK\v2.0\Bin`, can be used as well. You can also access the tool's path by clicking on Start ⇨ All Programs ⇨ Microsoft Visual Studio 2005 ⇨ Visual Studio Tools ⇨ Visual Studio 2005 Command Prompt. Keep in mind that your path may vary based on what version of .NET you are using. At the command prompt, type **gacutil.exe /i "<assembly path>"** to start the utility, as shown in Figure 2-9.

Figure 2-9: Launching gacutil.exe from the command prompt

The assembly must also be placed in the `C:\WINDOWS\Microsoft.NET\Framework\v2.0.50727` path (again, this final folder name may vary based on the version of .NET you have installed). This is where Visual Studio for Applications will look for references. When you have the Script Task in design mode, the assembly can be referenced by right-clicking References within the Project Explorer pane on the left, and then selecting Add Reference. You will then be presented with a list of available assemblies that can be referenced. You can add the reference by selecting the assembly's name and clicking the Add button. The added assembly is now listed on the Add Reference window, as shown in Figure 2-10. Click OK to accept this addition and close the window.

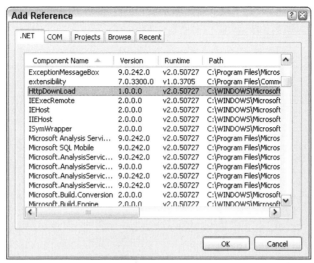

Figure 2-10: Adding a reference

After you have added a reference, the following code shows how to call a custom assembly from a Script Task. Two Script Task variables are passed to the custom assembly, SSIS.Utilities.HttpDownload, through the object's constructor. It's important to have the two variables already set in the ReadOnlyVariables property of the Script Task prior to using the following code.

```
Imports System
Imports System.Data
Imports System.Math
Imports System.Net
Imports System.IO
Imports System.Windows

Public Class ScriptMain

  Public Sub Main()
        Dim strUrl As String = CStr(Dts.Variables("varHttp").Value)
        Dim strFile As String = CStr(Dts.Variables("varSaveFile").Value)
        Using DownloadFile As SSIS.Utilities.HttpDownload = New
SSIS.Utilities.HttpDownload(strUrl, strFile)
            DownloadFile.GetFile()
        End Using
        Dts.TaskResult = Dts.Results.Success
  End Sub
End Class
```

Before running this package, be sure to set the values of the two variables to something useful, or else the code will not know which URL to visit and where to save the resulting file. Set these variables by opening the Variables window again and manually typing both a valid URL into the value for the strUrl variable and a valid file name into the value for the strSaveFile variable. Run the package and, after a while, you should see the file created in the specified location.

Any time custom assemblies are used, it is important to test them before they are implemented. An easy way to test functionality of assemblies is to add a Windows project to the same solution that the class library project belongs to that created the custom object (see Figure 2-11). To add a window project, right-click the solution of the class library project and click Add ⇨ New Project. Select Windows Application. Within the Windows project, right-click References ⇨ Add References ⇨ Projects to add the custom library project as a reference. All you need to add is a button to test the custom object. Note that the Windows project in the following code is in C#. This is a new feature within Visual Studio 2005 that enables you to add projects of different code types. The following code can be added to test the assembly.

```csharp
using System;
using System.Collections.Generic;
using System.ComponentModel;
using System.Data;
using System.Drawing;
using System.Text;
using System.Windows.Forms;
using System.Net;
using System.IO;
using SSIS.Utilities;
using System.Configuration;

namespace WindowsApplication1
{
    public partial class Form1 : Form
    {
        public Form1()
        {
            InitializeComponent();
        }

        private void GetFromWebClient()
        {
            using (HttpDownload httpDL = new
HttpDownload("http://localhost/CSVDownload/Delimited.txt", @"C:\Documents and
Settings\Administrator\Desktop\YouDidit.txt"))
            {
                httpDL.GetFile();
            }
        }

        private void button1_Click(object sender, EventArgs e)
        {
            try
            {

                GetFromWebClient();

            }
            catch(Exception ex1)
            {
                MessageBox.Show(ex1.Message);
            }
        }
    }
}
```

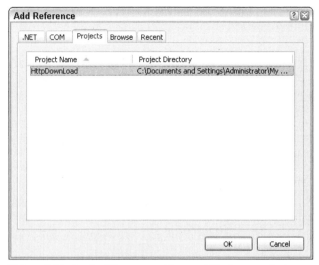

Figure 2-11: Testing the assembly as a Windows project

The method GetFromWebClient() instantiates the custom object, HttpDownload, and passes in a URL and file path. This method is then called from within the button1_Click event, which is called when the button on the form is clicked. Your button may be named differently, so change the name of this event to represent your name. Now that there are two projects, the Windows form project must be set up as the start-up project. To do this, right-click the Windows project and select Set as Startup Project. After the solution is run, if there are any problems, a message box will pop up with any errors that occurred.

When the code is functioning correctly, the assembly is ready to be referenced from within the Script Task.

Making Connections Configurable and Dynamic

Connections are the most common object within a package that needs to be updated. This is because packages in development most often point to development databases. When you are ready to deploy your package to a test machine or a production machine, then you must have that connection updated. The wrong answer is to manually open the package and hard-code the new connection string because when the package is modified, you introduce the possibility of new bugs creeping in.

Another common example that requires connection strings to be dynamic is when file names change because of a change of date or because you are given a set of identical files that you need to loop over.

Within SSIS, there are many ways to accommodate dynamic connection strings. A developer can choose from one the following options:

❑ **Package Configurations** — The connection string is stored somewhere external to the package (such as a file or database table) by leveraging SSIS Package Configurations. The connection can then be changed without touching the package. With this approach, the connection is updated once at the very start of the package execution. Setting up configurations is relatively straight-forward and the details can be found in Books Online, or in Chapter 16 of the *Professional SQL Server 2005 Integration Services* book.

❑ **Property Expressions** — The `ConnectionString` property of a package connection can be dynamically updated through the use of SSIS Property Expressions. When a property expression is implemented on a connection, then, when the connection is accessed during execution, instead of pulling the hard-coded value of the `ConnectionString`, the expression is run to generate the new `ConnectionString`. (Unlike configurations, the `ConnectionString` is updated when the connection is accessed, not when the package loads.) Chapter 3 of this book walks through an example where a set of Excel files is looped over with the For Each loop container and each iteration uses a Data Flow Task to pull in the Excel data, with the connection property updated through this mechanism.

❑ **Script Task** — Package connection properties are accessible at runtime. This means that you can add a Script Task to your control flow, and within the script, perform updates to the connections when the Script Task runs. The remainder of this section focuses on accessing and updating connections in the Script Task.

Making connections configurable through the Script Tasks is extremely useful when building packages that will be run in different environments. The Script Task can also provide the flexibility of updating more than one connection, or even of building new connections through code on-the-fly.

To better understand configurable connections, the best starting point is the `Microsoft.SqlServer` `.Dts.Runtime` namespace. A Connections collection within the namespace holds the connections that are set up within the connection manager. These connections can be iterated through using an index or the actual name of the collection created. Each collection exposes a property called `ConnectionString` that can be configured at runtime.

To begin with a simple example, the following code (inside of a Script Task) shows how to display a connection string that is stored in a package variable (the first line of code). The second line then gets a count of how many connections are available within the connection manager, and exposes the results via a message box. Next, the code sets the `ConnectionString` property of the first connection within the connection manager to the value from the variable `"strConnString"`. Note that this code uses an index or numeric value to get the connection object (the name of the connection object that was set when the connection was created can be used as well). In this simple example, the connection can be updated to run against different databases just by changing the variable that holds a connection string value.

```
Public Sub Main()
    Dim strCnStr As String = CStr(Dts.Variables("strConnString").Value)

    MsgBox(Dts.Connections.Count.ToString())
    Dts.Connections(0).ConnectionString() = strCnStr

    Dts.TaskResult = Dts.Results.Success
End Sub
```

This next example creates a new connection from scratch, which, as you will see, is also straightforward. The code in Listing 2-2 shows how to create a `SqlConnection` object. To take advantage of a connection object, the code also uses a `SqlCommand` object and a `SqlDataReader` object. In this case, the `SqlCommand` object runs a query as a text statement. However, it can also run stored procedures. It uses the connection object that was created and opened (based on the connection string) to return a `SqlDataReader`, which is a forward-only representation of the data returned. The `System.Data.CommandBehavior` has been set to `CloseConnection` to ensure that the connection is closed after the `SqlDataReader` is iterated or looped through.

Listing 2-2: Creating a New Connection

```
Public Sub Main()
        Dim SqlConn As SqlClient.SqlConnection
        Dim SqlCmd As SqlClient.SqlCommand
        Dim SqlReader As SqlClient.SqlDataReader
        Dim strCnStr As String = CStr(Dts.Variables("strConnString").Value)

        Dts.Connections(0).ConnectionString() = strCnStr
        MsgBox(Dts.Connections.Count.ToString())

        SqlConn = New SqlClient.SqlConnection(strCnStr)
        SqlConn.Open()
        SqlCmd = New SqlClient.SqlCommand(" _
            SELECT TOP 5 ADDRESSLINE1 FROM PERSON.ADDRESS", SqlConn)
        SqlReader = _
            SqlCmd.ExecuteReader(System.Data.CommandBehavior.CloseConnection)

        While (SqlReader.Read)
            MsgBox(CStr(SqlReader(0)))
        End While

        Dts.TaskResult = Dts.Results.Success
    End Sub
```

When using this approach, ensure that the package variable `strConnString` has been set to a valid connection string value (in this case, a table in the `AdventureWorks` database); otherwise, your package will fail!

In both of these examples (updating an existing package connection and creating a new connection), the dynamic connection strings were handled with only a few lines of code.

Raising Error Events

Sometimes the logic in your Script Task can be quite complex, and you may want to raise an error intentionally without causing the entire task to fail. For example, if you try to encrypt a file and the file name doesn't match what you expect even though your Visual Basic .NET syntax is fine, you may want to raise an error.

You can force the entire task to fail by using the `Dts.Results.Failure` method, but the error that is logged is not verbose to diagnose why the failure occurred. SSIS would only report a general failure.

In the `Microsoft.SqlServer.Dts.Runtime` namespace's interface, `IDTSComponentEvents` contains events that can be wired within the Script Task. When an error occurs, the `FireError` method can be used to raise the error. The parameters shown in the following table are passed to expose information about the error that occurred.

PARAMETER	DATA TYPE	DESCRIPTION
errorCode	Integer	Unique identifier of the error message
subComponent	String	Specific information as to where the event originated
Description	String	Explanation about why the error occurred
helpFile	String	Location of the file that gives specific information about the error
helpContext	Integer	Unique identification of the information source within the Help file

The following example shows how to throw an error through code:

```
Dts.Events.FireError(1234, "", "Here is an error!", "", -1)
```

After the code has been run, the error can be seen by switching over to the Progress tab during execution (see Figure 2-12), or to the Execution Results Tab within the design view of the package. It can also be seen in the SSIS Logs if you are producing those. This error will be seen whether the task would have succeeded or not.

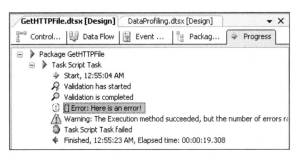

Figure 2-12: Viewing the error using the Progress tab during execution

When using error events, there are two important things to think about when deciding what information the event should know about:

❑   What type of error occurred?

❑   What information about the error needs to be raised?

When addressing errors, utilize the Try...Catch block. Within the Try...Catch block, errors can be caught by the type of error that is thrown. For example, in Listing 2-2, connections are opened and data is returned from the database. If an error is thrown when performing either task, a SqlClient .SqlException can be thrown and handled differently than if any other type of error is thrown.

The following code demonstrates how to handle the two different types of errors. If a SqlClient .SqlException occurs, then an error event is fired. If a standard exception is thrown, then a message box is raised to show the exception message. You obviously do not want to normally pop up message boxes in SSIS. Otherwise, you could inadvertently leave them, and your job would hang in production because no one is there to click OK.

```
Try
    'Do some stuff that may fail...
Throw New Exception("Here is a base Exception")

Catch Sqlex As SqlClient.SqlException
    Dts.Events.FireError(Sqlex.ErrorCode, "", Sqlex.Message, "", -1)
Catch ex As Exception
    MsgBox(ex.Message)
End Try
```

Encrypting Data Through Script Components

So far, most of this chapter has focused on the Script Task, which is in the control flow of your package. In the data flow, you use a Script Component, which morphs into a Script Source, Transform, or Destination. The code that's stubbed out for each of the components varies based on what role you want the Script Component to play. More information on this can be seen in the *Professional SQL Server 2005 Integration Services* book. This section shows you how to use the power of the data flow to transform data into an encrypted form.

As the world of technology matures, the unfortunate reality is that new methods of hacking mature as well. In earlier versions of SQL Server, there was nothing that handled encryption. Within SQL Server 2005, however, there is built-in functionality that handles encryption and decryption of data. Obviously, certain types of data should not be left in plain text within a database (data such as credit card numbers and Social Security numbers, for example). Wouldn't it be nice to have a component that handles encryption as well?

SSIS does not have a component that handles encryption and decryption out-of-the-box. However, the Script Component can be extended to use a custom library that encapsulates the encryption/decryption for you. The component can then be reused within other packages.

When using encryption, you should understand how it works, as well as what types of encryption are available. There are two types of encryption: symmetric and asymmetric.

Symmetric encryption means that there is one key that is shared by two different parties for encrypting and decrypting data. For example, if Party A needs to send encrypted data to Party B, then both parties must know a private key that can be used to encrypt and decrypt any data that is sent.

Asymmetric encryption uses a key pair. One key is private and one key is public. Party A sends a message request along with a public key to Party B. Party B can then encrypt a message over the wire with the public key supplied, so it cannot be compromised. After the message has been encrypted with the public key, it is then sent to Party A. The message can now be decrypted by Party A using the private key. The important part is that a public key can be re-created each time, thus changing the private key in case it is ever compromised.

The following table describes some well-known encryption algorithms.

Encryption Algorithm	Description	Key Size
Data Encryption Standard (DES)	Created by IBM, National Security Agency (NSA), and others as a standard back in the 1970s. In 2000, it was broken because of the growth in technology.	56 bits
Triple DES (3DES)	Superseded DES by implementing the DES algorithm three times over, therefore providing the name 3DES. Encryption experts feel that its days are numbered. However, it has not been broken.	156 bits
Rijndael (AES)	Advance Encryption Standard (AES) was created by Joan Daemon and Vincent Rijmen, and is currently the standard of the United States government. The algorithm used is called Rijndael.	126,192, and 256 bits (Standard)

Listing 2-3 is a `static` class that uses Rijndael's encryption algorithm. Since this is another example of custom code, it has been written with C# to show that it does not matter what language is used, as long as custom assemblies are written with .NET code. Listing 2-3 contains two public properties: `Key` (the symmetric key) and `IV` (the Initialization Vector). These properties can be generated by calling the `CreateSymmetricKey()` method. The properties can also be passed in using the two methods, `Encrypt()` and `Decrypt()`, along with the data to be encrypted or decrypted.

Listing 2-3: C# Code Using the Rijndael Encryption Algorithm

```csharp
using System;
using System.Collections.Generic;
using System.Text;
using System.Security;
using System.Security.Cryptography;
using System.IO;

namespace SSIS.Utilities
{
    static public class SecuringData
    {
        static private byte[] m_key;
        static private byte[] m_iv;

        /// <summary>
        /// Holds the Symmetric Key
        /// </summary>
        static public string Key
        {
            get
            {
                return Convert.ToBase64String(m_key);
            }
```

```csharp
        set
        {
            m_key = Convert.FromBase64String(value);
        }
}
/// <summary>
/// Holds the Init Vector
/// </summary>
static public string IV
{
    get
    {
        return Convert.ToBase64String(m_iv);
    }
    set
    {
        m_iv = Convert.FromBase64String(value);
    }
}

/// <summary>
/// Sets a key and iv for encryption
/// </summary>
/// <param name="key"></param>
/// <param name="iv"></param>
static public void CreateSymmetricKey(string key, string iv)
{
    Key = key;
    IV = iv;
}

/// <summary>
/// Creates a key and IV for encryption
/// </summary>
static public void CreateSymmetricKey()
{
    Rijndael RhineDal = new RijndaelManaged();

    try
    {
        RhineDal.GenerateKey();
        RhineDal.GenerateIV();
        m_key = RhineDal.Key;
        m_iv = RhineDal.IV;

    }
    catch (CryptographicException)
    {
        throw;
    }
    finally
    {
        RhineDal.Clear();
    }
}
```

(continued)

Listing 2-3: *(continued)*

```csharp
static public void Encrypt(ref string Data,
                          string key,
                          string iv)
{
    Rijndael RhineDal = new RijndaelManaged();
    CryptoStream cs = null;
    MemoryStream ms = null;
    Byte[] byt;

    try
    {
        if(key!=null)
            Key = key;

        if(iv!=null)
            IV = iv;

        KeySupplied();

        RhineDal.Key = m_key;
        RhineDal.IV = m_iv;

        ICryptoTransform RndlEncrypt = RhineDal.CreateEncryptor();
        byt = Encoding.UTF8.GetBytes(Data);

        ms = new MemoryStream();
        cs = new CryptoStream(ms, RndlEncrypt, CryptoStreamMode.Write);
        cs.Write(byt, 0, byt.Length);
        cs.FlushFinalBlock();
        cs.Close();
        Data = Convert.ToBase64String(ms.ToArray());
    }
    catch (ApplicationException)
    {
        throw;
    }
    catch (CryptographicException)
    {
        throw;
    }
    catch (Exception)
    {
        throw;
    }
    finally
    {
        RhineDal.Clear();
    }
}

static public void Decrypt(ref string EncryptedData,
                string key, string iv)
```

```
        {
            Rijndael RhineDal = new RijndaelManaged();
            CryptoStream cs = null;
            MemoryStream ms = null;
            Byte[] byt;

            try
            {
                if (key != null)
                    Key = key;

                if (iv != null)
                    IV = iv;

                KeySupplied();

                RhineDal.Key = m_key;
                RhineDal.IV = m_iv;

                ICryptoTransform RndlEncrypt = RhineDal.CreateDecryptor();
                byt = Convert.FromBase64String(EncryptedData);

                ms = new MemoryStream();
                cs = new CryptoStream(ms, RndlEncrypt, CryptoStreamMode.Write);

                cs.Write(byt, 0, byt.Length);
                cs.FlushFinalBlock();
                cs.Close();
                EncryptedData =  Encoding.UTF8.GetString(ms.ToArray());
            }
            catch (ApplicationException)
            {
                throw;
            }
            catch (CryptographicException)
            {
                throw;
            }
            catch (Exception)
            {
                throw;
            }
            finally
            {
                RhineDal.Clear();
            }
        }

        static private void KeySupplied()
        {
            if (m_iv == null || m_key == null)
                throw new ApplicationException("A Key and IV must be supplied");
        }

    }
}
```

After the `SecuringData` class is compiled (using a new C# class library project) and added to the GAC, it is ready to be referenced just as you did earlier in this chapter. Create or open an existing SSIS package within Visual Studio and add a new Data Flow Task. Create a new ADO.NET Connection Manager that connects to the `AdventureWorks` database. In the data flow, add a new Data Reader Source. Double-click the Data Reader Task to configure it. Figure 2-13 shows how the Data Reader Source should be configured to reference the AdventureWorks Connection Manager.

Figure 2-13: Creating a new connection manager that points to the AdventureWorks database

The Data Reader Source is the source for all records from the `Person.Address` table, where the person lives in the city of Bothell, and will initiate the data flow.

Prior to opening the Data Reader Source, create two new string variables, one called `Key` and the other called `IV` (which stands for Initialization Vector). These two variables will be used later to store the key that SSIS will use to encrypt the data. The values of each variable can be random bytes of data. To get started, use `THk5QMKX1HGVzSo8Pq7X6y1q6IjnVqR/inuZsaagVpY=` as `Key` and `bjsLiMoy6/mUsvuMdjMWhA==` as `IV`, as shown in Figure 2-14.

With the plumbing now complete, open the Data Reader Source, and in the Component Properties tab, set the `SqlCommand` property for the Data Reader Source to the following `SELECT` statement:

```
SELECT  *
FROM    Person.Address
WHERE   (City = 'Bothell')
```

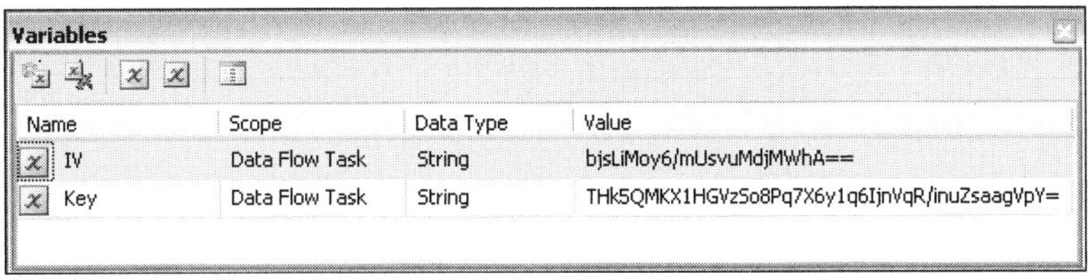

Figure 2-14: Creating the Key and IV variables

The Script Component can now be added (select Transformation as the script type after you drag it onto the design surface) and wired to the Data Reader Source component by using the green arrow. Double-click on the Script Component, and in the Input Columns page, check `AddressLine1` to pass it into the script and select `ReadOnly` for the usage type. Any columns you select here can be accessed inside the script and their values can be used in calculations or whatever the script needs them for. Setting their usage to `ReadOnly` means the column values cannot be changed in the script; setting them to `ReadWrite` allows the script to both read the current values of the column and then update them, too. Lastly, any columns you don't check here just pass right through the transform untouched.

There is an Add Output button that can be pressed to add new output columns and paths from the transform (additional green arrows). In this case, use the existing `Output 0` output. When you select the `Output Columns` folder, the Add Column button can be clicked to add new columns to be outputted from the transform. When creating a new column, be sure to set both the `DataType` property, which is the type of data the column will hold (Boolean, integer, string, and so on), and the `Name` property, which will be used to identify the output. For this example, create a new output column called `EncAddressLine1`, which is a 250-character string (see Figure 2-15). More space will be needed to store the `AddressLine1` column after it's encrypted, and the amount of space will vary based on the encryption type you use.

Note that, in this case, we have created what is called a *synchronous transformation*, meaning that as each row comes into the script, it is updated immediately with any new values (using the script code) and the new row is passed through to the output without copying any data. You could also have created an *asynchronous transformation*, which, in a nutshell, would mean that inside the script you actually copy each row from the input into the output. This copying would mean the operations would be slower, but the benefit is that the set of output columns could be quite different from the set of input columns in terms of number, type, and size.

To add the script that follows, select the Script page in the left pane of the Script Transformation Editor. The `Key` and Initialization Vector (`IV`) variables you created earlier must be passed into the custom assembly from the component. The property `ReadOnlyVariables` should be set to `Key, IV` (without spaces between the two variables) so that the script recognizes them as variables.

Also note that the custom assembly `SecuringData` has a `CreateSymmetricKey()` method. This can be called as well to create these parameters. However, just as with testing the assemblies within a Windows project, the `SecuringData` object could be embedded within the Windows app, which could then call the `CreateSymmetricKey()` method to display the generated `key` and `IV` on the form.

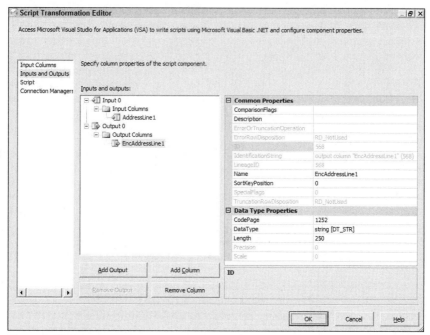

Figure 2-15: Output columns in the Script Transformation Editor

The script can now be added by clicking the Design Script button. When the Visual Studio Script Editor launches, paste the following code (available at www.wrox.com). After adding the code, add a reference to the code by right-clicking on References ⇨ Add Reference and selecting the name of the file created from Listing 2-3 that was added to the GAC earlier.

```
Imports System
Imports System.Data
Imports System.Math
Imports Microsoft.SqlServer.Dts.Pipeline.Wrapper
Imports Microsoft.SqlServer.Dts.Runtime.Wrapper
Imports SSIS.Utilities

Public Class ScriptMain
    Inherits UserComponent

    Public Overrides Sub Input0_ProcessInputRow(ByVal Row As Input0Buffer)
        'Encrypt AddressLine1 and save the result to EncAddressLine1
        Row.EncAddressLine1 = EncryptValue(Row.AddressLine1)
        'Then blank out the original (unencrypted) value from AddressLine1
        Row.AddressLine1_IsNull = True
    End Sub

    Private Function EncryptValue(ByVal RowVal As String) As String
        SecuringData.Encrypt(RowVal, Me.Variables.Key, Me.Variables.IV)
        Return RowVal
    End Function
End Class
```

Finally, add a Flat File Destination component and wire it up to the Script Component by dragging the green arrow and connecting it (see Figure 2-16). This component will accept the transformed or encrypted data, and write it to a specified file. Double-click the component to set the properties of what columns to write, as well as the type of file and where the file will be written (of course, there is no need to write the `AddressLine1` column to the file since every one of these values has been ensured to be `null` inside the script—but you do want to write out the `EncAddressLine1` columns). The package is now ready to be executed.

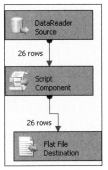

**Figure 2-16: Adding a Flat
File Destination component**

If you open the text file where you saved the encrypted data, you should see that all of the `EncAddressLine1` values are now encrypted, as shown in Figure 2-17.

**Figure 2-17: Viewing all EncAddressLine1 values
encrypted**

Similar code can be used to decrypt the data. To see how to decrypt the file in the pipeline, you could use the same steps, but this time, make the flat file the source. The code then for the Script Component would look like the following:

```
Imports System
Imports System.Data
Imports System.Math
Imports Microsoft.SqlServer.Dts.Pipeline.Wrapper
Imports Microsoft.SqlServer.Dts.Runtime.Wrapper
Imports SSIS.Utilities

Public Class ScriptMain
    Inherits UserComponent

    Public Overrides Sub Input0_ProcessInputRow(ByVal Row As Input0Buffer)
        'Decrypt EncAddressLine1 and save the result to AddressLine1
        Row.AddressLine1 = DecryptValue(Row.EncAddressLine1)
        'Then blank out the original (encrypted) value from EncAddressLine1
        Row.EncAddressLine1_IsNull = True
    End Sub

    Private Function DecryptValue(ByVal RowVal As String) As String
        SecuringData.Decrypt(RowVal, Me.Variables.Key, Me.Variables.IV)
        Return RowVal
    End Function
End Class
```

Data Profiling

Data profiling is becoming an increasingly important facet to a DBA or warehouse architect's job title. Data profiling can shave weeks off a few-month project by speeding up the requirements process and letting the business unit know what type of issues they're going to experience prior to starting the project. It also is extremely important if you want to do data validation or cleansing as data moves through the data flow.

Data profiling is the DBA's way of checking inconsistent user-entered data that falls through the cracks of being validated from the source that saved the data to the database. DBAs can use SSIS to assist in data profiling so that the format of data (such as credit card numbers, telephone numbers, e-mail addresses, residential addresses, and so on) follows the formatted guidelines for which the data is intended to be stored. You especially see this type of data cleansing with companies that perform mailings. The cost of mailing is much cheaper if you're able to presort and standardize the addresses.

Data profiling with SSIS provides the flexibility to direct bad data to text logs or other database tables, and to provide custom information or metadata, so that there is enough information for corrective action to be taken on such data.

The following demo profiles the `EmailAddress` and `Phone` columns from the `AdventureWorks` `Person.Contact` table. The data flow will separate good and bad records by placing them into two different flat files.

To get started, create a new package and add a Data Flow Task. Then, add a Data Reader Source. An Ado.Net connection manager is also needed to connect to the AdventureWorks database that must be wired up to the Data Reader Source, just as you did in previous examples. In the Component Properties tab of the Data Reader Source, set the SqlCommand property to the following query:

```
SELECT * FROM PERSON.CONTACT
```

A Script Component can now be added that will perform the profiling on the data (once again in a synchronous manner). Double-click on the component and check the ContactID, EmailAddress, and Phone columns as Input Columns, as shown in Figure 2-18. Ensure that ReadOnly is set for the UsageType property of all the columns.

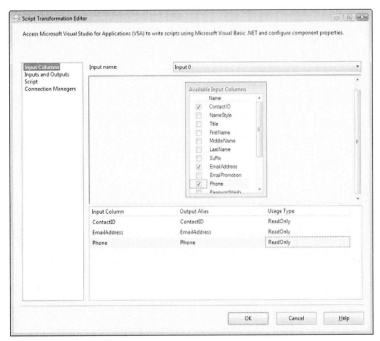

Figure 2-18: Input Columns

The extraneous columns that will be set as output can now be manually added to the Output 0 node; making sure that their data types and lengths match the corresponding input columns. Figure 2-19 shows ValidPhone as a Boolean, and ValidEmail as a Boolean. The values for ValidPhone and ValidEmail will be set by script within the component that uses Regular Expressions (RegEx) to validate the format of the data.

If the data is valid for each record, then the transform will set the ValidEmail or ValidPhone columns to true. If the data is not valid, then they will be set to false accordingly. You could then apply additional business logic in a Conditional Split or Derived Column transform to separate the good and bad rows. Next, click the Design Script button in the Script page to begin writing the code. Listing 2-4 shows the logic. Note that the RegularExpressions are part of the System.Text.RegularExpressions namespace, so be sure that the assembly is imported first.

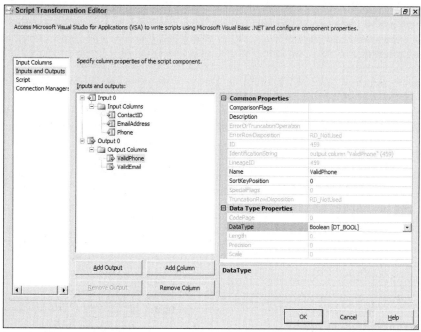

Figure 2-19: Output fields

Listing 2-4: Getting Input Values

```
Imports System.Data
Imports Microsoft.SqlServer.Dts.Pipeline.Wrapper
Imports Microsoft.SqlServer.Dts.Runtime.Wrapper
Imports System.Text.RegularExpressions

Public Class ScriptMain
    Inherits UserComponent

    Dim rgxEmail, rgxPhone As Regex

    Public Overrides Sub PreExecute()
        MyBase.PreExecute()
        rgxEmail = New Regex("\S+@\S+\.\S+", RegexOptions.Compiled)
        rgxPhone = New Regex("\(?\s*\d{3}\s*[\)\.\-]?\s*\d{3}\s*[\-\.]?\s*\d{4}",
RegexOptions.Compiled)
    End Sub

    Public Overrides Sub Input0_ProcessInputRow(ByVal Row As Input0Buffer)
        Row.ValidEmail = rgxEmail.IsMatch(Row.EmailAddress)
        Row.ValidPhone = rgxPhone.IsMatch(Row.Phone)
    End Sub
End Class
```

Listing 2-4 performs the cleaning operations discussed. Phone numbers and e-mail addresses are checked against regular expressions that validate the data's format. There are different regular expressions, and you will find that there is not just one regular expression that's a fix for all, even for phone and e-mail addresses. E-mail addresses and phone numbers that are valid for one application may be invalid for others. These expressions have been selected just for this demonstration. Note how the regular expressions have been instantiated in the PreExecute() phase of the component; this is so that we only initialize them once. An optional parameter is also passed in to the regular expression constructor to tell it to compile the expression, which provides some extra performance when using these objects.

A Conditional Split component is then used to separate the valid/invalid data coming out of the Script Component. Using logical operators of || represents an OR condition and && represents an AND condition.

Figure 2-20 shows that there are two conditions created by dragging a column from the Columns tree and adding them as a condition. The functions in the top-right window can be used when creating the condition's expression logic. The first condition, called Invalid Data, checks the output columns, ValidEmail or ValidPhone, which are passed from the Script Component. The Invalid Data condition checks if either flag is false. The Valid Data condition checks that both flags are true. In actuality, you could have just entered the first Invalid Data condition and then put the Valid Data condition as the Default output name. In essence, this would have created and If...Then...Else condition, but for this example, both conditions were left in to demonstrate how you can check for multiple conditions if your logic were more complex.

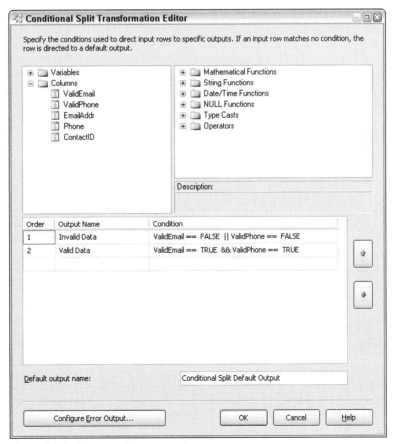

Figure 2-20: Creation of two conditions

As shown in Figure 2-21, by setting up this logic, the component can now be wired to handle both conditions. The conditions are wired up to Flat File Destination components. The columns used as outputs are then added to each of the flat files.

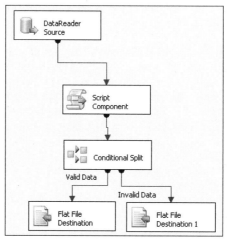

Figure 2-21: Component wired to handle both conditions

In Figure 2-22, you can see the BadData.txt file that was created. The component has been configured so that the column headers are added to the top. The first two fields are the flags, and the record shows that the phone number is not the correct format for the regular expression that was used to check it. The record has a phone number of 55-2555-0100, which is obviously invalid.

Figure 2-22: BadData.txt file

This type of example is very important when you're dealing with postal data. Companies can quantify the cost of each letter going out to a customer. If you can give your marketing department better quality data or more reliable data, you can save your company a lot of money. Also, it's useful for detecting fraud or data that you may want to have manually inspected.

Summary

This chapter has focused on building tasks and components to be configurable. SSIS tasks and components are even more powerful when they are designed so that they can be reused within other packages. When designing packages, it is good practice to use variables when there is a need to hold configuration settings. Tasks can then be configured to function differently within different packages and environments.

Not only are reusable tasks important, but creating reusable code is even more important. The examples in this chapter have shown how scripts can be extended by reusing custom functionality within assemblies. By extending SSIS scripts to use custom assemblies, custom logic is encapsulated into assemblies and referenced, rather than embedded within the script. The logic becomes easier to maintain, although, at the same time, allows more than one person to technically work on building scripts during a given time.

Now that you understand how to extend SSIS through scripts, you are ready to tackle extracting data from sources.

3

Data Extraction

A natural first discussion point for ETL is the extraction, the *E* in ETL. This chapter applies the concepts of the data extraction with using SSIS. As discussed in Chapter 1, ETL applies to a broad spectrum of applications beyond just data warehousing and ETL loading. Therefore, the discussion of this topic will include both generalized extraction concepts and data warehouse–specific concepts.

Data extraction is the process of moving data off of a source system, potentially to a staging environment or into the transformation phase of the ETL. Figure 3-1 shows the extraction process separated out on the left. An extraction process may pull data from a variety of sources, including files or database systems, as this figure highlights.

A few common objectives of data extraction include the following:

❑ Consistency in how data is extracted across source systems

❑ Performance of the extraction

❑ Minimal impact on the source to avoid contention with critical source processes

❑ Flexibility to handle source system changes

❑ The ability to target only new or changed records

This chapter is structured into the following three sections:

❑ **SSIS data flow source adapters** — Beyond just a review of the data flow sources, this chapter looks at performance and configuration options.

❑ **Incremental extraction** — Part of applying data extraction in SSIS involves seeing how to design SSIS packages that perform incremental extractions — extracting only changed records from a source.

❑ **Data lineage** — Many applications require that the source data being extracted include a mechanism that points back to the very records that were extracted, which provides valuable data validation.

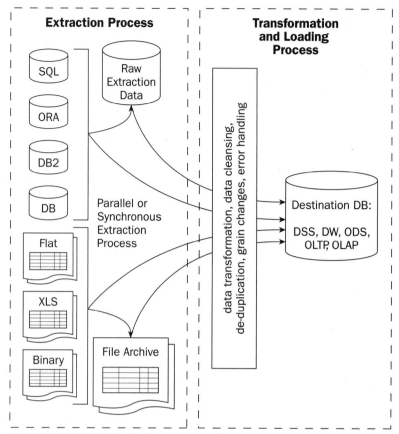

Figure 3-1: Extraction process

Package Connections and Data Flow Sources

The data flow sources in SSIS provide the ability to connect to most standard data repositories, such as delimited files, Excel files, Oracle databases, and so on. With these data sources, which rely on package connections, some of the connections included out-of-the-box with the Windows and SSIS install include SQL Server, flat files (of various code pages), Analysis Services, Oracle, MS Excel, MS Access, XML, and so on.

> It's important to note that many of the sources that SSIS can use come from the OS-level inclusion of Microsoft Data Access Components (MDAC). Go to www.microsoft.com/data for more information.

Both data flow and control flow components use separate objects at the package level to facilitate connectivity package connection, whether to connect to an FTP site, to a relational database, or to a file system folder. All data flow sources (except the Raw adapter) leverage package connections to extract data. As a review, the Connection Manager window appears at the bottom of the control flow and data flow, and right-clicking in the window allows a new connection to be created, as Figure 3-2 highlights.

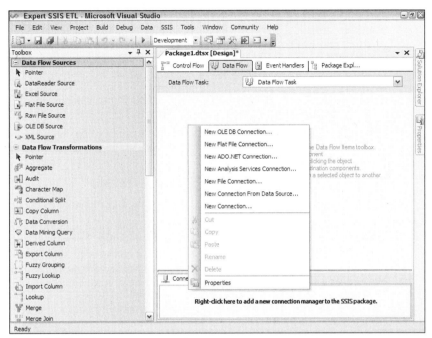

Figure 3-2: Creating a new connection

The choices include creating a connection from an existing project Data Source, plus the ability to create a data source from many other types of connection types, including flat file connections, ADO.NET connections, Analysis Services connections, and OLE DB connections. Creating a connection is the first step in extracting data, and the second step is typically to create a new Data Flow Task (in the same package) that will contain the source adapter (which references the connection). The next section examines all the different package adapters, but also be aware that when you create a new source adapter in the data flow, new connections can typically be created automatically right inside the specific adapter's editor.

> A Data Source created within an SSIS project (and viewable in the Solution Explorer window in BIDS) can be linked to and shared among packages. When using a Data Source in this manner, be aware that these shared Data Source connections are only updated in the designer, meaning that when you modify the project Data Source, you must open up all the packages that share that Data Source, then the linked connection can be updated with the new connection string. When you deploy packages from your development environment and run the package outside BIDS, the connection will no longer be shared among other packages or updated by the Data Source. Instead, you should use a package configuration to update connections and to share connection strings.

Source Adapters

Although connections in the package point to source systems or files, the adapters are the objects that define what is extracted. For example, a connection may reference an Oracle database or SQL Server database, and a source adapter would define which specific table (or view or query) to extract data from. For Excel connections, the adapter references which worksheet and data range to pull, and for flat files, the adapter simply references the flat file connection, because the connection already defines the columns and file format metadata. Figure 3-3 shows the data flow source adapters within the data flow toolbox.

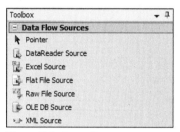

Figure 3-3: Data flow source adapters

It's only the raw file that doesn't have an associated connection, and that is because the file itself already contains all the details about the columns and data types defined within. *Professional SQL Server 2005 Integration Services* (Wiley Publications, 2006) summarizes the source adapters in Chapter 8. Therefore, this section simply summarizes this information, looks at some advanced features of these components, and discusses some best practices around the adapters.

Flat File Source

Flat files are a very common extraction source. This is because many source systems will push data to flat files (for various reasons) that can then be consumed by another process (such as SSIS) in a loosely coupled manner. The flat file source adapter is a powerful mechanism to bring data into the data flow. Flat files come in many different structures and formats. SSIS supports delimited, fixed-width, and fixed with ragged right, where the last column may have an undetermined number of characters. Even delimited flat files may have different column delimiters and different text qualifiers, and these can be set in the advanced properties of the connection.

Two important features of the flat file source give the adapter extra flexibility and great performance. First of all, the flat file adapter supports various code page formats. Figure 3-4 shows the General tab of the Flat File Connection Manager Editor, with the Code page drop-down selected.

The most common code page, of course, is ANSI 1252 – Latin 1. But beyond that, you may have files generated from legacy systems or applications, such as sources with double-byte characters, IBM EBCDIC files, or even other language-specific code pages.

Second, a little-known property of the flat file adapter is the FastParse property available for date, time, and integer source columns, as Figure 3-5 shows.

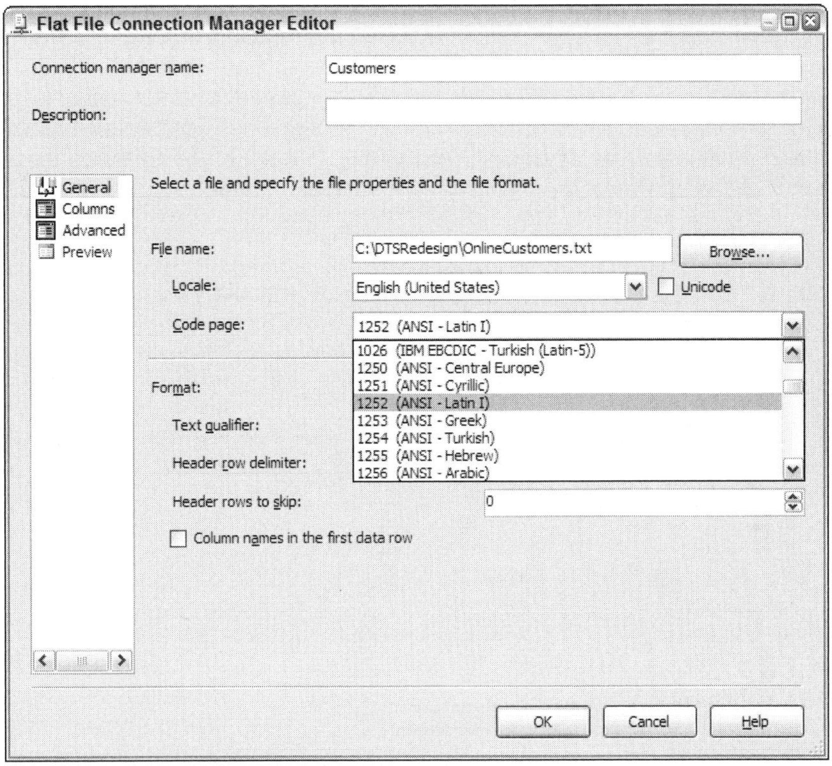

Figure 3-4: General tab of the flat file editor

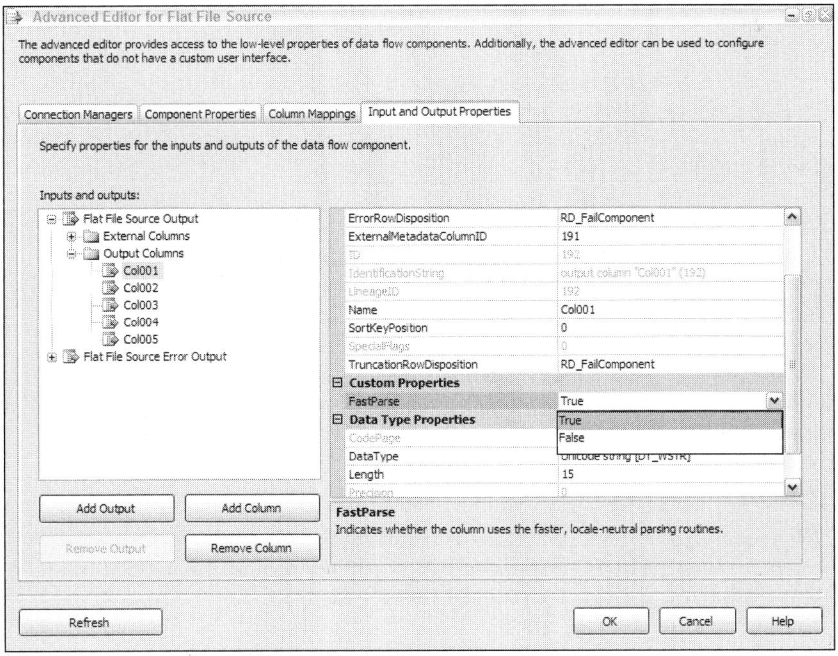

Figure 3-5: FastParse property

The `FastParse` property of output columns (found in the Advanced Editor, Input and Output Properties tab) reduces the conversion overhead of each column as it is imported into the data flow buffers, and overall gives generous performance benefits. By using the Fast Parse option, you are giving up the ability to translate the value to the local specific data, and you are forced to have date columns formatted in YYYYMMDD or YYYY-MM-DD format. But if you are dealing with large flat files, you will want to work through these limitations to take advantage of the setting. In essence, you are telling the connection that the data can be trusted in the source column to be in a standard format.

DataReader Source

The DataReader Source is the adapter used to connect to an ADO.NET source. There's nothing fancy about the user interface. Because the ADO.NET providers don't expose the database objects and metadata, the source query must be manually entered. Figure 3-6 shows the main editor of the DataReader adapter.

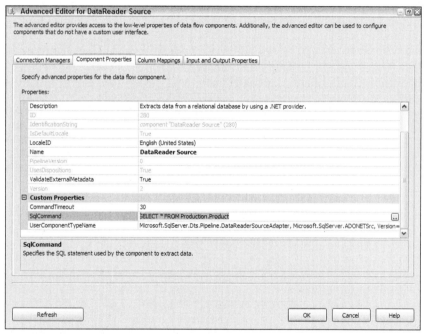

Figure 3-6: Main editor of the Data Reader adapter

Many have found that the ADO.NET provider is more often than not slower in SSIS as compared to an OLE DB provider for the same source. The reason is not that the ADO.NET providers are slow, but rather the overhead required to marshal data from a native source, through a managed provider, and into the native SSIS pipeline requires more steps.

OLE DB Source

The OLE DB source adapter provides the most flexibility, because it allows several mechanisms to customize the source query, including parameterization and variable bound queries, which are both covered later in this chapter in the section "Incremental Data Extraction."

When using the OLE DB source adapter to connect to SQL Server, leverage the SQL Native Client (SQLNCI), because it is the best choice for SQL Server sources, offering very fast extraction.

In addition, you can use OS-based Microsoft Data Access Component (MDAC) providers. Download updates for the generic providers at www.microsoft.com/data. These providers have been detached from SQL Server and are included with the operating system install.

Excel Source

With the release of Service Pack 2, there are now two providers to access Excel (or Access). The first version (now legacy) supports Excel 97-2005 and is merely a modified version of the JET provider (the OLE DB provider for connectivity to Access and Excel). New to SP2 is the latest provider for Office 2007 Excel and Access. This provider, called Microsoft ACE OLEDB 12.0, overcomes the 255-character limit when extracting cells. Both have a limitation in that they are only supported in a 32-bit execution mode (no native 64-bit). This doesn't mean that you cannot extract data from Excel on a 64-bit system; it just means that you must run the package in 32-bit mode, which will be a little more inefficient. (On 64-bit servers, both 64-bit and 32-bit versions of DTExec are installed to handle 64-bit compatibility issues.)

You can create an Excel connection in the data flow simply by using the Excel Source in the Data Flow Source adapter list, as shown earlier in Figure 3-3. The Excel source adapter interface will allow a new Excel connection to be generated, which includes the Excel file path property, shown in Figure 3-7.

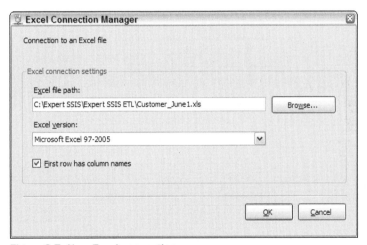

Figure 3-7: New Excel connection

The Excel connection references the Excel file, and the data flow adapter for the Excel connection then allows a specific worksheet to be selected.

One thing that may cause you issues when extracting from Excel sources is that all the text columns are pulled back as Unicode (DT_WSTR) data types in SSIS. Even if you try to modify the advanced input and output properties of these columns, the adapter will not accept a change to these types; therefore, another approach is required to maintain any native string (DT_STR) types. To change the data type of your columns, you must use the Data Convert transformation and add new columns for each Unicode column that needs conversion back to native strings. The initial data flow will look like Figure 3-8.

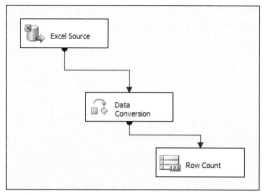

Figure 3-8: Initial data flow

When looking at the details of the conversion, Figure 3-9 shows that the Data Convert transformation is changing several of the data types from DT_WSTR to DT_STR, since, in many cases, your destinations may be non-Unicode. When converting to non-Unicode, you will need to specify the code page. Doing this is required to prevent destination errors.

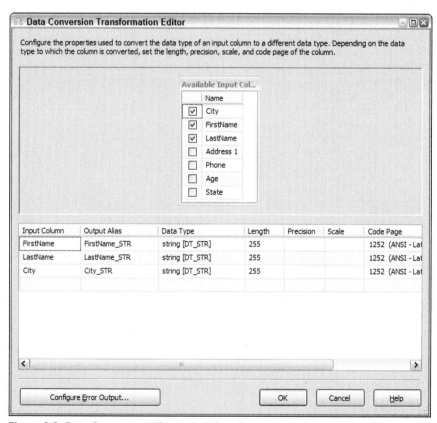

Figure 3-9: Data Convert transformation changing several of the data types

Any time you need to change the data type of a pipeline column, SSIS requires a new column to be added to the buffers, since the data type of an existing column cannot be changed in place. Therefore, new columns are added to the pipeline with adjusted data types. This makes the rows wider and the buffers less efficient with the extra columns.

Raw File Source

The raw file is a highly efficient file-based storage mechanism unique to SSIS in that it contains data created in the native format of the data flow. Therefore, the raw file can only be created by a Data Flow Destination. As mentioned earlier, the raw file does not include a reference to a package connection. The file internally contains all the metadata information it needs for columns and data types, but not having a connection means that the file location property cannot be added to a package configuration through a connection. Instead, the raw file allows the AccessMode to be set to File name from variable, which then allows the file path to be dynamic, based on the value of a variable. (Using this approach will allow the file path to be put in a package configuration.) When AccessMode is set to File name, then the file path is hard-coded in the adapter.

Uses of the raw file include the ability to temporarily stage data between data flows, which can be useful for restartability, and also the ability to share data between multiple packages. Chapter 7 reviews the Raw file in detail for these purposes. Additionally, the raw file can provide a data archiving mechanism for later processing, data lineage, or data validation requirements.

XML Source

Pulling XML data into the data flow may be valuable if you have large XML files that need to be imported into a database. By nature, XML files have the overhead of tags, which makes their file sizes larger, so XML files are not often used as a bulk data transfer means. Instead, delimited files are more common because they can be created, transferred, and read faster. Smaller data sets or B to B integration is more commonly XML-based. However, you may have to deal with XML as a source if the data comes from another department or from a vendor that supplies the data in this way.

The XML Source adapter enables you to import XML data into the data flow. The Data access mode property enables you to point to XML data in a few different ways:

- ❏ XML file location, when a hard-coded path to the XML file can be entered
- ❏ XML file from variable, if the path and file name pointing to the XML file is located in a variable
- ❏ XML data from variable, if the XML you are importing is embedded in a text variable

If you have an XSD schema, then you can enter it right in the XSD location property, or you can generate one right from the editor. The XML Source will present multiple outputs, depending on the schema. In some ways, the output acts like a Conditional Split, where multiple outputs are possible and the output needs to be selected when connecting it with the next transformation or destination. One final note is that you should go to the Advanced Editor and modify the input columns to be the right data type and length, because the XML source assigns every output column as a Unicode string (DT_WSTR) of length 255.

Advanced Features and Concepts

As mentioned in the discussion of the OLE DB source adapter, when you use this adapter, you have the ability to dynamically filter data from a source system. This dynamic query capability is reviewed in detail in the section "Incremental Data Extraction" later in this chapter. This section examines delaying the validation of the source and updating connections by using property expressions.

Delaying Adapter and Connection Validation

An important property of source adapters is the `ValidateExternalMedata` because it allows a source to be identified that may not exist at design time, or may change before execution. For example, if you are creating a database view in one data flow, and then connecting to the newly created view in the second data flow, the object will not initially exist. This property would need to be set to `False` to ensure that the package will run without failing validation. Connections in the Connection Managers window have a similar property called `DelayValidation`. This is similar except that it is applied to the entire connection.

Updating Connections with Property Expressions

It is often the case that the database used at design-time is not the same database that a production package will use. In such cases, it is useful to be able to dynamically tell the package at runtime which database it should point to instead.

Three general methods exist to update a connection at runtime. The most common way to update a connection is by leveraging Package Configurations (discussed in Chapter 16 of *Professional SQL Server 2005 Integration Services*), which can update a connection when the package loads. This provides the capabilities to change the connection strings without opening the package, such as for moving packages from a development server to a test server, and onto a production server.

The drawback to configurations when updating connections is that the connection can only be updated when the package loads. This approach will not work if you are looping through identical files in a folder and then using data flow to import the data. In this case, the connection must be updated every time the package loops. As an example, Figure 3-10 shows a control flow with a `ForEach` Loop Container that is looping over Excel files in a folder.

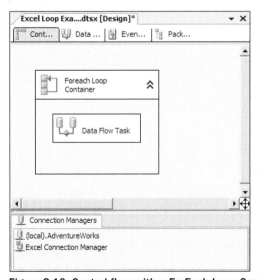

Figure 3-10: Control flow with a ForEach Loop Container

The Excel connection must be updated for every file. So, for this situation, a configuration will not work, since they are only applied when the package loads. Instead, a Property Expression is utilized. The ForEach Loop is updating a package variable called FileName every time the container loops, which can easily be used to update the connection. Property Expressions can be found in the sliding property grid window under the property called Expressions. Figure 3-11 highlights the Expressions property when selected on the Excel Connection Manager connection.

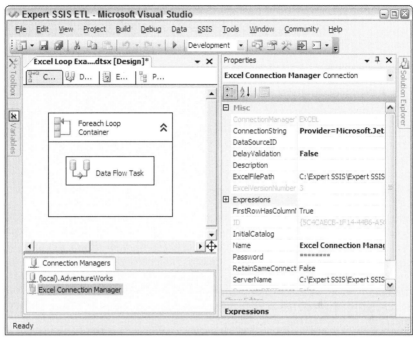

Figure 3-11: The Expressions property when selected on the Excel Connection Manager connection

To open the Property Expressions Editor, click the plus symbol to the left of the Expressions property name, and then the ellipse on the right-hand side of the property when it appears. This opens a window, allowing several properties of the connection to be updated by an expression. For the purpose of this example, the ExcelFilePath property is selected from the drop-down list, and the expression @[User::FileName] is selected, as Figure 3-12 shows.

In this case, the expression itself is only referencing a package variable, but property expressions can leverage the full SSIS Expression language. To create a more complicated expression, the ellipse next to @[User::FileName] will open the full SSIS Expression Builder window.

When the package shown in Figure 3-11 executes, the ForEach Loop iterates through every file in the designated folder, and the full name and path are passed into the FileName variable. When the data flow runs and the adapter calls the connection, the connection is then automatically updated by the property expression and the right file is extracted in the data flow, making the extraction flexible to handle multiple sources while using the same connection.

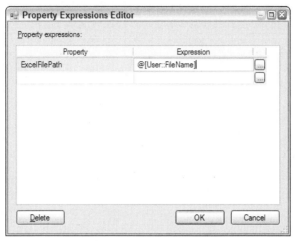

Figure 3-12: Selecting the expression @[User::FileName]

Optimal Data Staging Method

Data staging provides a valuable mechanism for data archiving and data validation. In some cases, a data warehouse may only be using a portion of the source data provided. However, at some later date, this information may become valuable to extend the solution. Having raw staged data can allow re-loading and data validation.

When dealing with flat files generated or pushed from a source, the flat file itself can be the archive mechanism. At times, however, it may be valuable to have your raw source data persisted into a database for tracking or validating with queries. In these cases, when you need to stage the data with SSIS, one of two approaches can be taken.

The data can be landed to the staging/archive table in one data flow, and a second data flow can then extract the data from the staged data back into the data flow for further processing. This approach would look like Figure 3-13, with the control flow and data flows, shown side by side.

The second approach is to handle both the staging and the transformation logic within the same data flow by using a Multicast transformation. Figure 3-14 shows the same process handled in this approach.

Both have their advantages and disadvantages. The second approach scales a lot better when dealing with large amounts of data. The reason is twofold. First, the staging process is handled in parallel with the transformation process, but also, the disk I/O is reduced in half because the staging table is only written to, as opposed to written to and then extracted from again.

However, if the transformation process fails, then the staging process will also stop. When taking the first approach, if the transformation process failed, the staged data would already be in the archive table, and then the data flow containing the transformation logic could be re-started after the data issue resolved.

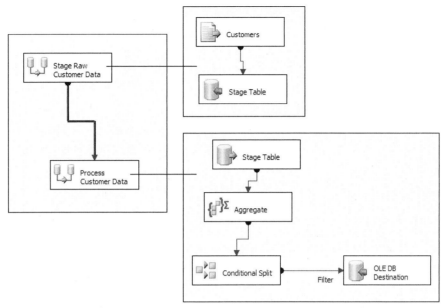

Figure 3-13: Data flow to stage data

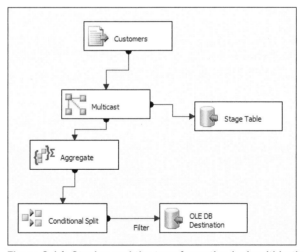

Figure 3-14: Staging and the transformation logic within the same data flow

Incremental Data Extraction

Incremental extraction is the process of targeting modified records and new records, and then tracking the last completed extraction. For example, as you process rows, you might track the last modified datetime value or last identifier for the rows that you've pulled. Then, the next time you extract from the same source system, you start where you left off, rather than extracting the entire process batch.

How you do incremental extraction depends on the source system design. In fact, certain source systems do not initially provide a mechanism to target changes and new rows. In these cases, sometimes you have the flexibility to make changes on the source system, sometimes you don't. SSIS can handle both scenarios.

Here are a few of the many ways that you may be able to identify changed source records:

❑　**Use a modified date or created date column from a database source** — These are called *change identifier* columns. In fact, many transactional systems already have change identifier columns that can be used for an incremental extraction. This is probably the most common approach to incremental extraction.

❑　**Use an auto-incrementing identifier** — If the source system doesn't have a modified date or created date, there may be an auto-incrementing column acting as a change identifier, which increases every time a row change happens. You can also use this approach to identify changed records.

❑　**Use an audit table** — Some source systems already have or allow a trigger (or similar mechanism) to capture the changes to an audit table. An audit table may track keys for that source table or the details of the change. However, this approach involves overhead, because triggers are expensive.

❑　**Log-based auditing** — Some database servers provide a log reader–based mechanism to automatically track changes in a similar way to the trigger-based mechanism, but with a much lower overhead. These log-based systems are often called *Change Data Capture features*, and in order to take advantage of this, you need a source system that supports these features.

Beyond these options, other scenarios may involve combinations or unique solutions. For example, a few years ago we worked with a client that allowed us to add a column (defaulted as NULL) to the source table, but we were not allowed to add a trigger to update that column on a transaction-by-transaction basis. However, we were allowed to batch-update this column during our extraction window. On a nightly basis, we would update the new column with a datetime value where the value had been NULL. Then we would extract the records that matched the new datetime value, and not worry about pulling the same record each extraction.

For the worst-case scenarios, if you do not have the ability to target changed rows, and the source system cannot be changed (or if your source is a flat file), then you will have to use SSIS to identify the new or changed records. This section reviews the case where the source can be filtered and where SSIS needs to handle the filter.

> It's important to understand the CRUD (Create, Read, Update, and Delete) operations for the source system. For example, an application might handle the `Modified DateTime` field. If other processes update rows (such as a batch system running at night), ensure that the source system is updating the `Modified DateTime`. If not, you may be missing rows that the source system needs to update. That can be a problem. In any warehouse design, the biggest risk is not having your end users trust the data because you have incorrect data. If users don't trust it and find bugs, then they don't use the system and the project fails.

Incremental Extraction Using a Change Identifier Value

If your source tables contain a change identifier value (such as a last modified `datetime`), or you are able to make small changes to your source tables to allow this, then the process in SSIS will involve three steps:

1. Targeting the changed records by making the source query dynamic. This process involves package variables and two methods in the data flow adapters.

2. Retrieving the incremental extraction values and updating package variables.

3. Capturing the last or maximum value of the change identifier value, so that the value can be tracked and used for the next extraction.

In addition to reviewing some standard approaches to handling this common scenario, this discussion examines an alternate approach if your source system is SQL Server. This approach does involve adding a column to the source tables. However, it doesn't require a table trigger or application logic to update the column value, and, therefore, can add some significant benefits without the overhead common to change identifiers. This approach involves using the SQL Server `timestamp` data type, and is discussed after the three aforementioned steps are examined.

Targeting Change Records Through Dynamic Source Queries

The core requirement when attempting to only pull a selected subset of data from a source is the ability to make the query change based on parameters. In the case of an incremental identifier value (such as last modified date), the goal would be to target the source table for the extraction by filtering on the last modified date. Using SSIS, a couple approaches are possible that use properties of the source adapter.

❑ Using an OLE DB source adapter may allow a parameterized query, where the query can reference package variables to filter the query.

❑ The OLE DB adapter also allows the source table name or query to be embedded into a package variable. The adapter can then point to the package variable and use its contents value as the source text of the query.

OLE DB Parameterized Source Query

An OLE DB parameterized source query has been reviewed in the *Professional SSIS* book, and is the method that the Chapter 1 step-by-step refresher used to target records from a source. It simply involves setting the source adapter Data access mode properties to SQL command and then using the parameterized method of the adapter to define the parts of the statement that should be based on the parameters. Figure 3-15 shows the OLE DB Source Editor with a parameterized query.

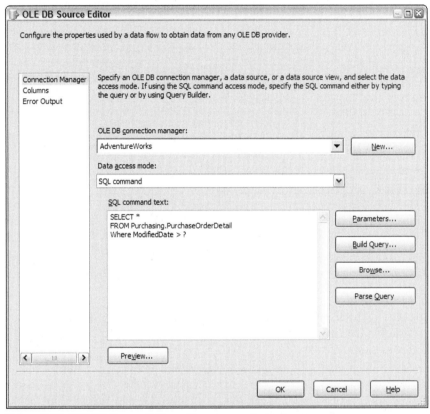

Figure 3-15: OLE DB Source Editor with a parameterized query

The second requirement of the parameterized query is to map the parameters to package variables, which is done using the Parameters button on the same screen. This example simply maps a package variable called `vdtLastModifiedDatetime` to the first parameter, as Figure 3-16 shows.

OLE DB parameters are 0 based, which means that the first ? in order is defined as the 0 parameter, the second ? in order is the 1 parameter, and so forth. Note that when you use parameterized queries, the statement cannot be parsed (using the Parse Query button) or previewed (using the Preview button). Therefore, to test the parameterization, the data flow must be executed. Figure 3-17 shows the executed data flow.

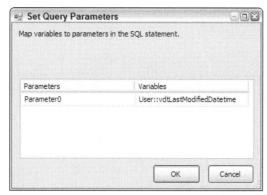

Figure 3-16: Mapping a vdtLastModifiedDatetime
package variable to the first parameter

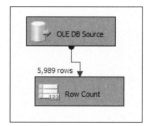

Figure 3-17: Executed data flow

A Row Count transformation is merely used as a development technique—a dummy destination to build and test the source adapter. The vdtLastModifiedDatetime variable has been defaulted to '1/1/2004', which caused 5,989 rows out of the 8,788 rows to be extracted. The next section discusses how to both update and retrieve the right variable value.

Variable Bound SQL Source

One major drawback to the OLE DB parameterized source query is that many of the non-SQL Server OLE DB source providers do not support parameterization. Therefore, an alternate approach will be needed that is also supported by the same source adapter.

The OLE DB provider also allows a source query to be based on the contents of a package variable. This is different from the parameterized source query in that the entire SQL statement is entered into the variable, rather than just the filter values. To exemplify, a string variable has been added to a package called vsExtractionSQL, and it contains the following SQL code:

```
SELECT *
FROM Purchasing.PurchaseOrderDetail
WHERE ModifiedDate > '1/1/2004'
```

The OLE DB source adapter is defined with the Data access mode property set to SQL command from variable, and the Variable name property is set to User::vsExtractionSQL, as shown in Figure 3-18.

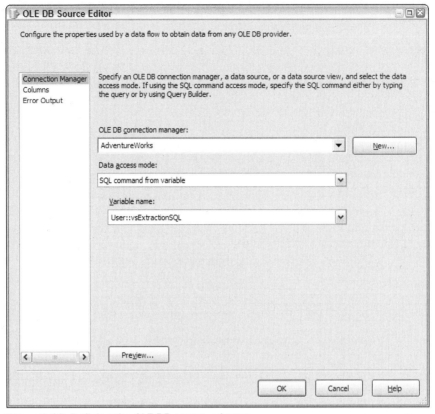

Figure 3-18: Defining the OLE DB source adapter

Alternately, if the variable only contained the name of the table or view, you could select the Table name or view name variable option in the Data access mode property. However, by only selecting a view or a table, you would not be able to filter the rows on the source.

Unlike the OLE DB parameterized statement, using this variable-bound feature, the parsing and previewing feature in the editor works, and when this data flow is executed, the results are identical to Figure 3-17, shown previously. The next section reviews how to update the variables.

Retrieving Incremental Identifier Values and Updating Package Variables

The first step showed how to enable the data flow to be able to run a targeted extraction, and this section reviews how to update the package variables that drive the targeted extraction. Both the OLE DB parameterized approach and the variable-bound source approach need variable values updated in order to extract the correct batch of data.

As an example, let's first update the vdtLastModifiedDatetime column, which is the only variable update that the OLE DB parameterized approach requires. Second, let's look at a couple of methods to update the `vsExtractionSQL` variable with the right `datetime` value from the `vdtLastModifiedDatetime` variable.

The current incremental identifying column value needs to be stored so that each ETL run can use a new value for the extraction. This can be done in various ways (such as keeping it in a file), but the most common way is to store the value in a database control table that contains only the extraction information. For the Last Modified Date example, a table named `cfgIncrementalExtraction` has been created with two fields with one entry row, which looks like the following.

SourceTable	LastModifiedDatetime
PurchaseOrderDetails	1/1/2004

The `SourceTable` column simply defines the source object, in case multiple configuration entries are made. The `LastModifiedDatetime` column contains the value of the last successful extraction.

Therefore, the first step is to retrieve the last extraction value and update the `vdtLastModifiedDatetime` column variable. To do this, the easiest way is to use an Execute SQL Task. Figure 3-19 shows the editor of an Execute SQL Task.

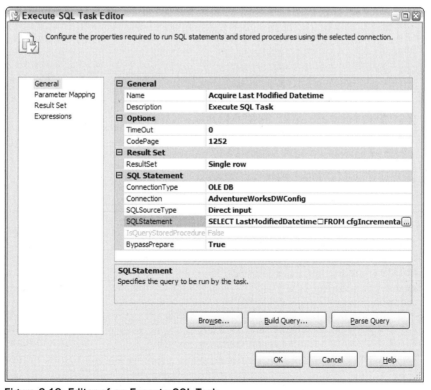

Figure 3-19: Editor of an Execute SQL Task

The SQLStatement executes the following query against the table defined previously:

```
SELECT LastModifiedDatetime
FROM cfgIncrementalExtraction
WHERE SourceTable = 'PurchaseOrderDetail'
```

The statement returns a single row where the resulting columns must update the variable. The ResultSet property of the task shown in Figure 3-19 has been set to Single row, and on the Result Set page of the editor, the LastModifiedDatetime column is mapped to the vdtLastModifiedDatetime variable, as Figure 3-20 highlights.

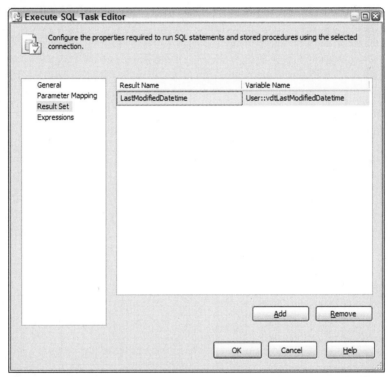

Figure 3-20: LastModifiedDatetime column mapped to the vdtLastModifiedDatetime variable

As an alternate approach, you could use the SQL logic to acquire the value that then could be embedded into a stored procedure and an output variable.

For the variable-bound source adapter method, a second step is required to update the vsExtractionSQL value for the variable-bound source adapter. In fact, two SSIS methods are available. The first is to have the variable updated by an expression, and the second is to use a Script Task to perform the update.

Variables have a little-known property called `EvaluateAsExpression`, which, by default, is set to `false`. When this is set to `true`, then an expression can be written that is evaluated any time the variable is read. Figure 3-21 shows that the `EvaluateAsExpression` property is viewable in the Properties window, when the variable is selected in the Variables window.

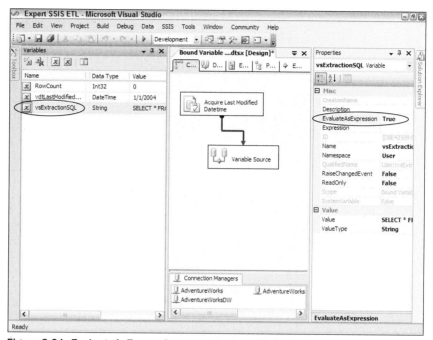

Figure 3-21: EvaluateAsExpression property viewable in the Properties window

Since the release of SQL Server 2005 Service Pack 1, the expression can be entered into an expression editor, allowing the statement to be built with the SSIS expression functions. To invoke the Expression Builder dialog box, the Expression property, which is right below the `EvaluateAsExpression` property, should be selected. Figure 3-22 shows the editor with the expression that builds the SQL statement added.

In this case, the expression updates the SQL statement by using the `vdtLastModifiedDatetime` value to update the string.

```
"SELECT * FROM Purchasing.PurchaseOrderDetail
WHERE ModifiedDate > '" + (DT_STR, 10, 1252) @[User::vdtLastModifiedDatetime] + "'"
```

The expression editor also allows the expression to be evaluated for accuracy and functionality.

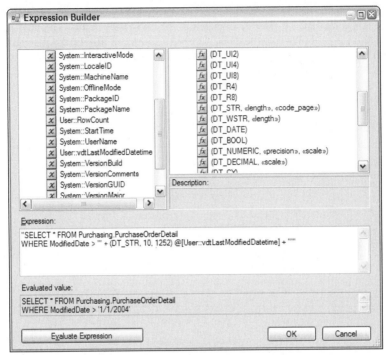

Figure 3-22: Editor with the expression that builds the SQL statement

One drawback of the `EvaluateAsExpression` feature of variables is that the property is difficult to find. Therefore, you may want to use a Script Task to manually update the value of the variable. To do this, be sure that the Script Task has the `vdtLastModifiedDatetime` entered in the `ReadOnlyVariables` list and the `vsExtractionSQL` in the `ReadWriteVariables` list. The script code that would be entered under the `Public Sub Main()` would look like this:

```
Dts.Variables("vsExtractionSQL").Value = _
  "SELECT * FROM Purchasing.PurchaseOrderDetail WHERE ModifiedDate > '" _
  + Dts.Variables("vdtLastModifiedDatetime").Value.ToString + "'"
```

When put together, the control flow would include the Execute SQL Task, an optional Script Task, and a Data Flow Task, as the control flow in Figure 3-21 demonstrated earlier.

Capturing the Maximum Change Identifier Value

So far, when dealing with incremental extractions, you have seen how to dynamically update the source query based on the value of a variable, which was updated from the value stored in a control table. The final part of targeting database records is to capture the final change identifier value so that it can be used for the next extraction.

A couple choices exist to handle this. An Execute SQL Task can be used to run a SQL MAX operation on the destination table. This requires either a staging table or keeping the change identifier column in the dimension or fact tables. With large volumes, this approach may require some time and resource overhead if the number of rows required to scan is too large.

A better approach is to handle the operation right in the data flow. In other words, the Aggregate transformation can be used to capture the maximum value. But can the aggregate be done at the same time as the rest of the transformation process? Yes, with the use of a Multicast, the rows can be sent to an Aggregate, while at the same time, the rows are flowing through the rest of the data flow operations. Figure 3-23 shows a data flow with this configuration.

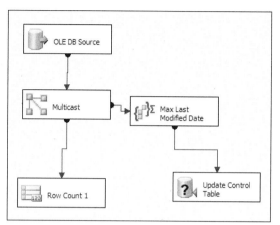

Figure 3-23: Handling the operation in the data flow

On the left side of the Multicast output, the rows are simply sent to a Row Count transformation. Once again, the Row Count transformation serves as a dummy destination for illustration purposes and, in reality, would be replaced by the actual data loading code. On the right side of the multicast, the rows are sent to an Aggregate transformation, configured to capture the maximum value of the ModifiedDate coming from the source. Figure 3-24 shows the Aggregate Transformation Editor.

Notice that there are no group-by columns in the Aggregate, which means that the maximum value of the ModifiedDate will be captured across the source data set. Because of this, only one row from the Aggregate will be sent downstream.

The next transformation used is an OLE DB Command transformation, which is updating the control table with the following statement:

```
UPDATE cfgIncrementalExtraction
SET LastModifiedDatetime = ISNULL(?, LastModifiedDatetime)
WHERE SourceTable = 'PurchaseOrderDetail'
```

The parameter (?) is mapped to the single row Modified Date output of the aggregate. This update statement will only be executed when given the single-row Aggregate output. Also, it's important to note that an ISNULL is used to trap for NULLs in the parameter. This is because the Aggregate will produce a single row NULL output even if there are no input rows from the source, since there are no group-by columns. This is expected, and without the ISNULL, the control table would be incorrectly updated with a NULL and affect the next run.

Figure 3-25 shows the data flow results when the extraction package is run in its entirety.

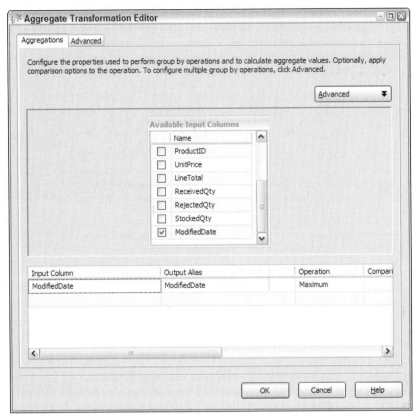

Figure 3-24: Aggregate editor

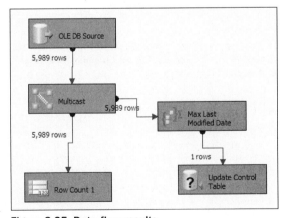

Figure 3-25: Data flow results

If the package is run again immediately, without any source rows being updated, then given the logic, the data flow results return what Figure 3-26 shows.

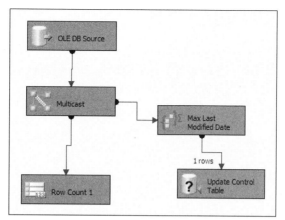

Figure 3-26: Data flow results after immediately running again

As expected, no rows were extracted, since the last run captured and tracked the maximum Modified Date, and there were, therefore, no rows left to pull.

Incremental Extraction from SQL Server Without a Trigger

Before looking at how to use SSIS to perform incremental extraction on text files and other sources (that is, sources that don't contain a change identification value), one other option exists for table extractions from SQL Server.

If you're using SQL Server as your source, then you may be able to perform an incremental extraction even though you don't have an explicit column that helps identify changes. SQL Server provides a timestamp data type that is automatically updated when a row is added or updated, without requiring a trigger.

Although the timestamp data type sounds like it is related to a date time, it is actually a misnomer. In reality, it is a row version column, which creates an auto-incrementing binary value. And, any time a row is modified within the source (or added), that column value is updated automatically. In fact, this timestamp is used by SQL Server for internal row checking for things like replication. Each table can have only one timestamp column, and when you add it to the table, you are really just exposing it in the table for another use.

In a nutshell, the timestamp can be used in SSIS to perform incremental extraction. To leverage this, SSIS requires converting the binary column so that it is useable.

To demonstrate, the Sales.Customer AdventureWorks source table has been altered with a new timestamp column, using the following TSQL code:

```
USE AdventureWorks
GO
ALTER TABLE Sales.Customer ADD
  CustomerTimestamp timestamp NOT NULL
```

In addition, a new row and column have been added to the control table. The new row contains the `Sales.Customer` source table column value, and a new `varchar` column has been added to capture the converted conversion number value of the binary `timestamp` value.

The difference between the `datetime` example reviewed earlier in this chapter and the `timestamp` being reviewed here is that the source query is also handling the conversion of the `timestamp` from binary to integer. Besides the normal columns being pulled, the `SELECT` statement includes the conversion and adjusted filter, with the following code:

```
SELECT *,
   CONVERT(BIGINT,CustomerTimestamp) as CustomerTimestamp_Int64
FROM sales.customer
WHERE CONVERT(BIGINT,CustomerTimestamp) > ?
```

Figure 3-27 shows the completed data flow for the first time that the process is run.

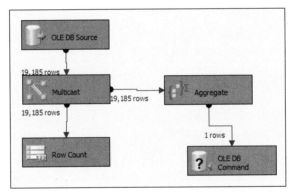

Figure 3-27: Completed data flow for the first time the process is run

And, as expected, when this package is run immediately a second time, no rows are extracted, as Figure 3-28 shows.

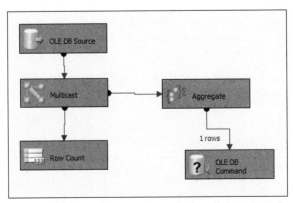

Figure 3-28: No rows are extracted when the package is run a second time

Since a trigger already exists on the `Sales.Customer` table, to illustrate this `timestamp` use, the trigger should be dropped. Secondly, the following updates are next performed on the table:

```
USE AdventureWorks
GO

UPDATE Sales.Customer
SET TerritoryID = 6
WHERE CustomerID = 13

UPDATE Sales.Customer
SET CustomerType = 'I'
WHERE CustomerID = 65
```

Then the package is run another time, with the data flow output shown in Figure 3-29.

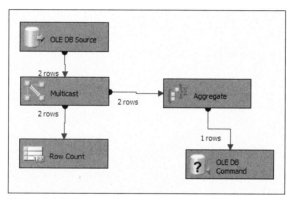

Figure 3-29: Output of running the package again

The two updated rows have been sent out. As you can see, this gives you a nice way to handle incremental extraction from a SQL source without requiring application changes or a table trigger. Yes, it does require the addition of an 8-byte column in the source, but the incremental extraction benefits may outweigh the additional table width.

Using SSIS to Handle All Aspects of an Incremental Extraction

Ideally, every source would have a method to capture only the new and changed records (and even deletes). But unfortunately, not every source has this capability, especially when dealing with flat files as your source. Therefore, this section looks at how to handle flat file sources and database tables that do not have change identifier values.

Flat Files that Contain Change Identifier Values

It is very possible that you may have a source flat file that contains a `LastModifiedDate` or similar column in the file (and the file contains both changed and non-changed rows from the last extraction). However, because of the nature of flat files, the data flow source adapter cannot issue a query against the file.

This scenario can actually be handled very easily in SSIS, with the use of a Conditional Split transformation as the first step in the data flow. Since the `vdtLastModifiedDate` variable cannot be used in the source, what can be done instead is the Conditional Split can filter the rows immediately as they are pulled into the pipeline from the file. Figure 3-30 shows the modified data flow.

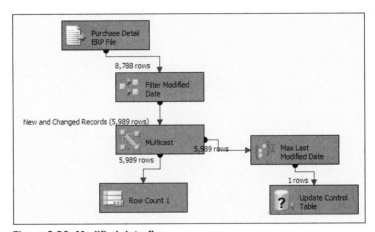

Figure 3-30: Modified data flow

The source adapter for the flat file is simply configured for the current structure of the delimited file. The Conditional Split checks the value of the Modified Date column for every row, and only allows rows through that are greater than the last incremental extraction value. Figure 3-31 shows the Conditional Split Transformation Editor.

Rows that do not meet the criteria would usually go out the default output. But, as you can see in the data flow that Figure 3-31 shows, the default output (named non-changed) is not being used. Therefore, the non-changed rows are discarded by the pipeline.

Notice in the data flow that the next identifier value is captured using a Multicast and Aggregate just like the dynamic query examples in the previous section. Also, not shown is the control flow that uses the same approach as before with an Execute SQL Task to update the `vdtLastModifiedDate` variable.

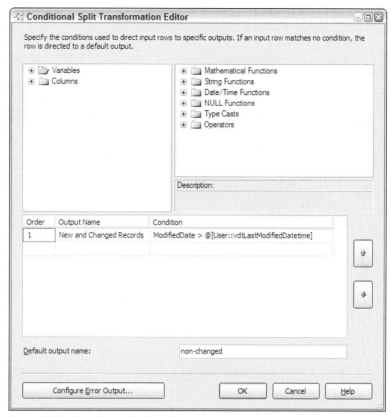

Figure 3-31: Conditional Split editor

Sources Without Change Identifier Values

Finally, you may have a situation where your source just doesn't have a change identifier value at all. In these cases, you will either need to use the data flow to determine which records are changed, or land the entire source to a temporary table and rely on the database to compare the records.

Focusing on the data flow approach, to handle this scenario, the source needs to be correlated with the destination, and based on the comparison, records need to be identified as new or changed and, in some cases, deleted.

> **Even in prior examples where a change identifier column is available, it may not indicate whether a record is new or updated. Even in these cases, a comparison of source and destination is required. Chapter 5 delves into more detail on the comparison between sources to identify changes. The review here is simply to identify whether the source record has a corresponding entry in the destination.**

A common theme throughout the book is how to do data correlation in the data flow to compare sources with destinations. The straightforward approaches are to use the Lookup or Merge Join transformations to perform the data association. The Lookup can identify matches with the output path and non-matches with the error row output. The Merge Join requires a Conditional Split to determine matches and non-matches.

In the following example, a flat-file source contains sales data, but does not indicate whether the sale had previously been added to the destination table. To identify whether the sale had been added previously, the source data is merged with the destination table, which, in this case, is the sales fact table within `AdventureWorksDW`. Figure 3-32 shows the first several steps of the data flow that performs the data association and comparison.

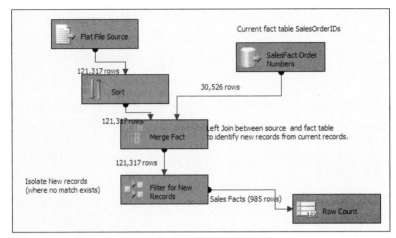

Figure 3-32: Beginning the data flow that performs the data association and comparison

Before the Merge Join is used, the flat file source is sorted on the `SalesOrderID`, which is also contained in the fact table. On the right side of the Merge Join, an OLE DB source adapter is used, which pulls the existing `SalesOrderID` from the existing fact tables, pre-sorted with an `Order By` statement. The advanced editors of this adapter are configured to recognize the pre-sort. Details of how to accomplish this are discussed in Chapter 4. Figure 3-33 shows the Merge Join configured as a left outer join.

Since this example is attempting to identify new records to add to the destination, the left outer join allows both matches and non-matches from the source to the destination to flow through the transformation. The `SalesOrderID` from the destination is aliased as `Fact_SalesOrderID` to differentiate the value in the Conditional Split transformation. Figure 3-34 highlights the Conditional Split, which performs the filter of records by checking for NULLs in the `Fact_SalesOrderID`.

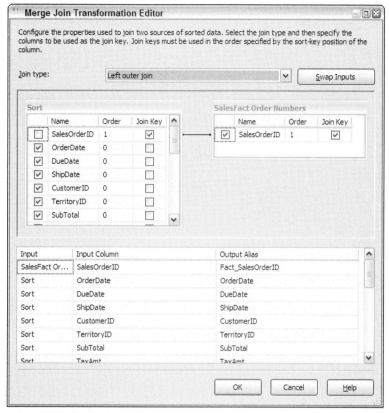

Figure 3-33: Merge Join editor

If a NULL exists in the Fact_SalesOrderID, it means that the source record is new to the fact table, and, therefore, should be allowed through the transformation process to be added to the fact table. Otherwise, the record already exists, and, in this example, is ignored by the Conditional Split since the default output is not used.

This approach and similar approaches with the Lookup transformation allow incremental data extraction by using SSIS data flow components to filter out rows early in the process.

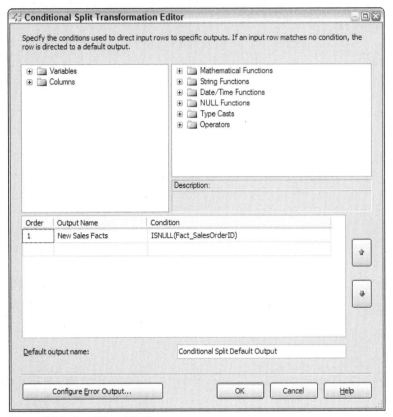

Figure 3-34: Conditional Split

Tracking Data Lineage Identifiers

Data lineage is a part of the metadata tracking in an ETL process associated with mapping data back to the source data points. But before considering an approach to data lineage tracking, to better understand data lineage requires understanding metadata in general.

Metadata is the data about the data. For ETL, it's the integrated tracking mechanism for the process and the core data. Metadata is very important for ETL and data warehousing — not just for administrators to understand what data got loaded, but also for system developers to validate data sources, for data administrators to find out what happened when failures occur, and for users to be confident in the data they are looking at. In fact, the latter may be the most important, because if the users do not trust the data, then their adoption of the solution will be slow going. Tracking data lineage is directly related to knowing where each data point came from, not just what system or table or file, but knowing which source row(s) they came from.

As with other requirements, data lineage can be handled several ways in SSIS. The most common way is to add an auto-incrementing number to the data flow that maps data points back to their sources.

If you are staging raw data, this can be leveraged by sending this lineage number to the staged data and also to the destination tables. With raw staging tables, instead of having to track back to a source system, which may be volatile, you are able to go back to the raw staging database and see what the data was at the point in time it was extracted.

To do this, add a lineage sequence identifier to the data flow right after the extraction so that it could then flow to both the stage table as well as the primary transformation processes. A simple Script component can handle the incrementing identifier. Figure 3-35 shows an extraction data flow that was presented earlier. This time, a Script component has been added after the extraction.

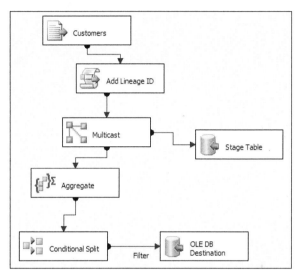

Figure 3-35: Extraction data flow with Script component added after the extraction

To configure the Script component to output a sequence lineage number, a new output column must be added to the Script component output properties. Figure 3-36 shows the Inputs and Outputs properties page, where a new integer column called `CustomerLineageID` has been added as an output column.

The script itself is very straightforward. For every row, the lineage is output and then the value is increased by 1 for the next row. The following code handles this lineage:

```
Public Class ScriptMain
    Inherits UserComponent
    Private CustomerLineageID As Integer = 1

    Public Overrides Sub Input_ProcessInputRow(ByVal Row As InputBuffer)

        Row.CustomerLineageID = Me.CustomerLineageID
        Me.CustomerLineageID = Me.CustomerLineageID + 1

    End Sub

End Class
```

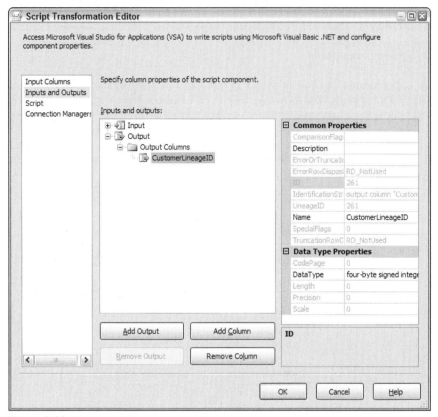

Figure 3-36: Inputs and Outputs properties page

With this sequence lineage approach, the added Customer Lineage ID would flow to both the raw staging table and the destination tables. Alternately, if the entire source data does not need to be staged, then the lineage ID could be landed to a staging table with only the business keys from the source, rather than every column. This would provide the necessary link between the source keys and the destination lineage ID. The SSIS data flow process would look very similar.

It's worth mentioning that in data warehousing, oftentimes a fact table will contain a *degenerate dimension* — or a granular-level number that is an attribute of the fact. But, instead of being broken out into a separate dimension table, it is stored in the fact table itself. Oftentimes this value is seen as a business key of the fact records. This is also a type of data lineage because the discrete values can relate back directly to the source system.

When the lineage ID is stored in the destination tables, the next step is to put a trigger or action in the destination database that can then reference the source data that is either stored in the raw staging environment, or links directly to the source. Tracking data lineage allows better data validation, but when you can enable the users to see the link between source and destination themselves by building that functionality into the application, you are ahead of the game. To get there requires adding it to your SSIS-based ETL.

Summary

SSIS includes the capability to connect to a wide variety of sources with functionality to make the extraction process scalable and flexible, including many ways to target and filter source data. Data extraction requirements are sometimes unique, and will require variations on the examples and design patterns presented here. For example, you may need to combine some of the incremental extraction approaches with dynamic connections and data lineage tracking. But even given the wide variety of requirements you may run into, SSIS provides the functionality to handle many extraction scenarios.

With the extraction component of ETL addressed, the next few chapters will now focus on the transformation and load aspects of ETL applied to data warehousing. Chapter 4 kicks off that discussion with an examination of the processing of dimension tables in SSIS.

4

Dimension ETL with SSIS

The next three chapters focus on the discussion of ETL for data warehousing and business intelligence processing. This chapter examines the processing of dimension tables in SSIS. Dimension tables are a data warehouse concept, which this chapter describes and then discusses how to move data from your data sources to your data warehouse dimension tables. Similar to this, Chapter 5 reviews the same things, but only applied for fact tables. Chapter 6 also covers business intelligence, but looks at the integration of SSIS with SQL Server 2005 Analysis Services (SSAS). Integration between SSIS and SSAS involves Online Analytical Processing (OLAP) cube and dimension processing, as well as SSAS data mining querying and training.

Dimension ETL Overview

Arguably, when looking at the development time investment required for a data warehouse ETL solution, dimension processing takes the longest, and is the most complex component. You may have experienced this, especially when the requirements call for tracking the history of changes that a dimension goes through.

Does this analyst requirement sound familiar: "I want to be able to look at the history of list price changes for a product to be able to understand the supply and demand curve"? In other words, what the business user is really asking is how the change in list price affects sales historically. To handle this type of request, a single product must have a new version created in the dimension table any time the list price changes. Furthermore, the sales activity (tracked in the appropriate fact table) must be associated with the right dimension record for the sales (the one with the list price at that point in time). Sound complicated? Add to that a second or third dimension attribute change (like department) that must be tracked historically, and pretty soon you will be pulling you hair out!

The good news is that SSIS comes with out-of-the-box functionality to handle dimension scenarios just like this. Specifically, it comes with a data flow transformation called the Slowly Changing Dimension (SCD) Wizard. As you will see, there are advantages to using the wizard, as well as some limitations you must consider, and ways to work through those limitations to create a scalable dimension process in your ETL.

But before going any further with how SSIS can be applied to dimension table ETL, you need to step back and review the basics of dimension, both in design and the tracking of history.

Dimensions: The Basics

This chapter focuses on dimension ETL, but in order to understand the full picture of dimension ETL, some dimension theory is required. The best resource is to read *The Complete Guide to Dimension Modeling*, Second Edition, by Ralph Kimball and Margy Ross (Wiley Publications, 2002), for a complete picture of a dimension. For the purposes of this discussion, here's a high-level summary.

The dimension itself is an organized grouping of categories and properties about a particular entity. These categories and properties are called *attributes*, and they form hierarchies with levels and members used to slice and query a cube or fact table.

For example, the following table shows data focusing on geography. The attributes are the Country, State/Province and City, which combine together because of their relationship to one another.

Country	State/Province	City
Germany	Bavaria	Augsburg
Germany	Bavaria	Munich
Germany	Niedersachsen	Hannover
United States	California	Palo Alto
United States	California	Woodland Hills
United States	New York	Cheektowaga
United States	New York	Lake George

Naturally, this data can be used together to create a hierarchy, which provides drill paths to data and the ability to slice and dice data based on certain records. Figure 4-1 shows one of the hierarchies within this geography dimension. The members are the names of the countries, state provinces, and cities. The hierarchy is made up of levels that usually correspond to the column names used in the hierarchy.

In this example, the hierarchy is made up of the levels Country, State, and City, in that order. When querying the dimension, the lower levels roll up to higher levels, so analysis can be done drilling up or down the hierarchy.

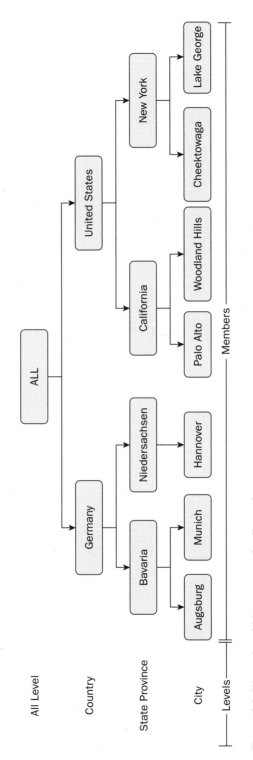

Figure 4-1: Hierarchy within a geography dimension

It is also important to understand how dimensions relate to fact tables. Chapter 5 examines the topic of fact table ETL, but some background in dimension to fact relationships will help you grasp the ETL requirements for dimension processing. Since the AdventureWorksDW sample databases will be used to illustrate this chapter, Figure 4-2 shows one of the fact tables with its related dimension. This is a picture of a single fact table, Reseller Sales Fact, one of the six fact tables in the AdventureWorksDW database.

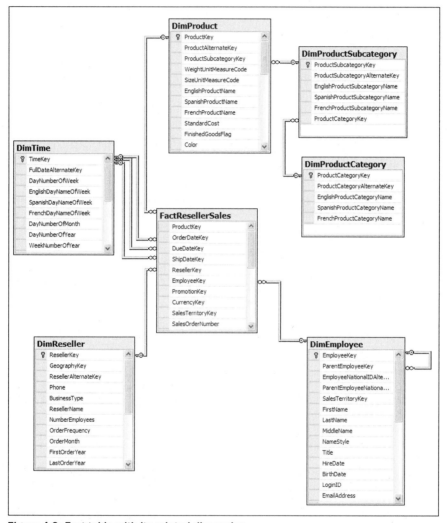

Figure 4-2: Fact table with its related dimension

Related to this fact table is a product dimension, a reseller dimension, an employee dimension, a time dimension, and a customer dimension (plus others not shown). In all, these are pretty typical dimensions. You'll notice that the product dimension has multiple tables associated with it in what's called a *snowflake design*. The employee dimension is also a different type of dimension, called a *parent-child*, given its self referencing nature.

Each dimension contains a *surrogate key*, as shown in Figure 4-2. The surrogate keys are identifiable by the `Key` suffix in the column name, such as `ProductKey`. This defines the primary key for the table itself and relates to the fact table foreign key field. Typically, these data types are numeric, most likely integer and auto-incrementing (called an `IDENTITY` column in SQL Server). Some designers prefer to use a unique identifier (GUID), but these column types are wider (16 bytes) and more difficult to read. The best practice recommendation is to use integer data types — either a 1-, 2-, 4-, or 8-byte integer based on the number of projected members within the dimension table.

The business keys are still tracked in the dimension table, but are not marked as the primary key to identify uniqueness, nor are they used for referential integrity in the database. Instead, they help identify source system data associations for the ETL. In the `AdventureWorksDW` database, each dimension's business key is called the `[DimensionName]AlternateKey` for standardization, but simply contains the source system's primary key value. This business key column is sometimes called the *candidate key*. Most dimension tables name the business key with the same name as the source system name.

A surrogate key, more precisely, is a single column with a value that is unrelated to the dimension table's members. These keys provide the central foundation to dimensional modeling, critical to tracking history and designing a business intelligence system that performs. Here are a few advantages to surrogate key usage:

❑ **Surrogate keys consolidate multi-value business keys** — A source table or file with multi-column business keys can be difficult to manage and will take up extra unnecessary space if used as the primary key. Some dimensions are sourced by multiple source systems, which also creates the situation of multiple business keys that a single surrogate key can handle.

❑ **Surrogate keys allow tracking of dimension history** — Tracking of a dimension attribute's history (such as the list price example discussed in the opening section of this chapter) is not possible without surrogate keys. The surrogate key allows multiple versions of a single source record to be tracked and associated with the fact table history.

❑ **Surrogate keys standardize dimension tables** — Having an identical relationship mechanism to every dimension creates simplicity in reporting and standardization or consistency in the design.

❑ **Surrogate keys improve query performance** — From an optimization standpoint, surrogate keys limit a fact table width. In other words, the combined total data type size for the fact table is small, allowing more fact table rows to fit in memory and, therefore, improving query performance.

> Make the surrogate key as narrow as possible. If you have a dimension table that only has 100 potential rows (considering future additions), a 1-byte integer (`tinyint`) would be the best choice. Based on the number of members in the dimension, make your data type as small as possible, but be sure you account for future rows! The performance gains will be pretty significant. Simply by going from a 4-byte `int` to a 2-byte `int` (just 2 bytes), you may improve performance by as much as 4–5 percent. And when all the dimension surrogate keys are optimized, it can translate into big performance gains on queries, which, in turn, reduces a server's resource load. In other words, don't make every dimension key a 4-byte integer. If you can take the fact table width and cut it in half, that's twice as many rows you can put in a SQL page that goes into memory. Inserts, updates, and queries will run much faster.

Later in this chapter, we will discuss the ETL for two advanced dimension forms:

❑ Snowflake dimension tables

❑ Parent-child dimension

Each of these requires unique handling in the ETL with SSIS.

Dimension ETL: The Challenge

As already mentioned, dimension ETL often consumes the largest portion of a data warehouse ETL effort. But even beyond the challenges presented of handling history, managing surrogate keys, and accounting for different dimension designs, dimension ETL must manage the source system complexities, and must consolidate them down from the source to the dimension structure in the data warehouse. Figure 4-3 compares the table structures of the product dimension destination in the AdventureWorksDW database with the multiple related product tables from the AdventureWorks database source.

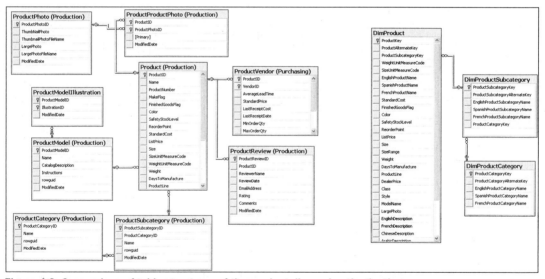

Figure 4-3: Comparison of table structures of the product dimension destination

The left side of the table layout represents the AdventureWorks transactional system, with nine related tables that focus on the product dimension. These tables involve many-to-many relationships and one-to-many primary to foreign key relationships, organized into a transactional third normal form. The challenge for the ETL process is taking the source data and transforming it to a structure that can be compared with the dimension in order to handle dimension history and changes. The challenge is also ensuring that the ETL is scalable and manageable, simple for people to follow when administering it, and flexible to handle changes.

The three tables on the right side of the table layout represent the product dimension organized into a snowflake structure. These tables are considered dimensionally normalized, which is a very different organization than the transactionally normalized tables from the source.

So far, this discussion has looked at the theory of dimension ETL and the challenges presented. As the discussion progresses, another consideration will be the preparation steps required to get your data ready for dimension ETL. Following that, the discussions will shift focus to the core dimension ETL, which requires looking at the built-in support within SSIS, looking at handling advanced dimension forms, and concluding with building your own dimension processing package that scales to your volume.

Preparing Your Source Data for Dimension ETL

Before diving into the details of applying SSIS to handle dimension changes, let's begin with data preparation.

As you saw with the challenge of dimension ETL, it was quite apparent that, in some situations, the source tables may not match one-to-one with the dimension table. In the case of the product dimension outlined earlier, several source tables must be combined to create a consolidated source recordset that matches the columns within the product dimension. Furthermore, data challenges may also require data cleansing and transformation logic to get the information in a consistent form that relates to the data within the matching dimension table.

With SSIS, several out-of-the-box transformations will become key to your transformation and data-cleansing steps, before even getting to the core of dimension processing. Here are some selective transformations that are very useful for this purpose:

❑ The Data Conversion transformation is valuable to handle data type conversions, such as conversions between Unicode and non-Unicode data types, numeric and float, or text and numeric.

❑ The Lookup transformation provides the ability to associate sources without requiring relational joins.

❑ The Derived Column transformation is especially useful in handling NULL values, performing calculations, or applying date functions.

Figure 4-4 shows several data preparation steps useful in the processing of the Product source data. The first objective is to take the third normal form of transactional system and transform it into a structurally equivalent copy of the dimension table in the data flow pipeline.

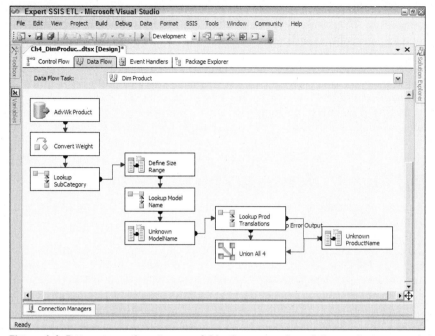

Figure 4-4: Data preparation steps useful in the processing of the product source data

Before you can even use the SCD Wizard, this package requires a series of preparation steps.

The first component is the source adapter, which extracts the source table (`Production.Product` in this example). Refer to Chapter 3 for a review of the SSIS source adapters. The very next component is a Data Conversion transformation, which changes the data type of the `ProductWeight` from a `Numeric` to a `Float`. This is because the destination table stores this attribute as a float, as opposed to a numeric. Figure 4-5 shows the Data Conversion Transformation Editor. The output column is aliased as `Weight` to match the column names of the product dimension table.

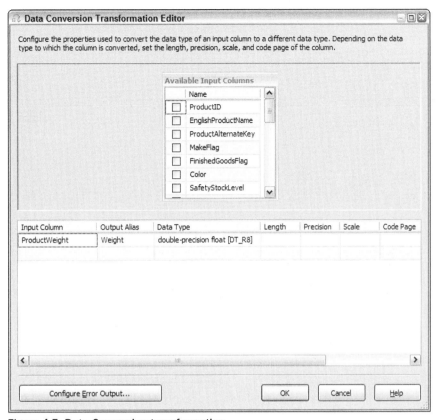

Figure 4-5: Data Conversion transformation

Second, in the product dimension table (which contains the products related to the sale of bicycles and bicycle parts, which AdventureWorks sells), a column exists called SizeRange. This dimension attribute is an example of a dimensional-modeling technique called *data banding*, where ranges are built from usually numeric sources that have several discrete values, but must be consolidated for grouping. Instead of reporting off of the bicycle sizes one size at a time (38, 40, 42, 43, 45, and so on), there are groupings of the discrete size values, such as 38–40, 42–46, and so on. To handle this requirement, a Derived Column transformation is employed, which considers the size and, based on certain values, how the output is grouped. Figure 4-6 shows the Derived Column transformation used.

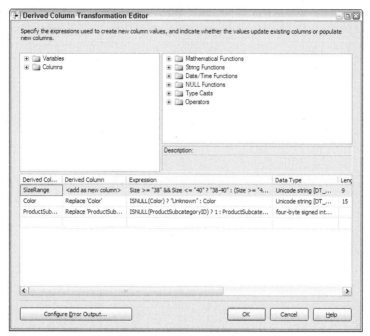

Figure 4-6: Derived Column transformation

The first column in the Derived Column transformation handles the banding by using an SSIS expression — the grammar of which is similar to C — to compare the size to groups of ranges, as shown in the following code. Critical to this expression is the use of an expression-based conditional statement, «boolean_expression» ? «when_true» : «when_false». In this case, the conditional evaluator is recursively embedded to perform multiple comparisons in one statement.

```
Size >= "38" && Size <= "40" ? "38-40" :
    (Size >= "42" && Size <= "46" ? "42-46" :
        (Size >= "48" && Size <= "52" ? "48-52" :
            (Size >= "54" && Size <= "58" ? "54-58" :
                (Size >= "60" && Size < "62" ? "60-62" :
                    ISNULL(Size) ? "NA" : Size
                )
            )
        )
    )
```

In the first condition, if the size for the row being evaluated is 38, then the output range is returned as 38-40. Otherwise, the next condition is checked; and so on, recursively.

The second column used in the example shown in Figure 4-6 deals with unknown values. If there's a NULL in the Color column, it is trapped and replaced by an Unknown. If the column is not NULL, the actual Color value is used. Note that the third column performs similar NULL-handling for the ProductSubCategory field.

The next transformation in the data flow is an example of data preparation. A Lookup transformation is used to query a second source table that contains an additional attribute needed for the product dimension. Because the Lookup transformation is referencing a source table, the AdventureWorks Connection Manager is selected. In this case, the attribute ModelName comes from a different table in the source. Figure 4-7 shows the Columns tab of the Lookup Transformation Editor.

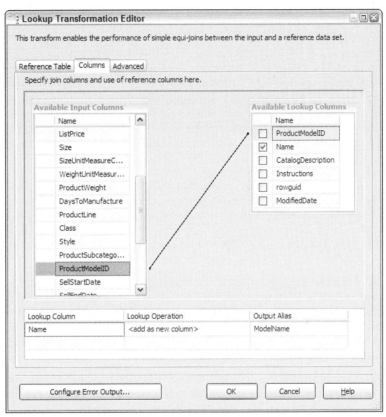

Figure 4-7: Columns tab of the Lookup editor

The available input columns shown on the left come from the Production.Product table that was defined in the source adapter. The available lookup columns on the right come from the Production.ProductModel table, also in the source, which was defined in the Reference Table tab in the same editor.

The lookup is done across the ProductModelID and the Name column is checked, which returns the column into the pipeline column list. The Name column is also aliased as ModelName to match the product dimension table column. In effect, what you have achieved is to take the incoming ProductModelID values and augment them with the corresponding Product Names from a separate table in the source.

The data flow highlighted in Figure 4-4 earlier also shows other transformations used for similar purposes of preparing the data. The output of all these transformations is a *pipeline*, or a set of columns that align with the dimension table itself. When that preparation process is achieved, then the source data is ready to be matched with the existing dimension data for the handling of dimension changes.

Dimension Change Types

The phrase *slowly changing dimension* refers to the tracking of dimension changes over time, and, although the phrase is specific to one of the types of tracking, the name has been used to identify the built-in transformation for SSIS.

> Much of dimension change tracking theory (including the slowly changing dimension) was driven by Ralph Kimball of the Kimball Group, Inc. Kimball and the Kimball Group have written extensively on the theory and practicalities of creating dimension models, handling ETL, and planning a data warehouse project. These theories have proven themselves critical to answering the challenge of business intelligence (BI) and data warehousing. In addition to theory, the Kimball Group has produced the *Microsoft Data Warehouse Toolkit* (Indianapolis: Wiley, 2006), which looks at applying data warehousing theory to the SQL Server 2005 BI technologies.

The question is, as information changes in your dimensions, how do you track those changes? In some situations, data may need to be updated, while other data needs to be tracked historically. Each different tracking requirement is classified as a certain *dimension change type*. Although there are several different change types, the following are the three most common ones that relate to dimension ETL with SSIS:

❑ **Change Type 0 (fixed)** — Also called a *fixed attribute*, this change type specifies an attribute that should not change over time. An example of this would be gender.

❑ **Change Type 1 (changing)** — Oftentimes, tracking the history of changes for a dimension attribute may not provide value. A Type 1 change, also called a *changing attribute*, is useful when you're not interested in the previous value of the attribute. For example, if the `Color` attribute of the product doesn't provide significant value, then when the color changes, its old value could be overwritten. This technique is also known as *Restating History*, since, for example, changing the product color from yellow to red would reflect the new color in all previous sales, too.

❑ **Change Type 2 (historical)** — A Type 2 change is the slowly changing type in dimension tracking. Also called a *historical attribute*, this change type is handled by adding a new row. If a customer location changes from New York to Atlanta, rather than overwriting the new location, a second record is created for the customer. Otherwise, if the location is overwritten, the sales history for New York will not include that customer, rather all the sales will appear to have come from Atlanta. This technique is also known as *Tracking History*, since all changes to dimension attributes can be accurately tracked through time without loss of fidelity.

Two other scenarios are also an important part of an SSIS-based ETL design:

❑ Creating new members when the data source presents a new record

❑ Handling missing dimension member processing, called an *inferred member*

Both of these other dimension processes are supported with SSIS and are discussed in detail later in this chapter.

Change Type 1, a Closer Look

As previously described, a Type 1 or changing attribute requires an in-place update. With this type, you are restating history, and once that update happens, there's no possibility of querying the older value. Overall, a Type 1 change proves fairly simple to understand and execute. Figure 4-8 shows one record from a source data set that matches a record in a dimension table.

Reseller Source			Reseller Dimension	
ResellerID	AW00000047		ResellerKey	10
Phone Number	141-555-0172		ResellerAlternateKey	AW00000047
BusinessType	Specialty Bike Shop		Phone Number	141-555-0172
Reseller Name	Greater Bike Store		BusinessType	Classic Bikes
			Reseller Name	Greater Bike Store

Figure 4-8: Record from a source data set that matches a record in a dimension table

In the reseller source record, the `ResellerID` matches the `ResellerAlternateKey` in the reseller dimension. The `BusinessType` attribute in the reseller dimension is identified as a changing attribute (change Type 1) and the current value is `Classic Bikes`. The reseller source record, however, indicates that this particular reseller store now is classified as a `Specialty Bike Shop`. Because the attribute is marked as changing, the value is simply updated. Figure 4-9 shows the updated dimension table record with the new value.

Reseller Dimension	
ResellerKey	10
ResellerAlternateKey	AW00000047
Phone Number	141-555-0172
BusinessType	Specialty Bike Shop
Reseller Name	Greater Bike Store

Figure 4-9: Updated dimension table record with the new value

Change Type 2, a Closer Look

A column that is identified as a Type 2 or historical attribute is a little more difficult because it involves adding a row and tracking details of the change. Figure 4-10 shows a record for the product source and the matching record in the product dimension table.

Product Source			Product Dimension	
ProductID	BK-T79U-60		ProductKey	576
Class	Mid Tier		ProductAlternateKey	BK-T79U-60
ModelName	Touring-1000		Class (Type 2)	High Perf
			ModelName (Type 2)	Touring-1000
			StartDate	7/3/2003
			EndDate	NULL

Figure 4-10: Source record for the product dimension, and the matching record in the product dimension table

Notice that two of the attributes, `ModelName` and `Class`, are marked as Type 2 historical attributes. In other words, if there is a change, you are interested in keeping the history of the change. In this example, the `Class` of the product changed from `Mid Tier` to `High Perf`. Because a change happened in a Type 2 historical attribute, a new record needs to be added, with a new surrogate key. Figure 4-11 shows the dimension table with the changes applied.

Product Dimension		
ProductKey	576	763
ProductAlternateKey	BK-T79U-60	BK-T79U-60
Class (Type 2)	High Perf	Mid Tier
ModelName (Type 2)	Touring-1000	Touring-1000
StartDate	7/3/2003	11/30/2006
EndDate	11/30/2006	NULL

Figure 4-11: Dimension table with the changes applied

The `High Perf Class` value remains in the original record, but is updated in the new record. Surrogate keys are the lynchpin to handling this, because they allow a new record to be created with the same business key, and all the history in the fact table references the first key, and any new fact records would reference the new surrogate key. This allows someone to run a query to say "show me the sales of the Mid Tier bicycles." If the change was not tracked historically, the `Mid Tier` sales would not be available for that bicycle, it would appear as if all the sales for that bicycle were `High Perf` if querying on `Class`.

Notice that there are metadata columns to help track the Type 2 historical change — a `StartDate` and an `EndDate`. The `StartDate` for the new record is set to `11/30/2006` and the `EndDate` is `NULL`, which indicates the dimension member is the current row. When this new record was added, the `EndDate` of the original record was updated to the date of that change. The `StartDate` and `EndDate` columns provide the capability to know when a dimension member was active, and the capability to identify the current record (that is, when the `EndDate` is `NULL`). In this example, there are now two records for this product. However, it is possible to have many different versions of this record.

Another common technique is to use a Boolean column that identifies the current record, which would be marked as `True`, and the outdated records, which would be marked as `False`.

Inferred Members

At times, the ETL system may need to handle missing dimension records. When the fact data is being loaded, if the dimension member is not available, the fact row should not just be ignored, but inserted into the fact table with a temporary dimension assignment. An *inferred member* is a dimension record that has been added during the fact load when the business key from the fact source doesn't have a match in the dimension table. You might have an inferred member for many reasons:

- If the data in the dimension source or fact source is dirty and the match is not available, then the dimension member may not be available or found in the dimension table.
- Depending on source system requirements, if the dimension source cannot be extracted as often or before the fact table source is extracted and processed, a missing dimension record may occur.
- If the dimension source is not updated as often as the fact source, it may result in missing dimension records during the fact load.

Having missing dimension members is a problem known as an inferred member, but is also commonly called a *late-arriving dimension* scenario.

For example, at some retailers, products may go on the shelf at a store to be sold before the master product table is updated at a corporate office. Store managers are often given autonomy to sell extra products in their stores outside of the corporate product list. Therefore, data may not enter into the centralized item inventory until later, but the sale is still recorded, causing a late arriving dimension scenario.

When dealing with inferred members, there are really two aspects of the ETL:

❑　*Inserting* the inferred member during the *fact load*

❑　*Updating* the inferred member during the *dimension load*

Adding Inferred Members During the Fact Load

The SSIS mechanisms for this aspect of inferred members is discussed in Chapter 5, but here are some of the basics of what must happen during the ETL. During the fact load, if a dimension record is not available, a placeholder record is added to the dimension table. If you get a business key for a product, but the product doesn't exist in the dimension table, instead of using a generic *unknown* that is not associated with any business key, you can add an *unknown* specific to the business key for the missing record. Later, if or when the dimension record comes in from the source, you can update it with all the attributes. Inferred members are the most complicated part of dimension processing.

Figure 4-12 shows a transactional source for a sales type fact table on the left, and a couple rows from a related dimension table on the right. The source contains a `ProductID`. However, there's no match in the dimension table itself. The `ProductID` (business key) BK-8006F sold for $439.99, but a matching dimension record is not in the dimension table.

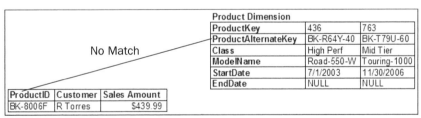

Product Dimension		
ProductKey	436	763
ProductAlternateKey	BK-R64Y-40	BK-T79U-60
Class	High Perf	Mid Tier
ModelName	Road-550-W	Touring-1000
StartDate	7/1/2003	11/30/2006
EndDate	NULL	NULL

No Match

ProductID	Customer	Sales Amount
BK-8006F	R Torres	$439.99

Figure 4-12: Transactional source for a sales type fact table (left) and rows from a related dimension table (right)

Handling this as an inferred member, you must add a record to the dimension table during this fact load. What you don't have are values for all the other attributes of the dimension, which must be set to an unknown value. Figure 4-13 shows the resulting dimension table after the load.

Product Dimension			
ProductKey	436	763	975
ProductAlternateKey	BK-R64Y-40	BK-T79U-60	BK-8006F
Class	High Perf	Mid Tier	Unknown
ModelName	Road-550-W	Touring-1000	Unknown
StartDate	7/1/2003	11/30/2006	11/30/2006
EndDate	NULL	NULL	NULL
Inferred Member Flag	No	No	Yes

Figure 4-13: Resulting dimension table after the load

Notice that the inferred member has been added with a new surrogate key, but the attributes in the dimension are set to Unknown. Furthermore, there's another column in the dimension table called the Inferred Member Flag column. This should be set to Yes (or True), because the dimension process needs to know this is an inferred member created during the fact load. That will impact how dimension processing handles that ETL.

Updating the Inferred Member During the Dimension Load

As just discussed, when you're loading the fact table, if there's a missing record, you add the record to the dimension table as an inferred member. When you process the dimension table later, if the dimension source becomes available for an inferred member, it can be updated with the missing dimension attributes. It works by essentially updating all the columns for that table. Every attribute becomes like a Type 1 changing attribute, even the Type 2 historical attributes. In other words, instead of creating a new record with the changes, the original record is updated. Figure 4-14 shows one row in the data source for a dimension (on the left), and a few rows from the dimension table. The source contains details for a record that currently exists in the dimension table as an inferred member.

Figure 4-14: Row in the data source for a dimension (left) and rows from the dimension table

If the matching record table in the dimension was added during a normal dimension load, the change in the Class or ModelName column (because they are Type 2 historical) would cause a new record to be generated. However, because the dimension member is marked as an inferred member, instead, every attribute is updated to the new values. Figure 4-15 shows the now updated dimension table.

Figure 4-15: Updated dimension table

Not only are all the attributes updated with the new value, but also the Inferred Member Flag column is marked as No (or false), because you now have the full details of that dimension member. An inferred member turns all the attributes into Type 1 changing until the dimension member details come in from the source.

You may have a scenario where you want the dimension table to act like an inferred member, even though the dimension is added from the dimension source. If you have a dimension source record that goes through lots of column value changes until at some point the record is stable, consider treating that dimension record as an inferred member until it stabilizes. The drawback in handling the dimension record like a normal dimension with Type 1 changing and Type 2 historical attributes is that every change to a Type 2 historical attribute causes a new record. Waiting until the stabilization will reduce the number of dimension records and, therefore, avoid too much confusion with so many records for a single member.

SSIS Slowly Changing Dimension Wizard

Now it's time to look at the built-in support for dimension ETL, called the Slowly Changing Dimension (SCD) Wizard. The SCD Wizard is a data-flow transformation and initially works like all the other transformations—simply drag and drop the transformation into the data flow and connect it to the upstream source or transformation. Figure 4-16 shows the data flow that was used earlier in the chapter with the SCD transformation now connected to the output of the Union All.

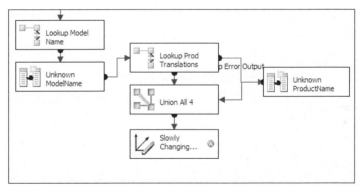

Figure 4-16: Data flow with the SCD transformation connected to the output of the Union All

Double-clicking the transformation will invoke the wizard. Like other user interface wizards, several windows will prompt you for configurations, in order to build the dimension ETL process. One of the nice advantages of the SCD Wizard is that it allows for very rapid ETL development.

The SCD Wizard supports Type 1 changing attributes, Type 2 historical attributes, inferred members, and Type 0 fixed attributes, all out-of-the-box.

When the source is connected to the SCD component, and the wizard invoked, the first screen will prompt you to identify the target dimension table, then the mapping of source columns from the data flow pipeline to the dimension columns in the dimension table, and, finally, the business keys in the source and dimension table. Figure 4-17 shows the mapping between the source rows generated for the product dimension and the dimension columns themselves.

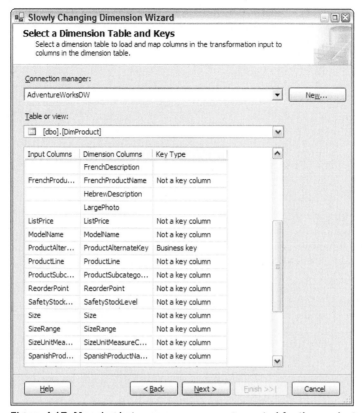

Figure 4-17: Mapping between source rows generated for the product dimension and the dimension columns

Note that the data types must match in order for the source columns to be compared with the dimension table columns, which may require use of the Data Conversion transformation in the upstream data cleansing logic. For the wizard to handle the matching automatically, the column names must be the same. Matching names is not a requirement, because the matching can be done manually. Furthermore, if you have any columns in the dimension table that are not attributes, but rather management or metadata columns (such as StartDate and EndDate columns that identify when the row is active), these will not be matched. Later options in the wizard will give you the opportunity to specify usage of these.

The final step in the first screen is to identify the business key or keys. In Figure 4-17, the ProductAlternateKey is the business key manually matched to the source column Product ID (which has been aliased as ProductAlternateKey). The business keys help identify dimension records that need to be added as new members. The business keys also provide part of the equation on identifying matching records that need to be evaluated for changes.

The next screen of the wizard is about associating the dimension columns that have just been matched with the dimension change type. The wizard does not use the common dimension changing type numbers (Type 0, Type 1, or Type 2); rather, it uses the descriptive terms to identify the type of change (fixed, changing, or historical).

Figure 4-18 shows the matching of the dimension changes. The column on the left contains any non-business key matches identified in the prior screen, and the column on the right is a drop-down of the three different change types.

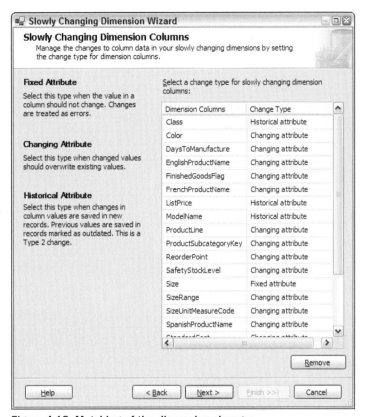

Figure 4-18: Matching of the dimension changes

In this example, the following groupings were made:

❑ **Fixed attributes** — Size (changes in size will generate a new product, therefore, this is fixed)

❑ **Historical attributes** — Class, ModelName, ListPrice

❑ **Changing attributes** — Color, DaysToManufacture, EnglishProductName, FinishedGoodsFlag, FrenchProductName, ProductLine, ProductSubcategoryKey, ReorderPoint, SafetyStockLevel, SizeRange, SizeUnitMeasureCode, SpanishProductName, StandardCost, Style, Weight, WeightUnitMeasureCode

> The matching shown in Figure 4-18 can be a tiresome process if you have dozens
> of dimension columns and you are using your mouse to select the column in the
> drop-down. A quicker way to fill in these values is to use the Tab key and the up
> and down arrow keys. After finishing a row, the Tab key will send the cursor to the
> next row and automatically select the next column in the list.

Now that you have defined the column matches and identified the change types, the next few screens
will help you to manage the advanced requirements for the dimension ETL process.

In the next screen, shown in Figure 4-19, some specific requirements are asked about Fixed attribute and
Changing attribute members.

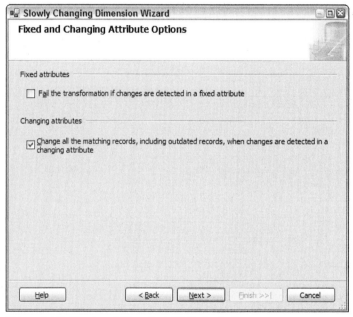

Figure 4-19: Fixed and Changing Attribute Options screen

If you do not identify any Fixed attribute or Changing attribute columns, then the respective detail questions shown in the screen shot will be grayed out.

The option for fixed attribute asks, "If there is a change in a fixed attribute, what should happen?"

❑ By leaving the box unchecked, the change will be ignored and the value in the dimension table
  will stay the same as it was originally.

❑ By selecting the box, if a change is detected in a Fixed attribute column, then the transformation
  will intentionally generate an error, so the data can be reviewed. This may be useful if, when a
  change is identified, it indicates a bigger problem.

The option for changing (Type 1) attributes identifies which records to update when a change happens. In other words, if the dimension record has any Type 2 historical attributes, there may be multiple records for the same business key.

❑ When the check box is selected, all the related records (the current dimension member and the outdated members) are updated.

❑ When the option is cleared, only the current record gets updated with the new value of the column. For example, if there's a change in Color from blue to aqua, and the particular business key had five historical changes, then only the last record would be updated with aqua. When the Changing attributes check box is cleared, and color is marked as a Type 1, only the Current record gets updated from blue to aqua. The rest of the historical records remain as blue.

If any historical attributes have been selected, then the next screen will prompt to identify how the current row is identified. Figure 4-20 shows the Historical Attribute Options screen.

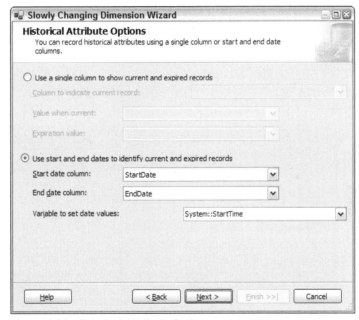

Figure 4-20: Historical Attribute Options screen

The two choices to identify a current row are:

❑ Use a flag column (usually Boolean) to identify whether a row is current or not. Besides just selecting the column that should be used, the SCD Wizard also supports defining what values identify a current record and expired record. Note also that the columns in the drop-down list are any dimension columns that have not been matched from the source. That is because these are considered metadata columns that are used for management purposes like this.

❑ Use a StartDate and EndDate combination to manage when a dimension record is active. The StartDate and EndDate column selections need to be dimension table columns defined with a datetime data type. Furthermore, one other option exists if taking the approach of start time and end time columns — that is, choosing which package variable should be used as the value to update the record with. In other words, when a new dimension member needs to be added, because there is a change in a Type 2 historical attribute, the prior record needs to be first updated with a new EndDate and the new record needs to be initiated with a new StartDate. Any system or user variable can be used. One good choice is to use the System::StartTime variable, which is automatically updated when the package is executed. And, in this example, the StartDate and EndDate columns are used in conjunction with the System::StartTime variable.

> **Choosing to use StartDate and EndDate columns will give you the advantage of knowing exactly when a particular dimension member was active, either for reporting purposes or even to handle the scenario when a fact record arrives late and a historical dimension record needs to be selected instead of the current member.**

The SSIS inferred member support is found in the next screen. As a reminder, inferred members are added during the fact ETL and updated during the dimension ETL. The built-in support for inferred members revolves around the dimension update. Figure 4-21 shows the options available for inferred members.

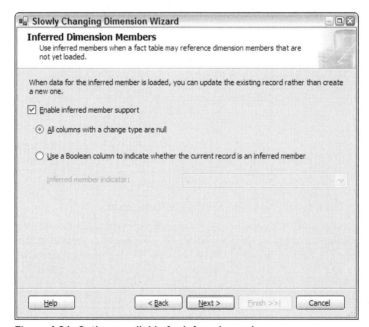

Figure 4-21: Options available for inferred members

First of all, inferred member support is either enabled or disabled. If enabled, the SCD Wizard needs to know how to identify whether a record is an inferred member. The two choices are to leave all the dimension columns in the dimension table as NULL, or to use an `Inferred Member` Boolean column in the table that identifies which rows are inferred members.

Since the product dimension table in the `AdventureWorksDW` database does not have an inferred member column, the first choice is selected.

> **Using the first choice for inferred members (all attributes contain NULL values) is not often practical, because, first of all, it assumes that the columns in the dimension table allow NULL values, and secondly, it makes for difficult querying. Using an unknown value, for example, is often a better way to see data for a reporting system. But in addition, if Analysis Services is used for analytics, NULL values are also not a good choice. The best practice is to define an inferred member column and handle the identification by setting the Boolean value to True or False.**

The final screen, not shown, presents a summary of the outputs that will be created. By selecting Finish on this screen, the SCD Wizard will take all the configuration options and create several downstream transformations and destinations. Figure 4-22 shows the end result of the SCD Wizard — the SCD transformation remains, but it contains several outputs to handle the different attribute types.

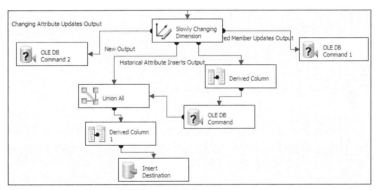

Figure 4-22: End result of the SCD Wizard

Since SSIS dynamically builds the data flow, the resulting layout in this example may not look exactly like your testing. However, the functionality is the same. For this example, on the left are changing attributes. Down the center are new members and historical attributes. On the right are inferred members. Starting with the SCD transformation, when a dimension row is processed, the SCD will determine which (if any) attribute changes occur, and whether there are new members to be added or inferred members to update. Consider the SCD transformation to be like a Conditional Split; it evaluates every row, one at a time, and routes the records to different outputs.

The simplest output to understand is the Changing Attributes Updates Output, which is linked to the OLE DB Command 2 transformation, connected to the AdventureWorksDW database. The following code shows the SQLCommand property, which defines the UPDATE statement:

```
UPDATE [dbo].[DimProduct]
SET [Color] = ?
,[DaysToManufacture] = ?
,[EnglishProductName] = ?
,[FinishedGoodsFlag] = ?
,[FrenchProductName] = ?
,[ProductLine] = ?
,[ProductSubcategoryKey] = ?
,[ReorderPoint] = ?
,[SafetyStockLevel] = ?
,[SizeRange] = ?
,[SizeUnitMeasureCode] = ?
,[SpanishProductName] = ?
,[StandardCost] = ?
,[Style] = ?
,[Weight] = ?
,[WeightUnitMeasureCode] = ?
WHERE [ProductAlternateKey] = ?
```

What you should note in the UPDATE statement is that only the columns that were defined as changing attributes (Type 1) are included in the UPDATE statement, simply because this output is only for the Type 1 changing attributes. Also notice that the SQL statement is an OLE DB parameterized statement with question marks, which is the way that the OLE DB provider handles the parameterization. Figure 4-23 shows the Column Mappings tab, which maps (in order) the pipeline input columns to the parameterized query.

The order of the question marks defines the order of the mappings.

The second output is the Inferred Member Updates Output. This output is very similar to the Changing Attributes Update Output because it also performs an UPDATE statement. Just like the first output, the inferred member output uses an OLE DB Command transformation to handle the updates (in this case, the OLE DB Command 1 transformation). The UPDATE statement defined in the SQLCommand property is as follows:

```
UPDATE [dbo].[DimProduct]
SET [Class] = ?
,[Color] = ?
,[DaysToManufacture] = ?
,[EnglishProductName] = ?
,[FinishedGoodsFlag] = ?
,[FrenchProductName] = ?
,[ListPrice] = ?
,[ModelName] = ?
,[ProductLine] = ?
,[ProductSubcategoryKey] = ?
,[ReorderPoint] = ?
```

```
,[SafetyStockLevel] = ?
,[Size] = ?
,[SizeRange] = ?
,[SizeUnitMeasureCode] = ?
,[SpanishProductName] = ?
,[StandardCost] = ?
,[Style] = ?
,[Weight] = ?
,[WeightUnitMeasureCode] = ?
WHERE [ProductAlternateKey] = ?
```

The difference, as you would expect, is that there are more columns in the UPDATE statement. Not only are the Type 1 changing attributes updated, but also the Type 2 historical attributes. Included in the UPDATE statement are the Class, ModelName, and ListPrice columns, which were defined as a Type 2 historical attributes. These are updated because of the nature of an inferred member, which requires updates to all the columns without generating a new record. Furthermore, if you had defined an Inferred Member Flag column, this is where the inferred member column would also be updated. Just like the first OLE DB Command transformation, the order of question marks defines the order of the mapping.

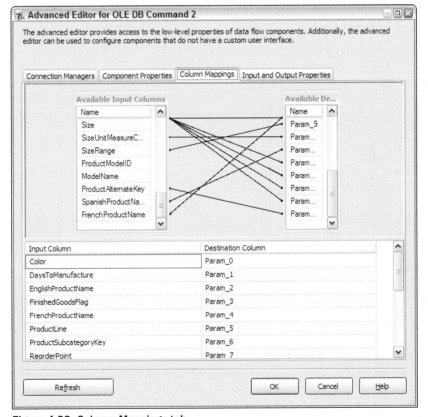

Figure 4-23: Column Mappings tab

The next two outputs to consider are also related. Both the New Output (new members to be added) and the Historical Attribute Inserts Output add rows to the dimension table. What you can see in Figure 4-22 earlier is that a Union All transformation is used to bring these two outputs together for a single destination insert.

If the business key from the source does not exist in the dimension table, it's identified as a new member that needs to be inserted. The New Output that handles new members goes directly to the Union All transformation. With the Historical Attribute Insert Output, before the records are brought together in the Union All, a couple of metadata management tasks need to happen. Whether the new historical attribute record is marked as current through a combination of dates or a separate column, the old record needs to be updated before the insert can happen. Either the End Date column is updated, or a current flag column is updated, which is handled in a two-step process:

1. The Derived Column transformation that is attached to the Historical Attribute Insert Output adds either an EndDate column to the data flow (as in this example), or it adds the expired flag value. Figure 4-24 shows the Derived Column editor that defines an EndDate column and then also uses the System::StartTime variable as specified in the SCD Wizard.

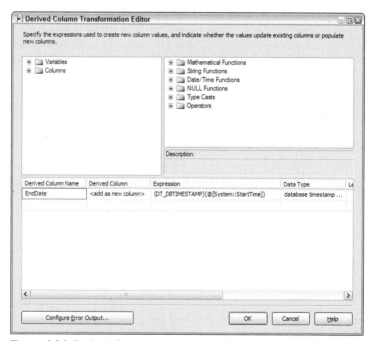

Figure 4-24: Derived Column editor

2. Another OLE DB Command transformation is used to update the End Date for the expired record, based on the business key and the current indicator (in this case, the record to be expired will currently have an End Date of NULL). The SQLCommand property of this OLE DB Command transformation is as follows:

```
UPDATE [dbo].[DimProduct]
SET [EndDate] = ?
WHERE [ProductAlternateKey] = ? AND [EndDate] IS NULL
```

One nice feature of the OLE DB Command transformation, as this example shows, is that the records from the pipeline can perform the UPDATE statement, and then still be available downstream for other purposes. After the expired record has been updated, then the record is ready to be "union-ed" with the new member output.

Before the final insert for the new members and Type 2 historical attributes, one final step is necessary — you need to add the Start Date (or current record flag). This is handled by a Derived Column transformation, which adds a column to the pipeline called StartDate (in this example). Figure 4-25 shows the details of the Derived Column transformation that falls just below the Union All transformation and before the OLE DB destination (from the data flow shown earlier in Figure 4-22).

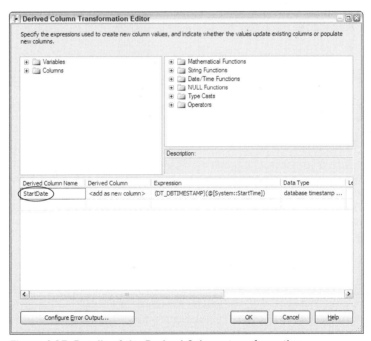

Figure 4-25: Details of the Derived Column transformation

Just like the EndDate, the StartDate uses the System::StartTime variable, which is used for the new record. New records that are new members or Historical-attribute inserts require the EndDate to be NULL. (If you have specified a current indicator, you put the indicator's current value in this Derived Column transformation.)

When executed, the SCD transformation routes the rows from the source to the different outputs. Notice in Figure 4-26 that the 504 input rows are not all sent out the outputs. This is because some of the records do not go through any changes, so they are effectively ignored.

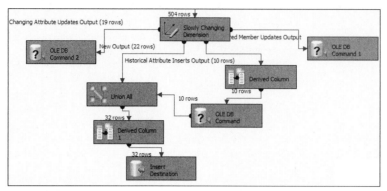

Figure 4-26: Input rows not sent out the outputs

Advanced Properties and Additional Outputs of the SCD

There are two advanced properties of the SCD that can be used to customize how the SCD transformation handles the processing:

❑   The CurrentRowWhere property identifies how the current dimension row for a source record is identified. If you have configured the SCD to use a Current Flag column, then, by default, this property would filter on the Current Flag where the value you defined in the wizard is current. Alternately, if you specified Start Date and End Date, then, by default, the property would assume that the End Date column IS NULL. This property can be changed if you need to re-define how the SCD transformation searches for the current record. For example, if your organizational standards do not allow NULL values, then you would have to modify this property to check the End Date for the default value set for the column (oftentimes, a date far out in the future is used to accommodate this, such as 1/1/2050).

❑   The SQLCommand property contains the SQL syntax used for the lookup against the dimension table to either determine if a new member needs to be created, or if there have been any changes in a Type 0 fixed attribute, Type 1 changing attribute, or Type 2 historical attribute.

Both of the properties referenced here can be found by reviewing the Properties window when selected on the SCD transformation, as shown in Figure 4-27, or by looking at the advanced editor of the SCD transformation.

Furthermore, the SCD transformation contains two additional outputs that are not used by default, but are useful for auditing and data validation.

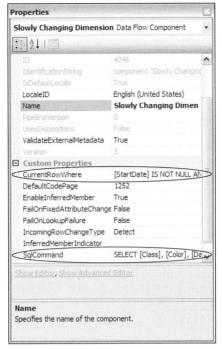

Figure 4-27: SCD Transformation Properties window

The first output enables you to capture the rows that have not gone through any change. Very likely, if you are pulling the entire dimension source (as opposed to just targeting new and changed records), you will have many dimension records from the source that are unchanged or are completely in synch with the dimension table. Although a change has not happened, you may have a need to count the number of rows that are unchanged, or capture the unchanged rows in a table or file for review. The Unchanged Output is accessible by selecting the green path output from the SCD transformation, and connecting it to another transformation or destination. When this is done, you will be prompted to choose the right output, and are prompted with the remaining outputs that are not used. In Figure 4-28, a Row count transformation is used to capture the number of rows that are unchanged into a variable that is later captured for auditing purposes.

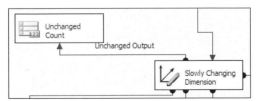

Figure 4-28: Row count transformation used
to capture the number of unchanged rows

The second additional output is the Fixed Attribute Output, which sends out any rows where a fixed attribute column has changed when it should not have. Rather than a Row count, a better use of this output is to capture the records to a staging table for review, since a change was not supposed to happen.

Only when the Ignore fixed attribute changes option is selected will this output be used. Otherwise, if a fixed attribute change occurred, the SCD would intentionally fail.

Slowly Changing Dimension Wizard Advantages and Disadvantages

The SCD Wizard is a very powerful tool, and will be appreciated by ETL developers who commonly deal with managing complicated ETL processes for dimensions. Several benefits will be achieved by using the built-in SCD support. However, there are also a few limitations surrounding the SCD that should be mentioned.

The advantages focus on management, development, and standardization, including the following:

❑   **Simplicity** — The SCD Wizard can handle most dimension scenarios. It makes the often complicated dimension processing straightforward, and helps standardize ETL development for dimensions.

❑   **Rapid development** — The SCD can save time in the development lifecycle by reducing the design and development time, and also easing the management and testing. This leaves more availability for other areas of an ETL process.

❑   **Wizard allows changes** — If the inputs entered into the SCD Wizard require changing, the wizard can be re-invoked, and these changes will propagate down to the downstream-generated components automatically. A caveat to this is presented in the limitations section.

❑   **Customized output transformations** — Since the SCD Wizard generates transformations rather than a black-box approach, the output can be customized. For example, the OLE DB Command transformation used for Type 1 changing attributes can be removed and replaced with a staging table in order to achieve set-based updates, which often perform faster than row-by-row updates.

❑   **Beyond dimension processing** — The SCD transformation can be used beyond just dimension processing, such as table synchronization. Even though the name suggests that the SCD Wizard focuses exclusively on dimension processing, one alternate use is to just leverage the Type 1 changing attribute support (and the included new member support).

The limitations of the SCD support focus mostly on scalability for large-dimension scenarios:

❑   **Dimension table lookup scalability** — The dimension table is not cached in memory. Therefore, for every row coming in from the source, a separate lookup statement is sent to the dimension table in the underlying relational engine.

❑   **All updates are row-based** — Relational updates are required for the Type 1 changing attribute output, the Inferred Member output, and the Type 2 historical attribute output (to expire the previous record). Because the OLE DB Command transformation is employed, every row coming through these transformations sends a separate UPDATE statement to the dimension table, in a cursor-like fashion. When dealing with several thousand updates, this can be limiting.

❑ **Customized outputs are overwritten by changes** — Although the wizard can be re-run (with the prior run's values remaining), if you have customized the output and then run through the wizard again, when the wizard finishes, it will overwrite any changes you made (the transformations will be orphaned by a new set of transformations). Be careful with that if you're making customizations. The wizard will overwrite them.

❑ **Locking issues and inserts** — All at the same time, data may be queried from the dimension table for comparison, it may be updated in the dimension table to handle a Type 1 change, and it may also be inserted for new members and Type 2 historical records. All this activity on the dimension table at one time can slow down the dimension ETL process. Furthermore, the inserts cannot take advantage of the Fast Load option because of the locking contentions, thus resulting in row-by-row inserts.

Optimizing the Built-in Slowly Changing Dimension Support

Later in this chapter, we examine writing an SSIS package for dimension ETL without using the built-in SCD Wizard support. However, if you are dealing with a large dimension table, a couple of techniques can be used to achieve better performance.

Index Optimizations

Since the dimension lookups and updates both are row-by-row operations, be sure to check the indexes on your dimension table to speed up the identification of the current record. If you are seeing very poor performance with the SCD (anything less than approximately 2,000 rows per minute), then chances are the SCD lookups are requiring relational table scans or bookmark lookups after identifying the record key. For best ETL optimization, create your dimension table's clustered index on the business key, rather than the dimension surrogate key. Including the current indicator flag or end date as the second column in the index will improve the performance even more.

> **Index optimization must be balanced between the ETL and the query usage. Optimization for query patterns should take priority over optimizations for ETL. However, some situations may require ETL-focused optimization as a priority to achieve the service-level agreements (SLAs) identified for processing times. Also, be cautious that too many indexes can slow down operations.**

Update Optimizations

Dimension table updates to handle Type 1 changing attributes are a common occurrence in any dimension table ETL process. Although the inferred member output also requires updates, the number of rows will typically be a fraction of the number of Type 1 changing attributes, since inferred members are considered an exception to the rule. Since the updates are row by row (this is the way the OLE DB Command transformation works), then dealing with thousands of updates will create a processing bottleneck. One way to improve performance is to replace the OLE DB Command update with a set-based update approach. In Figure 4-29, the OLE DB Command that handles the Type 1 changing output has been replaced with an OLE DB Destination to a staging table.

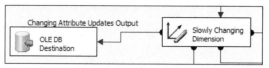

Figure 4-29: OLE DB Destination to a staging table

Using a staging table for this scenario improves performance, because it allows a single set-based UPDATE statement to be run. The UPDATE statement is handled with an Execute SQL Task in the control flow.

The set-based statement is comprised of an inner join between the staging table and the dimension table across the business key, where any matching rows (already identified as requiring a Type 1 changing update) will require the attributes to be updated. The following highlights the TSQL code that performs this operation:

```
UPDATE [dbo].[DimProduct]
SET
  [Color] = STG.[Color]
, [DaysToManufacture] = STG.[DaysToManufacture]
, [EnglishProductName] = STG.[EnglishProductName]
, [FinishedGoodsFlag] = STG.[FinishedGoodsFlag]
, [FrenchProductName] = STG.[FrenchProductName]
, [ProductLine] = STG.[ProductLine]
, [ProductSubcategoryKey] = STG.[ProductSubcategoryKey]
, [ReorderPoint] = STG.[ReorderPoint]
, [SafetyStockLevel] = STG.[SafetyStockLevel]
, [SizeRange] = STG.[SizeRange]
, [SizeUnitMeasureCode] = STG.[SizeUnitMeasureCode]
, [SpanishProductName] = STG.[SpanishProductName]
, [StandardCost] = STG.[StandardCost]
, [Style] = STG.[Style]
, [Weight] = STG.[Weight]
, [WeightUnitMeasureCode] = STG.[WeightUnitMeasureCode]
FROM [dbo].[DimProduct]
INNER JOIN [SSISOps].[dbo].[stgDimProductUpdates] STG
ON [DimProduct].[ProductAlternateKey]
  = STG.[ProductAlternateKey]
```

Be sure to truncate your staging table for every ETL run (by adding an Execute SQL Task at the start of the control flow); otherwise, you will be updating data from old rows from a prior execution.

Handling Advanced Dimension Processing with the Slowly Changing Dimension Support

This section examines how to handle the ETL for advanced dimension forms, combining the functionality of the SCD with other out-of-the-box transformations, focusing on snowflake dimensions, parent-child dimensions, and date dimensions.

Snowflake Dimension Tables

A *snowflake table*, as briefly described in the beginning of this chapter with the product dimension (see Figure 4-2 earlier), requires some unique ETL handling aspects. In a snowflake dimension, the higher-level tables (subcategory and category in this example) also have surrogate keys. With the product snowflake dimension, the `ProductCategoryKey` cascades down as a foreign key in the `DimProductSubCategory` table, and the `ProductSubCategoryKey` cascades down to a foreign key relationship in the `DimProduct` table. The `ProductKey` itself relates directly to the fact table, whereas the surrogate keys in the category and subcategory tables do not relate directly to the reseller fact table.

The design is called a snowflake because when viewed in relationship to the fact table, the table layout looks like a snowflake as opposed to a star. (A star schema has dimension tables one level out from the fact table. A single table dimension is often called a *star dimension*.) Generally, most dimensions are designed as a star dimension. However, there are two very valuable reasons to break out a dimension table into a snowflake design:

❑ When a dimension table has several attributes that relate directly to a higher level within a dimension hierarchy, managing those dimension changes can be a lot easier with a snowflake design. For example, say the product subcategory table contains the English, Spanish, and French names of the subcategory. If these columns were included in the base product table, and the subcategory changed for the dimension, it would be much more difficult to ensure that the Spanish and French names were in synch with the subcategory. Otherwise, if they were not, reporting of these attributes would be misleading with the incorrect association.

❑ A second and more compelling reason to use a snowflake is when you have multiple fact tables related to the same dimension table at different levels. For example, if the Reseller Sales fact table tracked sales at the Product Level, but the Sales Quota facts were assigned to a Product Category, if the Product dimension only had one table, the Category could not be effectively joined. Using a snowflake design, the fact tables can be related to one another because they share a common table at different levels of the product dimension hierarchy. Sharing dimension tables between fact tables is a driving emphasis of dimensional modeling called *conforming dimensions*.

> Analysis Services supports having a standard dimension relate to different measure groups, at different levels. (A *measure group* in Analysis Services is equivalent to a fact table in the database.) It understands how to do the right aggregations. The Analysis Services engine naturally understands how to associate this data and perform aggregations.

A straightforward method to processing snowflake dimension in SSIS is to use multiple SCDs embedded in different data flows, linked by precedence constraints in the control flow starting at the top level of the snowflake tables and working down to the lowest level. Figure 4-30 shows the control flow of the product dimension package. Note the very first task is an Execute SQL Task that truncates the staging table used for the set-based update, followed by the three Data Flow Tasks.

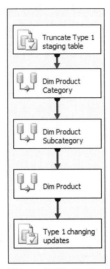

Figure 4-30: Control flow of the product dimension package

The first data flow shown is the product category dimension table, followed by the subcategory dimension table, and concluding with the product data flow. The final Execute SQL Task handles the set-based updates for Type 1 changing attributes as discussed earlier.

The product category data flow is the most straightforward because it only requires one Lookup transformation to get the category translation attributes, and, furthermore, it only contains Type 1 changing attributes. Figure 4-31 shows the product category data flow.

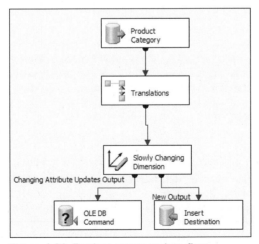

Figure 4-31: Product category data flow

Next, you process the product subcategory. When processing data within intermediate snowflake tables in the hierarchy, a lookup is also required to reference the parent table surrogate key. For example, as you process the product subcategory table, include a Lookup transformation to pull the surrogate key of the category, as shown in Figure 4-32.

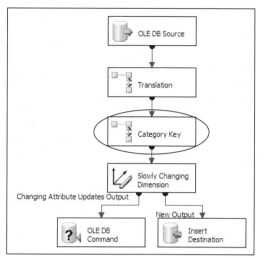

Figure 4-32: Subcategory lookup to pull the surrogate key of the category

The ETL processing in the lowest-level product table has already been discussed. Not mentioned, but also included in the data preparation steps for the product dimension, is the need to pull the surrogate key of the subcategory table.

Parent-Child Dimension ETL

The next dimension design that we will consider is the *parent-child dimension*. A parent-child is a self-referencing dimension table and also has special ETL requirements. Simply put, a parent-child dimension has a surrogate key and a parent surrogate key, which gives the dimension a self reference. In addition, parent-child dimensions usually have a business key and a parent business key. The self-referencing business key nicely illustrates the parent relationship in the table.

An organizational structure is a great example. An organization typically has common attributes for all the individuals in the organization, such as location, office, salary, and so on. All of these attributes relate to higher levels in the hierarchy. A parent-child enables you to build a hierarchy where members at different levels have common attributes. Secondly, a parent-child dimension also allows the hierarchy to be unbalanced, where not every drill path in the hierarchy goes down to the same level.

The Employee dimension table as shown in the beginning of the chapter (see Figure 4-2) is an example of an organizational structure. Figure 4-33 shows a subset of data and columns within the Employee dimension table.

Employee Key	Parent Key	Name	Title
112	NULL	Ken Sanchez	Chief Executive Officer
23	112	Peter Krebs	Production Control Manager
7	112	David Bradley	Marketing Manager
44	112	Jean Trenary	Information Services Manager
143	112	Laura Norman	Chief Financial Officer
275	7	John Wood	Marketing Specialist
276	7	Mary Dempsey	Marketing Assistant
214	23	Brenda Diaz	Production Supervisor - WC40
204	23	Hazem Abolrous	Quality Assurance Manager
188	23	Jack Richins	Production Supervisor - WC30
189	23	Andrew Hill	Production Supervisor - WC10
105	44	Dan Bacon	Application Specialist
120	44	François Ajenstat	Database Administrator
154	44	Stephanie Conroy	Network Manager

Figure 4-33: Subset of data and columns within the Employee dimension table

As you can see, some dimension members relate to other dimension members. For example, Dan Bacon reports to Jean Trenary (Dan's parent employee key is 44, which is the employee key of Jean). At the top of the table, the Chief Executive Officer, Ken Sanchez has no parent key and, therefore, no manager. Every member in the table is a member at a different level in the hierarchy. Taking this subset of data and building the hierarchy for the parent-child relationship turns into the hierarchy shown in Figure 4-34.

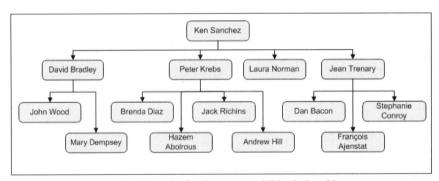

Figure 4-34: Building the hierarchy for the parent-child relationship

Note a few points about this parent-child dimension:

❑   This is an *unbalanced hierarchy*. The levels within this dimension don't all extend to the lowest level (Laura Norman, for example, has no direct reports). In a USA-based geography dimension, for example, everything typically goes to the same state or city level. Within an unbalanced hierarchy, there are levels that don't cascade all the way down.

❑   A parent-child dimension can also be a *ragged hierarchy*. A ragged hierarchy has holes in the hierarchy; you could be at the top level, skip the next level, and go directly to the level below. You must be aware of these variations when processing ETL.

❑   Parent-child dimensions have shared attributes. Most of the records, except at the top level, share common attributes, such as Employee Address.

When processing parent-child dimensions in SSIS, a couple of methods can be applied for acquiring the parent record key.

The first approach is to use a Lookup transformation to acquire the parent record for the parent-child relationship. Figure 4-35 shows the data flow used to process the Employee dimension table.

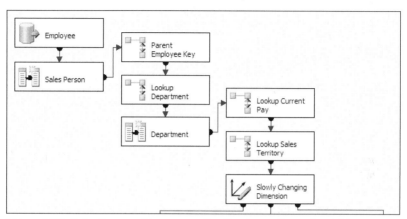

Figure 4-35: Data flow used to process the Employee dimension table

This data flow has similarities to the product dimension data flow, as the first several transformations are used to prepare the data for the SCD transformation. Note that the third data flow object is a Lookup transformation used to acquire the parent surrogate key. In this case, the Lookup transformation joins the parent employee business key of the source to the matching employee business key from the employee table. Figure 4-36 shows the Columns tab of the Lookup editor.

Besides the join being across the parent business key to the business key in the reference table, the surrogate key that is returned is aliased to match the `ParentEmployeeKey`.

A second approach involves using an Execute SQL Task in the control flow and performing a set-based update to associate the employee with the employee's manager record. This SQL Task needs to be run after the data flow that adds new dimension records. The following SQL code is used to perform the operation:

```
UPDATE dbo.DimEmployee
   SET ParentEmployeeKey = Parent.EmployeeKey
FROM dbo.DimEmployee
INNER JOIN dbo.DimEmployee Parent
      ON DimEmployee.ParentEmployeeNationalIDAlternateKey =
            Parent.EmployeeNationalIDAlternateKey
        AND Parent.EndDate IS NULL
WHERE DimEmployee.ParentEmployeeKey IS NULL
```

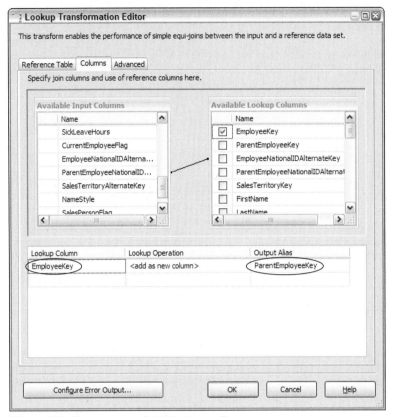

Figure 4-36: Columns tab of the Lookup editor

The query could be handled by a self join or a correlated subquery. In this case, a join is used between the Employee table and the Employee table (aliased as Parent) matching across the child employee with the parent manager record. The ParentEmployeeKey is updated with the EmployeeKey of the Employee table joined as the parent table. Also important to note is that the only records affected are those with the ParentEmployeeKey set to NULL, which targets and, therefore, optimizes the updates.

A final approach is to use a combination of a Lookup transformation and an Execute SQL Task. The Lookup transformation approach may fall short of handling all situations if an employee is added at the same time as the assigned manager. In this case, the parent employee key would not yet be available. This combined approach would give better scalability in higher-volume situations by reducing the rows affected by the update.

Date Dimension ETL

The *date dimension* is probably the most common and conformed dimension in any data warehouse or data mart structure. In other words, most fact tables have relationships to a Date table. In the sample AdventureWorksDW, the date dimension table is called DimTime. Honestly, it's poorly named. The word *Time* has connotations of time of day—hour or minute, not the date grain, which is actually what is stored in the DimTime table. DimDate would have been a better name.

A date dimension can have many different attributes, besides the year, month, and date. It might include the following:

- Day of week
- Week of year
- Holiday
- Fiscal hierarchy

The attributes combine to create different hierarchies. An example of a natural calendar hierarchy would be Year-Quarter-Month-Date or Year-Week-Date. In the natural calendar, weeks do not line up with months (a week can span two months). Therefore, there are two natural calendar hierarchies. Because of this challenge, organizations have come up with different, and often unique, fiscal hierarchies. Your organization may have its own fiscal hierarchy.

A common approach to a custom fiscal hierarchy is to break a quarter into three periods: four weeks in period 1, four weeks in period 2, and five weeks in period 3 (commonly called a 4-4-5 fiscal date hierarchy). A period essentially replaced a month to accommodate the week-month challenge. One organization we worked with had at least 10 different fiscal hierarchies—every branch of the organization wanted to see the sales data from a different perspective.

When it comes to handling the date dimension ETL, the dimension is relatively easy to process because once a new date record is added, it is usually never updated. The Date dimension is commonly not snowflaked into multiple tables.

> **The date dimension is not typically snowflaked even if you have higher-level fact tables and a multi-grained scenario. For example, account balances might be tracked at a week level, whereas sales come in at a day level, and inventory at a month level. The date dimension almost always uses the day for granularity. You would use the first period of that grain as the key. For example, if inventory is at the month level, use the first day of the month as the key for the month.**

There are a few different ways to process date-dimension ETL. The following are some common mechanisms:

1. Handle the date dimension population through a stored procedure. Whether you're calculating one date at a time every day or out into the future once a year, a stored procedure can load all of the records and handle all the date logic.

2. Use a data flow with Derived Column transformations and date part expressions. The data flow generates a set of dates where additional attributes are added using the date functions in SSIS updated.

3. Use a For Loop Container to iterate through a range of dates with SQL Inserts. The For Each Loop container could be configured to increase the date variable by one every loop and then leverage an Execute SQL Task to manage the inserts, one row at a time.

Any of these approaches are viable. Since the date dimension usually contains a small number of records, this package will process quickly regardless of the approach chosen.

As an example, if the second approach is taken, the process would involve identifying the first new date and the last date to add, followed by a data flow to handle the inserts. Figure 4-37 shows the control flow of a package with an Execute SQL Task followed by a data flow.

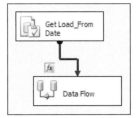

Figure 4-37: Control flow of a package with an Execute SQL Task followed by a data flow

Defined in the package are two user variables, `FromDate` and `ToDate`, which are populated by the Execute SQL Task using a single row resultset. The `FromDate` is populated by querying the MAX date in the time dimension plus one day, and the `ToDate` is populated from the MAX date in the sales header table source. As you would guess, the data flow only needs to run if the `ToDate` is greater than the `FromDate`. This is handled through the Precedence Constraint after the Execute SQL Task. Figure 4-38 shows the Precedence Constraint Editor.

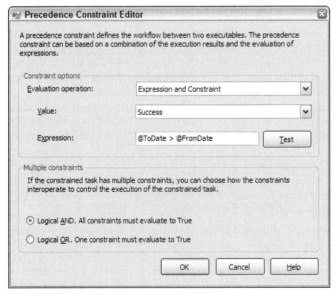

Figure 4-38: Precedence Constraint Editor

If the Execute SQL Task is successful *and* the @ToDate is greater than @FromDate, then the Precedence Constraint will allow the Data Flow Task to execute. At this point, if the criteria are met, then there are rows that need to be inserted into the time dimension table. The data flow, shown in Figure 4-39, contains five components:

- ❏ A Script Component that generates a row for every day starting with the Start Date and ending with the End Date

- ❏ A Derived Column transformation that adds the required date attributes

- ❏ Two Lookup transformations to pull in some date translations from a translation table

- ❏ A destination adapter that inserts the rows into the Time dimension table.

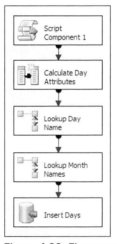

Figure 4-39: Five components of the data flow

Since the Script Component can be used as a source (as described in Chapter 2), it is a great candidate to generate rows from the FromDate to the ToDate values. The following code takes the SSIS variables and, using a Do While loop, iterates over the dates from the FromDate to the ToDate, adding a date for every loop:

```
Imports System
Imports System.Data
Imports System.Math
Imports Microsoft.SqlServer.Dts.Pipeline.Wrapper
Imports Microsoft.SqlServer.Dts.Runtime.Wrapper

Public Class ScriptMain
    Inherits UserComponent

    Public Overrides Sub CreateNewOutputRows()

        Dim vFromDate As Date = Me.Variables.FromDate
```

```
            Do While vFromDate <= Me.Variables.ToDate
                With NewDatesOutputBuffer
                    .AddRow()
                    .FullDateAlternateKey = vFromDate
                End With
                vFromDate = DateAdd(DateInterval.Day, 1, vFromDate)
            Loop

        End Sub

End Class
```

The second component to highlight is the Derived Column transformation. Figure 4-40 shows the Derived Column editor, which contains several additional columns using the DATEPART SSIS expression function to pull out common attributes.

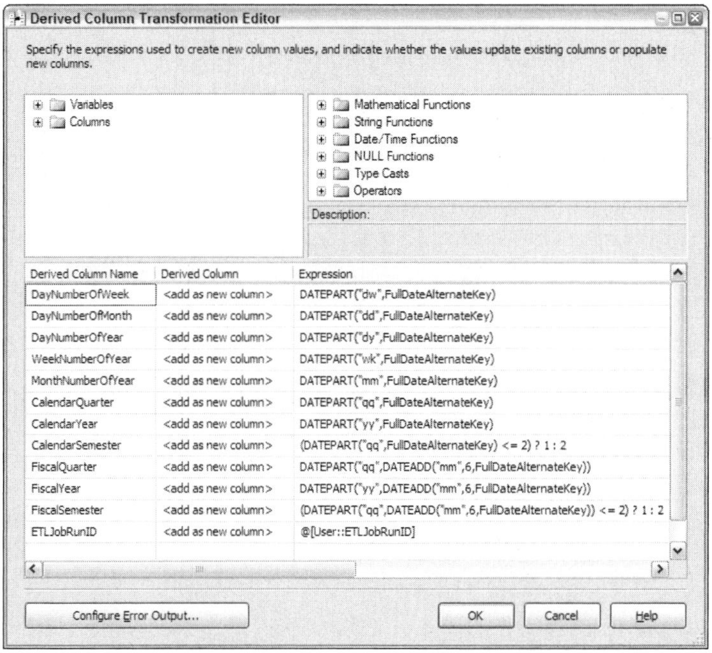

Figure 4-40: Derived Column editor

Before the OLE DB Destination, which is just an insert into the DimTime table, two Lookups handle the translation, because the time dimension table supports multiple languages for the month- and day-related attributes.

Overall, the package is straightforward, performs well, and leverages SSIS capabilities.

Creating a Custom Slowly Changing Package

After working with a couple of clients, it became obvious that the built-in SCD transformation would handle most, but not all, dimension processing situations, and its limitations have been pointed out earlier.

The question becomes: "How can we build a dimension ETL package that mimics the functionality of the built-in SCD support, but scales to handle high volumes?"

If you are now comfortable with the SSIS data flow features and the SCD concepts covered thus far, then the answer will be surprisingly easily. Before laying out a couple of variations, consider the different aspects of the dimension process:

❑   Data correlation between the source records and the dimension table

❑   Comparisons between the column values from the source and the dimension tables

❑   Updates to handle Type 1 changing records and inferred members

❑   Inserts to handle Type 2 historical changes and new dimension members

When considering the built-in SCD support, the SCD transformation (not including the downstream transformations) handles the first two aspects listed here. So, our objective first is to re-create this process by using out-of-the-box features.

Joining Source Data to Dimension Data

The first thing you want to do is correlate the data, comparing the source to the dimension. Within SSIS, there are two primary transformations that can help you correlate data: the Lookup transformation and the Merge Join transformation.

In both cases, you must use the business key in the source and associate it with the current record in the dimension. When you join those records together, you can then compare the different attributes to see if there are changes.

❑   Using a Lookup transformation, the dimension table can be fully cached, which will limit the RDBMS impact as opposed to the row-by-row lookup approach of the SCD transformation. However, on a 32-bit server with 4GB of memory, the Lookup cache will max out in the neighborhood of 2 to 6 million dimension members in the cache, depending on the availability of system memory, the data type of the surrogate key and business key, and the number of columns needed to be returned by the lookup for comparison.

❑   A Merge Join transformation will allow the dimension members to be joined with source records. When the source or dimension can be pre-sorted, this approach will allow greater memory scalability. Instead of keeping everything in cache, once a key match occurs, the row is sent downstream and no longer held up by the Merge Join. This approach requires a Left outer join, taking rows from the source on the left side, and the dimension on the right side, and merging across the business key.

Step B involves comparing the columns from the source to the dimension, and could be handled with a Conditional Split transformation.

Figure 4-41 shows the sample data flow for the customer dimension.

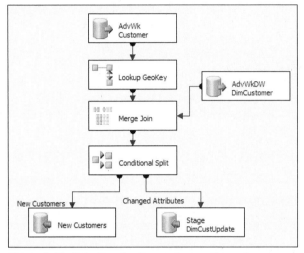

Figure 4-41: Data flow for the customer dimension

On the left, the customer source records are extracted (along with a Lookup to acquire the geography surrogate key), and on the right, the customer dimension records are pulled. Both of these sources are joined together with a Merge Join. As you recall, the Merge Join requires that the data sources are sorted. However, neither input is sorted using the Sort transformation. Rather, these sources use a SQL ORDER BY statement in the source adapter, sorting by the business key. To accomplish this, the Advanced Editor allows the sources to be flagged as pre-sorted. Figure 4-42 shows that the IsSorted property is set to True on the OLE DB Source Output of the dimension table source.

To be sure, the IsSorted property is only a flag. It does not perform any actual sorting itself. It is merely a contract by the developer to the component to state that it should "trust this source is already sorted."

The second required step to mark a source to be pre-sorted is to drill into the Output Columns folder in the same window, and change the SortKeyPosition (not shown) of the appropriate sorted column to an integer that delineates which columns are sorted in which order (negative indicates descending).

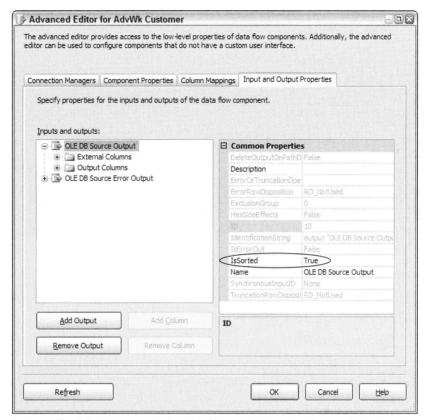

Figure 4-42: IsSorted property is set to True on the OLE DB Source Output of the dimension table source

As a reminder, both inputs into a Merge Join need to be sorted on the join column in order for the Merge Join to validate. Since both sources have been marked as pre-sorted, the Merge Join will recognize the sort columns. Figure 4-43 shows the Editor window of the Merge Join transformation.

The Left outer join Join type will allow the new source records to be identified. Notice also that the attribute columns are selected on both inputs. This is to allow the comparison of the columns in the next step. Because many of the column names are repeated, the columns from the right input (the Dimension table) are prefixed with a DW_.

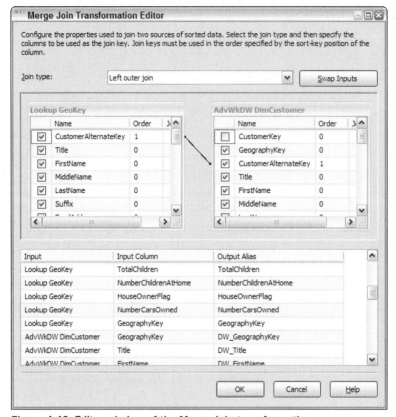

Figure 4-43: Editor window of the Merge Join transformation

Determining Data Correlation Approach

Before continuing with the review of this custom SCD package, here are a few considerations when determining what SSIS approach should be used to correlate data in the data flow. These approaches employ different uses of the Merge Join and Lookup transformation for bringing source and dimension data together.

❑ **Merge Join with Sort** — The Merge Join requires the sources be sorted on the joining keys. You could use a Sort transformation in each source before the Merge Join. However, this approach requires a lot of memory because the Sort must encapsulate all of the records and then sort them before sending the rows downstream.

❑ **Merge Join with Presorted Input** — Relational engines do a great job of sorting data because, in many cases, the join keys in the source are already indexed. If this is the case, use a simple ORDER BY statement in the source, and then tell the source adapter that the input is sorted (the approach identified in the last section).

❑ **Fully cached Lookup** — The Lookup transformation allows full cache, partial cache, and no cache. Partial and no cache don't scale well since database calls are expensive. However, if your dimension table size is manageable (less than a few hundred thousand members), then caching the dimension table in memory will provide great performance without the data sources having to be sorted.

❑ **Filtered Cache Lookup** — If you have millions of rows in your dimension table and are able to target only new and changed records during the dimension source extract, one option is to land the business keys from those dimension tables in a staging table, then use that staging table to filter the lookup itself. This will allow all the needed records to be loaded into the Lookup cache, but not the entire dimension table.

On a 64-bit server, the fully cached Lookup scales very well. The benefits of 64-bit are in both the size of the cache (millions of records) and the ability to load the records into cache much faster than a 32-bit environment.

Determining Dimension Changes

Now that the dimension source has been joined with the dimension table, the records now need to be routed to the appropriate output for the dimension change handling. As Figure 4-41 shows, the next step after the Merge Join is a Conditional Split, which will help determine where the records should go.

The Customer dimension in `AdventureWorks` contains only Type 1 changing attributes, which simplifies this example. Therefore, only new members and changes need to be accommodated. The comparison is handled through the Conditional Split transformation, the editor shown in Figure 4-44.

Figure 4-44: Conditional Split transformation editor

As you can see, the first criterion evaluated is whether the business key is NULL in the dimension table, ISNULL(DW_CustomerAlternateKey). If it is NULL, then this indicates the dimension record does not exist, and, therefore, the source record is New Customers as the output name indicates.

The second criterion is to determine whether a change has happened in any of the attribute columns, using an SSIS expression, as shown in the following code:

```
    (ISNULL(GeographyKey) ? 1 : GeographyKey) !=
    (ISNULL(DW_GeographyKey) ? "" : DW_GeographyKey)
 || (ISNULL(Title) ? "" : Title) != (ISNULL(DW_Title) ? "" : DW_Title)
 || FirstName != DW_FirstName
 || (ISNULL(MiddleName) ? "" : MiddleName) !=
    (ISNULL(DW_MiddleName) ? "" : DW_MiddleName)
 || LastName != DW_LastName
 || BirthDate != DW_BirthDate
 || MaritalStatus != DW_MaritalStatus
 || (ISNULL(Suffix) ? "" : Suffix) !=
    (ISNULL(DW_Suffix) ? "" : DW_Suffix)
 || Gender != DW_Gender
 || EmailAddress != DW_EmailAddress
 || TotalChildren != DW_TotalChildren
 || NumberChildrenAtHome != DW_NumberChildrenAtHome
 || HouseOwnerFlag != DW_HouseOwnerFlag
 || NumberCarsOwned != DW_NumberCarsOwned
 || AddressLine1 != DW_AddressLine1
 || (ISNULL(AddressLine2) ? "" : AddressLine2) !=
    (ISNULL(DW_AddressLine2) ? "" : DW_AddressLine2)
 || Phone != DW_Phone
 || DateFirstPurchase != DW_DateFirstPurchase
 || CommuteDistance != DW_CommuteDistance
```

The Logical OR operator (||) allows each column to be evaluated for changes. The ISNULL function helps to perform the comparison in the case that both of the values are NULL, which evaluates as not equal. In other words, if a change happens in any column, then the entire expression evaluates as TRUE, and the record is identified as meeting the Changed Attribute output.

Finally, if a row does not meet either of these criteria, then it is consider as not having changed, and therefore the Default Output is called No Changes.

You can also use the script component to do the conditional comparison, as it might be easier when dealing with a large number of columns or more complicated logic. The Conditional Split expression box does not allow a secondary editor window to generate more complicated expressions. Therefore, a Script Component would be potentially cleaner.

Handling Dimension Inserts and Updates

If a change exists or a new record needs to be created, the final step in the dimension table ETL is to handle inserts and updates.

The SCD Wizard approach also handles inserts and updates by using a series of OLE DB Command transformations and OLE DB Destinations. When considering how to deal with changes in a custom dimension process, the same options are available:

❑ **Dimension Updates** — Updates for Type 1 changing attributes and inferred members can be handled by the OLE DB Command transformation, or a set-based update approach, which would leverage a staging table and an Execute SQL Task, as described earlier in this chapter.

❑ **Dimension Inserts** — Inserts should use an OLE DB Destination adapter or other destination that optimizes the inserts. If updates are handled through a staging table approach, the OLE DB Destination can be configured with fast load support. Otherwise, database table locking contentions can happen if the updates are happening at the same time as the inserts.

Continuing with the previous example, a set-based approach is taken to handle the updates. Therefore, the output of the Conditional Split requires two OLE DB Destination adapters, as Figure 4-41 earlier demonstrated: one for the dimension inserts and a second for the staging table inserts.

Since the ETL process controls the data in the dimension table and the updates will not be happening at the same time, a Fast Load with a Table Lock is used to handle the inserts. Figure 4-45 shows the OLE DB Destination adapter editor for the dimension inserts.

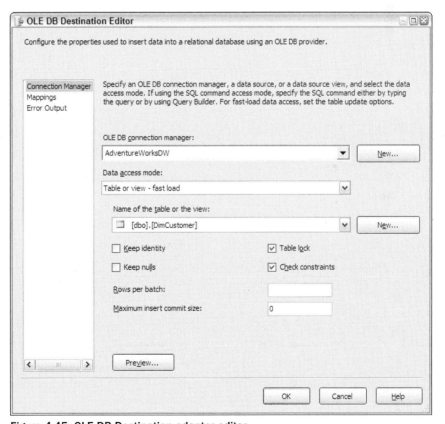

Figure 4-45: OLE DB Destination adapter editor

When it comes to the dimension updates, after the rows requiring an update are loaded to the staging table, the set-based update can be performed. Figure 4-46 shows the control flow of the Customer package, which ends in an Execute SQL Task to perform the update, called Batch Updates. This control flow also begins with a truncation statement to clear out the same staging table used for the updates.

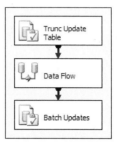

Figure 4-46: Control flow of the Customer package

The update itself is formed by joining the dimension table with the staging table, and replacing the values in the staging table with the current values in the dimension table.

```
UPDATE AdventureWorksDW.dbo.DimCustomer
   SET AddressLine1 = stgDimCustomerUpdates.AddressLine1
     , AddressLine2 = stgDimCustomerUpdates.AddressLine2
     , BirthDate = stgDimCustomerUpdates.BirthDate
     , CommuteDistance = stgDimCustomerUpdates.CommuteDistance
     , DateFirstPurchase = stgDimCustomerUpdates.DateFirstPurchase
     , EmailAddress = stgDimCustomerUpdates.EmailAddress
     , EnglishEducation = stgDimCustomerUpdates.EnglishEducation
     , EnglishOccupation = stgDimCustomerUpdates.EnglishOccupation
     , FirstName = stgDimCustomerUpdates.FirstName
     , Gender = stgDimCustomerUpdates.Gender
     , GeographyKey = stgDimCustomerUpdates.GeographyKey
     , HouseOwnerFlag = stgDimCustomerUpdates.HouseOwnerFlag
     , LastName = stgDimCustomerUpdates.LastName
     , MaritalStatus = stgDimCustomerUpdates.MaritalStatus
     , MiddleName = stgDimCustomerUpdates.MiddleName
     , NumberCarsOwned = stgDimCustomerUpdates.NumberCarsOwned
     , NumberChildrenAtHome = stgDimCustomerUpdates.NumberChildrenAtHome
     , Phone = stgDimCustomerUpdates.Phone
     , Suffix = stgDimCustomerUpdates.Suffix
     , Title = stgDimCustomerUpdates.Title
     , TotalChildren = stgDimCustomerUpdates.TotalChildren
  FROM AdventureWorksDW.dbo.DimCustomer DimCustomer
 INNER JOIN dbo.stgDimCustomerUpdates
    ON DimCustomer.CustomerAlternateKey
       = stgDimCustomerUpdates.CustomerAlternateKey
```

In this case, since the Customer dimension only contains Type 1 changing attributes, every non-key attribute is updated. In the case where Type 2 historical attributes are involved, the UPDATE statement would only target the Type 1 changing attributes and leave any changes in the Type 2 historical attributes to an insert.

When this package is run with a large volume, the differences will be stark compared to the built-in SCD Wizard. A customer dimension with hundreds of thousands or millions of records will process in a fraction of the time that the SCD would take, given how the SCD works.

Summary

As demonstrated, when working through your list of dimension change and processing requirements, SSIS provides great out-of-the-box support to handle a majority of the cases and data volumes in your organization. The SCD Wizard can deal with Type 0 fixed, Type 1 changing, and Type 2 historical attributes, and even handle the unique update requirements that inferred members require. But even in situations where the complexity or volume go beyond what the SCD Wizard can handle out-of-the-box, you can tweak the SCD outputs or even use other data flow features and components to build a custom solution that does scale and can deal with your unique situations.

As a natural extension to dimension ETL, Chapter 5 focuses on the requirements around fact table ETL practices using SSIS. Then, Chapter 6 shifts to taking your processed, loaded data in your dimension and fact tables, and processing it into the supporting Analysis Services objects that your BI solution leverages for analytics.

5

Fact Table ETL

When processing data warehouses, dimension table ETL is only half the story. The next major aspect of ETL involves fact tables. But the good news is that dimension ETL usually represents the majority of the complexity in the overall warehouse ETL. To be sure, a data warehouse involves more than just dimension and fact ETL (such as data lineage, auditing, and execution precedence), but in terms of business data, dimension, and facts, it contains the core information.

In this chapter, we focus on applying SSIS to fact table ETL. We discuss the theory and general concepts of fact table ETL, including data mapping, workflow, and precedence. We also identify dimension surrogate keys and measure calculations, and discuss how to manage data grain changes.

Fact Table Overview

Instead of containing attributes about an entity as dimension tables do, a fact table contains the metrics or numbers that the report presents and that the cubes aggregate, as well as trends. *Measures* include sales amount, account balance, discount amount, and shipping quantity. Figure 5-1 shows the Internet sales fact table, which contains several measures related to the direct sales to consumers, such as `OrderQuantity`, `UnitPrice`, `ExtendedAmount`, and so on.

In addition to the measures, a fact table also contains the relationships between the measures and the dimensions. As Figure 5-1 shows, the fact table contains the foreign key relationship from the dimension tables. Essentially, the primary key in the dimension table is the dimension's surrogate key. The surrogate keys from the related dimension tables are included in the fact table. This fact table also contains degenerate dimension values and lineage columns, which often overlap, to provide the transaction IDs to allow tracing back to the source data and filtering by transaction numbers.

Degenerate Dimensions and Lineage   Degenerate Dimensions

Dimension Surrogate Keys   Measures

FactInternetSales

Column Name	Data Type	Allow Nulls
ProductKey	int	☐
OrderDateKey	int	☐
DueDateKey	int	☐
ShipDateKey	int	☐
CustomerKey	int	☐
PromotionKey	int	☐
CurrencyKey	int	☐
SalesTerritoryKey	int	☐
SalesOrderNumber	nvarchar(20)	☐
SalesOrderLineNumber	tinyint	☐
RevisionNumber	tinyint	☑
OrderQuantity	smallint	☑
UnitPrice	money	☑
ExtendedAmount	money	☑
UnitPriceDiscountPct	float	☑
DiscountAmount	float	☑
ProductStandardCost	money	☑
TotalProductCost	money	☑
SalesAmount	money	☑
TaxAmt	money	☑
Freight	money	☑
CarrierTrackingNumber	nvarchar(25)	☑
CustomerPONumber	nvarchar(25)	☑
		☐

Figure 5-1: Internet sales fact table

The three types of columns in the fact table are dimension keys, measures, and metadata. These columns map directly to the ETL processing requirements for fact table ETL, mapping dimension keys, calculating measures, and adding metadata.

Mapping Dimension Keys

Data warehouse project plans should include some mechanism to map source tables or files to both the dimension and fact tables. The fact table mapping must include not just where and how the measures are calculated, but also how the dimension relationships are mapped to acquire the surrogate key. In other words, when you are loading a fact table, you need to have the business keys of the dimension available that are used to join to the dimension table to identify the surrogate keys that are inserted into the fact table. The business keys are sometimes called *candidate keys*. There may even be situations when one fact table uses one set of business keys to look up against a dimension, and a second fact table uses a second key or keys to identify the dimension record for the same dimension table.

Calculating Measures

Measures in fact tables may be generated from multiple source columns and tables, or files. At times, a measure may be derived in the ETL process without a direct mapping from a source value. A common example of this is when Analysis Services (or other cubing engine) is involved, and a counting or occurrence measure is needed. Such measures usually assume the values of 0 or 1, based on a source occurrence. These measures are additive in nature, and fit nicely with Analysis Services aggregations.

Adding Metadata

Fact tables (and dimension tables) often include metadata columns that provide information about the rows in the table. These metadata columns include `datetime` columns, batch identifiers, and lineage columns. `datetime` and batch identifiers help to identify when a row was added, and with what ETL processing run. Lineage, on the other hand, identifies where a record came from in the source system down to the source row or records.

> In contrast to fact table volumes, dimension tables typically don't have many records — most often fewer than a million records. However, fact tables can scale into millions of records, and even billions, depending on how much data is coming across from the transactional sources. Column optimization of the fact table is, therefore, critical to performance. Because of this, fact tables may not always have metadata in order to reduce the overall row width for performance reasons. By keeping the fact table narrow, you trade off the benefits of the metadata for better overall performance, both querying and loading data.

Fact Table Types

Dimensions ETL involved dealing with different change types and managing change history. Fact table ETL has similar concepts, which involve different types of fact tables, managing history and change, and data grain changes from the source to the fact table.

Figure 5-2 shows the primary sales fact tables within the `AdventureWorksDW` database: reseller sales and Internet sales.

These fact tables are *transaction fact tables*. This means that the fact tables contain transactional activity. In this case, the transactions are sales activity, but other transactional fact tables may have a different type of transaction, such as system alerts, shipping activity, and so on. Furthermore, in this case, both the reseller sales and Internet sales fact tables come from the same source tables. This is an example of a *data grain change*.

Another fact table type is called a *snapshot fact*. Figure 5-3 shows the schemas of the finance fact table and the currency rate fact table, which are examples of a snapshot fact table.

Figure 5-2: Primary sales fact tables within the AdventureWorksDW database

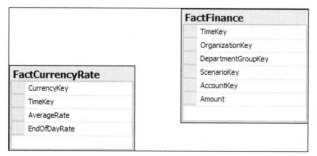

Figure 5-3: Schemas of the finance fact table and the currency rate fact table

A snapshot fact table is a point-in-time picture of the levels or balances of the source. The finance fact table, for example, contains account balance snapshots of the amounts on a monthly level. The advantage to this design is that it allows quick querying of the balances historically without having to compile the transactions in order to answer the query. But also, it also allows trending over time of the balances at different grains of the dimensionality.

Another common type of snapshot fact table targets inventory levels. Instead of account balances tracked over time, an inventory-level fact table tracks in-stock levels at different locations at various times.

Fact Table ETL

Processing fact records from the source system into the destination fact table involves some common ETL processes, which map to the fact table column types. Fact table ETL involves the following:

- ❑ Acquiring the dimension surrogate keys
- ❑ Calculating measures
- ❑ Identifying existing records for changes
- ❑ Managing changes in the data grain

This discussion of fact table ETL considers such aspects, applied with SSIS.

Fact Table ETL Challenge

Fact Table ETL is similar to dimension ETL in that the source system may come in a different structure than the destination dimensional fact structures. Figure 5-4 shows (on the left) the transactional tables that participate in the sales activity for AdventureWorks. On the right, it shows the table structures that are involved in the dimensional model.

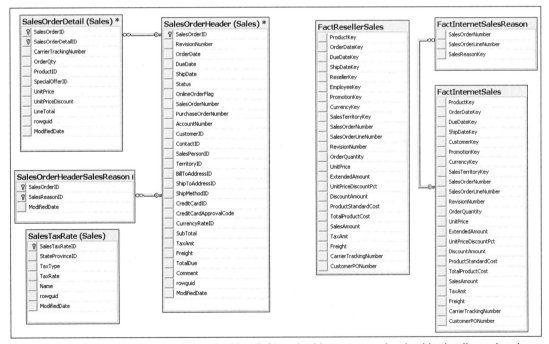

Figure 5-4: AdventureWorks transactional tables (left) and table structures involved in the dimensional model (right)

As you can see, the tables are different. There are two sales transaction tables in the source: a header and a detail. In the dimensional model, there are several fact tables, the two primary fact tables being the Internet sales fact and the reseller sales fact. Essentially, to perform the ETL, the header and detail transactional tables are combined, and then broken out based on whether the sale was direct-to-consumer (through the Internet) or sold to a reseller. The ETL performs both consolidation and a breakout (or partitioning) of the data. The challenge is to do this in a way that is scalable, manageable, and flexible.

To address the fact table ETL with SSIS, this discussion has been broken into the ETL basics of fact table processing and the advanced fact table ETL concepts. In all, this examination provides the tools and methods needed to move from requirements to SSIS package development.

Fact Table ETL Basics

The primary components in a fact table ETL process include acquiring the dimension surrogate keys, managing measure calculations, and identifying records for changes.

Acquiring the Dimension Surrogate Key

As you process fact source records (such as transactions or inventory), you must pull the surrogate key from the dimension. To accomplish this, you must have the business key from the transactional source that maps to the business key in the dimension table. This process of loading a dimension table involves looking up the surrogate key from the matching business key.

Type 2 Historical Changes and Late-Arriving Facts

If you are doing history on the dimension, it's important to pull the current surrogate key. In some situations, even the current surrogate key is not the most accurate association to make. Much like a late-arriving dimension, there's a situation called a *late-arriving fact*. Some systems hold a transaction for reporting until a pre-defined situation. In this case, the transaction may arrive in the ETL with an older transaction date than a strong majority of the records. When the related dimension record has gone through a Type 2 change since the transaction date, then the current dimension surrogate key would not be aligned with the transaction date of the fact record.

Missing Dimension Records or Inferred Members

Recall the Chapter 4 discussion on loading dimensions that reviewed the support for updating the dimension record when an inferred member exists. However, this was only half the story. When loading the fact records, it is possible to have a missing match within the dimension table. In other words, the business key does not exist in the dimension table. When this occurs, the inferred member must be added to the dimension, which generates a new surrogate key to be used for the fact table load.

In most cases, acquiring the surrogate key is straightforward, but as you can see, there can be exceptions to handle in the process.

Identifying the Dimension Surrogate Keys with SSIS

The best SSIS approach for acquiring surrogate keys is to take advantage of the data flow and use one of the following transformations:

❑ A *Lookup transformation* is the primary method to use, because it performs well when the dimension table can fit into the transformation cache.

❑ A *Merge Join transformation* works well if the dimensions are large and do not fit easily into memory for cache.

❑ A *Fuzzy Lookup transformation* is useful with dirty data. If no match exists when performing a lookup on the dimension, the Fuzzy Lookup can find the "best guess" match. It indexes and caches the data; it also requires some start-up time and overhead, so the best approach is to leverage the Fuzzy Lookup in tandem with the Lookup transformation, by handling the missing records from the Lookup transformation with the Fuzzy Lookup.

Another approach is to use the control flow and handle the dimension association to the fact table with an Execute SQL Task. This requires staging the fact data and using a SQL join to get the surrogate key. However, this approach is synchronous — it requires one step at a time:

1. Landing the fact source data to a staging table

2. Performing the joins across all the related dimension tables (and either performing an UPDATE to the staging, or taking the join results and loading the fact table)

3. Loading the fact table

A data flow approach will scale better by reducing the impact on the database (eliminating expensive joins) and reducing the steps involved in the dimension association.

Using the Lookup Transformation to Get the Dimension Key

As an example of using the Lookup transformation for the dimension key, Figure 5-5 shows the currency rate fact table package, configured with a data flow containing an OLE DB Source, pulling from the currency rate source table and a Lookup transformation to get the surrogate key from the time dimension.

The currency rate fact table defines the changes of currency matching with U.S. dollars (USD) for this company, which sells products inside and outside of the United States. The sales currency rate source tracks daily currency conversions for AdventureWorks. Therefore, the OLE DB Source is configured to reference the AdventureWorks connection, and point to the Sales.CurrencyRate table. Figure 5-6 shows the Lookup Transformation Editor that references the time dimension.

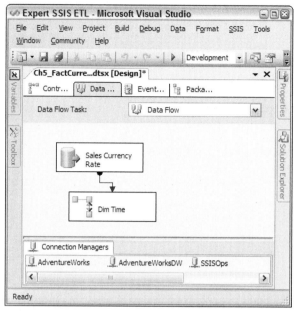

Figure 5-5: Currency rate fact table package

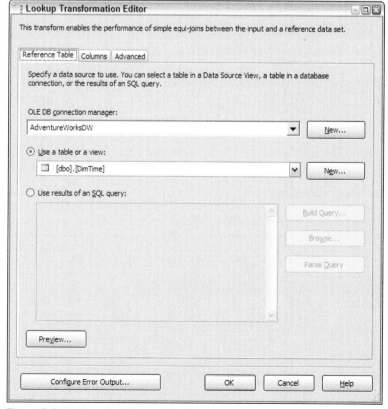

Figure 5-6: Lookup transformation editor

Configured with the `DimTime`, this Lookup transformation caches the complete time dimension table into memory. Figure 5-7 shows the Columns tab of the editor.

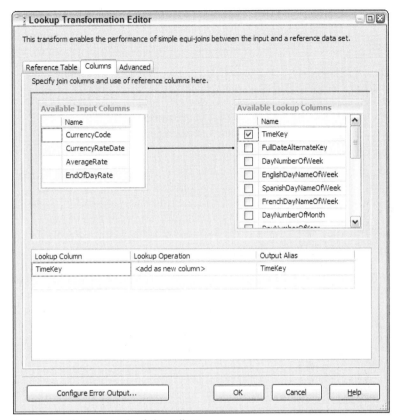

Figure 5-7: Columns tab of the editor

The `CurrencyRateDate` column from the source is matched to the `FullDateAlternateKey` in the dimension table. In both cases, the column contains a `datetime` value at the day level (as opposed to having values down to the minute, second, and sub-second). The surrogate key, `TimeKey`, is checked as the return column, which will add the surrogate key to the output of the Lookup transformation that will later be used for the fact table inserts.

The second dimension relationship for the currency rate fact table is the currency itself. There is only one currency lookup because, even though the currency rate is being converted between two currencies, the default conversion currency is USD. Therefore, the currency lookup is referencing what the conversion rate is coming from in order to achieve a USD baseline. Figure 5-8 shows an updated data flow with a second Lookup transformation.

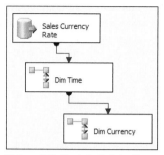

**Figure 5-8: Updated data flow with
a second Lookup transformation**

The Lookup transformation for the currency dimension is configured almost identically to the time dimension lookup. This lookup references the currency dimension table, joins the `CurrencyCode` from the source against the `CurrencyAlternateKey` in the dimension table, and returns the `CurrencyKey` to the pipeline. Since both the time dimension and the currency dimension are small (and, therefore, will fit in the Lookup cache) and the matching values are clean, this data flow solution to acquiring the dimension keys will run very quickly, and is preferred for most situations.

As a second, more complicated demo, Figure 5-9 shows the Sales fact table load package that contains several surrogate key lookups.

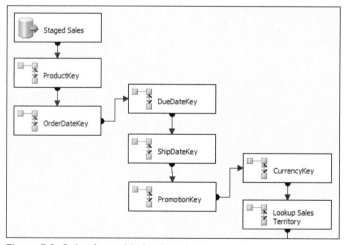

Figure 5-9: Sales fact table load package

This data flow is not complete, and in later sections, the measures will be handled, as well as the fact table loads. But this example highlights the setup of a fact table load with several dimension relationships. What you may be wondering is how efficient this will be, seeing that the lookups happen one after the other. Yes, this package runs efficiently if the Lookup is designed sequentially in this manner. Although it may appear that the data flow might require the first dimension Lookup to be completed before the second, what is actually happening is that the Lookup transformations are being handled in parallel. Figure 5-10 shows a mid-stream picture of the data flow execution, before the records are completely landed into the fact table.

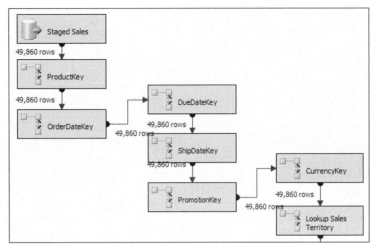

Figure 5-10: Mid-stream picture of the data flow execution

Based on the record count shown, note that the lookups are all happening at the same time, because the record count (49,860) is identical for all the Lookups. The reason this is an important point is that it underscores the architecture of SSIS. In this case, the Lookup transformation output is synchronous, meaning that the output of the Lookup is synchronously connected to the input of the next lookup. This means that as soon as a flat data buffer in the pipeline (typically representing about 10,000 rows) completes in one Lookup, it is immediately available to the next Lookup to perform its work. So rather than the multiple lookups having to be performed in serial, the data is actually being performed in parallel, which gives a tremendous advantage to how SSIS can scale, and makes for a compelling case to use the Lookup transformation for dimension key lookups. Although not shown, it will become apparent later that while rows are still coming in from the source, transformed data is already landing to the destination.

Also of note in this example, the sales fact table contains a product dimension relationship. If you remember, the product dimension includes Type 2 historical dimensions. This means that the lookup cannot be performed by including the entire table into memory, because it would generate duplicates with the product dimension business key, `ProductAlternateKey`. Instead of just selecting the Use a table or a view reference table option, the reference lookup uses a SQL Query to define which records should be loaded. Figure 5-11 shows the Lookup transformation editor for the product dimension lookup.

The lookup is configured to use the results of a SQL query, and the query entered into the text box is as follows:

```
SELECT ProductKey, ProductAlternateKey
FROM DimProduct
WHERE EndDate IS NULL.
```

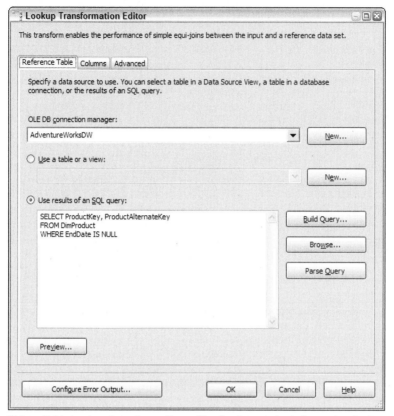

Figure 5-11: Lookup transformation editor for the product dimension lookup

Essentially, this configuration will assign the current surrogate key to the fact record. A NULL in the EndDate indicates that the dimension record is current, and the Lookup cache will, therefore, only be populated with the current records in the Product dimension, so the join across the business key will still yield the right current match.

The "Advanced Fact Table ETL Concepts" section later in this chapter examines three more complicated dimension Lookup scenarios:

❑ A *late-arriving fact scenario* has fact source records arriving late in the ETL with the current fact records. When a dimension with Type 2 historical changes is involved in this scenario, the late transaction date may require looking up an outdated dimension record to get the most accurate dimension association. In other words, the surrogate key of a non-current dimension record may be required.

❑ *Large dimensions* that don't fit in the Lookup cache (which varies based on physical RAM availability) require special handling to optimize the Lookup process for fact ETL processing.

❑ *Inferred members*, when the dimension member is missing, must be accommodated in scenarios when the data is dirty or the dimension member arrives late in the dimension table.

Using the Merge Join Transformation to Identify the Dimension Key

The Merge Join transformation presents another alternative to getting the dimension's surrogate key for the fact table load. With the Merge Join transformation, the source records can be merged with the dimension table across the business key, which makes the surrogate key available. The Merge Join transformation allows three join types:

❑ An *inner join* only brings across records that match from both sources. Any record without a match is discarded.

❑ The *left outer join* allows rows from the left source input to flow through the transformation either with a matching record or without a match on the right input.

❑ A *full outer join* brings rows from both the left and right, whether or not there is a match between sources.

If the source has the possibility of missing dimension records, then a left outer join should be used in the join with the source rows acting as the left input. A full outer join would not provide the right solution, since there may be many dimension records (the right input) that have no current match in the source, and, therefore, are not needed. Similarly, an inner join should not be used because it would filter out new dimension members that are in the source, but not yet in the dimension.

One aspect of the Merge Join to be careful of is the possibility of producing duplicates when the dimension source brings over too many matching records for a single business key. The Lookup transformation will ignore a duplicate record in the lookup reference table, while the Merge Join will create multiple records in the matching input based on the number of matches across the join columns.

The Merge Join requires sorted input. You can sort the data in the transactional source, or use a Sort transformation. The Sort transformation can also de-duplicate records based on the sort. If you have duplicates coming across from a set of keys, select the Remove rows with duplicate sort values check box in the Sort transformation editor.

Using the Fuzzy Lookup to Pull Dimension Keys Based on Similarity

Using a Fuzzy Lookup transformation for dimension lookups provides greater flexibility when the source data does not match absolutely with the source. In some cases, the match to acquire the surrogate key will not be across a single business key, but rather a column or several columns that may not have exact matches. Since the Fuzzy Lookup matches on column value similarity, its use allows non-equal matches. For example, Figure 5-12 shows a data flow for the sales quota fact table.

The source, in this case, is coming from a flat file generated from the customer relationship management (CRM) system, which does not have a single matching key for the employee lookup. Figure 5-13 shows the Lookup editor on the Columns tab. Several columns are used in the join to return the surrogate key.

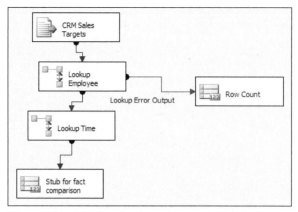

Figure 5-12: Data flow for the sales quota fact table

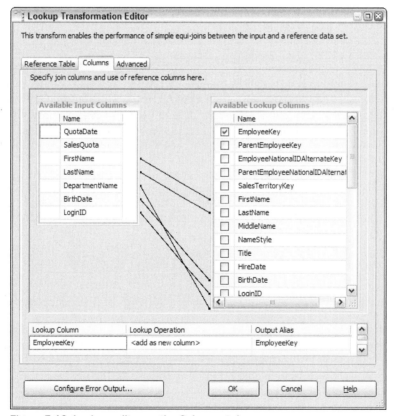

Figure 5-13: Lookup editor on the Columns tab

The challenge is that when this package is executed, several Employee dimension records do not return a match, even though the Employee record actually exists in the table. The difference is spellings and minor differences between the source and the dimension table itself. Figure 5-14 highlights the executed package, with the missing Employee matches sent to a Row Count transformation.

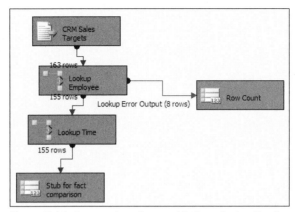

Figure 5-14: Executed package with the missing Employee matches sent to a Row Count transformation

Rather than mark these eight fact records with an unknown employee surrogate key, the output can be pushed through a Fuzzy Lookup to pull the unmatched records. The Fuzzy Lookup columns mapping is identical to the Lookup configuration, but this transformation has advance options to configure the thresholds for the comparison. Figure 5-15 shows the options available on the Advanced tab of the Fuzzy Lookup transformation.

The Similarity threshold, in this case, is set to 0.80 (or 80 percent), indicating that only employee matches will be identified that are over this threshold. Only the highest similar match is pulled, as indicated by the Maximum number of matches to output per lookup property set to 1. Although not shown, the Fuzzy Lookup outputs a confidence value, which identifies the overall possibility that the highest match selected is the right one. In other words, if multiple good matches are possible between the source and reference tables, the confidence value would be lower, because there would be some lack of surety on which match is the right one.

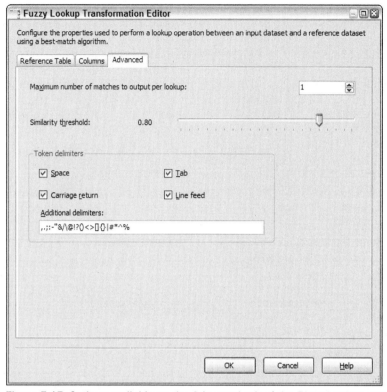

Figure 5-15: Options available on the Advanced tab of the Fuzzy Lookup transformation

All said and done, the sales quota fact table package uses both the Lookup and the Fuzzy Lookup transformations to accomplish acquiring the dimension surrogate keys. A Union All transformation brings the records back together in the data flow from both the Lookup and the Fuzzy Lookup outputs. Figure 5-16 shows the completed data flow for the dimension lookups and the execution results.

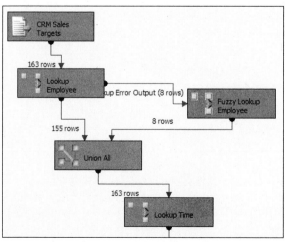

Figure 5-16: Completed data flow for the dimension lookups and the execution results

All of the eight unmatched records for the employee dimension Lookup are now matched with the Fuzzy Lookup, and the rows are "union-ed" back into the pipeline for the ensuing transformations.

As an alternate approach, the Fuzzy Lookup could have been used in place of the Lookup transformation. However, for optimization purposes, the error row output was used. This is because the majority of records do match directly (which the Lookup handles efficiently), and only the missing rows are sent through the Fuzzy Lookup (which, behind the scenes, requires staging, indexing, and `tempdb` overhead to perform the matches). The general rule of practice is to separate the exception to the rule to handle the one-off situations, and then bring the data back into the main stream of processing.

Measure Calculations

Another major component of a fact table ETL load involves calculating measures. And, in most cases, calculating measures is relatively straightforward.

Measure Calculation Types

Calculating measures involves a few different types of transformations from the source:

- ❏ **No change from a source column** — In the case where the source column matches one-to-one with the destination fact table column, the measure can be passed through form the source to the fact table without change.

- ❏ **Standard calculations** — Oftentimes a measure will involve standard arithmetic calculations, such as dividing one column from the another, or determining the difference between two values. For example, the number of items in the sale record times the price of the item returns the transaction subtotal, or the subtotal sales divided by quantity provides the average price.

- ❏ **Derived calculations** — In some cases, the measure must be derived in the ETL process. As mentioned in the introduction to this chapter, oftentimes a measure may simply be the value 0 or 1, based on certain conditions in the source feed. An example of this is an *occurrence* measure, where the measure indicates the happening of an event (1), or the non-happening of the event (0). Such measures are usable in additive scenarios when aggregating to determine the number of occurrences of the event.

- ❏ **Advanced calculations** — In rare cases, a calculation is required that goes beyond simple math or derivation, such as aggregating a subtotal of a group of records, divided by a part, or using advanced algebraic expressions, or parsing out values in a string.

Handling Measure Calculations in SSIS

The good news is that measure calculations are relatively straightforward in SSIS. Here are a few methods for handling the calculations:

- ❏ **Using a Derived Column transformation to perform the calculation with SSIS expressions** — SSIS provides many standard mathematical functions to perform calculations from associated columns in the same row of data.

- ❏ **Including the calculation in the source query** — If the source pull is a relational database, as opposed to a flat-file extraction, the calculation expression can be handled inline in the SQL statement. This typically has low impact on the source system, as long as the query is straightforward.

❑ **Using an aggregate to handle the calculation** — In the case where the measure is a SUM, MAX, MIN, or COUNT of a grouping of source rows, the Aggregate can perform this functionality. Combining the Aggregate transformation with an ensuing Derived Column transformation will enable both aggregates and calculations based on the aggregates.

> **Leverage the data flow Script Component as a transformation to handle advanced calculations. The Script Component unlocks a full-featured Visual Basic.NET environment, which can take advantage of many more functions and the ability to compare values across rows of data. When dealing with more advanced situations, consider the Script Component to provide that extended capability beyond what the SSIS expression language can provide.**

To exemplify measure calculations, the sales fact table load package referenced earlier requires some common calculation. Figure 5-17 shows an updated data flow with a Derived Column transformation added as the next in-line transformation after the dimension lookups.

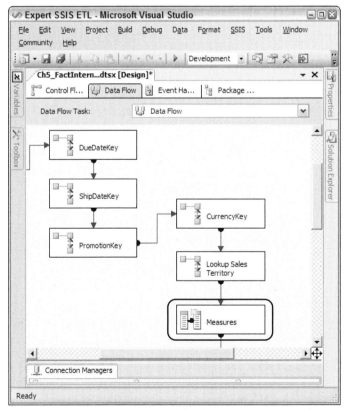

Figure 5-17: Updated data flow with a Derived Column transformation

Because the Derived Column transformation also contains a synchronous output, the calculations contained within will be handled in parallel with the upstream lookups and the next downstream transformation. In the Sales fact table process, seven calculations are required. Figure 5-18 shows the Derived Column editor, which contains the calculation logic.

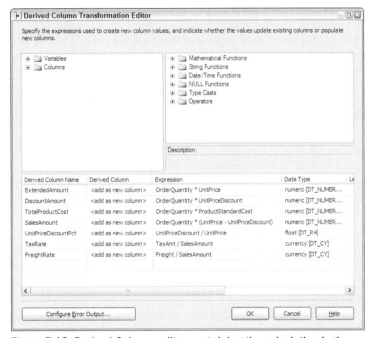

Figure 5-18: Derived Column editor containing the calculation logic

As you can see, these calculations use common mathematical equations that generate the needed output for the destination measure. The ExtendedAmount involves multiplying the OrderQuantity times the UnitPrice. The UnitPriceDiscountPct involves dividing the UnitPriceDiscount by the UnitPrice.

In summary, measure calculations are often easy to handle in SSIS. But when the situation requires more advanced computations, SSIS also provides the Aggregate transformation and the Script Component.

Managing Fact Table Changes

At times, a matching fact table record in the source may change, which, therefore, needs to propagate through to the fact table. To handle the change, a few different data warehousing approaches are common:

❑   A simple UPDATE to the fact table to modify the existing record with the change

❑   A newly generated record in the fact table with the new values, and a flag in the table to indicate the status of the record (current or expired)

❑   An offset change record that calculates the difference between what was in the fact record and the new value

Each approach comes with its advantages and disadvantages, including the following:

❑   UPDATE changes can be very expensive in large scenarios

❑   Adding a second record can increase the fact size

❑   Change records are not possible with non-additive measures

The right approach is situational. Since the goal of this book is applying SSIS to ETL, the right fact table design choice is left for other forums. However, to enable you to deal with the design, this discussion will focus on the common aspect of identifying changes, and, also, how to best perform fact table updates when required in the ETL.

Approaches to Identifying Changed Fact Records

If you are lucky, the source feed will include a way to identify whether the record requires a change or a new fact row. For example, a source column may provide the Data Manipulation Language (DML) type. DML is the cause for the row being sent to the ETL, commonly a value of I (insert), U (update), or D (delete). Alternatively, the source feed may include both a create date and a modified date. Comparing these dates together in conjunction with the last incremental change identifier (as discussed in Chapter 3) will allow the identification of the row as a new row or a modified row.

> **A new row would be when the creation date is greater than the last incremental change identifier date. A modified row would be when the create date is less than the incremental extraction date, and the modified date is greater than the last incremental extraction date.**

In both of these cases, the source records do not need to match the source rows to existing records in the fact table. Unfortunately, when a fact source goes through changes, most cases will not provide this capability, and the source row will need to be matched with the fact row to identify the DML type of the record.

Just like the other aspects of dimension and fact ETL, two general categories exist to associate source rows with fact rows in SSIS:

❑   **Database joins between the source data and the fact table** — These enable the comparison of the source to the fact table. This approach comes with several drawbacks. For starters, it requires the source data to be in a table in the same database engine and on the same server as the fact table in order to perform the join efficiently. If the source data is already on the same server, then the join can be performed. However, it will impact the source database and create potential locking issues when the comparison is run (and the fact table will also be impacted during the expensive join operation). If the source data is on a different system or is in a flat-file form, then the data needs to be staged, which generates more disk IO and creates a multi-step process. On the other hand, fact tables often contain millions of rows and would consume tremendous memory consumption if brought completely into the SSIS pipeline buffers. When dealing with large volumes, an RDBMS can provide invaluable help in scaling an ETL solution. See the section, "Handling the Fact Updates, Inserts, and Deletes," later in this chapter for more on leveraging the RDBMS to handle comparisons.

❑ **Data correlation with the data flow** — As mentioned before, two primary data transformations exist that assist in associating sources together: the Lookup transformation and the Merge Join transformation. Using these, the source feed can be correlated with the fact table, which is the first step in processing changes. The general benefit of these transformations is that the source feed can come from any source system or files, and still be joined to the fact table. The Lookup will have more memory overhead when the fact table is fully cached. However, the Merge Join requires the inputs to be sorted, which would use just as much memory as the Lookup if the Sort transformation is used (because of the Sort's data blocking nature). However, sources can be marked as pre-sorted, which gives the Merge Join an advantage when the source can be sorted efficiently.

Here is an example: The sales quota fact source doesn't have the capability of identifying whether a source record is a change or a new fact record. Furthermore, the source does not provide a modified date column to filter the extraction. Therefore, the source feed will include non-changed rows along with changed, new records, and deletes.

To handle this example, two data flow methods are presented:

❑ The Lookup transformation

❑ The Merge Join transformation

Using the Lookup to Identify Fact Change Records

Using the Lookup approach, Figure 5-19 shows the sales quota fact data flow, which includes the dimension key lookups and a new Lookup transformation for the fact table. A Conditional Split transformation immediately follows the Lookup transformation.

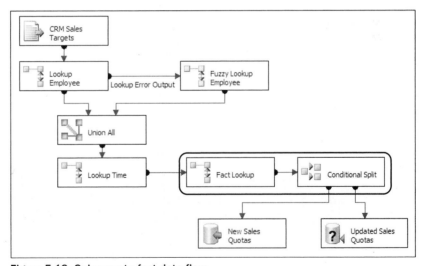

Figure 5-19: Sales quota fact data flow

The Lookup transformation is configured with the fact table as the reference table, and the dimension keys that make up a unique record (the `EmployeeKey` and `TimeKey`) are joined with the corresponding fact table keys. Figure 5-20 shows the Columns tab of the fact table Lookup transformation.

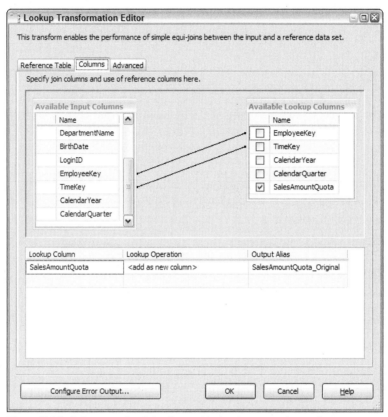

Figure 5-20: Columns tab of the fact table Lookup transformation

The Lookup is configured to pull back the `SalesAmountQuota` measures, aliased as `SalesAmountQuota_Original` to indicate that it came from the fact table. This measure will be used in the next step. The Lookup is also configured to ignore failure in the event of an error. Figure 5-21 shows the Configure Error Output editor of the Lookup transformation.

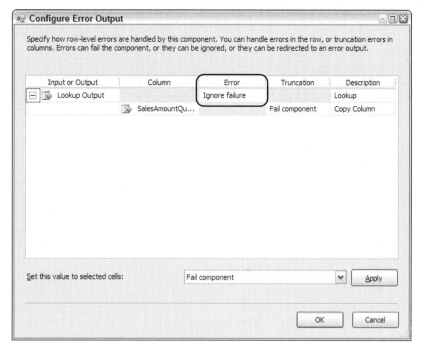

Figure 5-21: Configure Error Output editor of the Lookup transformation

Ignore failure means that, when the Lookup does not find a match, the record will still be sent down the Lookup output path, but the returned column(s) will be NULL. In this case, the SalesAmount Quota_Original will be marked as NULL when a match from the fact table does not exist.

The Conditional Split will now provide the DML identification of the records. Figure 5-22 shows the Conditional Split editor, which has three outputs defined.

The Conditional Split is like a CASE statement in that the criteria are checked in order until the first TRUE is reached in the WHEN condition. The first condition evaluated, called Sales Quota New, determines whether a match has been found in the fact table. The condition, ISNULL(SalesAmountQuota_Original) evaluates the returned column in the fact lookup to see if the value is NULL. In this case, a NULL indicates that the Lookup did not find a match and, therefore, the record must be inserted into the fact table. The SalesAmountQuota column in the fact table is defined as NOT NULL, thereby ensuring that a NULL in the SalesAmountQuota_Original indicates a non-match.

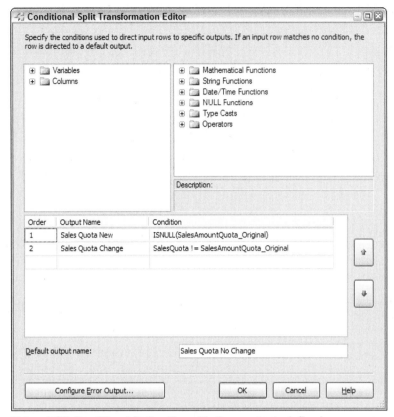

Figure 5-22: Conditional Split editor with three outputs defined

The second condition, called `Sales Quota Change`, checks the value of the measures between the source and the fact table. The output of this Boolean expression, `SalesQuota != SalesAmountQuota_Original`, will evaluate to `TRUE` if the measures do not match. When this is the case, the value has changed and needs updating in the fact table (or a change record needs to be generated).

The final condition is merely the default output, called `Sales Quota No Change`. With the Lookup approach, if the first two criteria do not apply, then by default there is no change. This is because the sales quota example pulls all the records from the source and, in many cases, a change hasn't happened.

Following are a couple of drawbacks that inhibit using the Lookup for many cases:

❑ Since the Lookup cache has a practical memory limitation, the fact volume may not fit in the private Lookup cache. This is accentuated by the nature of fact tables, which are commonly large.

❑ The solution does not handle deletes. Deletes are rarer with fact processes, so this limitation may not apply to your situation. The lookup rows in cache are only used if the input to the Lookup contains a match to the reference table. Therefore, there is no way to know which fact row in the Lookup cache was not used and should be deleted.

Using the Merge Join to Identify Fact Changes

Before discussing the update and insert process, an alternate approach for identifying fact changes involves the Merge Join transformation. Figure 5-23 shows the identical fact ETL process, sales quota fact, only with a Merge Join used to correlate the fact source rows to the fact rows.

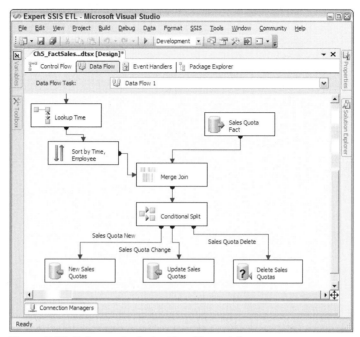

Figure 5-23: Sales quota fact with a Merge Join

This data flow uses a combination of the Merge Join, the Sort, and the Conditional Split transformations. The Merge Join requires two sorted inputs, and, in this case, the source rows are sent through the Sort transformation (sorted by `TimeKey` and `EmployeeKey`) as the first input. The second input brings the fact rows into the Merge Join, only the OLE DB source is pre-sorted with an `ORDER BY` statement and configured as pre-sorted.

Figure 5-24 shows the Merge Join editor configured as a Full outer join type to bring across both matching and non-matching rows from both inputs.

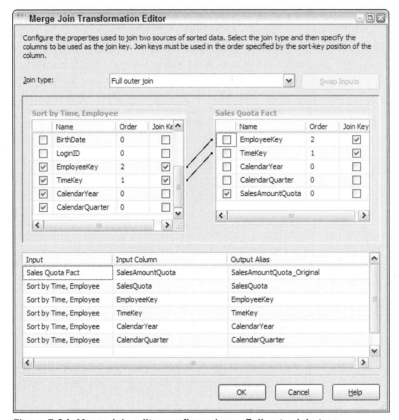

Figure 5-24: Merge Join editor configured as a Full outer join type

The keys and measures are brought across from the source input, along with the `SalesAmountQuota` from the fact table, aliased as `SalesAmountQuota_Original` to distinguish it from the source (just like the Lookup approach). The next component, a Conditional Split, identifies the row DML type: no-change, new, deleted, changed. Figure 5-25 shows the Conditional Split editor.

The only difference from the previous Conditional Split reviewed with the Lookup approach is that a new condition has been added as condition 2. When the condition `ISNULL(EmployeeKey)` evaluates to `TRUE`, then the row exists in the fact table, but was deleted in the source. This Employee Key comes from the employee Lookup transformation and is used to join the source rows to the fact table. Therefore, a `NULL` indicates the row must be deleted in the fact table.

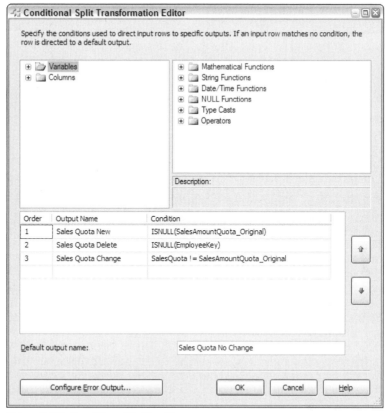

Figure 5-25: Conditional Split editor

Overall, this approach allows identifying all types of row changes — new, changed, no change, and deleted. Because source adapters can be pre-sorted, this solution will scale with larger fact volumes. Typically, an index will exist on the columns used in the join pattern of the Merge Join. Be sure to evaluate the query plan, and, if possible, tweak the index to avoid table scans with the ORDER BY added to the fact query.

> **Don't forget about historical dimension changes. If you had a historical dimension change, you can't always compare across surrogate keys, because the surrogate key might have gone through a change. Otherwise, you may have duplicated data in the fact table.**

Handling the Fact Updates, Inserts, and Deletes

The final step in the fact ETL is to load new records and handle updates, if necessary. Data inserts are relatively straightforward and will be handled with a destination adapter configured to load the rows into the fact table. Chapter 12 discusses scaling data loads and how to choose and configure the destination adapters.

Updates and deletes present a more difficult challenge. With SSIS, two primary options exist for updating and deleting rows in a table from data in the data flow:

❑   Using an OLE DB Command transformation, rows flowing through the pipeline can be mapped to RDBMS statements. In other words, for every row flowing through, the column values can be used to call a statement such as an UPDATE or DELETE statement or a stored procedure.

❑   Pipeline data can be staged to a table in the same RDBMS, which can be used to perform a set-based UPDATE or DELETE.

Figure 5-23, highlighted earlier, shows the sales quota fact data flow with components added to handle inserts, updates, and deletes.

For the sales quota source records that are new records, an OLE DB Destination has been chosen using the SQL Native Client. The destination adapter has been named New Sales Quotas. The output from the Conditional Split to handle deletes is called Delete Sales Quotas. Because these deletes only account for a small percentage of rows in this example, an OLE DB Command has been chosen. In other words, not many rows are coming through the Delete Sales Quotas output; therefore, the row-by-row deletes will be handled fine without any major performance penalty by using an OLE DB Command. The SQLCommand property of the OLE DB Command contains the DELETE statement, as shown here:

```
DELETE FROM dbo.FactSalesQuota
 WHERE EmployeeKey = ?
   AND TimeKey = ?
```

Remember, the OLE DB Command uses a parameterized OLE DB statement. The question marks are parameters in the statement mapped to columns and rows in the pipeline. Figure 5-26 shows the Column Mappings tab of the OLE DB Command editor.

The two question marks in the SQL statement are mapped to EmployeeKey and TimeKey in the DELETE output.

> **Performing an update or delete with the OLE DB Command transformation and, at the same time, inserting into the same table in the same data flow may cause locking issues. Be sure to turn off the table lock in the data flow destination used. If locking still becomes an issue, fast load may need to be turned off, in which case, it may be better to use a set-based approach for the OLE DB Command operation, such as the update output will demonstrate next.**

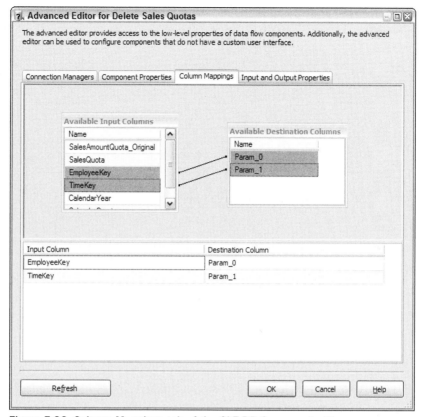

Figure 5-26: Column Mappings tab of the OLE DB Command editor

The final Conditional Split output requires rows to be updated in the fact table. Updates are more common in this scenario, so rather than using the OLE DB Command transformation, the rows are staged to a table called stgFactSalesQuota_Updates through a second OLE DB Destination adapter named Update Sales Quotas.

Two additional control flow steps are needed to complete the set-based update. Figure 5-27 shows the completed control flow tasks.

The first Execute SQL Task, which runs before the data flow, clears out the rows in the staging table with a TRUNCATE TABLE statement. Rows are typically preserved in the staging table until the next ETL run to allow auditing and troubleshooting. This is why the TRUNCATE statement happens before the data flow, as opposed to after the UPDATE statement.

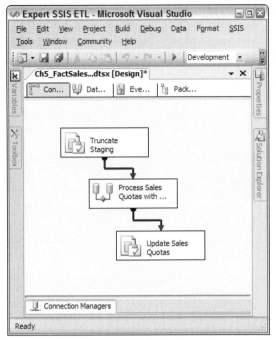

Figure 5-27: Completed control flow tasks

The UPDATE statement happens after the data flow since the new staged records are added to the staging table in the data flow, as already shown. The Execute SQL Task used for the update performs a SQL UPDATE statement with the staging table joined to the fact table with the new measure value being handled in the update, as the following code shows:

```
UPDATE dbo.FactSalesQuota
   SET SalesAmountQuota  = STG.SalesQuota
  FROM dbo.FactSalesQuota
 INNER JOIN SSISOps.dbo.stgFactSalesQuota_Updates STG
    ON FactSalesQuota.EmployeeKey = STG.EmployeeKey
   AND FactSalesQuota.TimeKey = STG.TimeKey
```

Essentially, this is a very similar process used to scale dimension updates as discussed in Chapter 4.

Advanced Fact Table ETL Concepts

The advanced topics in fact table ETL involve changing data grain from the sources to the fact table, handling missing dimension records, and dealing with late-arriving facts.

Managing Fact Table Grain

Many fact table scenarios require data grain changes. This means that the source data coming into the ETL process must be modified to match the record detail in the fact table. For example, you may have a source feed with a certain level of data like *product sales at a store for a day*. This is called the *grain* of the data. The fact table destination for the same data coming into the process might be at a different level, such as rolled-up to the week level. In this case, the data grain has changed from day to week. Rolling up data may not always be based on time. For example, a product may be rolled up to a sub-category or category level.

Data Grain Change Scenarios

Grain changes come in many different forms, including some of these common scenarios:

❑ **Consolidating sources**, such as combining multiple tables or files together or joining sources to produce a complete set of business keys needed for the fact table. A common situation is when multiple locations within an organization use different copies of the same system. To report off of a combined fact table, these sources must be consolidated together.

❑ **Breaking out sources** may be required if you have a single table that populates multiple fact tables. For example, an ERP system may export a file that is the transactions for two different fact tables, based on transaction category. In this case, the rows would need to be divided.

❑ **Roll-up summarizations** are a common grain change, where the source feed is at a lower level of detail than the required fact table based on reporting needs. Many situations do not require the detail grain of the source for reporting, which has a side benefit of performance gains and reduced storage requirements.

❑ **Allocating down or blowing-out the grain** is a less common, but interesting, grain change. This is when the level of detail in the fact table is actually a lower grain than what the source system is providing. This may sound impossible, and, in reality, the exact detail cannot be achieved. As an example, an industry data provider may be sending a summarization of sales at a category level, but this detail can be broken down to a sub-category or product level if the percentage breakout is known.

❑ **Pivot or un-pivot dimensionality** takes a source data and converts columns to rows or rows to columns. The most common pivoting needed for fact table data is when the source is coming from a fourth-normal form design, or key-value pair. This data may need to be un-pivoted to de-normalize the data for the fact table match.

Other types of grain changes and scenarios are common, and this transformation requirement (data grain changes) will need to be handled for many fact table ETL processes.

Handling Data Grain Changes with SSIS Transformations

How are these grain changes handled with Integration Services? SSIS includes several built-in transformations to help manage fact table grain changes from the Aggregate transformation to the Pivot. The following table describes several transformations and potential uses to handle different grain changes.

Transformation	Data Usage
Pivot	Converts columns to rows. Useful in a flattened recordset to normalize the grain of a source that will be used for a fact load.
Unpivot	Converts rows to columns. Useful for key-value pairs that are common in auditing tables, to collapse rows to columns, and de-normalize the grain.
Conditional Split	Allows data routing and filtering. Useful when a source feed needs to be filtered for a fact load, or a single source needs to be split to different fact loads.
Aggregate	Summarizes source data. Useful for sources that need to be rolled up to a higher level grain for the fact table load. Can also be used to aggregate across multiple key sets for multiple fact table outputs.
Sort	De-duplicates data (and sorts). Provides the ability to remove duplicates across the sort key columns. Useful for sources that need to be pared down based on duplicate records.
Union All	Stacks rows of data from multiple sources. Useful when more than one source table or feed matches in structure and is required to be combined for a fact table load. Rows are not joined, but rather passed through. Provides similar semantics to a relational UNION ALL operation.
Merge	Combines two identical sources with matching sorted inputs. Similar to the Union All, this transformation can also combine source data for a fact load, especially when the sources are sorted, while preserving the sort order.
Merge Join	Joins two sources on a set of keys. Useful when several sources' entities need to be consolidated for a single fact load. Joins across rows, rather than stacking rows, which allows for columns from both inputs to be included in the output. Also allows the ability to allocate rows to a lower grain by providing multiple output rows across matches. Provides similar semantics to relational JOIN operations (INNER JOIN, LEFT OUTER JOIN, FULL OUTER JOIN).
Lookup	Includes Augments columns from a reference table to the output. Useful to also correlate sources, by providing the ability to augment columns from a relational table to the pipeline based on matching source key columns. Can also be used as a filter mechanism to identify matches and non-matches.
Derived Column	Allows calculations for allocation with a row. Useful when combined with other transformations.
Term Extraction	Provides word-to-text column matching. Useful for text mining–based fact tables to do analysis on words within a source text column. Allocates the grain to the word level of a source.

Transformation	Data Usage
Term Lookup	Provides English noun-to-text column matching. Similar to the Term Extraction transformation, allocates records down to the word level of a text column, based on an input word list.
Script Component	Provides advanced grain-changing capabilities. Useful for many complex scenarios not included in the out-of-the-box capabilities, such as advanced pivoting, filtering, combining, and so on.

Even beyond what is listed, grain changes can also be achieved by combining these different out-of-the-box transformations together, thus allowing for a fairly comprehensive toolset to handle unique scenarios.

Grain Change SSIS Example

The sales fact tables are a good example of a common grain change from a data source to a fact table destination. In the source AdventureWorks database, the sales transactions are kept in the sales header and sales detail tables. These tables need to be combined together to generate a source record that matches the fact table records. Furthermore, the destination fact tables, Internet sales fact, and reseller sales fact come from the same source, so a separation of the source rows is needed to load these two fact tables separately.

In order to load the fact tables, several steps are involved in the process:

1. The sales header and sales detail records need to be combined to generate all the business keys needed for the load.

2. Records already loaded into the fact tables need to be filtered.

3. The transformed fact records need to be routed to the Internet sales and reseller sales fact tables, respectively.

To demonstrate this, the rest of the sales load package will be shown, picking up where Figure 5-17 left off. At the point in the data flow shown earlier, you are now ready to complete the data flow load. First of all, the dimension lookup and measure calculation discussion earlier in this chapter considers the sales fact table load scenario, which included several dimension lookups and several measures that needed calculations. With the sales fact tables, any record marked as an online order is a direct-to-consumer sale that originated through the Internet. Therefore, these rows must be inserted into the Internet sales fact table. Alternately, any record that is not an online order originates from a reseller transaction and, therefore, should be loaded into the Reseller fact table. Figure 5-28 shows the completed data flow for the sales load package.

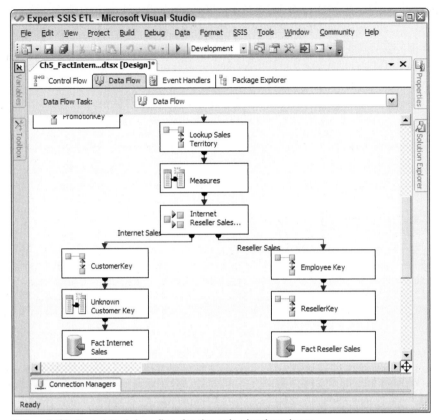

Figure 5-28: Completed data flow for the sales load package

The Conditional Split handles the routing of the fact records to the appropriate fact table. Figure 5-29 shows the Conditional Split editor, which contains the condition `OnlineOrderFlag == TRUE`.

The rows that meet this criterion are Internet sales orders routed to one output. Every other record is a reseller sale. Therefore, these records are sent out the default output, which is named Reseller Sales.

You will notice that the output of the Conditional Split contains a couple of Lookup transformations on the Internet Reseller Sales output, and one Lookup transformation on the Internet Sales output. This is because the two sales fact tables contain a couple of several different dimension keys. A Customer dimension relationship exists in the Internet Sales fact and a reseller and employee dimension relationship exists in the Reseller Sales fact. Finally, the data flow destinations perform fast loads into the two fact tables, respectively.

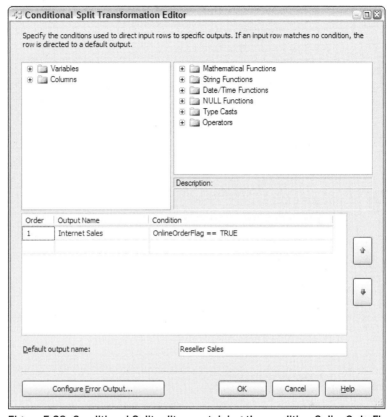

Figure 5-29: Conditional Split editor containing the condition OnlineOrderFlag == TRUE

Consolidating Source Feeds Example 1

So far, the sales fact table package reviewed in this chapter handled the key lookups and loaded the data into the fact tables. However, this data load package is the second package involved in the sales fact table ETL. The first package that is run for the sales fact is a staging package that consolidates source rows, cleanses data, and filters the records required for the load. Because of the complexity of the data cleansing and correlation, an intermediate staging table was chosen to simplify the ETL and provide a data restartability point.

In the incremental extraction discussion in Chapter 3, Figure 3-32 shows the method used to identify new fact records. In that example, the source records were being pulled from a flat file. But suppose that the source for the sales came from a relational database in two tables, a header and detail, which happens to be the case in the AdventureWorks database. In this scenario, the header and detail tables would need to be combined. Figure 5-30 shows the OLE DB Source adapter editor, which highlights the SQL statement used.

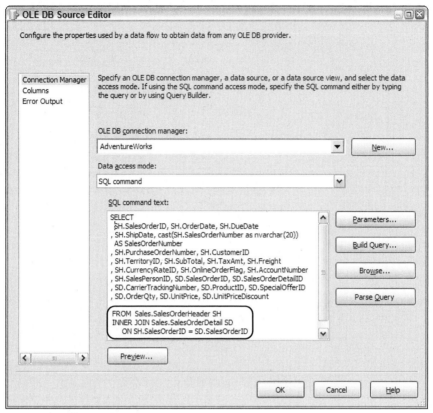

Figure 5-30: OLE DB Source adapter editor

The reason a SQL join was used in this case is because the source system tables are directly related and supported by foreign keys and indexes. The relational database query optimizer efficiently handles the join of the sales header and sales detail tables. However, in the case when the source feed does not come from a database system, or the database cannot optimize the join effectively enough without either straining the source system or slowing down the extraction, then an alternate approach should be taken. Figure 5-31 shows the same extraction package with the sales header and sales detail tables separated into different source adapters.

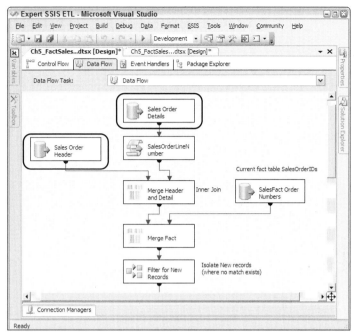

Figure 5-31: Same extraction package with the sales header and sales detail tables separated into different source adapters

To perform the correlation from both source files, a Merge Join transformation is used. Figure 5-32 shows the Merge Join editor. Both source adapters contain SQL statements with explicit ORDER BY operations on the SalesOrderID key, and the adapter is marked as pre-sorted, as described in Chapter 4.

An Inner join is used in the Merge Join transformation, since the source system that created the files uses referential integrity. Therefore, no records will be lost in the join. A Lookup transformation could have been used in this example with the sales header in the Lookup transformation reference table, because the lookup would be across the SalesOrderID and the SalesOrderID, which has a unique constraint as the primary key. However, if your sales header and sales detail tables were coming from files, a Merge Join approach would be required since the Lookup component is unable to directly read in flat file data.

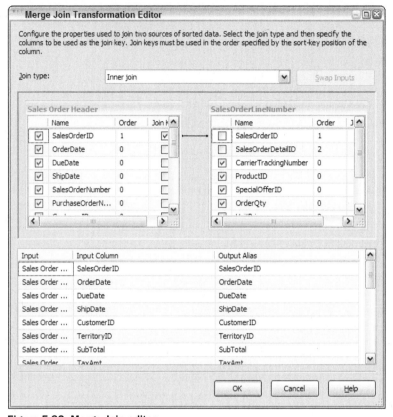

Figure 5-32: Merge Join editor

Consolidating Source Feeds Example 2

Do you have a scenario where you are processing multiple identical source files from different company locations? Given one of the goals of data warehousing, which is to bring related data together, a common situation is dealing with multiple feeds from the same application installed in different locations. In other words, you may have several identical files or need to run several identical queries from different installations of the same application.

Briefly, two approaches are possible. The first is to use a ForEach Loop Container to iterate through the files, updating the connections in each loop and running the same data flow multiple times with the updated connections. Chapter 3 discussed a method of looping through files (see Figure 3-10) and updating the connections. Essentially the ForEach Loop Container iterates through the files in a folder, and for every file the connection is updated by a property expression (or alternately a Script Task).

Alternately, a second approach combines the source files in the data flow. In Figure 5-33, three identical files are brought together with a Union All transformation. If your data files are pre-sorted, a Merge transformation would accomplish the same thing, with the benefit of maintaining the sorting downstream.

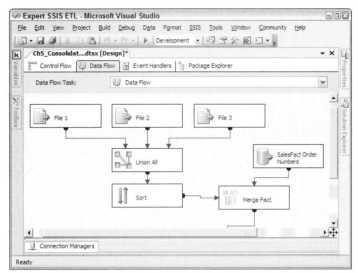

Figure 5-33: Three identical files brought together with a Union All transformation

This approach is useful for smaller files and smaller file counts. The addition of the Sort will add memory overhead, and the file count needs to remain static. However, this approach can be effective when dealing with a contained number of feeds that are very consistent in availability. Otherwise, consider a looping approach.

Handling Missing Dimension Lookups

When the fact table is being loaded and a dimension match is not available, then the fact ETL needs to assign a placeholder surrogate key for the row to be successfully inserted. Dimension foreign keys in the fact table usually do not allow NULL values. Two common approaches exist. Option 1 involves using a generic unknown surrogate key for the missing key. Commonly a surrogate key value of 0, 1, or -1 is reserved for the missing key. Option 2 involves adding a placeholder record in the dimension table with the business key that previously did not exist in the dimension.

Option 1 can be handled through a Derived Column, replacing any NULL values in the surrogate keys with the generic unknown surrogate key. However, this choice will not allow the fact row to ever be updated with the right dimension key, should the dimension source record be available at a later date.

The second option, called an inferred member, offers greater flexibility and will be the focus of this section. In Chapter 4, consideration is given to updating the inferred member dimension record when the missing dimension source is available. This section looks at creating the inferred member during the fact load.

Before looking at how to handle inferred members with SSIS, here's a quick visual reminder from Chapter 4 about inferred members.

There are at least three ways to handle inferred member creation during the fact-loading process:

❑ Create a *pre-data flow check* of the source rows to see if any missing dimension members exist, and subsequently load them first, before you load the primary data flow for the fact table.

❑ Use a *post-data flow process*. During the primary fact load data flow, only fact source records that have every dimension match immediately available are loaded into the fact table. Any row with at least one missing dimension member is staged to a temporary table. After the primary fact load data flow, the inferred members are added to the dimension table, and then the staged fact source rows are re-processed with complete matches.

❑ Use an *in-line data flow approach*. During the fact row processing, if a missing dimension record exists, add the dimension record mid-stream in the data flow, and bring the new surrogate key back so that all the fact source records can be added to the fact table.

Unfortunately, none of these approaches comes with an Easy Button. Each has its complexities, benefits, and drawbacks. The pre-data flow choice works well when only one or two dimensions require inferred members, and it is okay to scan the source file or table two times (the first to check for inferred members, and the second to load the fact rows). It would involve an initial data flow with dimension Lookups, where any missing lookup records are sent to a dimension destination. The post-data flow requires a few steps: Staging records with missing dimensions, adding the inferred members, and then running the fact load process a second time to associate the newly created inferred member keys and load the rows into the fact table.

The in-line data flow choice comes with some advantages, but requires more complex data flow component configuration. One thing to keep in mind is that, if a dimension record is missing for one fact source row, it is possible that the same dimension record may come across a second time (or more) during the same load. In this common case, the inferred member should be added only once; otherwise duplicates will be generated in the dimension table.

Using out-of-the-box transformations, one data flow approach involves redirecting the missing record, handling the inferred member, and joining back the new record into the data flow. Figure 5-34 shows the sales fact data flow, with inferred member handling of the product dimension.

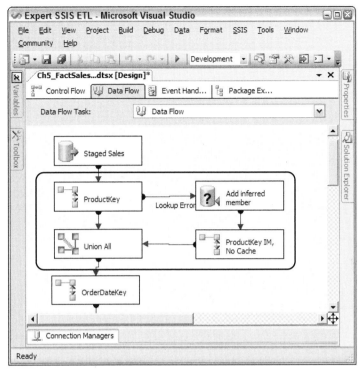

Figure 5-34: Sales fact data flow with inferred member handling of the product dimension

The product dimension lookup is configured as a full cached lookup, and the error output is set to redirect error rows, in the event of a missing record. All error rows are sent out the red path into an OLE DB Command transformation. This component calls a SQL stored procedure, passing in the `ProductAlternateKey` (or `ProductID` from the source). The following code shows the details of the TSQL procedure:

```
CREATE PROCEDURE upCreateProductInferredMember
@ProductAlternateKey nvarchar(25)
AS

IF NOT EXISTS
  SELECT ProductAlternateKey
  FROM AdventureWorksDW.dbo.DimProduct
  WHERE ProductAlternateKey = @ProductAlternateKey)
BEGIN

INSERT INTO AdventureWorksDW.dbo.DimProduct
    ( ProductAlternateKey, ProductSubcategoryKey
    , EnglishProductName, SpanishProductName
    , FrenchProductName, FinishedGoodsFlag
    , Color, StartDate, EndDate, Status)
VALUES
```

```
        (@ProductAlternateKey
        ,0,'NA','NA','NA',1,'NA'
        ,GETDATE(),NULL,'Inf')

END
```

Within the stored procedure, the IF NOT EXISTS line checks to see if the business key already exists, in which case, the procedure does not need to re-add it. If the business key does not exist then the procedure adds the inferred member with the business keys and unknowns for attributes.

Because the OLE DB Command cannot receive any returned value, the surrogate key needs to be acquired in a second step. The output of the OLE DB Command is passed to a second Lookup transformation. This Lookup is configured with a disabled cache, as Figure 5-35 highlights. Disabling the cache has the effect of forcing the Lookup component to query the database directly for the required values, instead of utilizing an in-memory cache. A partial-cache could also be used in this context, where the cache is built as new matches are received from the lookup reference table.

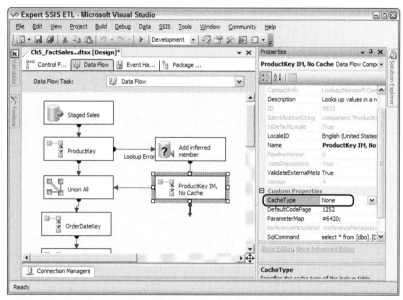

Figure 5-35: Lookup configured with a disabled cache

Every row passed through the OLE DB Command transformation needs the product surrogate key. The Lookup queries the product dimension and returns the right surrogate key. Figure 5-36 shows the Lookup editor Columns tab with the returned surrogate key added as ProductKey_inferred to the data flow.

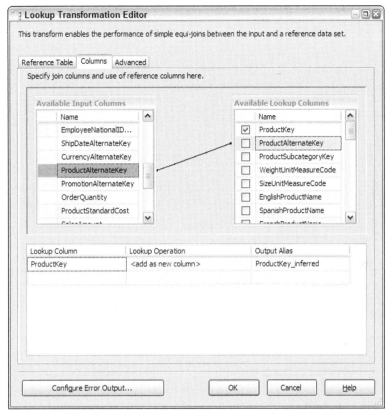

Figure 5-36: Lookup editor Columns tab with the returned surrogate key added

The final step is to bring the fact row back into the main pipeline of records that initially matched the dimension records. This is handled with a Union All transformation. Figure 5-37 shows the Union All editor.

Of note, the `ProductKey` column from the product Lookup is matched with the `ProductKey_inferred` from the inferred member Lookup, thus giving a complete set of product surrogate keys from the source fact rows that can then be inserted into the fact table destination.

If you have been counting, this model requires three queries against the product dimension table for a new inferred member. The first checks for the record, the second adds the record, and the third gets the surrogate key. Furthermore, every time the same `ProductAlternateKey` comes through the inferred member process, the product dimension is queried again to check for the record, and again to return the key. When considering that the inferred members should make up a very small minority of source records, this solution may work well and not pose scalability issues. However, a second choice is available that presents a more efficient in-line approach to inferred members.

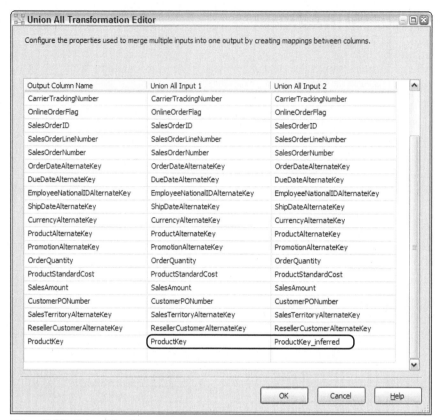

Figure 5-37: Union All editor

A Script Component can be used to perform a similar process, but at the same time, increasing the performance by reducing the queries against the dimension table. Rather than describe the solution here, Microsoft has included the code and examples in the Project REAL solution, available for download on the Project REAL site (www.microsoft.com/sql/bi/projectreal), and written up in the Project REAL "ETL Design Practices" paper, also available for download. In brief, the Script component (acting like a transformation) also calls a procedure. However, the procedure returns the surrogate key in the same step and maintains its own cache of ProductAlternateKey with matching surrogate keys in the event the same business key resurfaces.

The bottom line is that choices are available to handle inferred members, and although the processes and code may add complexity to the ETL, the overall benefits are significant for missing dimension handling.

Handling Late-Arriving Facts

Like it sounds, a *late-arriving fact* is when a fact source row comes through the ETL process at some amount of time after the source row was actually generated. Perhaps a sales record is delayed for a day or so for verification purposes, and then made available to the ETL. The only reason this may require special handling is when a dimension contains Type 2 historical attributes. If the associated record in the dimension table has gone through a Type 2 historical change, then the late-arriving fact row may need to look back to an outdated dimension record for the most accurate dimension association.

One approach for this scenario is to check the current dimension `StartDate` with the fact transaction date and, if the dimension `StartDate` is later than the fact transaction date, then send the row out for special handling. Figure 5-38 shows an example of the sales fact load data flow, again focused on the product dimension Lookup.

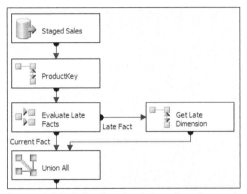

Figure 5-38: Sales fact load data flow focused on the product dimension Lookup

The Lookup for the product dimension returns both the product surrogate key along with the `StartDate` (aliased as `ProductStartDate`) of the dimension, since the product dimension contains Type 2 historical attributes. The very next transformation, a Conditional Split, compares the dates. Figure 5-39 shows the Conditional Split editor.

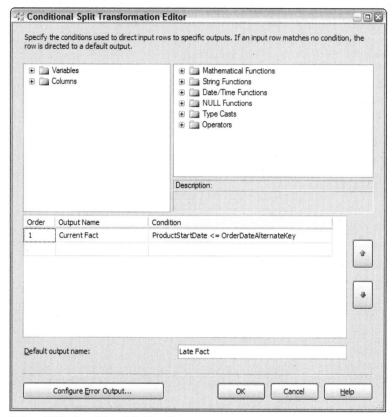

Figure 5-39: Conditional Split editor

If the order date of the sale (`OrderDateAlternateKey`) is less than or equal to the dimension's start date, then the surrogate key must be replaced with the correct outdated surrogate key. The rows redirected to the default output called Late Fact are sent into another Lookup transformation, with special configuration to handle the date range. Figure 5-40 shows the Advanced tab of the second Lookup transformation.

Notice that the Enable memory restriction and Modify the SQL statement check boxes are selected, which allow a custom query to be entered. The query is redefined with parameters to handle the date range. These parameters are mapped to the `ProductAlternateKey`, the `OrderDateAlternateKey`, and the same `OrderDateAlternateKey` again, as Figure 5-41 shows (by clicking the Parameters button).

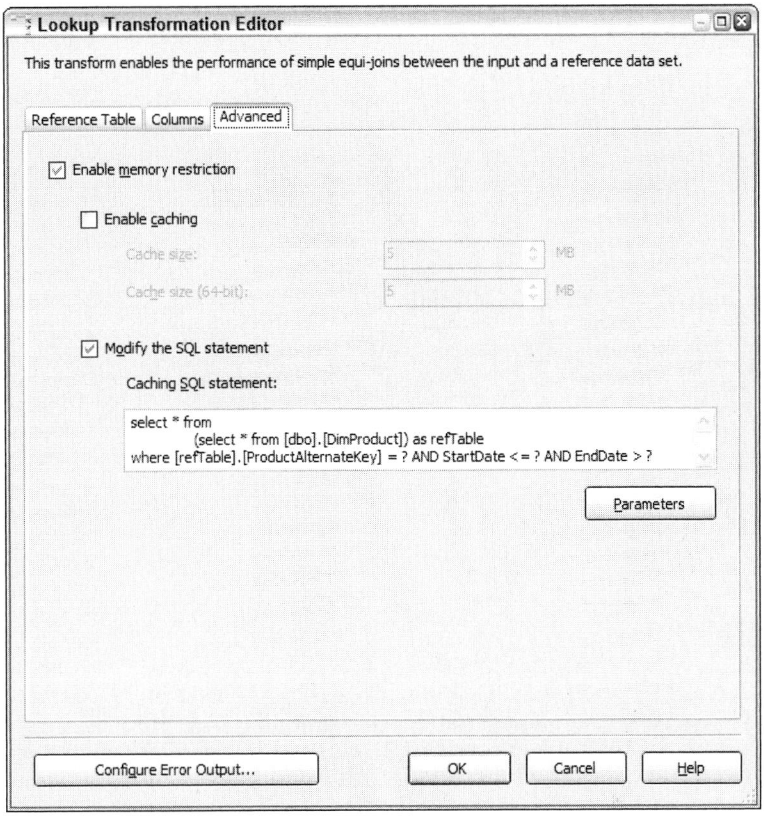

Figure 5-40: Advanced tab of the Lookup transformation

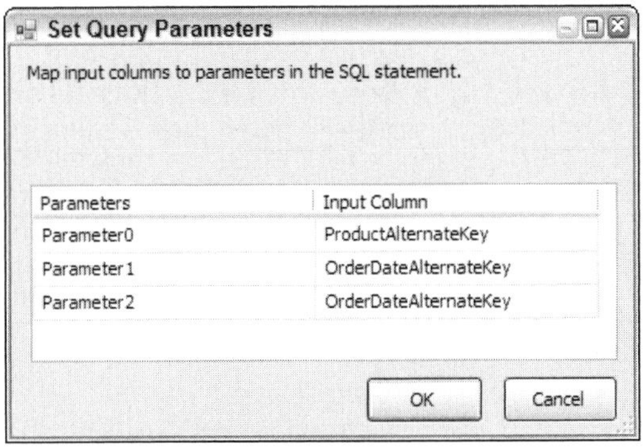

Figure 5-41: Mapped parameters

Using this approach does not allow caching. However, the number of records requiring this handling is usually significantly small. One trick is required to get the modified SQL statement to work. The Column Mappings tab needs to include the `OrderDateAlternateKey` mapped to a column in the reference table (mapped to `StartDate` because it made the most sense) so that the lookup can see the `OrderDateAlternateKey` for parameterization. Without this, the transformation will fail with the error referencing the `OrderDateAlternateKey` as not existing. Also note, because the SQL statement is being modified, the configured column mapping will not apply, so it is, therefore, okay to map the `OrderDateAlternateKey`.

Advanced Fact Table Loading

Fact table loading is an important discussion point for scalability and performance. And when dealing with large volumes in the hundreds-of-millions of rows, data flow destination optimization will be a key performance point.

Chapter 12 discusses optimizing destinations for heterogeneous data and bulk loading, respectively. Choosing the right provider and optimizing the settings are reserved for that discussion, including partitioned table data load optimization.

Summary

Fact table ETL involves several central (but simple) aspects, such as dimension key lookups and measure calculations. Beyond these two common components, many fact table processes require changing source data grain, which adds a layer of difficulty. And in more rare occasions, unique dimension processing requirements (such as inferred members and late-arriving facts) are more complex and require more planning, development, and testing. But in all, SSIS provides the tools to meet your fact table ETL requirements successfully.

As an extension to this chapter and Chapter 4, Chapter 6 focuses on SSAS integration, mainly processing SSAS dimensions and cube partitions.

Processing Analysis Services Objects with SSIS

This chapter targets the integration points between SSIS and SQL Server 2005 Analysis Services (SSAS). Business Intelligence (BI) solutions that involve SSAS cubes typically include a method for processing the objects from the data warehouse or data mart database sources into the OLAP cube structures. With the focus of Chapters 4 and 5 on handling dimension and fact table ETL, the final step in the process is to load the related SSAS objects, which, in most cases, will be the responsibility of the ETL process.

Since a big portion of SSAS integration in SSIS involves processing data and managing measure group partitions, the focus of this chapter is on processing and partition management techniques and best practices, starting with the out-of-the-box basics and followed by handling more complicated situations. The chapter concludes with a consideration of dimension change type implications with SSAS attribute relationships.

SSAS ETL Processing and Management Overview

Enterprise BI systems often have recurring ETL schedules that are predicated on the availability of source data. Often, these schedules are set to run nightly when either a source system is idle or has downtime, or when some prior batch process or precedence is complete. However, there are times when scheduling is required more or less frequently, such as when an inventory system sends data updates weekly or monthly, or on the flip-side, when data is made available several times a day. You may even have a situation that contains a diversity of processing schedule requirements, from monthly to near real-time.

The common thread in most of the enterprise ETL processes is that the load times are known. The ETL schedules kick off at either pre-defined times, or by scheduling tools that work in conjunction with other environment precedence. This can be for ETL jobs that run every five minutes to once a month. And, when a job finishes, the scheduling tool or package that coordinates execution can spawn off another process.

ETL scheduling is important in a discussion on SSAS processing because, in the majority of cases, when an Enterprise BI system involves SSAS, the processing of the SSAS objects is the responsibility of the ETL subsystem. Therefore, you must take into consideration the aspects and methods involved in it.

To be sure, a handful of BI solutions are real-time or very near real-time, meaning the transactions that are happening from the source systems are trickled through to the BI solution throughout the day as they happen. This scenario requires leveraging some of the real-time and near real-time features of SSAS, including Relational Online Analytical Process (ROLAP) storage for objects and proactive caching. These are both out of the scope of this chapter, but important in describing the overall picture of SSAS processing. You can refer to SQL Server's online documentation on Proactive Caching for more information on near real-time processing.

SSAS Objects and Processing Basics

Before jumping into the details of SSAS processing, here's a quick refresher on the concepts and components involved in SSAS processing.

To begin, the main types of objects in SSAS that must be processed are dimensions and partitions. If you are using the data mining features of SSAS, you will also be processing data mining objects. You may ask, "What about processing the SSAS database, cubes, and measure groups?" True, these objects can be processed, but they are just containers for subordinate objects, and when you choose to process them, you are really identifying the set of dimensions, partitions, and mining objects to process.

> Note that even though a cube doesn't contain data itself (only its related dimensions and measure group partitions), when a cube is processed, that cube does have a script cache that is refreshed. In other words, you should process the cube object itself if you made any changes to calculations or to the MDX script.

Dimensions

An SSAS dimension, as you would guess, maps very closely to a dimension table in the database. In fact, when you have a dimensionally structured modeled data warehouse or data mart (with an ETL process, as described in Chapters 4 and 5), then the SSAS dimensions are loaded directly from their underlying dimension tables. However, it's not always the case that the mapping is exactly one-to-one, because at times you may need to combine multiple tables or use a single source dimension table for more than one SSAS dimension. Furthermore, an SSAS solution can be built on top of a transactional system where several source tables are involved. However, a transactionally sourced SSAS solution is limited in size and the tracking of history, and this is mostly reserved for proof-of-concept, specialized, or smaller-scale solutions.

Figure 6-1 shows the Employee dimension in the `AdventureWorks` example SSAS solution.

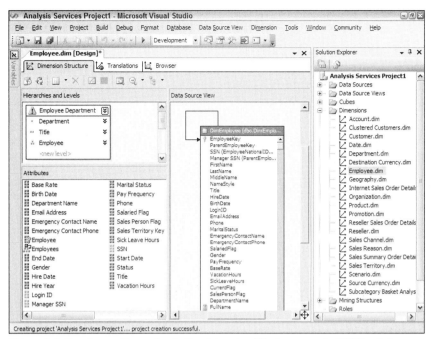

Figure 6-1: Employee dimension in the AdventureWorks example SSAS solution

The main Business Intelligence Development Studio (BIDS) designer window shows the dimension editor. The Solution Explorer (on the right) shows the list of dimensions created in the SSAS solution. Dimensions contain attributes and defined hierarchies, which come into play when loading the underlying table data into the SSAS objects.

Several processing types exist for SSAS dimensions, including the following:

❑ **Full process** — A full process involves a rebuild of the data structure underlying the SSAS dimension, which requires full rescans of the dimension table to populate the attribute's structures, hierarchies, and indexes created for optimization. A full process is required when you make any structural change to the dimension (such as adding attributes and hierarchies, and moving or adding attribute relationships).

When you perform a full process, the data is dropped in any associated measure group partitions because the structures are rebuilt.

❑ **Process update** — A process update is similar to a full process, in that the underlying dimension table is rescanned. However, the attribute, hierarchy, and index structures in the SSAS dimension are merely updated with changes and additions. This is the best choice when processing an SSAS database because it will preserve the related structures.

Some dimension changes, including deletes, may not be allowed based on the design, which has implications in dimension ETL change types. This is discussed later in this chapter when reviewing the implications of rigid and flexible attribute relationships.

❑ **Unprocess** — Occasionally, you may want to *unprocess* your dimension to perhaps free space, or perhaps to force a full rebuild of a partition with the full processing.

❑ **Process data** — Process data is similar to the process update, but only involves processing the data structures for the attributes and the hierarchies, excluding the attribute bitmap indexes.

❑ **Process index** — The complement to process data is process index, which only processes the indexes. The requirement for this is that the SSAS dimension must first be processed, because process index does not require re-scanning the dimension table.

❑ **Process add** — Process add enables you to add dimension members to the SSAS dimension without requiring the entire dimension table to be rescanned. This option is not available in the UI processing features found in SQL Server Management Studio (SSMS) or SSIS, but is a method that can be used programmatically or through XML for Analysis (XMLA), which is the industry specification message for interacting with OLAP structures.

Partitions

The second SSIS object involved in processing is the measure group partition. A measure group partition is most often sourced from a fact table when loading data from a data warehouse or mart. If loading data from an active transactional database system, your partitions would map to your primary transaction tables. But again, enterprise scale solutions are best designed with a dimensionally normalized underlying database.

When associating SSAS objects with fact tables to SSAS objects, the mapping is at the measure group level. The partitions are a subordinate object to the measure group, and provide the data storage for the measure group. Therefore, when a measure group contains more than one partition, the partition only contains a subset of the measure group's entire data set.

As already mentioned, SSAS has the capability to drive the scheduling and processing times of the partitions; this feature is called *proactive caching*. Furthermore, you may have some partitions that act like database views where the structure allows queries but the queries are passed through to the database that contains the cube data. This is called *relational OLAP* (ROLAP), which is useful for a rapidly changing subset of data. For most of your partitions (if not all) you will be using Multidimensional Online Analytical Process (MOLAP) storage, where the underlying data is completely pulled into the partition structure and aggregates can be added.

Figure 6-2 shows the cube designer in BIDS, with the Partitions tab selected, which highlights the partition management UI for SSAS.

As you can see, the partitions are associated with measure groups, and, furthermore, each partition has a different name and, although not shown, also a different underlying query to keep the partition data separate from one another.

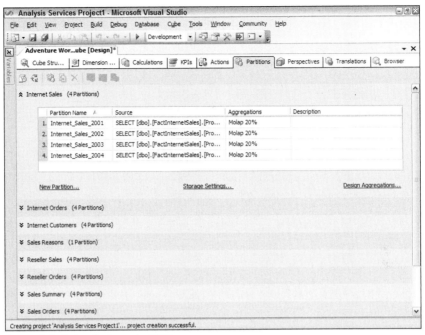

Figure 6-2: Cube designer in BIDS

When processing partitions, the following options are available:

❏ **Process full** — A process full for partitions is equivalent to both the process update and process full for dimensions. The underlying partition's data is rescanned and the partition is rebuilt with any changes and updates. When process full is complete (or the transaction that it is contained in), the new data will be made available, and during processing, the old data is still online.

❏ **Incremental process** — An incremental process is the equivalent of *process add*, where data can be added to the partition without the need to rebuild it. However, process add does not update any data currently in the partitions; it only brings in new underlying fact rows. In other words, if you have a fact record that is updated, you will need to perform a process full. Alternatively, you could use a change-record approach to offset the original value in the partition.

❏ **Unprocess** — Unprocess drops the data, aggregates, and indexes from the partition.

❏ **Process data** — Process data, just like the equivalent on the dimension side, only loads the detailed data into the partition's MOLAP structure without processing the indexes or aggregates. Since ROLAP and Hybrid Online Analytical Processing (HOLAP) keep data in the underlying database, this only applies to MOLAP structures.

❏ **Process index** — Process index processes both the bitmap indexes and the aggregation, provided that at least the partition's core data is already loaded. In other words, the process index does not need to access the underlying table data.

Mining Structures

When processing data mining objects in SSAS, you are really dealing with processing mining structures and mining models, which are very different in regard to what the processing is doing.

The *mining structure* is the base organization of data that the mining models are built upon. Mining structures define the organization of data that will be mined (hence, *structure*), as well as the training data that give the mining models the ability to perform predictions and associations. Figure 6-3 highlights the Targeted Mailing mining structure in SSAS, which contains a series of columns that will be used in the mining.

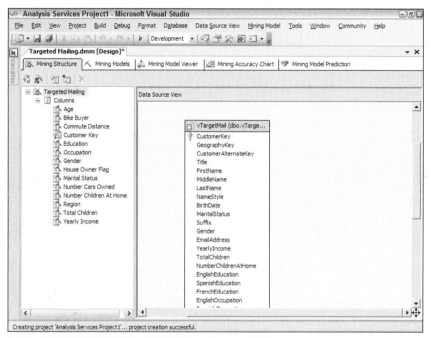

Figure 6-3: Targeted Mailing mining structure in SSAS

When processing the mining structures in SSAS, what you are doing is loading the training data into the structure so that the mining models can perform their analysis. When you process the mining models, you are applying the chosen mining model algorithms to the content of the mining structures.

Both mining structures and mining models have only two general processing types: *process full* (called *process structure* for mining structures) and *unprocess* (called *process clear* for mining structures). As you would expect, a process full rebuilds the structures or models. However, be aware that a process full on a mining structure does not automatically perform a process full on the associated mining models; therefore, if you process a mining structure, you must then process the mining models created on top of that structure.

Methods to Process SSAS Objects Through SSIS

Here's where it starts to come together. When you have an SSAS solution involved in your BI solution, just what are the different methods that you can use to process these related objects in your SSIS-based ETL process?

There are several, which involve leveraging different aspects of SSIS in the data flow and control flow:

❑ Using the control flow object Analysis Services Processing Task is the most straightforward approach, and is discussed in the next section. This allows any SSAS objects (that involve processing) and their processing method to be selected. A few drawbacks are listed in the next section.

❑ Although the Analysis Services Execute DDL Task may sound as if it only allows objects to be modified, created, or deleted, its functionality goes way beyond Data Definition Language (DDL). This task will run an SSAS XMLA script. XMLA includes the ability not just to run DDL, but also query and process. Therefore, this task will become very useful for SSAS processing because the XMLA can be modified in an SSIS package before it is executed.

❑ The data flow in SSIS includes two destinations: the *Dimension Processing destination* and the *Partition Processing destination*. These allow data directly from the pipeline to be pushed into either an SSAS dimension or SSAS partition, respectively. Unlike all the other SSIS approaches discussed here, this is the only approach where data is pushed directly to SSAS. The other approaches essentially tell SSAS to start pulling the data from a data source. Like the other SSIS approaches, this approach is described later in this chapter.

❑ The programming API for SSAS, called *Analysis Management Objects* (AMO), allows the interface into the SSAS object model, and can leverage the processing methods to process any of the SSAS objects described. To use AMO for processing, you must leverage either the Script Task in the control flow, or the Script Component in the data flow.

❑ A final mainline approach involves using the Execute Command Task to call the ASCMD executable that comes with SSAS. This executable can run Multidimensional Expressions (MDX), Data Mining Expressions (DMX), and XMLA, but also contains some command line switches to make your processing more dynamic.

When it comes down to it, your situation may use a combination of approaches as the needs arrive, or even a one-off derivative of these choices.

Creating and Modifying Partitions

When discussing SSIS integration with SSAS, just reviewing partition processing is not the complete story. Any enterprise BI solution involving SSAS almost always requires more than one partition per measure group for data management, processing, and performance reasons.

In other words, in your ETL, you will often have to create new partitions before processing them. The easy way out may be to create several partitions a couple years out into the future. Just don't give them your phone number if you leave the project or organization, because you might get a call in two years asking why the processing is breaking!

To create and manage SSAS partitions within an SSIS process, the methods available are merely a subset of the processing options:

❑ The Execute Analysis Services DDL Task is the most natural choice for managing and creating partitions because these are DDL-type operations, and XMLA provides all the needed operations to handle partition operations.

❑ Since AMO allows objects to be created, modified, and deleted, it can be used with the scripting features in SSIS, the Script Task and Script Component.

❑ Finally, the ASCMD.exe executable also provides partition-management functionality since it can run XMLA code and handle parameterization within the XMLA, therefore allowing partitions to be managed. Within SSIS, the ASCMD is run from an Execute Process Task.

SSAS Integration Basics Within SSIS

To make an informed decision on how you will handle your SSAS processing, it is important to understand the uses, benefits, and drawbacks of the built-in SSAS components in SSIS. This section is followed by examples of the various choices reviewed, which, in some cases, use these features.

The two built-in control flow components already mentioned that interact with SSAS are the Analysis Services Processing Task and the Analysis Services Execute DDL Task. The two data flow components that interact with SSAS are the Dimension Processing destination and the Partition Processing destination. All of these components leverage an Analysis Services connection that must be defined in the Connection Managers window pane.

To create a new connection, right-click in the Connection Managers window pane and select New Analysis Services Connection, which brings up the Add Analysis Services Connection Manager window with a connection string. When you select Edit next to the connection string, it opens up the standard Connection Manager editor, as shown in Figure 6-4.

The Server or file name entry is the name of the SSAS server, and the Log on to the server selection defines how the connection should pass its authentication to the SSAS server. SSAS only supports Windows authentication (local machine or Active Directory security), so the two choices for security both relate to Windows security.

❑ The Use Windows NT Integrated Security option uses the existing security account for the user who is logged in during either design or execution. When a package is executed through the command line, it is the account that runs DTExec, which may be a service account or a proxy account when using SQL Agent or Windows scheduler, or a third-party scheduling tool.

❑ The Use a specific user name and password option allows a Windows account and password to be entered, so that you can define a different Windows account that the connection uses. Because a password must be entered, even if you select the Allow saving password check box, you must still handle the password storage or un-encryption (through an SSIS configuration entry, or command line switch or property expression).

Chapter 9 discusses package security and package roles in more detail.

Figure 6-4: Standard Connection Manager editor

Control Flow Tasks for SSAS

As mentioned, the two control flow tasks are the Analysis Services Processing Task and the Analysis Services Execute DDL Task.

Analysis Services Processing Task

The Analysis Services Processing Task is designed to process objects selected in a list with the ability to set processing types, handle errors, order and relate objects, and manage transactions. Figure 6-5 shows the Analysis Services Processing Task Editor.

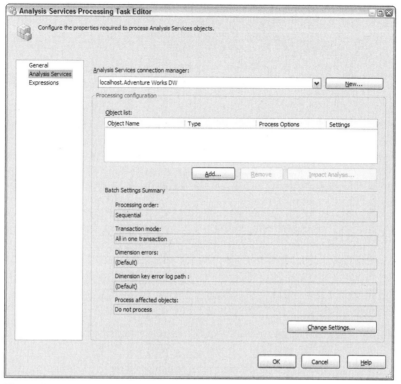

Figure 6-5: Analysis Services Processing Task Editor

Adding objects to the Object list is very straightforward. Selecting Add below the Object list will enable an entire SSAS database to be selected, or specific cubes, dimensions, or mining models. When selecting a cube or mining model, you are merely instructing the task to process the underlying measure groups and partitions or mining structures. These can also be selected individually, as Figure 6-6 shows.

When the objects are selected, the task will return them to the Object list on the main screen. Here is where the processing types can be selected. For each item in the list, choose the processing option from the drop-down list. Figure 6-7 shows some of the choices for the Product dimension.

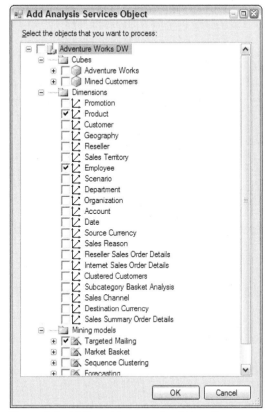

Figure 6-6: Adding objects to the Object list

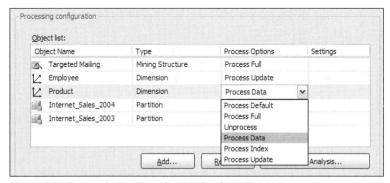

Figure 6-7: Processing options for the Product dimension

If you have selected a parent container with the intention of processing the underlying objects, the list will only show the processing options that are in common with all the objects. So, you may need to select the different objects individually. Also, if you have selected the Process Incremental option for a partition, you will be prompted to configure some advanced settings. This is because when adding data to a partition incrementally, you must define which data should be added. The configuration screen (not shown) allows for a table, view, or query to be specified as the source for the rows being added to the partition.

The second aspect of this task involves setting how the processing batch will be handled. The lower half of the task editor window shown earlier in Figure 6-5 has settings related to the batch. Selecting Change Settings opens a window to modify the advanced properties, with a Processing options tab and a Dimension key errors tab. The first tab allows some general settings to be updated, such as whether to run the processing sequentially or in parallel, and how to handle SSAS transactions initiated by the task. Also, a writeback table selection exists, along with the option to process affected objects.

Figure 6-8 shows the Dimension key errors tab, which controls the action taken when a partition is being processed, and a dimension key is referenced in the underlying fact, but the associated key doesn't exist in the SSAS dimension itself.

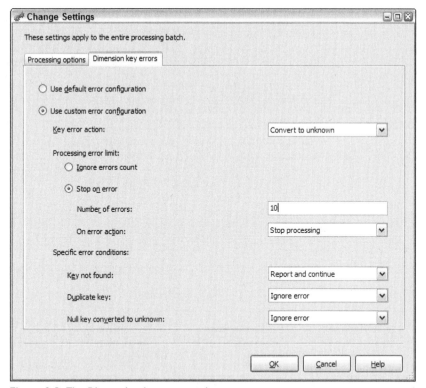

Figure 6-8: The Dimension key errors tab

Similar settings can be defined within a given measure group and the Use default error configuration option will then default to those settings. The Use custom error configuration option enables you to override these settings. For example, you are able to set a threshold number (property Number of errors) so that if processing errors reach the threshold, either the task can fail, or it can stop reporting the errors.

Several key errors will also cause issues in processing, including missing keys, duplicates, and NULL values. These settings can ignore, report, and continue processing, or report and stop the processing. In this case, you are able to define what types of errors you allow to happen, and which indicate a bigger issue that may need to be addressed (and, therefore, stop the processing).

The following are some drawbacks to the Analysis Services Processing Task:

❑ Although some of the general properties are configurable through property expressions or SSIS Configurations, what is not changeable is anything related to the list of objects and the batch setting. In essence, when you use this task, you are hard-coding the list of objects and how the objects should be processed. In many cases, this will not meet your requirements, especially if partitions are involved. The good news is that even if you have multiple partitions, typically your dimension list doesn't change, nor the processing type. This makes the processing task a good choice for defining dimension processes.

❑ A second drawback is that the SSAS Processing Task either requires every object to be processed one at a time (in separate transactions), or the entire process set to run in parallel in the same transaction. The drawback when choosing to run the processing in parallel is that the processing is an all-or-nothing proposition. Therefore, you need to consider other choices that allow for better granular control over which objects get run in which order, and how things are batched for transactions for restartability.

Analysis Services Execute DDL Task

The Analysis Services Execute DDL Task is relatively simple in form, but provides excellent functionality. Figure 6-9 shows the task editor with the DDL property page selected.

There are only three properties. The Connection property, as you would guess, defines which SSAS package connection should be used. The SourceType property allows three different methods to input the XMLA statement:

❑ Choosing Direct Input changes the third property to SourceDirect, where the XMLA can be hard-coded into the task.

❑ Selecting File Connection changes the third property to be Source, so that a file connection manager can be selected, which identifies the file system file that contains the XMLA to run.

❑ Choosing Variable in the SourceType means that the XMLA will be embedded in a variable of type string. The Source property becomes the package variable that the task will use.

Because these properties are exposed, you are able to modify them through expressions and configurations, which will be the pivotal use of the Analysis Services Execute DDL Task as we look at some dynamic examples.

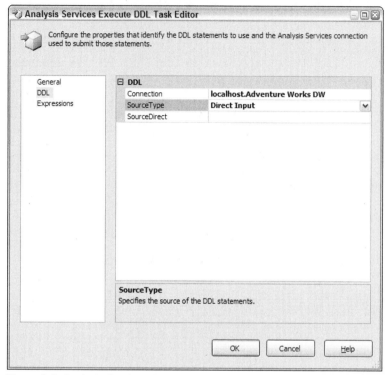

Figure 6-9: Analysis Services Execute DDL Task Editor

Data Flow Destinations for SSAS Objects

Besides the data mining components discussed later, the final consideration for the built-in features involves the data flow destinations: Dimension Processing and Partition Processing.

As briefly mentioned earlier, these two data flow destinations are the only SSIS methods where the ETL process is actually pushing the data into SSAS. The other choices listed earlier instruct SSAS to begin its processing, which causes the SSAS engine to pull data in from defined sources for the various objects being processed. As discussed later, these destinations are a very powerful mechanism to load data into SSAS from non-standard sources and for near real-time processing.

Dimension Processing Data Flow Destination

The Dimension Processing destination is connected directly to the data flow pipeline, which allows any type of transformation to influence the data before it is pushed into the SSAS dimension structures. Figure 6-10 shows a data flow where source rows from a flat file are being loaded into the Geography dimension.

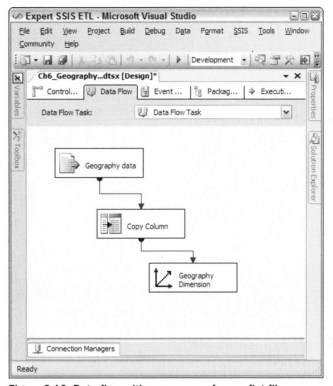

Figure 6-10: Data flow with source rows from a flat file

The Dimension Processing destination provides property pages for specifying the dimension (and processing option), column mappings from the source data into the dimension attributes, and dimension key error handling. Figure 6-11 shows the Connection Manager property page in the Dimension Processing Destination Editor, which identifies the SSAS connection manager, the dimension (in this case, Geography), and the type of processing (described earlier).

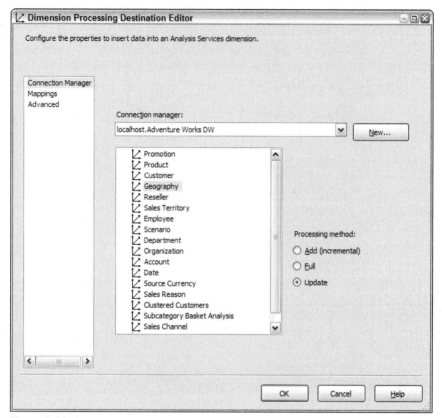

Figure 6-11: Connection Manager property page in Dimension Processing destination

Mapping the source columns from the pipeline to the dimension attributes is handled in much the same way as any other source-to-destination mapping within the pipeline. Figure 6-12 shows the Mappings page of the Geography Dimension Processing destination.

Attribute names and keys are required for the processing to be successful. The keys are defined within SSAS, which may be a collection of more than one column. The Copy Column transformation shown in Figure 6-10 is creating duplicates of the columns that are used for attribute keys so that they are available in the destination. Not shown, the Advanced tab allows key error handling, identical to the details shown earlier in Figure 6-8.

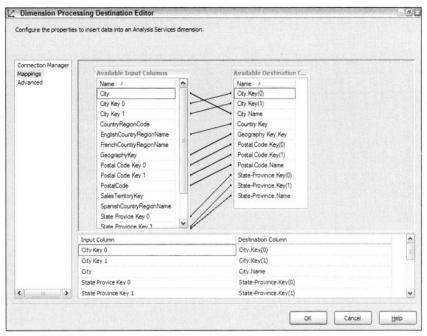

Figure 6-12: Mappings page of the Geography Dimension Processing destination

Partition Processing Data Flow Destination

The Partition Processing destination is very similar to the Dimension Processing destination. As with any destination, the data flow can pull from any source and perform a variety of transformation logic before the Partition Processing destination.

Figure 6-13 shows the Connection Manager tab of the destination, which is selected on the sole partition of the currency rate measure group. This page includes processing options to handle additions, full process (which includes aggregations), or data loading only.

The Mappings tab and the Advanced tab are identical to the Dimension Processing destination, where the columns are mapped and key error handling can be defined.

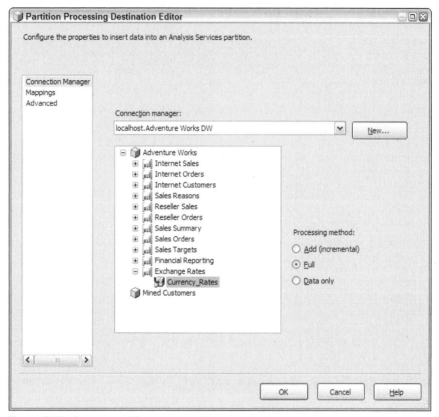

Figure 6-13: Connection Manager tab of the destination

Advanced Processing and Partition Management Examples

When it comes to an enterprise BI solution, rarely is the status quo applicable for processing objects. Usually, there are unique precedent requirements or complicated partition management and processing needs to get the performance and agility essential for successful BI applications. Earlier, this chapter discussed the different ways that SSAS objects could be processed and managed within SSIS. The prior section looked at the basic out-of-the box functionality. So, now it's time to consider leveraging some of the other approaches and learning how to take advantage of the Analysis Services Execute DDL Task by making the XMLA dynamic.

Dimension Processing

Dimension processing is generally straightforward, except for some potential unique precedence handling or transaction management. Because of this, even though many of the prescribed approaches would work for dimension processing, the keep-it-simple corollary dictates that some of the approaches would be overkill.

Leveraging the Analysis Services Processing Task is often sufficient, and has already been described. The other straightforward approaches involve creating an XMLA script for processing the dimensions. Rarely do dimension structures change, and, in most scenarios, a process update is performed on the dimensions. In most cases, the XMLA script doesn't need to be dynamic. Therefore, the XMLA can be generated and then just executed either by using the ASCMD executable or the Analysis Services Execute DDL Task. Here's an example of a small XMLA script that performs a parallel process update on the Product, Employee, and Time dimensions:

```xml
<Batch
    xmlns="http://schemas.microsoft.com/analysisservices/2003/engine">
  <Parallel MaxParallel = "2">
    <Process xmlns:xsd="http://www.w3.org/2001/XMLSchema">
      <Object>
        <DatabaseID>Adventure Works DW</DatabaseID>
        <DimensionID>Dim Employee</DimensionID>
      </Object>
      <Type>ProcessUpdate</Type>
      <WriteBackTableCreation>UseExisting</WriteBackTableCreation>
    </Process>
    <Process xmlns:xsd="http://www.w3.org/2001/XMLSchema">
      <Object>
        <DatabaseID>Adventure Works DW</DatabaseID>
        <DimensionID>Dim Product</DimensionID>
      </Object>
      <Type>ProcessUpdate</Type>
      <WriteBackTableCreation>UseExisting</WriteBackTableCreation>
    </Process>
    <Process xmlns:xsd="http://www.w3.org/2001/XMLSchema">
      <Object>
        <DatabaseID>Adventure Works DW</DatabaseID>
        <DimensionID>Dim Time</DimensionID>
      </Object>
      <Type>ProcessUpdate</Type>
      <WriteBackTableCreation>UseExisting</WriteBackTableCreation>
    </Process>
  </Parallel>
</Batch>
```

This code was generated in SSMS by connecting to SSAS. The Processing dialog box (right-click any dimension and choose Process) contains the ability to script out the processing settings.

To run this XMLA script with the Analysis Services Execute DDL Task, the XMLA can just be entered directly into the task as described earlier, or captured into a package variable identified within the task. (A later discussion of partition processing will involve dynamic XMLA with the Analysis Services Execute DDL Task.)

A second approach to executing this XMLA script is to leverage the ASCMD.exe executable that was first shipped with SQL Server 2005 SP1 and with an updated version in SP2. As mentioned earlier, the ASCMD contains the ability to run XMLA scripts, MDX queries, and DMX queries. Refer to the following URL for an article that describes the full feature set of ASCMD.exe:

    http://msdn2.microsoft.com/en-us/library/ms365187.aspx

In its basic use, the ASCMD can be used in SSIS through an Execute Process Task. For example, the prior XMLA script can be saved to a local directory file, and the Execute Process Task can be used in the control flow to run ASCMD.exe, identifying the file containing the XMLA script. Figure 6-14 shows an example package designed in this manner executing in the designer with the command window open.

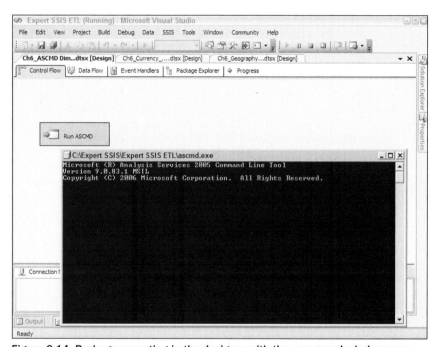

Figure 6-14: Package executing in the designer with the command window open

When looking at the properties of the Execute Process Task, the task is configured to run the ascmd.exe executable and pass in three primary arguments. Figure 6-15 shows the editor being used to execute the Execute Process Task.

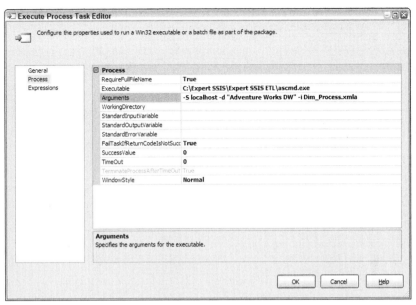

Figure 6-15: Execute Process showing ASCMD editor settings

The first argument, -S localhost, specifies the server to run the script. The second argument, -d "Adventure Works DW", identifies which SSAS database the script should be run against. The third argument, -i Dim_Process.xmla, specifies the name of the file containing the XMLA script to run.

ASCMD.exe also supports the ability to dynamically update the contents of the XMLA, MDX, or DMX code with variables passed into the command line through the arguments. This will be discussed later during an examination of processing partitions with ASCMD.exe.

Partition Creation and Processing

If you have an SSAS solution that does not contain more than one partition per measure group, or your design has a static set of partitions and you do not have the need to dynamically add or process them, then you can use one of the prior solutions demonstrated with the following:

- ❏ The Analysis Services Processing Task
- ❏ The direct input use of the Analysis Services Execute DDL Task
- ❏ The ASCMD.exe utility with a static XMLA file

If you have the need to dynamically process partitions, the following are your choices:

- ❏ A parameter-driven ASCMD.exe (or a dynamic build of the XMLA file)
- ❏ Dynamic XMLA code in conjunction with the Analysis Services Execute DDL Task
- ❏ AMO code embedded in a Script Task or Script Component

Parameter-Driven ASCMD

Among other benefits (such as more comprehensive logging), the ASCMD.exe utility also contains the capability to accept parameters as arguments, and then apply those parameters to the XMLA code being executed. To demonstrate, a new XMLA file has been generated with the following XMLA code. Included in the code are parameters identified by the reference $(parameter_name).

```
<Batch
   xmlns="http://schemas.microsoft.com/analysisservices/2003/engine">
   <Parallel MaxParallel="$(parallel_count)">
     <Process xmlns:xsd="http://www.w3.org/2001/XMLSchema">
       <Object>
         <DatabaseID>Adventure Works DW</DatabaseID>
         <CubeID>Adventure Works DW</CubeID>
         <MeasureGroupID>Fact Internet Sales 1</MeasureGroupID>
         <PartitionID>$(partition_1)</PartitionID>
       </Object>
       <Type>ProcessFull</Type>
       <WriteBackTableCreation>UseExisting</WriteBackTableCreation>
     </Process>
     <Process xmlns:xsd="http://www.w3.org/2001/XMLSchema">
       <Object>
         <DatabaseID>Adventure Works DW</DatabaseID>
         <CubeID>Adventure Works DW</CubeID>
         <MeasureGroupID>Fact Internet Sales 1</MeasureGroupID>
         <PartitionID>$(partition_2)</PartitionID>
       </Object>
       <Type>ProcessFull</Type>
       <WriteBackTableCreation>UseExisting</WriteBackTableCreation>
     </Process>
   </Parallel>
</Batch>
```

Three parameters have been defined: $(parallel_count), $(partition_1), and $(partition_2). This file has been saved as is with the name Part_Processing.xmla.

The host package will be calling this XMLA script, which contains four matching package variables, and an Execute SQL Task, which updates the variables just before the Execute Process Task, as shown in Figure 6-16.

Since the package variables must update the argument switches for the executable, a property expression will be used to handle this within the Execute Process Task. The property expression is defined in the Execute Process Task on the Expressions property page, as shown in Figure 6-17. Since the goal is to modify the command line switches, the Arguments property is updated with an expression.

The following SSIS expression integrates the package variables with the ASCMD switches needed to execute the XMLA file. Remember that package variable references are case-sensitive.

```
  "-S " + @[User::SSAS_Server]
+ " -d \"Adventure Works DW\" -i Part_Process.xmla
-v parallel_count=\"" + @[User::Parallel_count]
+ "\" -v partition_1=\"" +  @[User::Partition_1]
+ "\" -v partition_2=\"" +  @[User::Partition_2] + "\""
```

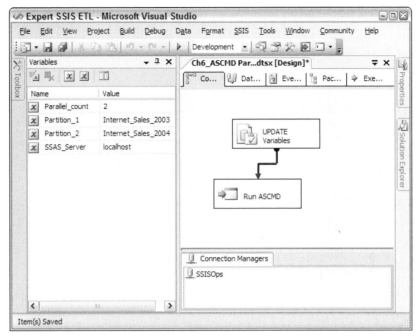

Figure 6-16: Host package

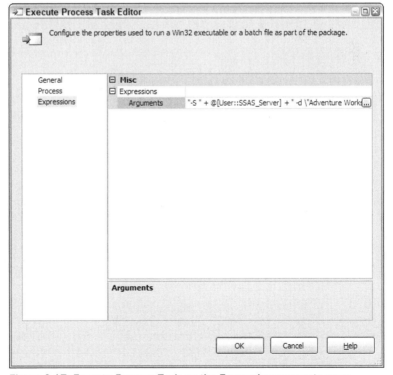

Figure 6-17: Execute Process Task on the Expressions property page

When the Execute Process Task runs, the Arguments property is updated with the evaluated value for the expression.

```
-S localhost -d "Adventure Works DW" -i Part_Process.xmla
-v parallel_count="2" -v partition_1="Internet_Sales_2003"
-v partition_2="Internet_Sales_2004"
```

In conclusion, this approach works well in the case where a fixed number of partitions must execute, and the XMLA can be parameterized to handle the fixed number, which would map to pre-defined package variables. The drawback is that the parameterization requires a fixed number of partitions. To circumvent this, the file could be updated with the correct number of partitions before the execution, if needed, or the Analysis Services Execute DDL Task could be used, as described next.

SSAS Execute DDL Task for Dynamic Processing

The next choice works well for cases where the partition count is dynamic. Using the Analysis Services Execute DDL Task, the XMLA can be modified before the DDL task is run. Figure 6-9 earlier showed how the Execute DDL Task works, by reading the XMLA (or MDX or DMX) either through the direct input, a package variable, or from a file.

Since the SSIS expression language does not support iterative functions, using a property expression with the direct input option will not allow the partition count to be dynamic. Instead, the Script Task is a good alternative to dynamically generate the XMLA and either outputting the script to a file, or the contents into a variable. If you are proficient with TSQL, the XMLA could be generated within a stored procedure and returned with the Execute SQL Task. But be mindful of output parameter length limitations.

Taking the approach of embedding the XMLA inside a variable (which is updated by a script) and using the variable in the Execute DDL Task, your control flow would look similar to Figure 6-18.

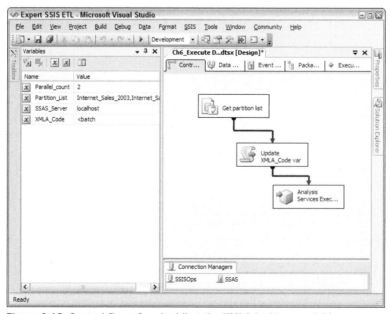

Figure 6-18: Control flow of embedding the XMLA inside a variable

The Execute SQL Task here is returning a comma-separated list of partitions that must be processed into a package string variable called `Partition_List`. With the following code, the Script Task takes the list, plus the other inputs, and builds the XMLA, returning it to a string variable named `XMLA_Code`.

```
Imports System
Imports System.Data
Imports System.Math
Imports Microsoft.SqlServer.Dts.Runtime
Imports System.Text

Public Class ScriptMain

  Public Sub Main()

    Dim sPartitionList As String = Str(Dts.Variables("Partition_List").Value)
    Dim sParallel_count As String = CStr(Dts.Variables("Parallel_count").Value)
    Dim sb As StringBuilder = New StringBuilder()

    sb.Append("<Batch xmlns=""http://schemas.microsoft.com")
    sb.Append("/analysisservices/2003/engine"">")
    sb.Append("<Parallel MaxParallel=""")
    sb.Append(sParallel_count)
    sb.Append(""">")

    For Each sPartition As String In sPartitionList.Split(","c)
      sb.Append("<Process xmlns:xsd=""http://www.w3.org/2001/XMLSchema""")
      sb.Append(" xmlns:xsi=""http://www.w3.org/2001/XMLSchema-instance""")
      sb.Append(" xmlns:ddl2=""http://schemas.microsoft.com")
      sb.Append("/analysisservices/2003/engine/2""")
      sb.Append(" xmlns:ddl2_2=""http://schemas.microsoft.com")
      sb.Append("/analysisservices/2003/engine/2/2"">")
      sb.Append("<Object><DatabaseID>Adventure Works DW</DatabaseID>")
      sb.Append("<CubeID>Adventure Works DW</CubeID>")
      sb.Append("<MeasureGroupID>Fact Internet Sales 1</MeasureGroupID>")
      sb.Append("<PartitionID>")
      sb.Append(sPartition)
      sb.Append("</PartitionID></Object>")
      sb.Append("<Type>ProcessFull</Type>")
      sb.Append("<WriteBackTableCreation>UseExisting</WriteBackTableCreation>")
      sb.Append("</Process>")
    Next

    sb.Append(" </Parallel></Batch>")

    Dts.Variables("XMLA_Code").Value = sb.ToString()

    Dts.TaskResult = Dts.Results.Success

    End Sub

End Class
```

When you are using the Script Task to perform the XMLA and integrating package variables, be sure to add the package variables to either the ReadOnlyVariables or ReadWriteVariables list as appropriate in the Script property page of the task. In this case, the XMLA_Code variable was added to the ReadWriteVariables list, and the Partition_List and Partition_count were added to the ReadOnlyVariables list.

At this point, the XMLA now in the variable can be used by the SSAS Execute DDL Task to process the partitions. Figure 6-9 earlier showed the editor of the DDL Task. In this package, the SourceType is set to Variable and the Source property is set to User::XMLA_Code.

A Preview of the Script Task with AMO

Processing SSAS objects can also be handled programmatically by using the Analysis Services object model API, called AMO (see the complete object model reference at http://msdn2.microsoft.com/en-us/library/ms345088.aspx). AMO contains all the methods, properties, and objects needed to perform many tasks such as creating SSAS partitions or other objects (which is discussed briefly in the next section), modifying settings at all levels, performing administrative operations such as backups and restores, and processing objects.

As a preview to using AMO, the following code in the Script Task loops through all the SSAS dimensions in the AdventureWorks DW cube database and performs a process update on each one:

```vb
Imports System
Imports System.Data
Imports System.Math
Imports Microsoft.SqlServer.Dts.Runtime
Imports Microsoft.AnalysisServices

Class ScriptMain

  Public Sub Main()

    ' Get Server and Database name from SSIS connection managers
    Dim oConnection As ConnectionManager
    oConnection = Dts.Connections("SSAS")
    Dim sServer As String = _
        CStr(oConnection.Properties("ServerName").GetValue(oConnection))
    Dim sDatabase As String = _
    CStr(oConnection.Properties("InitialCatalog").GetValue(oConnection))

    ' Connect to the requested server
    Dim oServer As New Microsoft.AnalysisServices.Server
    oServer.Connect(sServer)

    ' Connect to the database
    Dim oDB As Database = oServer.Databases.FindByName(sDatabase)
    Dim oDimension As New Microsoft.AnalysisServices.Dimension

    'Process update each dimension
    For Each oDimension In oDB.Dimensions
      oDimension.Process(ProcessType.ProcessUpdate)
    Next
```

```
        Dts.TaskResult = Dts.Results.Success
        End Sub

End Class
```

Note that the `Microsoft.AnalysisServices` namespace reference has been added to the script to allow interaction with AMO references. With the release of SQL Server 2005 SP2, this reference is available with the .NET Framework 2.0. However, if you are running a prior release, you will need to copy the `Microsoft.AnalysisServices.dll` assembly (found in `%Program Files%\Microsoft SQL Server\90\SDK\Assemblies`) to the .NET Framework build folder (`%windows%\Microsoft.NET\Framework\v2.0.[build#]`) in order to interact with the references during design time.

The script also references the SSAS connection (named *SSAS* as the script references) within the SSIS package, which prevents the need to hard-code the server or database. The full AMO reference can be found in Books OnLine or online at MSDN.

Figure 6-19 shows the control flow with the single Script Task used in this example, but the code can also be used in a Script Component in the data flow, with the connection information included in the `PreExecute` subroutine.

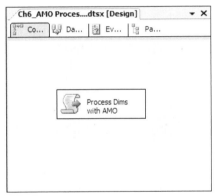

Figure 6-19: Control flow with the single Script Task

Partition Management

When it comes to managing SSAS partitions (creating, modifying, and deleting), here are your choices in SSIS:

❑ Use an Analysis Services Execute DDL Task to run a dynamically built XMLA script, which uses the `Alter` and `ObjectDefinition` commands of XMLA, and dynamically modifies the partition list that must be created.

❑ Leverage the `ASCMD.exe` executable to run the same XMLA DDL statement, and parameterize the XMLA file with the partition and measure group names.

❑ Use AMO in a Script Task or Script Component to create or modify the partition.

With the first two choices, the following XMLA example would be the basis for creating a partition. In this example, a new partition is generated in the Fact Internet Sales measure group with the name `Internet_Sales_2005`. This XMLA was generated in SSMS by scripting a create partition statement dialog to the query editor window.

```
<Alter AllowCreate="true" ObjectExpansion="ObjectProperties"
       xmlns="http://schemas.microsoft.com/analysisservices/2003/engine">
  <Object>
    <DatabaseID>Adventure Works DW</DatabaseID>
    <CubeID>Adventure Works DW</CubeID>
    <MeasureGroupID>Fact Internet Sales 1</MeasureGroupID>
    <PartitionID>Internet_Sales_2005</PartitionID>
  </Object>
  <ObjectDefinition>
    <Partition xmlns:xsd=http://www.w3.org/2001/XMLSchema
            xmlns:xsi="http://www.w3.org/2001/XMLSchema-instance">
      <ID>Internet_Sales_2005</ID>
      <Name>Internet_Sales_2005</Name>
      <Annotations>
        <Annotation>
          <Name>AggregationPercent</Name>
          <Value>20</Value>
        </Annotation>
      </Annotations>
      <Source xsi:type="QueryBinding">
        <DataSourceID>Adventure Works DW</DataSourceID>
        <QueryDefinition>
        SELECT *
        FROM [dbo].[FactInternetSales]
        WHERE OrderDateKey &gt;= '915'
        AND OrderDateKey &lt;= '1280'
        </QueryDefinition>
      </Source>
      <StorageMode>Molap</StorageMode>
      <ProcessingMode>Regular</ProcessingMode>
      <AggregationDesignID>AggregationDesign</AggregationDesignID>
    </Partition>
  </ObjectDefinition>
</Alter>
```

As with the other examples provided earlier in this chapter, the XMLA can be generated in a Script Task, or used in a file with ASCMD parameters to update the properties.

The third choice for creating or modifying partitions is to use AMO. One advantage of AMO is the ability to clone an existing partition to a new partition. In other words, you can have a template partition in each of your measure groups that is used as the basis for any new partition that must be created; then the AMO code is a simple template-copy operation. The following AMO code embedded in a Script Task demonstrates cloning an existing partition named `Internet_Sales_2001` to new partitions contained in the `Partitions_List` package variable (in this case, as a comma-delimited string of names). The script first checks for the existence of the partition before cloning the identified template partition.

```
Imports System
Imports System.Data
Imports System.Math
```

```
Imports Microsoft.SqlServer.Dts.Runtime
Imports Microsoft.AnalysisServices
Imports System.Text

Class ScriptMain

  Public Sub Main()

    Dim sPartitionList As String = _
        CStr(Dts.Variables("Partition_List").Value)
    Dim sCube As String = "Adventure Works"
    Dim sMeasureGroup As String = "Internet Sales"
    Dim sPartitionTemplate As String = "Internet_Sales_2001"
    Dim sb As StringBuilder = New StringBuilder()

    ' Get Server and Database name from DTS connection object
    Dim oConnection As ConnectionManager
    oConnection = Dts.Connections("SSAS")
    Dim sServer As String = _
        CStr(oConnection.Properties("ServerName").GetValue(oConnection))
    Dim sDatabase As String = _
    CStr(oConnection.Properties("InitialCatalog").GetValue(oConnection))

    ' Connect to the requested server
    Dim oServer As New Microsoft.AnalysisServices.Server
    oServer.Connect(sServer)

    ' Connect to the database, cube, measuregroup, and partition
    Dim oDB As Database = oServer.Databases.FindByName(sDatabase)
    Dim oCube As Cube = oDB.Cubes.FindByName(sCube)
    Dim oMeasureGroup As MeasureGroup = _
        oCube.MeasureGroups.FindByName(sMeasureGroup)
    Dim oPartitionTemplate As Partition = _
        oMeasureGroup.Partitions.FindByName(sPartitionTemplate)

    For Each sPartition As String In sPartitionList.Split(","c)

      ' Check for the partition existence, clone as needed
      If Not oMeasureGroup.Partitions.Contains(sPartition) Then
        Dim oNewPartition As Partition
        oNewPartition = oPartitionTemplate.Clone()
        oNewPartition.Name = sPartition
        oNewPartition.ID = sPartition
        oMeasureGroup.Partitions.Add(oNewPartition)
        oNewPartition.Update()
        oNewPartition = Nothing
      End If

    Next

      Dts.TaskResult = Dts.Results.Success

    End Sub

End Class
```

To be sure, this AMO example needs error handling for object existence and does not completely update every property necessary for the new partition (such as the source filter or slicer), but can be used as a starting point for more complex partition management needs.

Putting it all together, you will end up with several steps that comprise your SSAS processing requirements. Figure 6-20 shows a control flow containing four tasks to acquire partitions, process dimensions, manage partitions, and then process your partitions.

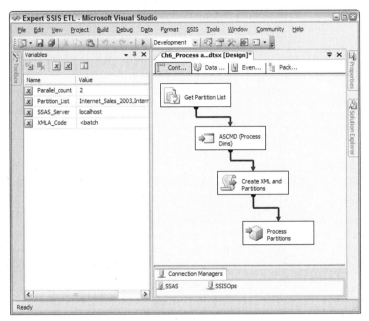

Figure 6-20: Control flow containing four tasks

In Step 1, SQL has tracked the partitions that need processing, and this step returns a comma-separated partition list to the variable XMLA_Code. Step 2 runs the ASCMD executable, which calls an XMLA file configured to perform a process update on the dimensions. Step 3 handles both the creation of the partitions, as well as composes the XMLA code to process the partitions, which is captured in the XMLA_Code package variable. The final step runs the generated XMLA to process the affected partitions.

Processing SSAS Cubes from Non-SQL Server Sources

Oftentimes, you may have an SSAS cube that is sourced from a data warehouse or mart that is stored in a non-SQL Server RDBMS (such as Teradata, Oracle, or DB2), and you are tasked with coming up with the right processing architecture to load the cubes and dimensions as quickly as possible.

The problem you run into is that the data access providers perform very slowly when taking the standard approach to processing the objects, or worse, SSAS does not support the source for SSAS objects.

The solution to this challenge is to leverage the SSAS data flow destinations. In other words, you may have your SSAS database objects built on top of an Oracle schema living on a remote database, but instead of loading your partitions directly from Oracle (which can be painfully slow), instead you can dump the data to a flat file, copy the file over the SSAS server, and then use the Partition Processing destination to load your partitions (potentially a much faster approach). The Dimension Processing and Partition Processing destinations were reviewed earlier (see Figures 6-10, 6-11, and 6-12). Figure 6-21 shows the Mappings tab of the Partition destination.

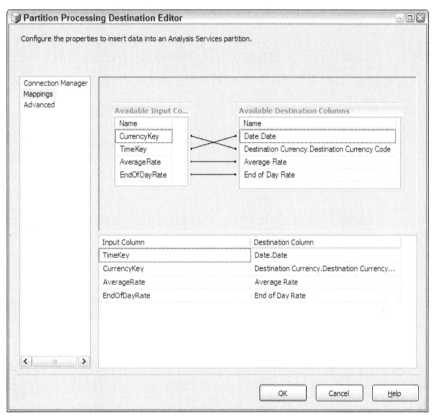

Figure 6-21: Mappings tab of the Partition destination

Since dimensions are comparatively small, it may make sense to continue processing dimensions directly from the source system and only leverage this strategy for fact data. That design choice will depend on the complexity, dimension data volume, and performance of your solution.

If you have a data warehouse built on a non-supported source for SSAS (such as IBM DB2), then you can base your cubes on an empty SQL Server schema in a template-like fashion, but still load the IBM DB2 data in the SSAS objects through these SSIS destinations.

Implications of Type 1, Type 2, and Inferred Members on Attribute Relationships

Since we talked about Type 0 fixed, Type 1 changing, Type 2 historical, and inferred member when looking at dimension ETL in Chapter 4, it is worth mentioning the processing implications with SSAS attributes. Figure 6-22 shows the dimension designer in SSAS with the `Product Line` attribute relationship highlighted for the `Model Name` attribute of the Product dimension. Also highlighted on the right is the `RelationshipType` property, which contains two selection choices, `Flexible` and `Rigid`.

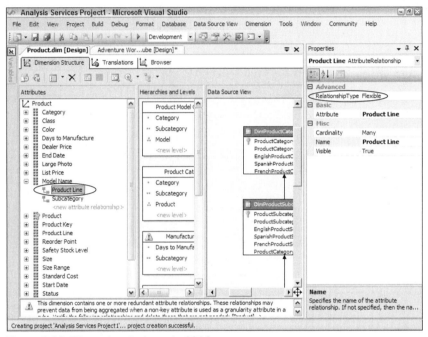

Figure 6-22: Dimension designer in SSAS

An attribute relationship associates one attribute with another for several reasons, one of them being aggregations. Choosing Rigid means that the relationships between the attributes never change over time. In other words, the value of one attribute in a member compared with the value of the related attribute doesn't change. In this example, if you have a Model Name member of StreamLine 2000 and a Product Line name of Road Bikes, and you define the relationship type as Rigid, then StreamLine 2000 should always reference Road Bikes (and will never get moved under another Product Line such as Mountain Bikes). This doesn't work the other way, since Road Bikes will have many Model Names underneath its hierarchy node.

When it comes to dimension ETL changes and the impact on SSAS, here are some things you need to consider:

❑ For Type 0 fixed attributes, all of the attributes can be marked as Rigid for the attribute relationship, because they will not change.

❑ Any dimension attribute that is processed as a Type 1 changing attribute in the dimension table must be marked as Flexible for all the attribute relationships it participates in, because the value can be changed or overwritten.

❑ Dimension attributes that are Type 2 historical can be marked as Rigid for attribute relationships that are associated to the key attribute.

❑ If you have any Type 2 historical attributes that have attribute relationships assigned to non-key attributes, then a Type 2 historical change may break the relationship when processing. Why? Attribute relationships are many-to-one or one-to-one when going from the attribute to the attribute relationship. A new Type 2 historical record may create a many-to-many relationship between values at the higher levels and, therefore, that attribute may need to stay as an attribute relationship only at the key attribute level.

❑ If you have a dimension that has inferred members, then you must mark every attribute relationship as Flexible, because each one can change when the inferred member is updated.

The exception to all of this is when you can perform a full process of your entire SSAS every time you need to process data. All the dimension attribute relationships can be defined as rigid if the dimension structures can be rebuilt. But rebuilding the dimension structures drops all related partition data. Therefore, the entire cube would need processing. For more on SSAS Attribute Relationships and the `RelationshipType` property, see the following MSDN links:

```
http://msdn2.microsoft.com/en-us/library/ms166553.aspx
http://msdn2.microsoft.com/en-us/library/ms176124.aspx
```

Summary

The built-in support for Analysis Services object processing handles some situations, but overall doesn't provide the flexibility needed to handle many enterprise BI processing requirements (such as transaction grouping or dynamic partition processing and creation). But SSIS does include the tools to create much more robust solutions to processing your SSAS objects. Specifically, by using a combination of the SSAS Execute DDL Task, the Script Task, and the Execute Process Task, you can then take advantage of dynamic XMLA, AMO, or the `ASCMD` executable, respectively.

Now that we have covered SSIS principles in loading data warehouse structures and processing cubes, the focus in Chapter 7 will shift to stabilizing your packages (through error handling, restartability, and transactions).

7

Package Reliability

What sets enterprise ETL solutions like SSIS apart from just writing your complete process in a TSQL script is how SSIS handles problems. This chapter walks you through several scenarios on how to trap an error that makes your system go bump in the night without having to receive that call or page. In SSIS, you can develop a package that can self-heal or, at worst, roll back to a predictable state where you can fix things in the morning. If you must get a 4 a.m. call, you will want to be able to fix the problem and re-execute the package without having to worry about your data being in an inconsistent state. This chapter walks you through a number of examples on how to stabilize and make your packages bulletproof.

Error and Event Handling

Event handling is, at its root, the main differentiating factor between SSIS and writing a 10-page TSQL script to transform your data. With event handlers, you can watch certain areas of the package or the complete package and react to errors. This section also shows you how to use event handlers in a few more advanced ways.

Types of Event Handlers

When you create an event handler, you must specify what type of event you want to trap. The main types of events to watch are going to be PreExecute, PostExecute, OnError, and OnWarning. The PreExecute event is executed any time a package, container, or task starts. If you were to have a package that had a sequence container with two tasks, you would see the PreExecute event executed four times in the packages execution: once for the package beginning, another time for the container starting, and once for each task. The PostExecute works much the same way, but is executed for every time a package, container, or task completes.

The OnWarning and OnError events are executed any time a warning or error is executed. In the same theoretical package mentioned earlier with a package, container, and two tasks, an OnError event handler would only be executed once if only a single task inside the container were to fail. You can also trap any type of informational event with the `OnInformation` event handler. This is generally going to be overkill, though, since the event is executed dozens of times (typically) for a small package and provides little value to someone looking at the log.

For auditing purposes, you may have the requirement to trap any time a variable is changed. You can do this by first creating an `OnVariableValueChanged` event handler. Then, you must set the `RaiseChangedEvent` property on each variable that you want to trap the event for to `True`. By default, this property is set to `False`. To change the property, select the variable, then go to the Properties window. This event handler comes in handy sometimes if your auditors require such detailed information.

Auditing Through Event Handlers

The most common use for event handlers is for auditing. Events can be scoped to the entire package, a container, or a granular and an individual task. Generally, you're going to scope the event handler to the entire package, but occasionally you may have a sensitive part of your package that needs special attention. Using event handlers for auditing gives you a lot of power to consolidate your logging into a single table for your entire SSIS enterprise environment. For example, you could have all 2,000 packages in your environment writing into a central log table, and you could then write reports on the table to detect hung tasks or errors.

First, you'll need to create a table to store your errors. The `AdventureWorks` databases will be a fine place to create this table for the purpose of this example, but ideally, if you consolidate your log for many packages, you'll want to centralize this table into an optimized table in its own database. The last thing you want is your packages being bottlenecked by auditing processes.

The following table is a good start on an auditing table (you can download all the scripts from this chapter from the book's web site at www.wrox.com). You'd ideally want this table as descriptive as possible to help an operations person diagnose a problem. This table may not have all the columns your operations DBAs need to diagnose an issue, but it's a great down payment.

```
CREATE TABLE [dbo].[SSISEnterpriseLog](
    [LogID] [int] IDENTITY(1,1) NOT NULL,
    [PackageName] [varchar](150) NULL,
    [EventType] [varchar](15) NULL,
    [ExecutionID] varchar(50) NULL,
    [PackageID] varchar(50) NULL,
    [SourceName] [varchar](150) NULL,
    [SourceID] varchar(50) NULL,
    [ErrorCode] [varchar](15) NULL,
    [ErrorDescription] [varchar](1000) NULL,
    [InteractiveMode] [bit] NULL,
    [MachineName] [varchar](50) NULL,
    [UserName] [varchar](50) NULL,
    [EventDateTime] [datetime] NOT NULL CONSTRAINT
[DF_SSISEnterpriseLog_EventDateTime]  DEFAULT (getdate()),
 CONSTRAINT [PK_SSISEnterpriseLog] PRIMARY KEY CLUSTERED
(
    [LogID] ASC
)WITH (PAD_INDEX  = OFF, IGNORE_DUP_KEY = OFF) ON [PRIMARY]
) ON [PRIMARY]
```

This table stores the events that occur any time you'd like to trap a problem, and the table will be inserted using an Execute SQL Task in the Event Handler tab. Let's create an event handler to simulate this example. After you've created the example SSISEnterpriseLog table in the AdventureWorks database, create a new SSIS package called EventHandler.dtsx. In the package, create a connection manager to the AdventureWorks database that holds the table you just created.

Next, go to the Event Handler tab and create a new OnError event handler that is scoped to your entire package. Do this by selecting OnError from the Event Handler drop-down box and EventHandler from the Executable drop-down box. Drag an Execute SQL Task onto the page and name it OnError. Open the task and connect it to the AdventureWorks connection manager. Go to the Expression page in the task and add a new expression by clicking the ellipse button. The expression should be on the SQLStatementSource and should read like the following code:

```
"INSERT INTO [dbo].[SSISEnterpriseLog]
           ([PackageName]
           ,[EventType]
           ,[ExecutionID]
           ,[PackageID]
           ,[SourceName]
           ,[SourceID]
           ,[ErrorCode]
           ,[ErrorDescription]
           ,[InteractiveMode]
           ,[MachineName]
           ,[UserName]
           )
     VALUES
           ('"+ @[System::PackageName] +"'
           ,'"+ @[System::TaskName] +"'
           ,'"+ @[System::ExecutionInstanceGUID] +"'
           ,'"+ @[System::PackageID] +"'
           ,'"+ @[System::SourceName] +"'
 ,'"+ @[System::SourceID] +"'
     ,"+ (DT_STR, 15 , 1252) @[System::ErrorCode] +"
       ,'"+ @[System::ErrorDescription] +"'
       ,'"+ (DT_WSTR, 6) @[System::InteractiveMode] + "'
 ,'"+ @[System::MachineName] + "'
 ,'"+ @[System::UserName] +"'  )"
```

The challenge of this statement is managing the double and single quotation marks. Luckily, you can download this complete package at www.wiley.com to avoid the trial and error of having to write it from scratch. This INSERT statement will insert a row into the auditing table any time an error occurs. You could also have used a parameterized query in the Execute SQL Task, but it would ultimately have been more complex to manage the ordinal question marks representing all the parameters. Usually, with more complex queries as shown here, it's easier to just create an expression to make the query dynamic.

The INSERT statement makes extensive use of system variables to determine what task has failed. The TaskName variable is used to read the task name of the event handler's Execute SQL Task. So, in this case, this would return the word OnError. This is going to be why you'll want to name your task based on what type of event handler it is. Then, the task will help you self-document the INSERT statement without having to go into each INSERT statement and configure it for the individual INSERT statement.

The `SourceName` variable stores what task, container, or package threw the error, and is mandatory information for any auditing table. The `ErrorCode` and `ErrorDescription` variables are only available for an `OnError` or `OnWarning` event, and would have to be removed from this expression in events such as the `OnPostExecute`. For event handlers other than the `OnError` and `OnWarning`, you would want your `INSERT` statement to read like this:

```
"INSERT INTO [dbo].[SSISEnterpriseLog]
          ([PackageName]
          ,[EventType]
          ,[ExecutionID]
          ,[PackageID]
          ,[SourceName]
          ,[SourceID]
          ,[ErrorCode]
          ,[ErrorDescription]
          ,[InteractiveMode]
          ,[MachineName]
          ,[UserName]
          )
      VALUES
          ('"+ @[System::PackageName] +"'
     ,'"+ @[System::TaskName] +"'
          ,'"+ @[System::ExecutionInstanceGUID] +"'
          ,'"+ @[System::PackageID] +"'
          ,'"+ @[System::SourceName] +"'
 ,'"+ @[System::SourceID] +"'
      ,NULL
      ,NULL
      ,'"+ (DT_WSTR, 6) @[System::InteractiveMode] + "'
 ,'"+ @[System::MachineName] + "'
 ,'"+ @[System::UserName] +"'  )"
```

The `InteractiveMode` system variable contains a Boolean value on whether the package was run interactively by a user. If it was run interactively, you'll also see the name of the user who ran the package in the `UserName` variable. Lastly, you can see what machine name ran the package in the `MachineName` variable.

The next step would be to copy the task over to the `PreExecute` and `PostExecute` event handlers for the package. You then must rename the Execute SQL Task to the type of event handler so the `INSERT` statement would use the value of `OnWarning`, `OnPostExecute`, or `OnPreExecute`. To test the solution, drag a few tasks over in the control flow and execute the package.

Areas to Grow This Solution

The solution that is described in the previous section is a great starter kit for your own auditing solution. In Chapter 8, you'll learn how to develop SSIS templates that can be used by everyone in your company. After you come up with an enterprise auditing solution as shown in this section, consider deploying it as a template to all of your developers so each one won't have to reinvent the wheel.

There are some areas where the solution may need to be improved to make it functional for your company. For example, you're currently constrained to 1,000 characters for the event description. If you want to fix that, you could just increase the table definition from a `varchar(1000)` to a larger field. A thousand characters is more than adequate to catch most (if not all) errors.

Another area that could be grown is where there is a lot of redundant data in the auditing table because of its denormalized form. To improve on this, you could create a schema in third normal form and perhaps use stored procedures from within the Execute SQL Task to insert into the table.

Disabling Event Handling

There is going to be overhead with doing event handling. In most cases, it won't be noticeable, since the event is only executed any time a task fails in the `OnError` event handlers. If you have the requirement to use the `OnInformation` event, you may execute the event handler hundreds of times, and the overall package performance may suffer. To test that theory, you could temporarily disable the event handlers for the entire package, or for certain portions of the package.

To disable a single event handler, you can go to the individual event handler and go to the Properties window. Then, change the `Disable` flag to `True`. This property disables that single event handler from ever executing.

You can also disable the entire event handling structure at a package, container, or task level. To do this, go to the control flow and to the package Properties. You can then set the `DisableEventHandlers` to `true`. This will only disable package event handlers, but the ones that are specified to execute on an individual task will still execute. If you have event handlers on an individual container or task, you would have to set the `DisableEventHandlers` property to `true` on each of those tasks or containers, too.

Integrating Snapshots into SSIS

Another excellent use of event handlers is for increasing your package's reliability. One way to do this is to integrate snapshots into your SSIS package. *Snapshots* are a SQL Server 2005 Enterprise Edition high-availability feature that takes a point-in-time, read-only image of your database. This image would include all tables, stored procedures, and data from the database. From a high-availability perspective, snapshots can act as a backup file, allowing you to quickly recover from a user error or data integrity issue. Because snapshots only hold the data that has changed since it was created, it will be an incredibly small file, and will be faster to create than a backup file.

Wouldn't it be great if you could create a snapshot image of your database prior to a package running, and then, if any problem occurred, roll back from the snapshot? With the help of event handlers and a little code, that's exactly what you can do. Snapshots don't get rid of the need for backups, but in specialized situations like this, it can really help out. Let's start by creating a new package for this example.

You will want the first step in this package to create the snapshot. You could, of course, place it in front of strategic areas instead of the first step, but for the purpose of this example, let's protect the entire package with a snapshot. Drag over an Execute SQL Task to create the snapshot and name the task Create Snapshot. Point the task to a connection manager that uses the `AdventureWorks` database on your test machine. When you create a snapshot, the syntax looks much like a `CREATE DATABASE` Data Definition Language (DDL) statement, with the exception of the last line, where you specify that it will be a snapshot of a given database. Configure the query in the task to run the following statement to create the snapshot (note your directory structure may vary from this one):

```
CREATE DATABASE AdventureWorks_PreETL_Snapshot ON
( NAME = AdventureWorks_Data, FILENAME =
'C:\Program Files\Microsoft SQL
Server\MSSQL.1\MSSQL\Data\AdventureWorks_data_PreETL_Snapshot.ss' )
AS SNAPSHOT OF AdventureWorks;
```

Next, create one more task in the control flow to simulate a failure. Create an additional Execute SQL Task and call it Generate Error. Connect the task to the AdventureWorks connection manager and create an intentionally bad TSQL statement like this:

```
SELECTTTTT BAD QUERY
```

It's important to note that the Execute SQL Task that creates the snapshot should always be the first task in the control flow, and that there should be some sort of precedence constraint between it and the first true task of your package. This can be seen in the example shown in Figure 7-1.

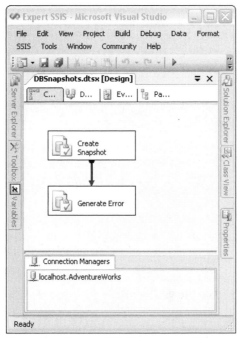

Figure 7-1: Execute SQL Task creating the snapshot appears first in the control flow

Before leaving the control flow, create a new variable called FailureFlag that is a Boolean data type with the default value of 0. Creating intentionally bad code is always the easy part of a solution, but now comes the challenging part of the solution. First, you must create an OnError event handler that is scoped to the entire package. Drag a single Script Task onto the event handler and name the task Set FailureFlag.

In the Script page of the Script Task, set the `ReadWriteVariables` option to `FailureFlag` (it is case-sensitive). Then click Design Script. In the code window, you want to add code to set the `FailureFlag` variable by using code such as the following:

```
Public Sub Main()
    Dts.Variables("FailureFlag").Value = True

    Dts.TaskResult = Dts.Results.Success
End Sub
```

Any time a failure occurs anywhere in the package, this script will set the `FailureFlag` variable to `true`, and this variable will come into play later in another event handler. The next step is to create a `PostExecute` event handler that's scoped to the entire package. After creating the event handler, drag a Script Task onto the design pane and rename the task **Stub**. This task will do absolutely nothing at all, other than to help you do conditional logic on the precedence constraint you are about to create.

You now need to create the logic that will restore the database from the snapshot in case of a failure. You'll create the conditional logic in a moment, but in the meantime, drag an Execute SQL Task over to the design pane to perform the restore. Drag the precedence constraint out of the Stub Script Task and onto the newly created Execute SQL Task. Name the Execute SQL Task Rollback DB and configure it to use the `AdventureWorks` connection manager. Lastly, use the following query to roll back the database from the snapshot:

```
use master
GO
RESTORE DATABASE AdventureWorks from
DATABASE_SNAPSHOT = 'AdventureWorks_PreETL_Snapshot';
GO
```

The assumption of this script is that there are no users in the database at the time of the restoration. If this assumption is incorrect, you must write code to disconnect all the active users prior to the `RESTORE` command. Luckily, something like that has already been written in many locations and a similar script can be downloaded at www.wrox.com (it is a stored procedure called `usp_killusers`).

With the database now restored, you can dispose of the snapshot that was created earlier. To do this, create another Execute SQL Task and name it **Drop Snapshot**. Again, connect it to the `AdventureWorks` connection manager and configure it to run the following script to drop the snapshot by using the `DROP DATABASE` command:

```
Use Master
go

DROP Database
AdventureWorks_PreETL_Snapshot
```

You're now ready to build the conditional logic to only execute the tasks if a failure had occurred. First, drag the precedence constraint from the Rollback DB Execute SQL Task to the Drop Snapshot Execute SQL Task that you just created. Also, drag over another precedence constraint between the Stub Script Task and the Drop Snapshot Execute SQL Task. You should now have two precedence constraints coming out of the Stub Script Task.

As it stands now, this series of tasks will execute every time a `PostExecute` event is triggered, which is every time any task, container, or package completes. You obviously can't have the database restoring for all of these events, so you want to only selectively have the database restore if the package is completing and there was a failure.

To do this, double-click the precedence constraint connecting the Stub Task to the Rollback DB Task to edit the constraint. Change the Evaluation operation option to Expression and Constraint. Then type the following expression into the Expression text box:

```
@FailureFlag == True && @SourceName == @PackageName
```

This expression evaluates whether the `FailureFlag` was set to `True` from some type of `OnError` event. It also ensures that the source that triggers the `PostExecute` event is the package's completion and not just a task. The two `&&` signs are a logical AND condition for the expression. Click OK to save this expression and note the FX box to the side of the precedence constraint.

You now need to build the opposite logic. If the package completes and no error occurs, you still need to gracefully drop the snapshot. Double-click on the precedence constraint connecting the Stub to the Drop Snapshot Task to edit the precedence constraint. Again, you will want to change the Evaluation operation option to Expression and Constraint, and type the following expression into the Expression text box:

```
@FailureFlag == False && @SourceName ==@PackageName
```

This code will only execute the `DROP SNAPSHOT` if the `OnError` event was never executed and the package has finished running. Before exiting the Precedence Constraint Editor, change the Multiple constraint option to Logical OR, as shown in Figure 7-2. This will allow either the Stub Task or the Rollback DB Task to conditionally execute the Drop Snapshot Task. If you did not do this, the cleanup step would never execute, since both tasks would have to execute (which is impossible with the expression logic you put in place).

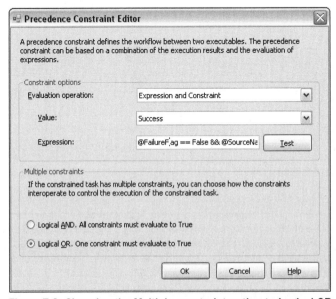

Figure 7-2: Changing the Multiple constraint option to Logical OR

Your final solution will look like Figure 7-3. If no problem occurs in the package, the Drop Snapshot Task will execute, cleaning up the earlier created snapshot. If a problem does occur, then both the Rollback DB and Drop Snapshot Tasks will execute sequentially. This solution can easily be built on to only watch certain tasks, or to disconnect the users prior to the rollback of the database. The assumption is made in this solution, though, that you have exclusive access to the target database. That may be a poor assumption and if so, you would want to use some of the other solutions mentioned later in this chapter (such as transactions). If you do have the luxury of being the only user making changes to the database (such as in a nightly ETL batch process), then the snapshot solution is an effective and quick way to ensure your data is in a consistent state if a problem occurs. If a problem does occur, you would simply fix the data quality, database space, or any other type of problem, and then rerun the package from the beginning. For more information on snapshots, refer to Books Online under the topic "Database Snapshots."

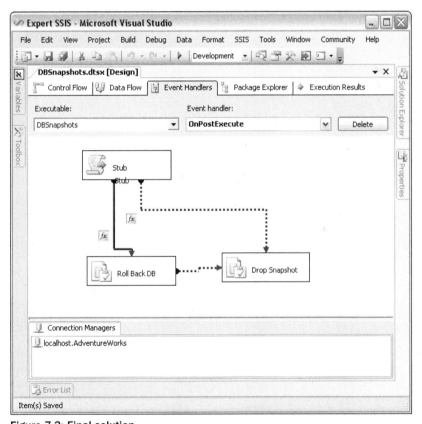

Figure 7-3: Final solution

Logging

SSIS has extensive logging built into its architecture to log into a variety of destinations, but typically you would log into a SQL Server table or a text file. If you were to log into a SQL Server table, you could have multiple packages all logging into the central table.

233

The standard table that SSIS will use for logging is called `sysdtslog90`. A big weakness of this logging provider for SQL Server is that you cannot log into a custom table, and some of the columns that would be real useful for ease of use aren't there. That's typically why you should use event handlers for logging. Regardless, logging using the logging providers is extremely easy to configure, and it does contain more information in some cases than can be obtained through an event handler like the pipeline events.

This section walks you through some common scenarios and shows you how to get over some of the obstacles with the logging providers. Let's start by creating a new package called `Logging.dtsx`. Drag over a single Script Task and name it **Write to Log**. Inside the script of the Script Task, add the following code inside the `Main` subroutine:

```
Public Sub Main()
    Dim emptyBytes(0) As Byte
    Dts.Log("Script error has occurred.", 10003, emptyBytes)
    Dts.TaskResult = Dts.Results.Success
End Sub
```

Close the Script Task to save the code. This code will write to whatever log provider you eventually select. This type of logic could be used to conditionally write data to your logging provider.

Your next step is to create the logging provider by selectingLogging from the SSIS menu. From the Providers and Logs tab, select the Text File provider and click Add. Select New Connection from the Configuration drop-down box and type **C:\ExpertSSIS\LogFile.txt** (make sure you have a `C:\ExpertSSIS` folder). Check the provider and all the containers in tasks on the left Containers tree, as shown in Figure 7-4.

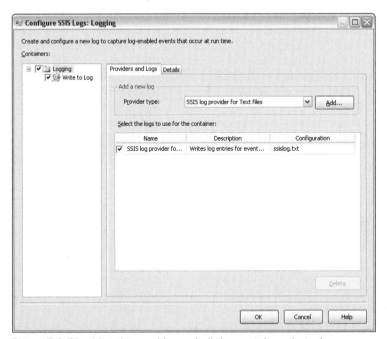

Figure 7-4: Checking the provider and all the containers in tasks on the left Containers tree

After you check the containers, go to the Details tab. Click the Write to Log Task in the left Containers box. Note that you have an additional event that you can check now. The `ScriptTaskLogEntry` traps any type of log event that the script designer has built into the task. Select that event and click OK to exit.

You're now ready to run the package. Execute the package and then view the `C:\ExpertSSIS\LogFile.txt` file in your favorite text editor. If everything executed successfully, you'll see an additional new event with the log entry the script created, as shown in this sample message:

```
User:ScriptTaskLogEntry,BRIANKNIGHT,BRIANKNIGHT\bknight,Write to Log,{8212956D-
A1FC-438C-9E64-D974190E3A7F},{3145FD4A-8959-4630-BB6F-C43FD0D0D41A},10/14/2006
1:07:37 AM,10/14/2006 1:07:37 AM,10003,0x00,Script error has occured.
```

For regulatory reasons, oftentimes you must monitor the data flow to determine how many rows are transformed from step to step in the data flow. The logging providers offer such a feature to help you meet that requirement. To experiment with the feature, drag over a Data Flow Task onto the control flow of the current package. Optionally, you can create a simple data flow to move data from a random table in the `AdventureWorks` database.

With the package now redesigned, go back to the Logging dialog box and to the Details tab. Notice now that the Data Flow Task is in the Logging tree on the left (shown in Figure 7-5). In the Details tab, click `OnPipelineRowsSent` and click OK. You're ready to execute the package again and look at the results.

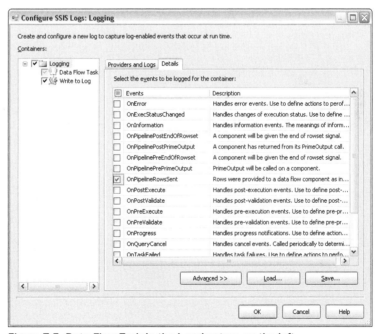

Figure 7-5: Data Flow Task in the Logging tree on the left

The `OnPipeline` events that you see here give you a view into the data flow pipeline. The main one you'll use is the `OnPipelineRowsSent`, which tells you how many rows go from step to step in the Data Flow Task. These events are not visible in the event handlers, and the most useful way to use them is to output the results into a table for parsing. Parsing of this output may be a little complex, since it outputs each step to a single row in your text file or table. The row count is shown in the Message column and is delimited by a colon, as shown in the following log file row:

```
OnPipelineRowsSent,BRIANKNIGHT,BRIANKNIGHT\bknight,Data Flow Task,{63B525E0-D4AB-
4878-BCC8-1A55918D5B50},{815870CF-51F3-4F19-B426-B637033A4752},11/8/2006 8:07:12
AM,11/8/2006 8:07:12 AM,0,0x,Rows were provided to a data flow component as input.
:  : 21 : OLE DB Source Output : 16 : FFD Employees File : 17 : Flat File
Destination Input : 290
```

What you see in this log snippet is that there is an OLE DB source that sends data to a Flat File Destination called FFD Employees File. The number you see before each name is the object's lineage ID, which may prove useful in a later discussion. The last number you see (290) is how many rows moved between both the source and destination. If you had transformations in the middle of the source and destinations, you'd see multiple rows in the log file.

On the Wiley web site (www.wiley.com), you can download ParsePipeline.sql to parse the row if it's in the standard sysdtslog90 table to something more usable. The function enables you to write a query like the following one to read data out of the message column into a report. This query is also available in the same script file as the function at the end.

```
SELECT      source, sourceid, executionid, dbo.ParsePipeline(message, 1) AS PathID,
dbo.ParsePipeline(message, 2) AS PathIDName,
                    dbo.ParsePipeline(message, 3) AS ComponentID,
dbo.ParsePipeline(message, 4) AS ComponentIDName, dbo.ParsePipeline(message, 5) AS
InputID,
                    dbo.ParsePipeline(message, 6) AS InputIDName, CONVERT(int,
dbo.ParsePipeline(message, 7)) AS RowsSent, starttime
FROM        dbo.sysdtslog90
WHERE       (event LIKE 'onpipelinerowssent%')
```

Creating a Unique Log File

Currently, in this example, the package log will always be called LogFile.txt. This is probably not going to be acceptable, since you may have 50 packages all running and writing to LogFile.txt. Instead, a common request for log files is to name the file based on the package name and timestamp the file. For example, a package named LoadDW.dtsx running on 1/24/2006 would be named LoadDW01242006.log.

Let's expand the previous example slightly to achieve this technical goal. To do this, you want to make the connection manager you created in the last example for the log file to be dynamic using expressions. Select the connection manager for the log file and create a new expression in the Properties window. Select the Connection String property, then click the ellipse button to enter the Expression Builder window. In the Expression box, type the following expression to fulfill your requirements. This code can also be downloaded at www.wiley.com.

```
"C:\\ExpertSSIS\\" +  @[System::PackageName] + "_" +
(DT_STR,4,1252)DATEPART( "yyyy" , @[System::StartTime]   ) + "_" +
RIGHT("0" + (DT_STR,4,1252)DATEPART( "mm" ,  @[System::StartTime] ), 2) + "_" +
RIGHT("0" + (DT_STR,4,1252)DATEPART( "dd" ,  @[System::StartTime] ), 2) + "_" +
RIGHT("0" + (DT_STR,4,1252)DATEPART( "hh" ,  @[System::StartTime] ), 2) +
RIGHT("0" + (DT_STR,4,1252)DATEPART( "mi" ,  @[System::StartTime] ), 2) +
RIGHT("0" + (DT_STR,4,1252)DATEPART( "ss" ,  @[System::StartTime] ), 2) +
".log"
```

This code will name the file based on the package name, and then append a timestamp at the end separated by underscores. The double backslashes are required in the path, since a single backslash is an escape character. The RIGHT function enables you to easily guarantee that you will always have two characters for the month and day, for example. Otherwise, months like January would be trimmed to only a single digit (1) instead of two digits (01). When you run the package again, you'll now see that the log file is timestamped.

Reporting on the Logging Providers

Ideally, you'll want to send all the package logs to a single database that is used for auditing of your entire environment. You can create a nice flexible data structure as shown in the previous section and log through event handlers, or you can log into the sysdtslog90 table for all the packages in your environment. If you do the latter option, you must create reports to slice the events by package and drill into the events.

Luckily, though, Microsoft has already created such a series of reports called the SQL Server Integration Services Report Pack. If you search the site for this (or go to www.microsoft.com/downloads/details.aspx?FamilyID=526e1fce-7ad5-4a54-b62c-13ffcd114a73&DisplayLang=en), you'll be able to download a series of reports to help you slice the newly created mountains of diagnostic data. If nothing else, it will carry you 90 percent to your goal of enterprise ETL reporting.

One such report is shown in Figure 7-6. In this report, you can see which packages are being logged, then you can drill into each execution instance of the package and see whether it succeeded or failed. Then, you can drill into the package and see how long each step took. Some SQL Server Reporting Services reports give you graphs of the execution times, and others show you the OnPipelineRowsSent data. The Reporting Services project includes a series of reports, documentation, and a backup of a database that's already populated. You'll be able to customize it from there.

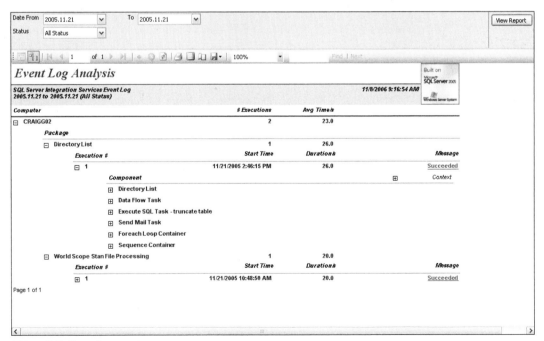

Figure 7-6: Sample report

Checkpoint Files

If you're a production DBA or have been a support person at one point, it's certain that you've had a middle-of-the-night call because of an ETL failure of some sort. You probably had to go into the server while you were groggy from lack of sleep, and try to make the necessary changes to get the package working again. For example, you may have had to clean up space on the server in order for the package to complete its load. Now comes the ultimate problem: Do you re-run the entire package or just a piece of the package, and if you only ran a piece, what piece?

If you choose the wrong answer to that question, you can accidentally reload data, causing duplication or not load data at all. It's a bad spot for a DBA to be in, and is highly contingent on experience with the package that failed. This experience is great until the DBA who has the experience goes on vacation or quits, and someone else has to come up to speed quickly.

Checkpoint files are a tool in your SSIS arsenal to mitigate this problem. Essentially, these files allow you to rerun a package from the point of failure, and they save the state of the package at failure. That state file, which is XML, will contain which container or task last successfully executed, as well as other state information (such as the variable values). When you fix the problem that caused the package to fail and re-run the package, it will start at the step that failed, and skip over the successful tasks.

There are a few points to bring out before trying an example. Checkpoint files can only be generated in the control flow. For example, checkpoint files cannot be used to capture the state of the data flow to restart on a given transformation. To do this, you'll need to use raw files. They can, however, capture the fact that they finished a data flow task and start the package after that step.

Let's now illustrate how to use checkpoints through an example. In this example, you will load three records into a table. If one statement fails, you want to be able to correct the issue and then start at the failed task. First, create a simple table to load with a single column by using the following syntax in SQL Server Management Studio while connected to the AdventureWorks database:

```
CREATE Table RestartabilityExample
(Column1 int)
```

Next, create a new package called Restartability.dtsx and drag three Execute SQL Tasks onto the control flow. Connect each of the three tasks sequentially using Success precedence constraints. Also, create a connection manager that points to the same AdventureWorks database in which you created the RestartabilityExample table. As a last preparatory step, create a string variable called strTestVariable that is scoped to the entire package and has a value of Test Value. This variable will only be used to demonstrate some data in your checkpoint XML file later.

You must now configure each of the Execute SQL Tasks. Name the first Execute SQL Task that executes in the package Purge Table and double-click it to configure it. Point the task to the AdventureWorks connection manager and type the following query into the SQLStatement property:

```
DELETE FROM
RestartabilityExample
```

This will purge the table prior to inserting into it, because it will be used in further examples in this chapter. Click OK to exit the task editor. The final configuration should look like Figure 7-7.

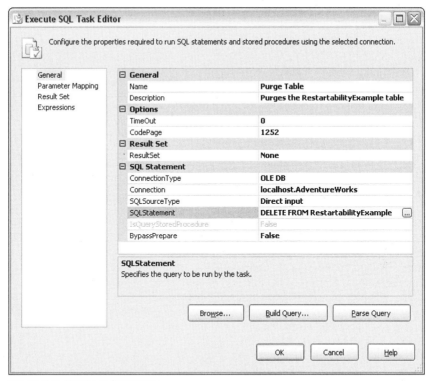

Figure 7-7: Final configuration

Rename the task that connects to the Purge Table Task, Insert Record 1, and open the task to configure it. This time, you want to insert a single row into the example table. Point the task to the AdventureWorks connection manager and then use the following query in the SQLStatement property:

```
INSERT INTO RestartabilityExample
    Values(1)
```

Lastly, rename the final task to Insert Record 2 and again point it to the AdventureWorks connection manager. This time, set the SQLStatement property to the following query:

```
INSERT INTO RestartabilityExample
    Values(2)
```

With the package now configured to run without checkpoints, run the package to confirm that all the components work properly. The successful creation and execution of the package should look like Figure 7-8. After executing the package, go to Management Studio and confirm that you have two records in the RestartabilityExample table.

**Figure 7-8: Successful creation
and execution of the package**

Let's now add the checkpoint logic into the package to detect a failure. This is a two-step process: Configure the package for checkpoints and then configure the tasks to trigger the checkpoint.

First, go to the Properties window for the package (make sure nothing is selected before going to the Properties window). In the top of the Properties window, change the CheckpointFileName to C:\ExpertSSIS\Checkpoint.xml. This property tells SSIS where to output the checkpoint file. The XML extension is optional, but most people decide to go with that format since it is an XML file. Next, change the CheckpointUsage property to IfExists and the SaveCheckpoints property to True. The IfExists property tells SSIS to use the checkpoint file if it exists. The checkpoint file will not be created until a failure occurs, and that's why you want to use the IfExists versus Always. The SaveCheckpoints property tells SSIS that if the package were to fail, then create the checkpoint file.

The next step is to configure each task that you want to participate in the checkpoint. Click each of the three tasks and go to the Properties window for each task. Then set the FailPackageOnFailure property to True for each task in the package (this is not to be confused with the FailParentOnFailure property). With this property set, the checkpoint file will be created if a failure occurs in any of the three tasks. Without this set, the checkpoint file will never be created, since a package failure event was never escalated. Execute the package again and note that the C:\ExpertSSIS\Checkpoint.xml file was never created. This is because the package successfully executed. In a moment, you'll be shown a way to trigger errors without having to alter the TSQL code, and we'll conclude this example by showing you the checkpoint file.

Dynamic Checkpoint File Name

In the example so far, you have hard-coded a checkpoint file name, which may be the same file being used by another package. C:\ExpertSSIS\Checkpoint.xml is a very generic name, and there's a very good chance of a collision. Instead of doing this, it is a best practice to name your checkpoint files based on the package name like RestartabilityCheckpoint.xml.

You can do this easily dynamically by going back to the Properties window for the package and then using the Expressions dialog box to create an expression for the file name that will automatically override the static file name you set earlier. The expression will need to set the CheckpointFileName property to the following expression code, and can be seen in Figure 7-9:

```
"C:\\ExpertSSIS\\Checkpoint" + @[System::PackageName] + ".xml"
```

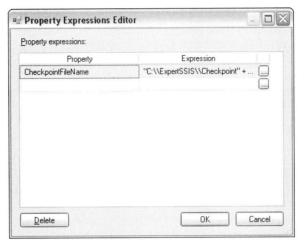

Figure 7-9: Creating an expression

Testing Your Error Logic

With the package now complete and the checkpoint file name now dynamic, let's intentionally cause an error. You can do this by using two mechanisms. One way is to change the TSQL statement in the second task to something like the following syntax. Since an A is an invalid character to pass to an integer field, the syntax will fail, causing a package failure.

```
INSERT INTO RestartabilityExample
     Values(A)
```

By taking that tactic, though, you may forget to set the syntax back to the way it was previously. A more elegant solution is to change a single property that simulates a failure. To do this, select the Insert Record 1 Task and go to the Properties window. Then, change the ForceExecutionResult property to Failure. This will cause the task to report a failure no matter if the task succeeds or fails. It's important to note that this mechanism to simulate errors does not trigger any event handlers. It is great for testing failure precedence constraints and to test your checkpoints.

Execute the package again and notice that the package now fails on the second task. This time, you'll also see that C:\ExpertSSIS\CheckpointRestartability.xml was created. When opening the file, you'll see it contains the information about what task last executed successfully and information about the variable you created earlier, too. An example of the checkpoint file can be seen here, but your data may vary:

```
<DTS:Checkpoint xmlns:DTS="www.microsoft.com/SqlServer/Dts" DTS:PackageID=
"{69774E8E-65E0-4C07-8C12-813FA5252747}">
<DTS:Variables DTS:ContID="{69774E8E-65E0-4C07-8C12-813FA5252747}">
 <DTS:Variable>
  <DTS:Property DTS:Name="Expression" />
  <DTS:Property DTS:Name="EvaluateAsExpression">0</DTS:Property>
  <DTS:Property DTS:Name="Namespace">User</DTS:Property>
  <DTS:Property DTS:Name="ReadOnly">0</DTS:Property>
  <DTS:Property DTS:Name="RaiseChangedEvent">0</DTS:Property>
```

```
  <DTS:VariableValue DTS:DataType="8">TestValue</DTS:VariableValue>
  <DTS:Property DTS:Name="ObjectName">strTestVariable</DTS:Property>
<DTS:Property DTS:Name="DTSID">{0EBB88DE-5910-46EC-BAB6-D1D2E75998EA}
</DTS:Property>
  <DTS:Property DTS:Name="Description" />
  <DTS:Property DTS:Name="CreationName" />
  </DTS:Variable>
  </DTS:Variables>
  <DTS:Container DTS:ContID="{61F576F2-D759-42A5-B6D0-19879E30E8E7}" DTS:Result="0"
DTS:PrecedenceMap="" />
  </DTS:Checkpoint>
```

With the file now created, fix the simulated problem by changing the `ForceExecutionResult` property on the second task to `None`. This will set the task to its natural state. Execute the package again and you'll see that the first task that successfully executed the first time is skipped over, as shown in Figure 7-10. When you go back to the `C:\ExpertSSIS` directory, you'll see that your checkpoint file is now gone, as your package successfully executed and the checkpoint file is no longer needed.

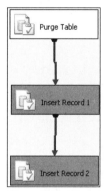

Figure 7-10: First task that successfully executed the first time being skipped over

Keep in mind that in checkpoint files, you must plan your packages very carefully. You must ensure that the package's purpose can still be served if you skip over the first few tasks. For example, if you have an on completion event that cleans up work from a failed previous task, but then jumps over that previous task on the next run, you may leave your data in an unknown state.

Transactions

Checkpoint files are only the first tool in your SSIS arsenal to help with restartability and those middle-of-the-night calls. A more important problem is managing data state. For example, if you were to run a package that loads three tables and the third table was to fail, ideally, you would want all three tables to roll back. Otherwise, you may not know what state your data is in to fix the problem and rerun the package.

Transactions in SSIS allow you to protect your data and envelope any data change that occurs in the package in that protection. Transactions can be either on the entire package, a container, or an individual task. They can be nested just like in TSQL. What is important to note about transactions is that only data-related tasks are protected. If your package were to archive a file, for example, that file would not be un-archived upon a package failure (unless you explicitly created some kind of compensating action to perform such duties).

Let's take the previous package you created and wrap the package in a transaction. First, let's disable the checkpoint from the previous example by changing the `CheckpointUsage` package property to Never and the `SaveCheckpoints` property to `False`. Next, delete all the records from the `RestartabilityExample` table.

With the example now reset back to its original state, you're ready to enable transactions on the package. In the Properties window for the package, change the `TransactionOption` at the bottom of the window to Required. By changing this from `Supported` to `Required`, you have created a transaction that envelopes the package. Any task or container that has this same property set to Supported will join the transaction. By default, each task is set to join the transaction with the `TransactionOption` of Supported set.

For you to enable this type of transaction, though, you need the Microsoft Distributed Transaction Coordinator (MSDTC) started on each server that you want to participate in the transaction. So, if you have a server that changes data on two servers and runs on a third server, you would need MSDTC running on all three servers. Transactions can then protect data nearly from any database like SQL Server, Oracle, and UDB, since you have externalized the transaction-handling to another service. The caveat with this, though, is the database must be running on a Windows machine, since MSDTC is a Microsoft service.

Before executing a package that has transactions enabled, you must ensure that MSDTC is started. You can start the MSDTC service in the Services applet, or you can type the following command from a command prompt: **NET START MSDTC**. If you did not have the service started, you would receive the following error when executing the package:

```
Error: The SSIS Runtime has failed to start the distributed transaction due to
error 0x8004D01B "The Transaction Manager is not available.". The DTC transaction
failed to start. This could occur because the MSDTC Service is not running.
```

After having the service started, let's break the package yet again. Select the last task, which is named Insert Record 2, and change the `ForceExecutionResult` package property to Failure. Execute the package again and you should see the results as shown in Figure 7-11. This time, if you were to view the records in the `AdventureWorks` database, you should see no new rows. This is because the purging of the table occurred, then the first record was inserted, and when the final task failed, both it and the first two operations (within the same transaction) were rolled back.

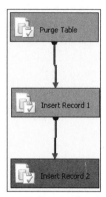

Figure 7-11: Result of package execution

Let's now try a slight variation of the package. This time, select the Insert Record 1 Task and change the `TransactionOption` property to `NotSupported`. Execute the package again, and note that this time it will hang on the second step because there is a table lock currently on the table from the first step (because the task is deleting all the records). If the Execute SQL Task were only reading data out of the table, then you could have changed the `IsolationLevel` property to `ReadUnCommitted` and the process could have continued, since it would be allowed to read dirty data. Since this operation is writing to the table that has a lock, you cannot fix this problem without addressing the first task.

To fix this problem, stop the execution and then select the first Package Properties window and change the `IsolationLevel` property to `ReadUncommitted`. Rerun the package again, and the package should still fail on the last task, as it did previously. You can now go to Management Studio and see that the first record is now in the table. This is because setting the `TransactionOption` property to `NotSupported` tells the task to not participate in the transaction. Run the package again and you'll see the 1 record in the table twice, showing that the `DELETE` statement rolled back as well.

As you can see, transactions are an incredible way to protect your data. They ensure that if a problem happens you do not end up in a state with half of your data not loaded and the other half in limbo, leaving you to figure out what to undo. You can also nest transactions inside of other transactions just like TSQL. To do this, you could use sequence containers, as shown in Figure 7-12.

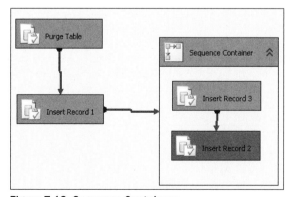

Figure 7-12: Sequence Containers

Figure 7-12 would represent the following set of TSQL statements:

```
BEGIN TRAN
DELETE FROM RestartabilityExample
INSERT INTO RestartabilityExample Values (1)
        BEGIN TRAN
                INSERT INTO RestartabilityExample Values (2)
                INSERT INTO RestartabilityExample Values ('a')
        COMMIT
COMMIT
```

This statement will fail on the last INSERT statement, since you're inserting a character value into an integer column. The results would be that the table would be completely put back to its original state because the inner transaction rolls back the outer transaction. The same thing would occur in the package shown in Figure 7-12. If the container and package had the TransactionOption set to Required and all other tasks were set to Supported, then all the data changes would be rolled back, even though the problem occurred inside the container.

However, if you were to change the container's TransactionOption to NotSupported, and the package's TransactionOption to Required, you would see that transaction never rolled back and the records are in the table. This is because any task inside the container would not participate in the transaction, since the tasks inherited the container's transaction or lack of transaction.

> **This is probably a good spot to give you a word of warning about using these restartability features in SSIS. When you use transactions and checkpoint files together, it's important to really plan well prior to development. There is a danger that when you use them in conjunction and don't plan the package well, the transaction may roll the data back, but then the checkpoint starts on the third or fourth step in the package, skipping over the data that needs to be reloaded. The only way to solve this problem is proper planning and some good whiteboard sessions.**

Raw Files

Raw files are proprietary sources and destinations in the SSIS data flow that are only accessible through SSIS. The files are binary files that contain all the metadata information for the file (data types and column names) in the file header. Because this file is proprietary to SSIS, it's the fastest source and destination. When you must stage data, it's an excellent choice because of its speed. It's also great from a reliability perspective, since you may use these sources and destinations in a complex data flow to capture images of your data at any point in time. For example, if you have a four-hour data flow process, you may want to stage the load at different points in time for recovery reasons; breaking up the extract and transformation from the load. This is common in a dimension load, where you may have to massage the data to be loaded into the dimension before applying the slowly changing dimension logic.

Another use for raw files is to break up a mainframe extract into more practical files. Oftentimes, you will receive files from a vendor or mainframe group as one unified file, when it should have been separated into individual files. For example, imagine the extract file shown in the following table.

RecordType	OrderID	Item	Quantity	Price
1	1			
1	2			
2	1	Soap	1	2.24
2	1	Firewood	2	4.5
1	3			
2	2	Pepper	1	1.58
2	3	Soap	1	2.24
2	3	Cola	5	4.5

In this file, you can see there is an order entry for RecordType 1 and the details are in RecordType 2. This file would generally be a fixed-width file or a ragged-right file, but to keep it simple, this file is delimited by commas. It can be downloaded from www.wiley.com (Chapter7SalesExtract.csv).

In this example, you would have two options for processing the file into the two tables based on the RecordType column. You could process the entire file in a single data flow, but keep in mind the file would generally be much more complex than the one shown here. You may also have a timing problem if the tables are related, as these are. The timing problem is going to exist with the foreign key relationship between the Order and OrderDetails tables. You want to ensure that you never process a detail record without the parent order record being processed first.

Your second processing option is to process the file as three data flows. The first Data Flow Task would break the file into multiple files and the other Data Flow Tasks would load each table.

For reliability, let's take the second option where you break the file into more usable files prior to load. You may also decide to add more logic into that data flow as well while you have the data in memory (such as data conversions and standardization). For this simple example, you'll want to have the Chapter7SalesExtract.csv file in your C:\ExpertSSIS folder and you'll want to create a new package called RawFile.dtsx.

Create two connection managers: one that points to the AdventureWorks database and another that points to your Chapter7SalesExtract.csv. The first row in the Chapter7SalesExtract.csv contains the column names, and the file is comma-delimited. Before exiting the connection manager for the Chapter7SalesExtract.csv file, go to the Advanced page and click Suggest Types. Accept the defaults and click OK. This option will read the file and perform its best guess on what the data types should be for the file.

With all the initial steps now done, drag over a Data Flow Task and name it **Break Up File**. In the data flow, drag over the Flat File source and point the source to the Chapter7SalesExtract.csv connection manager. Name the extract file **Initial Extract**.

Next, drag over a Conditional Split and connect the Initial Extract source to the Conditional Split. Name the transform **Read Record Type**. As you already know, the Conditional Split is going to take data from a single input and break it up conditionally into multiple outputs much like a CASE statement in TSQL would do. The first case you will need to create should be called Order and the expression should be set to RecordType == 1. The second should be called Order Detail and the expression should be set to RecordType == 2. The Default output name option should just be called Unhandled. Your final configuration should resemble Figure 7-13.

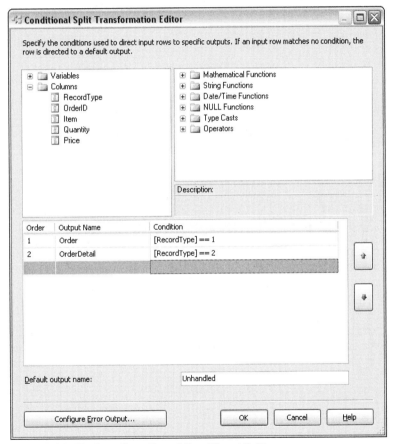

Figure 7-13: Final configuration of Conditional Split

Finally, drag over two Raw File destinations. Rename one of the destinations to Order Extract and the other to Order Details Extract. Connect one output from the Conditional Split to the Order Extract destination and the other to Order Details Extract. Each time you drag the green arrow from the Conditional Split down to the destination, you will be prompted to define which output you want to send to the destination, as shown in Figure 7-14. Choose the output that corresponds with the destination that you are sending the data. The unhandled output won't have anywhere to send the data to at this time, but in reality, you may send this data to an error queue.

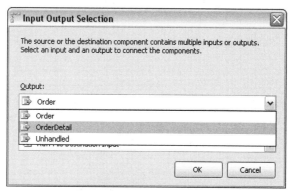

Figure 7-14: Prompt to define which output you want
to send to the destination

Raw files are a little unusual to configure, since they break a few of the standard rules for SSIS. For example, they don't use connection managers. Inside the Order Extract destination, change the `WriteOption` property to Create Always. Change the `FileName` property to `C:\ExpertSSIS\OrderData.raw`, as shown in Figure 7-15. Even though you can't use connection managers from within this destination, you could optionally set the destination to a variable that is dynamically set somewhere else. Next, go to the Input Columns tab and check only the `OrderID` column to send to the file.

Figure 7-15: Changing the FileName property

For the Order Details Extract raw file destination, change the `FileName` property to `C:\ExpertSSIS\OrderDetailsData.raw` and the `WriteOption` to Create Always. The in the Input Columns tab, check every column except the `RecordType` column. Exit the editor and execute the package. The package execution should look like Figure 7-16 with three records being written to the `Orders` file and five being written to the `Order Details` file.

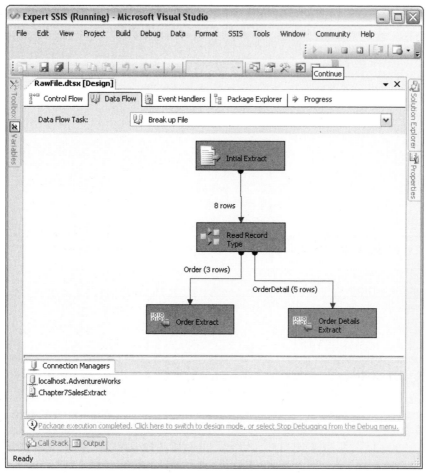

Figure 7-16: Package execution with files written to Orders and Order Details files

The hard work of the package is now complete. You can download the rest of the package at
www.wiley.com to see the complete example. The script to create the target tables is called
Chapter7ExampleOrderTables.sql. There are two more Data Flow Tasks to add to complete the
example. One Data Flow Task would load the parent table (ExampleOrder) and the other would load
the child table (ExampleOrderDetails); both Data Flows would load their respective tables using the
newly created raw files as sources.

Note that for the ExampleOrderDetails table, you will need to add a Lookup transform, as shown in
Figure 7-17, to look up the primary key from the Orders table to populate the child table. This OrderSK
column is an identity column that represents a unique order.

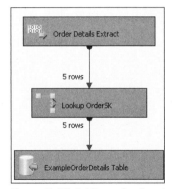

Figure 7-17: Adding a Lookup transform

As you can see, raw files provide a fast way to provide reliability in your data flow. In this example's case, raw files helped to separate the extract, transform, and load steps into distinct steps in the package.

Proactive WMI Integration

SSIS has extensive hooks into Windows Management Instrumentation (WMI). WMI is an object that allows you to interface with Windows easily to add reliability to your package. For example, prior to attempting a large move of a file from one server to another by using the File System Task, you could use the WMI integration to check to ensure there's enough space on the target server. If there's not enough space, you could then just send an email to the administrator and gracefully exit.

This integration is achieved through the WMI Data Reader Task and the WMI Event Watcher Task. Each task uses the Windows Query Language (WQL) to look into the Windows operating system and determine things like the amount of disk space, the services that are running, if there are any errors in the event log, and if a file exists. The sky is really the limit. If you can click it in Windows, you can achieve the function through WQL. An example WQL query looks like the following one, which retrieves all the space information about the hard drives:

```
Select * from Win32_LogicalDisk
```

You can use tools like Scriptomatic to help you write WQL queries, or you can go to the following URL to find a list of samples that you can tweak. At the same URL, you can find Scriptomatic:

```
www.microsoft.com/technet/scriptcenter/scripts/storage/default.mspx.
```

There are two tasks that help you interface with the WMI objects. The WMI Data Reader Task will run a WQL query and then return the results to a variable or file. For example, you can run this task to determine how much RAM is available before running a large ETL process. The WMI Event Watcher Task watches and waits for a given WMI event to occur before running the next task. For example, you can use the WMI Event Watcher Task to look for a file to be written into a directory before running the ETL.

Building a File Watcher Task

Now that you know about the WMI tasks, let's try a real-world common problem. In this example, you want to create a process to constantly watch a directory awaiting for any file to arrive. You'll do this through the WMI Event Watcher Task. It's important to note that before you create this example, you would never want to create a process like this to endlessly loop. You'd instead want to have some sort of timeout so the package has deterministic start and stop times.

Let's start by creating a new package called `FileWatcher.dtsx` and create a directory under `C:\ExpertSSIS` called `temp` (`C:\ExpertSSIS\temp`). Start the package by dragging over a WMI Event Watcher Task and name the task **Watch for File**. Open the task to configure it. In the WMI Options tab, select <New Connection...> for the `WMIConnection` property. This opens the WMI Connection Manager Editor. Name the connection `Localhost` and then select the Use Windows Authentication check box, as shown in Figure 7-18.

Figure 7-18: Naming the connection in the WMI Connection Manager Editor

Click Test to confirm the connection is valid and click OK to go back to the task editor. In the WMI Options tab, copy the following query into the `WqlQuerySource` property. You can download this query from the Wiley web site (`Chapter7WMIFileWatcher.sql`):

```
SELECT * FROM __InstanceCreationEvent WITHIN 10 WHERE TargetInstance ISA
"CIM_DirectoryContainsFile" and TargetInstance.GroupComponent=
"Win32_Directory.Name=\"c:\\\\ExpertSSIS\\\\temp\""
```

This query looks in the `C:\ExpertSSIS\Temp` directory for any file to be created. Change the `Timeout` property to 60 (seconds). This causes the event to wait for 60 seconds prior to causing a failure. The final screen will look like Figure 7-19.

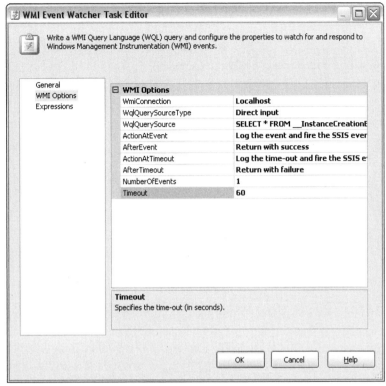

Figure 7-19: Final screen

Back in the control flow, drag over a Script Task and name it **Stub Code**. Connect the precedence constraint from the WMI Event Watcher Task to the Stub Code. Execute the package and then create or copy any file into the `C:\ExpertSSIS\temp` directory. You will have to do this within 60 seconds of the package execution in order to see the package succeed, as shown in Figure 7-20. When you do this, within 10 seconds the Watch for File Task will succeed and the next task will execute.

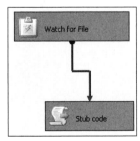

Figure 7-20: Seeing the package succeed

Of course, the Stub Code Task does nothing at all, but in reality, would be a data flow or a container of tasks to transform the newly arrived file. This example is a common problem that every SSIS developer must, at some point, solve, where a mainframe or partner may be sending you a file through FTP and you want to kick off the process after that. If you want to simplify this process, you can also download a free task for watching for files from www.sqlis.com.

Summary

In this chapter, you've learned how to make your packages more reliable. This is primarily done through event handlers and by the two restartability features: transactions and checkpoint files. Event handlers trap events like errors and warnings, and execute a control flow for each event. Checkpoint files enable you to restart a package at the point of failure, and scoped transactions selectively roll back any data changes.

With your package now ready for the enterprise, Chapter 8 discusses how to deploy your packages and how to handle the various software environments like Development QA and Production.

8

Deployment

Most enterprise environments rely on consistent and reproducible patterns in development to keep cost down and deployments predictable. Whether your environment is an enterprise-sized company or a smaller company, you want minimal work in order to move your solution through development, quality control, and production. This chapter shows a number of options to help you with development of your SSIS solution, and shows how to lower your total cost of development by creating simple, easy migrations from environment to environment.

Working with a Team in SSIS

As you can imagine, in most companies, there isn't just a single person developing SSIS packages for a single project. Generally, for most medium and large companies, there would be a few people developing the project's ETL, and they would need to collaborate on the solution. Because of this, source control becomes mandatory for keeping one developer from coding on a package that another developer is already working on. Another tactic is to break large packages into smaller, more modular packages to allow for multiple components to be worked on at the same time. Additionally, package templates can create consistency between the developers.

Source Control Integration

A key ingredient to a stable development environment is going to be source control. *Source control* ensures that only a single developer can work on a package at any given point in time, and, if a problem occurs, you can roll back code to a previous version. The great thing about the SSIS development environment in BIDS is that it can take advantage of the Visual Studio 2005 source-control integration. One of the most popular source control systems is Visual Source Safe (VSS). In this section, you'll see how easy it is to integrate your SSIS project into Source Safe 2005. You can also use Visual Studio Team Systems, a concept that is covered in the book Professional SQL Server 2005 Integration Services (Wiley Publications, 2006).

First, however, a word of caution about source control. As with any proper development process, as you add control, you sometimes lose flexibility. The advantage of source control systems is knowing who made changes and when, but the disadvantage is you lose a little of the "cowboy development" that you may be used to (where you can make whatever changes you want). However, the benefits of source control far outweigh the negatives.

With Visual Studio, you can either create a fresh project that integrates into VSS from the onset of the project's creation, or you can add an existing project into VSS. If you have VSS installed, the integration options automatically show up in BIDS. The VSS architecture will allow you to store your project locally on your machine, or on a central server for all the developers to check code in and out of. It is most certainly recommended that you install the VSS repository on a central server that is regularly backed up.

Adding a New Project

Assuming that you already have VSS installed, let's create a new project that will be checked into the repository. Open BIDS and create a new SSIS project called TestVSSProject. Ensure that the Add to Source Control option is checked and click OK. The Add SourceSafe Database Wizard will then open. On the first screen, choose the Create a New Database option and click Next. On this first screen, you could also add the project to an existing VSS database. In the Location tab, find a good location to place the files. However, if your VSS repository is installed locally, type **C:\ExpertSSIS\VSS**. In the next screen, type **ExpertSSIS** for the Connection Name option.

The next screen is the Team Version Control Model, shown in Figure 8-1. This screen is where you choose whether you want the file to be locked when your developers are modifying it, or whether you want for them to operate off of a local copy and then merge the packages back in. In SSIS package development, even though it's less functional, it is recommended to select the Lock-Modify-Unlock Model option. SSIS packages are not the type of program that can be easily merged, and it can result in errors if you do this inappropriately.

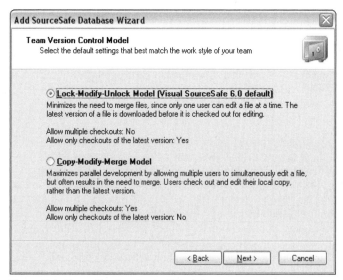

Figure 8-1: Team Version Control Model

After the confirmation screen, click Finish. The VSS database will then be created behind the scenes, and you'll be prompted for your Windows credentials to log in to the database. After you log in, you'll see the Add to SourceSafe dialog box shown in Figure 8-2. Click OK to add it to the root.

Figure 8-2: Add to SourceSafe dialog box

The solution, project, and default `package.dtsx` file will now be added into VSS under a folder called `TestVSSProject.root`, and potentially a directory under that. In the Solution Explorer, you will see a new icon to the left of each package, project, and solution (shown in Figure 8-3). This icon represents the state of the file. A check mark means the file is checked out, and no one can access it if you selected exclusive mode earlier in the project's creation. A plus sign represents a new file, and a lock means that the file is checked in and no one is accessing the file for write access.

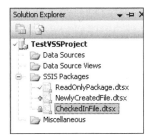

Figure 8-3: New icon to the left of each package,
project, and solution in Solution Explorer

You can right-click any file to see a menu structure that now includes source control integration. If you are just starting your day, it is wise to right-click the project or solution and select Get Latest Version. This will ensure that the local copy on your machine is up-to-date with VSS. If a file isn't up-to-date, you'll be prompted to replace your local copy. Only get the latest version of files if you have already checked in your files. Otherwise, you can overwrite your files inadvertently.

As you make changes to the packages, the files will check out automatically and no one else can access them. When you're finished with your changes at the end of each day, right-click the package and select Check In. This will open the Check In dialog box shown in Figure 8-4, where you can add comments about what you're checking in. This will show up later in reports, or when other developers are trying to figure out what changes you made in a build.

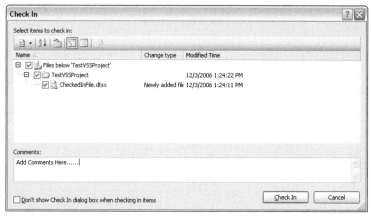

Figure 8-4: Check In dialog box

One of the most useful screens you can use is the Pending Checkins window shown in Figure 8-5. You can access the window under the View menu. The screen enables you to see everything that you have not checked in. You can also quickly add comments to each file here. If you check each file and then click the Check In button, everything will be checked in for you.

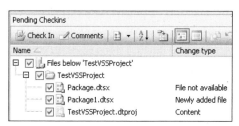

Figure 8-5: Pending Checkins window

It's important to note that when you create a new package or rename a package, your project is automatically checked out behind the scenes, and no one else can create a new package or rename a package until you check in the project. The same applies when you create a new project under the solution. Because of this, ensure that you only have the project checked out for a very limited period of time.

After you've created multiple versions of a file, you can right-click the file and select View History. This opens the History dialog box, which enables you to select which release you'd like to retrieve by clicking the Get button. You can click Diff to see the difference between two releases. This is not as useful in SSIS, though, because VSS will detect changes between the back-end XML files, which are not very readable.

VSS is a powerful way to ensure that one developer doesn't step on another developer's code. It also helps you properly document builds and roll back from a mistake. You can also add an existing project to VSS by going to File ➪ Source Control and following the same prompts that you followed to add a new project.

As you open a file and make a slight change, BIDS will automatically check out the package and lock others from editing the package. Some find this quite annoying, as they may only want to have made a quick change locally uncoupled from VSS. One tactic to fix this is to go to Tools ➪ Options. Then, under Source Control ➪ Environment (shown in Figure 8-6), you can set the On Edit option to Do Nothing, which will not automatically check out the package any time you happen to make a small change. The risk with doing this, however, is that you may make several small or large changes and forget to check them in. So, changing this option requires that you have discipline to check the packages in and notify the other developers manually.

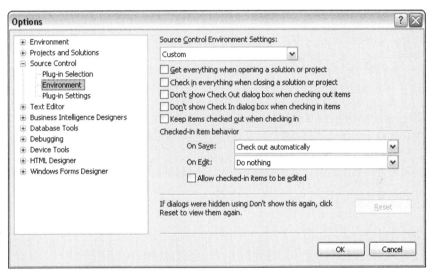

Figure 8-6: Environment Options screen

Reusable Packages

Some developers are familiar with the concept of object-oriented programming (OOP). In OOP, you break up large pieces of a program into its smallest unit of work. So, instead of having one big class file that performed every function in a program, you would, for example, have a class that handled data access. Then, you could refer to this object from any other program, rather than having to re-create the logic over and over again.

In SSIS, you use the concept of parent-and-children packages to perform a similar function, although it's not quite as elegant as OOP. The concept of parent-and-children packages is where you would break up a large SSIS package into smaller packages based on units of work, and then have a parent package tie the children packages together. How large the unit of work in the child package should be is based on a manageability compromise. Oftentimes, SSIS developers will create a package for each table they want to load; at other times they will create a package per subject area. A favorite way to componentize the package is to have one set of packages for the extract and transformation of the data, and another for the final load of data into the final destination. This way, you can stage your data throughout the day without affecting production. Then, when your production window allows, run the load package to move the data into the production database.

As discussed in the previous section, modularization also helps with development and maintenance. For example, if the entire solution were encapsulated in one single package, then only one developer could work on it at a time for fear of overwriting another developer's concurrent changes. On the other hand, if the solution was broken into more modular packages, then multiple developers could work on different packages at the same time, thus improving productivity and isolating regressions.

When maintaining packages or fixing bugs, a modular approach will lend itself toward being able to replace just the problematic areas, as opposed to the whole solution. If you compare this approach to compiled programming languages; this is similar to fixing just a specific library component, rather than replacing the whole program every time you fix a bug.

The reason why some people break packages up by a subject area or by an individual table load is so they can run the table load individually in production. Keep in mind that after you deploy a non-modular package to production, you will not be able to run pieces of the package unless you build the package to be dynamic this way, or re-open them in BIDS from your development machine. If you were to break the package up by table, then you could load each table by itself if one piece of the package were to fail. Of course, checkpoints, discussed in Chapter 7, could also help with this.

In the parent package, you can execute the package by using the Execute Package Task and try to run as much as you can in parallel. The children packages can then read the variables from the parent packages by using the configuration feature of SSIS. This feature is discussed later in this chapter. A typical solution would actually have multiple levels of packages calling a sub-package, in a hierarchy several levels deep.

Creating a Package Template

When you go through the trouble of developing the perfect shell or blueprint of a package to use repeatedly, you don't want to have to do it again. Templates in SSIS can help you prevent having to do repetitive boilerplate work inside the package (such as setting up your configuration, event handlers, logging, or annotation). They also enforce the same best practices across your entire development team, and strengthen time-to-market and cross-training. As developers move from project to project, they'll be able to read another developer's package.

To create a template, you must create the package that you want to use as a template, then copy the package to the following directory:

```
%ProgramFiles%\Microsoft Visual Studio
8\Common7\IDE\PrivateAssemblies\ProjectItems\DataTransformationProject\DataTransfor
mationItems
```

The %ProgramFiles% directory is an environment variable that redirects you to the proper drive for your Program Files folder (and would typically resolve to c:\Program Files).

When the file is copied into each developer's template folder, they can use the template by right-clicking the project and selecting Add ➪ New Item. Then, they select the file name for the template. A new package will be created that is an exact duplicate of the one created earlier.

The problem with this newly created package being exactly like the original package is that the new package has the same ID as its parent. This same predicament occurs when you copy and paste a package to clone a package in Solution Explorer. This is not really an issue until your packages are moved to production. At that point, you'll have multiple packages with the same PackageID potentially logging in to the same database. If a problem occurs, you won't be able to trace which package is having the issue, since the PackageID is how you map back to the package's name.

The problem can easily be fixed by generating a new PackageID in BIDS. You can do this by going to the Properties Window for the package and selecting <Generate New ID> for the ID property. This can also be done with the DtUtil.exe utility by using the -I switch. This particular command line utility is discussed in more detail in Chapter 9.

Package Configuration

Now that you have your set of packages complete, the challenge is trying to migrate them to your testing environment or to production without having to manually configure it for that environment. For example, your production server may not have the same directory to load extract files from, or the same user name to use to connect to the database. Configuration files help you make the migrations seamless and the configuration automated to reduce your risk of errors. In this section and the next, you'll see two different methods for configuration. One is to create a configuration repository and the other is to create your own repository, which mimics configuration files, but gives you more flexibility.

SSIS Package Configurations

The SSIS Package Configuration option enables you to write any SSIS property for the package, connection, container, variable, or any task into an XML file or a table, for example, and then read the setting at runtime. You could deploy the configuration file to multiple servers and point the setting inside the file to a new SQL Server database on the second server, and when the package runs, it will shift its connection to the new database automatically. Configuration files will also come in handy later when you deploy the packages to production using the deployment utility. Because they're just XML files, you can compare them with your favorite comparison tool such as VSS to determine what settings are different between the environments.

Let's do a quick example to show you the strengths and weaknesses of package configurations. This example creates a simple Script Task that will pop up a message with the configuration value instead of its normal, hard-coded value. Then you'll create multiple configuration files and see which configuration file wins.

First, create a new package called `ConfigFiles.dtsx`. Drag a new Script Task onto the Control Flow tab in the newly created package and name the task **Popup Value**. Next, create a new string variable called **strMessage** that is scoped to the package and not the Script Task. Seed a default value of Hard Coded Value for the string variable. Double-click the Script Task to configure it, and in the Script page, type **strMessage** for the `ReadOnlyVariables` property. Click Design Script to add your code to the task. The code you're going to add will pop up the value from the `strMessage` variable by using the following code:

```
Public Sub Main()
    '
    ' Add your code here
    '
    MsgBox(Dts.Variables("strMessage").Value)

        Dts.TaskResult = Dts.Results.Success
End Sub
```

If you execute the package at this point, you should see the pop-up dialog box that states, "Hard Coded Value." If you see that value, you're now ready to set this variable from a configuration file instead. Select Package Configurations from the SSIS menu, or right-click it in the control flow. This opens the Package Configurations Organizer where you will create and arrange the priority of your package configurations. Click Enable Package Configurations to enable this feature.

To add your first package configuration, click Add. This will take you to the Package Configuration Wizard. You can set your package configuration to use an XML file, SQL Server table, environment variable, or registry setting, or to read a variable from a parent package. Most people choose to use XML files or a SQL Server table. In this example, though, use an XML file and type **c:\expertssis\configuration.xml** for the Configuration File name property. The default extension for the configuration XML files is `.dtsConfig`, but use an XML extension so that it is easily registered to most XML editors.

You can even make the path and file name of the XML file dynamic by reading it from an environment variable. Otherwise, the file must be in the `C:\ExpertSSIS` folder on each server that you want to deploy the package to, which may not be allowed in your production environment. You can also change this later during deployment, but that will be discussed in a moment in the section, "Deployment Utility."

Click Next to go to the Properties to Export screen in the wizard. If the `c:\expertssis\configuration.xml` file had already existed on your server, you would be prompted as to whether you want to reuse the existing file or overwrite the file (shown in Figure 8-7). If you had chosen to reuse an existing file, the next screen would be the final summary screen. This option is fantastic if you want to have all of your packages in your project reuse the same configuration file.

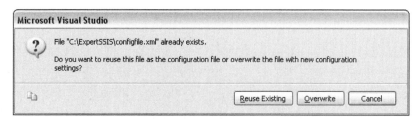

Figure 8-7: Prompt as to whether you want to reuse the existing file or overwrite the file

Back in the Properties to Export screen, you can check any property that you want to have read and populated from the configuration file. In this case, drill down to Variables ➪ strMessage ➪ Properties and finally check the Value option (as shown in Figure 8-8). Click Next to proceed to the next screen.

Figure 8-8: Checking the Value option

You are then taken to the summary screen where you should name the configuration **Variable File**. Click Finish, which takes you back to the Package Configuration Organizer. Click Close to exit the organizer and execute the package. You'll notice that the pop-up dialog box should still have the same old message. Note that the configuration file was created after you closed the wizard.

Open the configuration.xml file in your favorite XML editor or Notepad and replace the old variable value of Hard Coded Value with a new value of Config File Changed Value, as shown in the following code. The other pieces of the configuration file contain lots of metadata about who created the configuration file and from what package.

```xml
<?xml version="1.0" ?>
- <DTSConfiguration>
- <DTSConfigurationHeading>
  <DTSConfigurationFileInfo GeneratedBy="BRIANKNIGHT\bknight"
GeneratedFromPackageName="ConfigFiles" GeneratedFromPackageID="{437BD1AA-6A94-4CCB-
89B8-781BADB81686}" GeneratedDate="12/10/2006 7:24:25 PM" />
  </DTSConfigurationHeading>
- <Configuration ConfiguredType="Property"
Path="\Package.Variables[User::strMessage].Properties[Value]" ValueType="String">
  <ConfiguredValue>Config File Changed value</ConfiguredValue>
  </Configuration>
  </DTSConfiguration>
```

When you execute the package again, notice that this time the message has changed. You can also create multiple configuration files. For example, you may want a configuration file that contains your corporate logging database for all of your packages to use, and then another configuration file for the individual package. As you add more package configurations, they stack onto each other in the Configuration Organizer screen. At runtime, if there is a conflict between two configurations, the lowest configuration displayed in the Package Configurations Organizer will win.

To demonstrate this, create one additional configuration. This time, when asked for the configuration type, select SQL Server. For the Connection property, select New and point the connection to the `AdventureWorks` database, which will create a connection manager. Lastly, click New for the Configuration Table property. The table can be called whatever you'd like, as long as you have the four core fields. Name the table `ctrlConfigurations`, as shown in the following script:

```
CREATE TABLE [dbo].[ctrlConfigurations]
(
      ConfigurationFilter NVARCHAR(255) NOT NULL,
      ConfiguredValue NVARCHAR(255) NULL,
      PackagePath NVARCHAR(255) NOT NULL,
      ConfiguredValueType NVARCHAR(20) NOT NULL
)
```

Type **Development** for the Configuration filter. When the package reads from the `ctrlConfigurations` table, it will read all the properties where the `ConfigurationFilter` column is equal to Development, as shown in Figure 8-9. Typically, you'd want to have this filter set to either the package name or group of packages with which you want to share the same configuration settings.

Figure 8-9: Setting the Development configuration filter

Select the same `strMessage` variable value as in the previous configuration file. Finally, go to the next screen and name this configuration **SQL Server Config**. You should now have two package configurations, as shown in Figure 8-10. Set the variable's value by going to the `ctrlConfigurations` table in the `AdventureWorks` database and setting the `ConfiguredValue` column to SQL Server Config Value. When you execute the package, notice that now the value that pops up is SQL Server Config Value. This is because there were two configuration packages that set the same variable, but the one at the bottom will set the value last (see Figure 8-10).

Figure 8-10: Two package configurations

Package configurations make it easy to migrate a package from environment to environment. For the most part, it's going to be easier to store your configurations in the SQL Server, since you can write some sort of front end to modify the settings, and you can create reports to view the settings. The main problem with package configurations is that data is not encrypted, so you should not store anything that should be secure inside package configurations (such as passwords). It is important to migrate your configuration files with the package.

There are a few methodologies you can employ when you use configuration files. One is to group all the like configuration properties together into files, or with filters, if you choose to store the settings in a table. The other (which many developers prefer) is to store each property in its own file, or with its own filter. If you choose the latter option, you'll incur higher maintenance in creating your package, since you may have to create dozens of files. However, it does allow you to cherry-pick which settings you'd like and reuse the settings repeatedly.

Configuration Repository

As mentioned, the preferred method is to use tables to store the bulk of your configurations. You may have to use, in reality, a mix of XML files and tables, but that will be addressed in a moment. The major weakness with storing data in package configurations is that the data is unencrypted, which is mandatory in some cases. The schema is also very rigid and may not fit your needs.

This is why you may sometimes find it useful to create your own configuration repository and build a user interface around it. Let's start with a more flexible schema. In the schema shown in Figure 8-11, the model you would normally use has been simplified to three basic tables. The goal here is to build an example that you can add to and customize to your environment. This complete example can be downloaded at www.wiley.com.

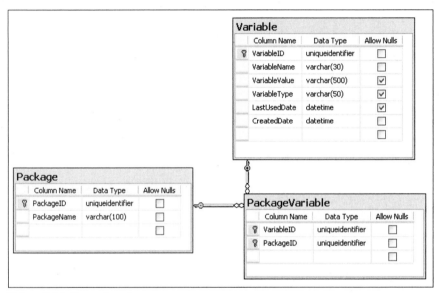

Figure 8-11: Example schema

In this configuration repository, the goal is to build a repository of variables that could be used by multiple packages. To accomplish this, a `Variable` table has been created to hold each variable, its value, and type. Also stored in this table is when the variable was last used, so you can later clean up older variables that are no longer active. The `Package` table holds which packages can eventually access the variables, and the packages are granted access to the variable in the `PackageVariable` table.

You may be wondering why `uniqueidentifier` columns (which store GUIDs) have been used. Even though they will be slightly slower in performance in comparison to an identity column, they will allow you flexibility when you want to migrate from environment to environment.

For example, when you migrate these variables from development to production, you don't have to worry about reseeding identity columns or regenerating new `VariableID` values. Values such as `VariableID` are artificially generated by using the `newid()` function, but other ones such as the `PackageID` column use the `PackageID` in the actual package. While on the topic of GUIDs, as an aside, there's a bit of an unexpected surprise in the package when you go to use the `PackageID`. The `PackageID` system variable in SSIS is actually a string value and not a `uniqueidentifier`.

The solution provides you with some stored procedures to begin, but there are some gaps. For example, you will have to create stored procedures to insert, update, and delete variables. These were not completely provided to allow you the flexibility of encrypting the values going into the database if you want.

Getting Started

To begin, create a new database called `SSISOps` and run `Chapter8_SSISOps.sql` to create the necessary schema and stored procedures. This database would eventually exist in each environment and, as you migrate a package from environment to environment, the package would read the environment's repository and set the variables appropriately. The repository only sets variables in this example, and you'll need to create expressions on other properties that you want to set to tie them to the variable.

Next, create a new package called `ConfigRepository.dtsx` in BIDS. Drag over a new Sequence container and rename it to **Configure Package**. Create two new string variables that are scoped to the new container called `tmpVariableName` and `tmpVariableValue`. Create one additional object variable `objTmpVariableList` scoped to the container as well. At this point, there should be no variable scoped to the package level, and two string variables and an object variable. The final step of the package setup is to create a new connection manager that points to the newly created `SSISOps` database.

Let's walk through the stored procedures. In the `Chapter8_SSISOps.sql` file on the Wiley web site, you'll find a very simple stored procedure to populate the `Package` table. The stored procedure only requires the `PackageID` and name as mandatory parameters, and the code looks like the following:

```
CREATE PROC AddPackage
@PackageID uniqueidentifier,
@PackageName varchar(100)
as

INSERT INTO Package
(PackageID, PackageName)
Values(@PackageID, @PackageName)
```

The other simple stored procedure populates the variable table. This stored procedure requires that you have a `@VariableName` input parameter that is an exact match to the one in the package that you'd like to use the parameter. This variable name is case-sensitive. The `@VariableValue` parameter stores the actual value for the parameter. The `@VariableType` parameter stores the data type of the variable. It's not really used in this example, but will be useful metadata for later usage. The valid data types are `String`, `Integer`, `DateTime`, and `Numeric`.

```
CREATE PROC
    AddVariable
        @VariableName varchar(30),
        @VariableValue varchar(500),
        @VariableType varchar(50)
as

INSERT INTO [dbo].[Variable]
```

```
        ([VariableName]
        ,[VariableValue]
        ,[VariableType]
        )
VALUES
        (@VariableName
        ,@VariableValue
        ,@VariableType
        )
```

After the variable is created, you must allow the package to use the variable. You do this by populating the PackageVariable table using the ScopeVariable stored procedure. This stored procedure uses both the PackageID and VariableID columns to grant access to the variable. This is most certainly not a secure system, but it can easily be built onto to add additional security.

```
CREATE PROC
        ScopeVariable
    @VariableID uniqueidentifier,
    @PackageID uniqueidentifier
as


INSERT INTO [dbo].[PackageVariable]
        [VariableID], [PackageID])
    VALUES
        (@VariableID, @PackageID)
```

The last step is to load the tables with some sample data so that the example package works. Inside the script file you downloaded, you'll see a section of code commented out that you can execute to do this if you'd like, or you can add real variables. Note the variables that you add to the tables, though, if you choose to venture off the path of the canned example values.

You'll want to create two variables in the database for this example: one variable called strMessage and another called strBadMessage. The following code, which shows you the sequence, should do the trick, but your IDs will not match and must be altered. This is the code that you will find commented out of the Chapter8_SSISOps.sql file:

```
AddVariable
        @VariableName='strMessage',
        @VariableValue='From the SSISOpsDB',
        @VariableType='string'
go
AddVariable
        @VariableName='strBadMessage',
        @VariableValue='From the SSISOpsDB',
        @VariableType='string'
go

AddPackage
    @PackageID ='{33E9278D-6288-4D01-83CB-BDC2FA0558ED}', -- Change this ID to
your package's ID
```

```
        @PackageName= 'Config Repository'
go
-- Capture the GUIDS from the Variable table to run this
ScopeVariable
        @PackageID = '{33E9278D-6288-4D01-83CB-BDC2FA0558ED}', --This should be the
same package ID used above
        @VariableID = '023B43AC-9D3C-48E5-81FD-503660841B36' --Run this procedure
twice, once for each GUID from the Variable table
go
```

Reading the Variables

The most important stored procedure is the `GetVariables` stored procedure, which reads all the variables that are stored in the repository that the package has access to. The only parameter needed for this stored procedure is the `@PackageID`, which is the string `PackageID` from the package. This stored procedure will be the one called from the packages that are using the repository. Notice that when the variables are read, the row is also updated, so you can track the metadata of when the variable was last used, and eventually remove old variables.

```
CREATE PROC
GetVariables
@PackageID varchar(38)
as

SELECT      PackageVariable.PackageID, Variable.VariableName,
Variable.VariableValue, Variable.VariableType, Variable.LastUsedDate
FROM            PackageVariable INNER JOIN
                      Variable ON PackageVariable.VariableID = Variable.VariableID
WHERE       (PackageVariable.PackageID =@PackageID)


UPDATE Variable
SET LastUsedDate = Getdate()
WHERE  VariableID in (
SELECT      Variable.VariableID
FROM            PackageVariable INNER JOIN
                      Variable ON PackageVariable.VariableID = Variable.VariableID
WHERE       (PackageVariable.PackageID =@PackageID)
)

GO
```

With the stored procedures and schema now complete, expand the package to use the repository. First, drag an Execute SQL Task onto the control flow and into the Sequence container. Configure the task to use the `SSISOps` database and set the `SQLStatement` property to the following query:

```
EXEC GetVariables @PackageID = ?.
```

The question mark in this query represents the input parameter that you will configure the task to pass. Before leaving the screen to do that, you must first set the `ResultSet` property to Full result set, as shown in Figure 8-12. This outputs the results of the `GetVariables` stored procedure to an object variable.

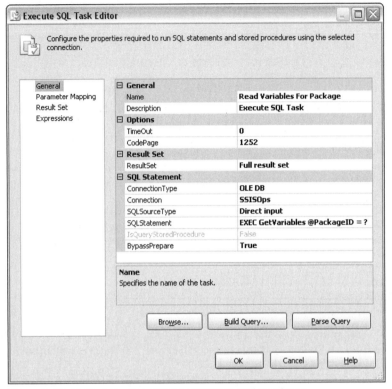

Figure 8-12: Setting the ResultSet property to Full result set

In the Parameter Mappings page, you will specify the input variables (represented as the previously mentioned question mark). Select System::PackageID from the Variable Name column and Input for the Direction column. For the Data Type column, select VARCHAR, even though the data looks like it should be a GUID. Lastly, set the Parameter Name property to 0 and the Parameter Size property to 38. The final result should look like Figure 8-13.

General	Variable Name	Direction	Data Type	Parameter ...	Parameter ...
Parameter Mapping	System::PackageID	Input	VARCHAR	0	38
Result Set					
Expressions					

Figure 8-13: Setting the Parameter Mappings

The last item to configure in this task is in the Result Set page. The result sets are zero-based, ordinal, like the parameters. Because of this, the Result Name should be set to 0 and the object variable you want to output to is User::objTmpVariableList, as shown in Figure 8-14. This variable should have been created in the earlier setup steps. Click OK to save the task.

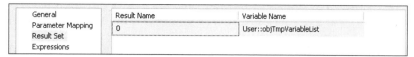

Figure 8-14: Setting the Result Set

The Execute SQL Task that you just created retrieves all the variables that are stored in your SSISOps table and stores them in a list inside the User::objTmpVariableList variable. You're now ready to loop through those results and set the variables in your package to what is in the database. You'll do this through a ForEach Loop container. Drag it into the Sequence container and below the Execute SQL Task you created earlier. Connect a precedence constraint between the Execute SQL Task and the newly created ForEach Loop container. Name the container Loop Through Variables.

In the Collection page (shown in Figure 8-15), change the Enumerator to Foreach ADO Enumerator and set the source variable to User::objTmpVariableList. This will read the User::objTmpVariableList variable and loop through the results list that you have stored in it during the Execute SQL Task.

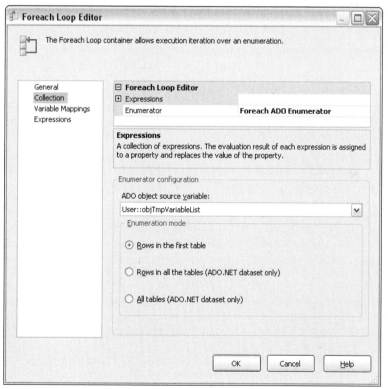

Figure 8-15: Collection page

The last step to configure this container is to specify where you want each column to be output to. This, too, is zero-based, ordinal, meaning that the first column has an index of 0, the second column has an index of 1, and so on. You can specify this mapping in the Variable Mappings page. Set User::tmpVariableName to an index of 1, User::tmpVariableType to an index of 3, and User::tmpVariableValue to an index of 2, as shown in Figure 8-16. The last output, which would have had an index of 0, is PackageID and it will not be used at this time.

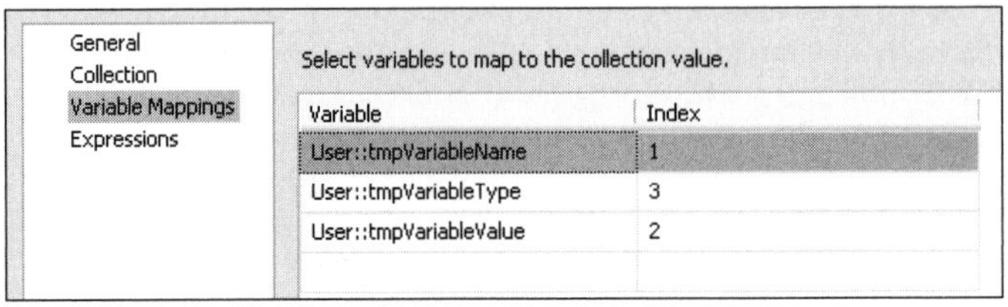

Figure 8-16: Specifying the container to use for output

Setting the Variables

You have now loaded your variables into an object variable and have a loop to perform some sort of action on each variable you pull from the database. The action you're going to perform is to read from the set of temp variables you set in the previous step, and then set the final variables using a Script Task.

Start by dragging the Script Task into the loop and naming it **Set Variables**. In the Script page of the task (shown in Figure 8-17), set the ReadOnlyVariables to tmpVariableType, tmpVariableName, tmpVariableValue. By doing this, the variables get locked in the designer, which simplifies the code later. It would be a better practice to use the VariableDispenser object throughout the script code to refer to the variables, but for this small of a function, using this method is fine.

Click Design Script to begin writing the script. The script is broken into two subroutines. The first one actually does the heavy lifting in the script and sets the variable. Here the VariableDispenser object is used, since you can't predict the variable's name that you want to lock. Prior to locking the variable, you want to ensure that the variable actually exists in the package by using the Containers method. This will ensure that someone hasn't mistyped a variable in the Variables table of the SSISOps database. If you don't have this line of code, and the variable is in the table but not in the package, the script will fail. With the line of code, if the variable doesn't exist in the package, it is ignored. This may not be the behavior you want to see. To set the variable, you must first lock the variable by using the LockForWrite method, then you set it. Also note that the Try...Catch code that wraps the inner code is only a stub for more advanced code that you could write to catch errors. Add whatever logic you want to handle this situation.

```
Private Sub SetVariable(ByVal varName As String, ByVal varValue As Object)
    Try
        Dim vars As Variables
        If Dts.VariableDispenser.Contains(varName) = True Then

            Dts.VariableDispenser.LockOneForWrite(varName, vars)
            Try
                vars(varName).Value = varValue
            Catch ex As Exception
                Throw ex
            Finally
                vars.Unlock()
```

```
            End Try
        End If
    Catch ex As Exception
        Throw ex
    End Try
End Sub
```

The last subroutine calls the variable setting and just does some of the light setup work.

```
Public Sub Main()

    Dim vars As Variables

    Dim strVariableName As String
    Dim strVariableValue As String


    strVariableName = Dts.Variables("tmpVariableName").Value.ToString
    strVariableValue = Dts.Variables("tmpVariableValue").Value.ToString

    SetVariable(strVariableName, strVariableValue)

    Dts.TaskResult = Dts.Results.Success
End Sub
```

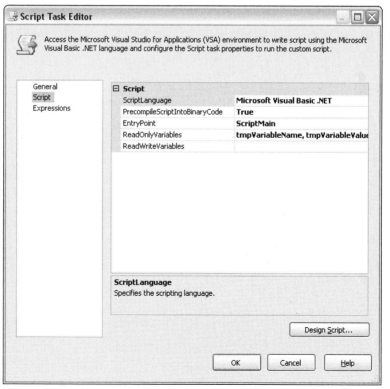

Figure 8-17: Setting ReadOnlyVariables of the script

The final solution should look like Figure 8-18. The great thing about wrapping it into a single Sequence container is that it can be minimalized, so it doesn't have visual impact, and you can create event handlers on the container. This container would need to be the first item in your package in order for the configuration to work, and then any item that you'd like to make dynamic would use the variables to set the properties with expressions.

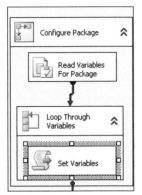

Figure 8-18: Final solution

Areas to Grow the Solution

This solution is surely not turnkey, but it does start you in your pursuit of a seamless configuration of your packages. The first area to improve this solution is to encrypt the VariableValue column in the Variable table. This can be done with the native encryption functions that are out-of-the box in SQL Server 2005. After this, you can rest assured that only SSIS and other approved applications can see the values for the variables.

You may also decide to add a task prior to the variable retrieval to add the package to the Package table if it doesn't yet exist. This can be done through an Execute SQL Task calling a new stored procedure that checks to see if the PackageID is already in the table and, if it is not, creates the row. This may help with usability for your users.

Another thing that may be useful is to expand the model to where the Script Task sets the final connection property as shown in Chapter 2. Tying a variable to the property with an expression may be more work than people are willing to give for the configuration of a package. A final rule of thumb is that if you plan on using a Script Task more than a few times, it's a wise idea at that point to create a custom task to perform all the script's functionality. The same could hold true here where you could replace both containers and everything inside of them with a single task.

Deployment Utility

In SSIS, you can create a deployment utility that will help a user install your project of packages and any dependencies such as configuration files. This deployment utility is similar to creating a program like InstallShield, and is perfect for times when you want to pass a set of packages to a customer or a production DBA who may not know how to install SSIS packages the manual way. When you create a deployment utility, all the files that are necessary to install the project are copied into a centralized directory, and a .SSISDeploymentManifest file is created for the installer to run, which opens the Package Installation Wizard.

To create a deployment utility, simply right-click the project in BIDS and select Properties. In the Property Pages dialog box, go to the Deployment Utility page and change the CreateDeploymentUtility to True, as shown in Figure 8-19. This is set to False by default. The AllowConfigurationChanges property is a useful setting as well, and when set to True, will prompt the installer to see if he or she would like to change any settings that may be exposed via a configuration file at installation time. The DeploymentOutputPath property shows you where the deployment utility will be outputted to underneath the project folder.

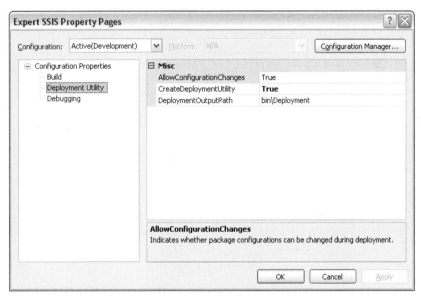

Figure 8-19: Changing the CreateDeploymentUtiliity to True

Next, under the Build menu, select Build *<Project Name>*, where *<Project Name>* represents your project's name. This will open each package and build the package. If there are any errors in the package, then you will see them at this point. As it builds the project, each package is outputted into the \bin\deployment directory under your project's folder.

The Package Installation Wizard

Now that you have created a deployment .SSISDeploymentManifest file, you're now ready to send the entire contents of the \bin\deployment folder to the installation person. The installation person would then need to copy the contents of the folder to the server he or she wants to deploy to, and double-click the .SSISDeploymentManifest file. The installer could also run it remotely, but it is preferred to run it on the same server as the target deployment server to simplify the installation.

After skipping over the introduction screen, you are asked where you want to deploy the packages, as shown in Figure 8-20. You can either choose a File system deployment or a SQL Server deployment. A File system deployment just copies the files to a directory on the server. A SQL Server deployment stores the packages in the MSDB database on the target server. Chapter 9 discusses the pros and cons to each option. You can also have the wizard validate each package after you install the package. This ensures that the package that was delivered to you is valid on your machine, including the data sources and configurations.

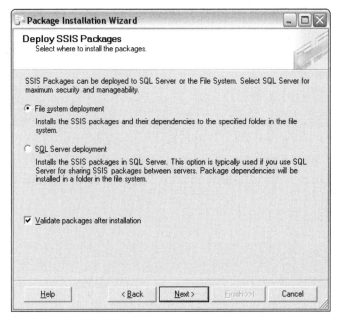

Figure 8-20: Prompt to where you want to deploy the packages

If you're following this example, select SQL Server Deployment and click Next. The next screen prompts you for which SQL Server 2005 machine you want to deploy the packages. You cannot deploy SSIS packages to SQL Server 2000. If you had selected a File System Deployment, the next screen prompts you for the file path to which you want the packages to be deployed. The last option in the SQL Server Deployment screen is to specify if you want to rely on SQL Server for protecting the package by encrypting the package. This is the preferred option, and will automatically change the `ProtectionLevel` package property to `ServerStorage` as it installs each package. Chapter 9 provides more information about the `ProtectionLevel` property.

Even though you have selected a SQL Server Deployment, there may still be files that must be deployed, such as configuration files and readme files. The next screen prompts you for where you'd like to put these files. Generally, they'll go under a folder named after the project under the `C:\Program Files\Microsoft SQL Server\90\DTS\Packages\` path.

After you click Next, the packages will be installed in the package store on the server. After the packages are installed, if the developer selected `True` to the `AllowConfigurationChanges` in BIDS (shown in Figure 8-19), then you will receive an additional screen giving you (as an installer) a chance to edit the values in the configuration file at deployment time. This can be seen in Figure 8-21, and you can pull down the drop-down box to see multiple configuration files. Unfortunately, it does not show which specific packages these files are tied to.

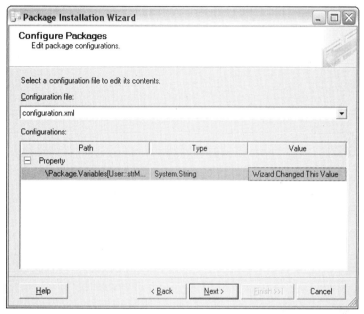

Figure 8-21: Chance to edit the values in the configuration file at deployment time

The only other additional screen you would see is a pop-up dialog box if there were a user password on any package. After the packages have been deployed, they are validated, as shown in Figure 8-22. If there were a problem, you would see it in the Packages Validation screen, and you could redeploy after the problem was corrected. The last screen is a summary screen to complete the wizard.

There are other ways to deploy packages, examined in Chapter 9, but this is a great way to deploy packages in bulk. If you want to deploy a package in Management Studio, as you'll see in Chapter 9, you have to do it one package at a time. The file system, however, is much easier. With this method of storage, you can just copy the files into a specific directory and they'll be seen from Management Studio.

The main thing to remember about the deployment utility is that when it is used, every package and dependency is deployed. You may not want to deploy this many packages at once all the time. The `.SSISDeploymentManifest` file can be edited in a text editor to remove any extra files you do not want to migrate. Some developers find it useful to create a project in the same project solution that contains a subset of the packages that they want to deploy if this is too aggressive for them.

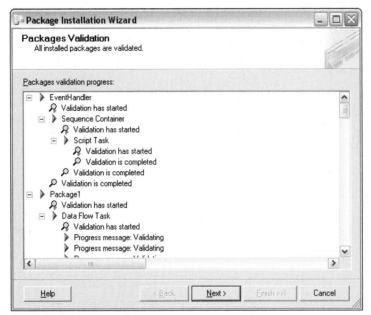

Figure 8-22: Validated packages

If you did want to edit the .SSISDeploymentManifest XML file before sending the folder to a client, you could just remove one of the <Package> lines, as shown in the following XML example. You can also see, in the header of the XML file, who created the deployment tool for you, and when. This information will be useful for tracking down who to ask questions later if the project doesn't install appropriately. If you do not want to deploy a configuration file with the wizard, you can remove or comment out the <ConfigurationFile> line to prevent the configuration file from overwriting the older one that may already be on the server file.

```xml
<?xml version="1.0" ?>
- <DTSDeploymentManifest GeneratedBy="BRIANKNIGHT\bknight"
GeneratedFromProjectName="Expert SSIS"
GeneratedDate="2006-12-15T23:39:54.7343750-05:00" AllowConfigurationChanges="true">
  <Package>EventHandler.dtsx</Package>
  <Package>Package1.dtsx</Package>
  <Package>Restartability.dtsx</Package>
  <Package>ConfigFiles.dtsx</Package>
  <!--Package>Chapter1.dtsx</Package-->
  <Package>RawFile.dtsx</Package>
  <Package>DBSnapshots.dtsx</Package>
  <Package>Logging.dtsx</Package>
  <Package>FileWatcher.dtsx</Package>
  <Package>ConfigRepository.dtsx</Package>
  <ConfigurationFile>configuration.xml</ConfigurationFile>
</DTSDeploymentManifest>
```

A final deployment technique is simply to copy the packages over by using a command such as XCOPY. This is often used for .NET application deployments and is a simple solution that your developers will understand. As you'll learn in Chapter 9, if you deploy to the file system, there is no record in SQL Server that contains metadata about packages in the file system. Because of this, the packages can simply be copied into a directory, and the package store will be aware of them. More on the package store and the benefit of the file system deployment technique is discussed in Chapter 9.

Summary

In this chapter, you've seen how to make it easier to migrate a package from environment to environment. This ease is the result of using configuration files, or by creating your own configuration repository, which gives you more flexibility. You can also simplify migrations by creating a deployment utility.

Chapter 9 will complete the deployment picture by showing you how to administer SSIS and deploy packages manually.

9

Managing SSIS

So, you have a set of packages and are ready to run the package in production. This chapter focuses on how to administer packages after they're deployed to production. The discussion also examines how to create a stand-alone ETL server and some of the command line utilities you can use to make your job easier.

The Package Store

When you deploy your packages, they are stored into what is called the *SSIS Package Store*. The Package Store, in some cases, will actually physically store the package, as in the msdb database option. Or, in the case, of the file system, the Package Store just keeps a pointer to a specific top-level directory and enumerates through the packages stored underneath that directory. To connect to the Package Store, the SSIS Service must be running. This service is called SQL Server Integration Services, or MsDtsServer. There is only one instance of the service per machine, or per set of clustered machines.

You can configure the SSIS service in the Services applet in Control Panel ⇨ Administrative Tools. Double-click on the SQL Server Integration Services item. As you can see, the service is set to automatically start by default and starts under the NT AUTHORITY\NetworkService account. In the Recovery tab, you may decide that you want the service to automatically restart in the event of a failure — you can specify how to react if the service fails the first, second, and subsequent times. As you can see in Figure 9-1, the service has been changed to restart if a failure occurs twice. The failure count in this figure is also reset after two days.

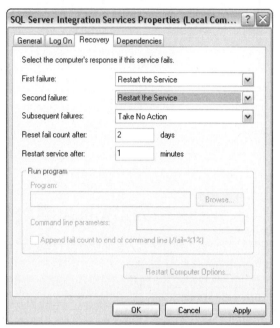

Figure 9-1: Configuring the service to restart in the event of a failure

Although you can run and stop packages without the service, the service makes running packages more manageable. For example, anyone who wants to interrogate the service can find out which packages are running. It can also aid in the importing and exporting of packages into the Package Store. Other uses for the service will be discussed throughout this chapter, but one last great use for the service is to enable you to handle centralized management, enumeration, and monitoring of your packages throughout your enterprise.

The `MsDtsServer` service is configured through an XML file that is located, by default, in the following path:

```
C:\Program Files\Microsoft SQL Server\90\DTS\Binn\MsDtsSrvr.ini.xml
```

This path will vary if you're in a cluster. If you cannot find the path, go to the `HKEY_LOCAL_MACHINE\SOFTWARE\Microsoft\MSDTS\ServiceConfigFile` Registry key in RegEdit. By default, the XML file should look like the following:

```xml
<?xml version="1.0" encoding="utf-8" ?>
- <DtsServiceConfiguration xmlns:xsd="http://www.w3.org/2001/XMLSchema"
xmlns:xsi="http://www.w3.org/2001/XMLSchema-instance">
  <StopExecutingPackagesOnShutdown>true</StopExecutingPackagesOnShutdown>
- <TopLevelFolders>
- <Folder xsi:type="SqlServerFolder">
  <Name>MSDB</Name>
  <ServerName>.</ServerName>
  </Folder>
- <Folder xsi:type="FileSystemFolder">
```

```
<Name>File System</Name>
<StorePath>..\Packages</StorePath>
</Folder>
</TopLevelFolders>
</DtsServiceConfiguration>
```

There really isn't a lot to configure in this file, but there are some interesting uses for the file. The first configuration line tells the packages how to react if the service is stopped. By default, packages that the service is running will stop upon the service stopping or being failed over. You could also configure the packages to continue to run after the service is stopped until they complete by changing the StopExecutingPackagesOnShutDown property to False, as shown here:

```
<StopExecutingPackagesOnShutdown>false</StopExecutingPackagesOnShutdown>
```

The next configuration sections are the most important. They specify which paths and servers the MsDtsServer service will read from. Whenever the service starts, it reads this file to determine where the packages are stored. In the default file, you will have a single entry for a SQL Server that looks like the following SqlServerFolder example:

```
- <Folder xsi:type="SqlServerFolder">
<Name>MSDB</Name>
<ServerName>.</ServerName>
</Folder>
```

The <Name> line represents how the name will appear in Management Studio for this set of packages. The <ServerName> line represents where the connection will point to. There is a problem if your SQL Server is on a named instance where this file will still point to the default non-named instance (.). If you do have a named instance, simply replace the period with your instance name.

The next section shows you where your File System packages will be stored. The <StorePath> shows the folder where all packages will be enumerated from. The default path is C:\program files\microsoft sql server\90\dts\Packages, which is represented as ..\Packages in the following default configuration. The .. part of the statement navigates one directory below the SSIS service file, and \Packages then traverses into the Packages folder.

```
- <Folder xsi:type="FileSystemFolder">
<Name>File System</Name>
<StorePath>..\Packages</StorePath>
</Folder>
```

Everything in the Packages folder and below will be enumerated. You can create subdirectories under this folder and they will immediately show up in Management Studio. Each time you make a change to the MsDtsSrvr.ini.xml file, you must stop and start the MsDtsServer service in order for the changes to take effect.

Creating a Central SSIS Server

Many enterprise companies have so many packages that they decide to separate the SSIS service from SQL Server and place it on its own server. The advantages of this are that your SSIS packages will not suffocate the SQL Server's memory during a large load, and you have a central spot to manage them.

The disadvantages of this are now you must license the server separately, and you add another layer of complexity while you're debugging packages. When you do this, you create a fantastic way to easily scale packages by adding more memory to your central server, but you also create an added performance hit because all remote data must be copied over the network before entering the data flow buffer.

To create a centralized SSIS hub, you must only modify the MsDtsSrvr.ini.xml file and restart the service. The service can read a UNC path such as \\ServerName\Share and it can point to multiple remote servers. In the following example, the service will enumerate packages from three servers: one that is local and another two that are on a named instance. After restarting the service, you will see a total of six folders to expand in Management Studio. (The Management Studio aspect of SSIS is discussed in much more detail later in this chapter.)

```xml
<?xml version="1.0" encoding="utf-8" ?>
- <DtsServiceConfiguration xmlns:xsd="http://www.w3.org/2001/XMLSchema"
xmlns:xsi="http://www.w3.org/2001/XMLSchema-instance">
  <StopExecutingPackagesOnShutdown>true</StopExecutingPackagesOnShutdown>
- <TopLevelFolders>
- <Folder xsi:type="SqlServerFolder">
  <Name>Server A MSDB</Name>
  <ServerName>localhost</ServerName>
  </Folder>
  <Name>Server B MSDB</Name>
  <ServerName>SQLServerB</ServerName>
  </Folder>
  <Name>Server C MSDB</Name>
  <ServerName>SQLServerC\NamedInstance</ServerName>
  </Folder>
- <Folder xsi:type="FileSystemFolder">
  <Name>Server A File System</Name>
  <StorePath>P:\Packages</StorePath>
  </Folder>
- <Folder xsi:type="FileSystemFolder">
  <Name>Server B File System</Name>
  <StorePath>\\SQLServerB\Packages</StorePath>
  </Folder>
- <Folder xsi:type="FileSystemFolder">
  <Name>Server C File System</Name>
  <StorePath>\\SQLServerC\Packages</StorePath>
  </Folder>
  </TopLevelFolders>
  </DtsServiceConfiguration>
```

Your next issue is how to schedule packages when using a centralized SSIS hub like this example. You can schedule your packages through SQL Server Agent, or through a scheduling system such as Task Scheduler from Windows. Since you're already paying for a license of SQL Server, it's better to install SQL Server on your server and use Agent since it gives you much more flexibility, as you will see later in this chapter. You can also store configuration tables and logging tables on this SQL Server to centralize its processing as well. Both scheduling mechanisms are examined later in this chapter.

Clustering SSIS

Making your SSIS service highly available can be done by clustering SSIS. Before proceeding, however, we need to clarify what a highly available SSIS service gives you. In the event of a server failure, the SSIS service will start on another server in the cluster, and packages can begin to be managed as if the failure never occurred. If there is a package running during the server failure, the package will not automatically begin running on the other server. So, the service is highly available, but the package itself will not continue to work uninterrupted.

The unfortunate news is that SSIS is not a clustered service by default. Even though it does not cluster in the main SQL Server setup, it can still be clustered manually through a series of relatively easy steps. This section walks you through those steps, but makes the assumption that you already know how to use Windows clustering and know the basic clustering architecture. Following are the high-level steps required to set up SSIS as a clustered service, which will then be explored in more detail:

1. Install SSIS on all nodes that can use the service.
2. Create a new cluster group (optional).
3. If you created a new group, create a virtual IP, name, and drive as clustered resources.
4. Copy the `MsDtsSrvr.ini.xml` to the clustered drive.
5. Modify the `MsDtsSrvr.ini.xml` file to change the location of the packages.
6. Change the Registry setting to point to the `MsDtsSrvr.ini.xml` file.
7. Cluster the `MsDtsServer` service as a generic service.

Let's begin by looking at a minor decision you'll have to make prior to clustering. You can choose to cluster the `MsDtsServer` service in the main SQL Server cluster group for a given instance, or you can create its own cluster group. Although it's easier to piggyback the main SQL Server service, you will find that it adds complexity to management.

Recall that you can only have a single SSIS service between the entire Windows cluster. If you have a four-instance SQL Server cluster, where would you place the SSIS service then? This is one reason why it makes the most sense to move the SSIS service into its own group. The main reason though is a manageability one. If you decide that you need to fail over the SSIS service to another node, you would have to fail over the SQL Server as well if they shared a cluster group, which would cause a data outage. Moving the SSIS service into its own cluster group ensures that only the SSIS service fails over and does not cause a wider outage.

Placing this in its own group comes at a price, though. The service will now need a virtual IP address, its own drive, and a name on the network. Once you have those requirements, you're ready to cluster. If you decided not to place SSIS in its own group, then you would not need the drive, IP address, or name.

The first step in clustering is to install SSIS on all nodes in the Windows cluster. If you installed SSIS as part of your SQL Server install, you'll see that SSIS installed only on the primary node. You'll now need to install it manually on the other nodes in the cluster. Ensure that you make the installation simple, and install SSIS on the same folder on each node.

If you want to have the SSIS service in a different group from the database engine, you'll first have to create a new group called `SSIS` in Cluster Administrator (it can be called something else). This group will need to be shared by whichever nodes that you would like to participate in the cluster. Then, add to the group a physical drive that is clustered, an IP address, and a network name. The IP address and network name are virtual names and IPs.

From whichever node owns the SSIS group, copy the `MsDtsSrvr.ini.xml` file to the clustered physical drive that's in the `SSIS` cluster group. Generally, it's best to create a directory called `<Clustered Drive Letter>\SSISSetup` in which to place the file. Make a note of wherever you placed the file for a later configuration step. You'll also want to create a folder on the same clustered drive for your packages (called `Packages`) to be stored. This directory will store any packages and configuration files that will be stored on the file system instead of the `msdb` database.

Next, open `regedit.exe` or your favorite Registry editing tool and change the `SOFTWARE\Microsoft\MSDTS\ServiceConfigFile` key to point to the new location (including the file name) for the `MsDtsSrvr.ini.xml` file. Be sure to back up the Registry before making this change.

After this change, you're ready to cluster the `MsDtsServer` service. Open Cluster Administrator again and right-click on the `SSIS` cluster group (if you're creating it in its own group) and select New ➪ Resource. This opens the Resource Wizard, which clusters nearly any service in Windows. On the first screen, type **Integration Services** for the name of the clustered resource and select Generic Service. This name is a logical name that is only going to be meaningful to the administrator and you.

Next, on the Possible Owner screen, add any node that you want to potentially own the SSIS service. On the Dependencies page, add the group's Network Name, IP Address, and Drive as dependencies. This ensures that the SSIS service will not come online prior to the name and drives being online. Also, if the drive were to fail, the SSIS service will also fail.

The next screen is the Generic Service Parameters screen, where you will want to type **MsDtsServer** for the service to cluster. The last screen in the wizard is the Registry Replication screen, where you will want to ensure that the `SOFTWARE\Microsoft\MSDTS\ServiceConfigFile` key is replicated. If a change is made to this Registry key, it will be replicated to all other nodes. After you finish the wizard, the SSIS service will be almost ready to come online and be clustered.

The final step is to move any packages that were stored on the file system over to the clustered drive in the `Packages` folder. The next time you open Management Studio, you should be able to see all the packages and folders. You'll also need to edit the `MsDtsSrvr.ini.xml` file to change the SQL Server to point to SQL Server's virtual name and not the physical name, which will allow failovers of the database engine. In the same file, you will need to change the path in the `StorePath` to point to the `<Clustered Drive>:\Packages` folder you created earlier as well. After this, you're ready to bring the service online in Cluster Administrator.

It's important to note now that your SSIS service is clustered, you will no longer connect to the physical machine name to manage the packages in Management Studio. Instead you will connect to the network name that you created in Cluster Administrator. If you added SSIS as a clustered resource in the same group as SQL Server, you would connect to the SQL Server's virtual network name.

File System or the msdb Deployment

As discussed earlier, you can store your packages in two places: on the file system or in the msdb database. Each storage option has its own pros and cons, and which option you choose will be based on what is more important to you. These pros and cons are examined in much more depth in this section, but to summarize, the following table provides a high-level idea of which storage option is best based on what functionality you're most interested in. Just because a given storage option is not checked does not mean that it doesn't have that functionality. The ones checked are simply most optimized for the given functionality.

Functionality	Best in File System	Best in msdb
Security		X
Backup and recovery		X
Deployment	X	
Troubleshooting	X	
Availability	X	
Execution Speed	X	X

If security concerns you greatly, you may want to consider placing your packages in the msdb database. To secure your packages on the file system, you could have multiple layers of security by using the NT File System (NTFS) security on the folder on the file system where the packages are located. You could also then place a password on the packages to keep users who may have administrator rights to your machine from executing the package. This does add extra complexity to your package deployments in some cases.

If you store your packages in the msdb database, you can assign package roles to each package to designate who can see or execute the package. The packages can also be encrypted in the msdb database, which strengthens your security even more. This is examined in much more depth later in this chapter.

Backup and recovery is simpler when you store your packages in the msdb database. If you were to store your packages in the msdb database, then you must only wrap the msdb database into your regular maintenance plan to back up all the packages. As packages are added, they are wrapped into the maintenance plan. The problem with this is that you can't restore a single package using this mechanism. You'd have to restore all the packages to a point in time, and that would also restore the jobs and history.

The other option is a file system backup, which would just use your favorite backup software to back up the folders and files. If you do this, you must rely on your Backup Operator to do this for you, which makes some people uneasy. At that moment you could restore individual packages to a point in time. In reality, you can just redeploy the packages from Source Safe if you can't retrieve a backup file.

File system deployments are much simpler, but less sophisticated. To deploy packages onto the file system, you must only copy them into the directory for the package store. You can create subdirectories under the parent directory to subdivide it easily. You can also copy a single package over easily as well, in case you need to make a package change. To import a package into the package store using the msdb database, you must use Management Studio (or the DTUtil.exe command line tool) and import them package by package. To do a bulk migration, you could use the deployment utility discussed in Chapter 8.

Along the same lines as deployment is troubleshooting. If something were to go bump in the night, and you wanted to see if the packages in production were the same release as the packages you thought you had deployed, you must only copy the files down to your machine and perform a comparison using Source Safe or another similar tool. If the files were stored in the msdb database, you would have to right-click each package in Management Studio and select Export. If the same packages were stored in the file system, you must only copy the files to your machine or open BIDS on the remote machine.

Availability of your packages is always on the top of the list for DBAs. If you were to store the packages in the msdb database and the database engine were to go down, the packages would be unavailable. If they were stored in the file system, then your packages would be available for execution. Of course, if the database engine is down, then probably one of your key data sources would also be down at the same time.

The good news is no matter what storage option you choose, the performance will be the same. As you can see, there are many pros and cons to each storage option, and neither wins overwhelmingly. The main reason that you should generally choose to use the file system is for simplicity of deployment.

Management Studio

In SSIS, there's delineation between development and administration. This makes the development model much more like developing a regular program. In a web application, you would never make a code change to the C# application on the production server. Instead, if you wanted to make a change, you would check it out of Source Control, make the change, and then redeploy. The same C# model applies to SSIS.

When you open Management Studio, select the Connect drop-down box in the Object Explorer window and select Integration Services. When you connect, you will see all the different stores that are available for you to explore.

A connection to that store isn't made until you expand one of the folders, as shown with the File System store in Figure 9-2. At that point, you may experience a timeout if you're trying to connect to an msdb database that isn't online, or when the server is offline. Otherwise, when you expand the folder, you will see a list of folders and packages that are stored in that particular store.

You can also access all the packages that are running under the Running Packages folder. From there, you can stop packages that are running too long by right-clicking the package and selecting Stop. You can also right-click the folder and select Reports ⇨ General to see a report of all the packages running and for how long. This method of accessing the Reports menu is only available in SQL Server 2005 Service Pack 2. Previously, you'd have to access the reports through the Reports drop-down box in the right Summary pane.

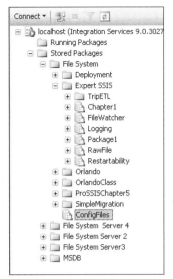

Figure 9-2: File System store

In Figure 9-3, you can see that there are two instantiations of the FileWatcher package. Both were executed by the bknight account and the Execution Duration is the number of milliseconds since the start time.

Figure 9-3: Two instantiations of the FileWatcher package

The package name shown in this report is the package name from the package properties in BIDS. If your package's file name is Package1.dtsx, but the package name in properties is called FileWatcher, then FileWatcher will show in this window, not Package1.dtsx. Because of this, it's very important to keep your package's name in synch with the file. Otherwise, it can become quite complex to have to find and manage your packages.

You can right-click any item or folder in the tree to produce item-specific reports. At a package level, you can see all the details for the package that the designer has exposed in BIDS. At the folder level, you can see all the packages in the folder and their build numbers.

Running Packages with DTExecUI

The primary way to manually execute a package is with DTExecUI.exe. This utility is a graphical wrapper for DTExec.exe and provides an easier way to produce the necessary switches to execute the package. Nearly all the same tabs and options you see in DTExecUI.exe will also be available when you schedule the package.

The quickest way to open the utility is from within Management Studio. To open it from there, right-click any package that you want to execute and select Run. You can also open the utility in Windows by selecting Start ⇨ Run and typing **DTExecUI.exe**.

Before beginning the discussion of this utility, it's important to note that the utility is a 32-bit utility. The utility will run on a 64-bit machine, but it will wrap the 32-bit version of DTExec.exe. Later in this chapter, you'll learn about some tricks to use to run the package in 64-bit mode.

When you right-click a package and select Run, the first screen in DTExecUI.exe is filled out for you automatically. The first page (shown in Figure 9-4) points to the package you want to execute, and indicates where the package is located. If you select the Package Store to connect to from the Package source drop-down list box, you'll be able to see all the packages stored on the server, no matter where they are stored. Your other options are SQL Server or the File System. With the SQL Server option, you will only see packages stored in the msdb of the server that you name. The File System option enables you to point to any arbitrary .dtsx file to execute.

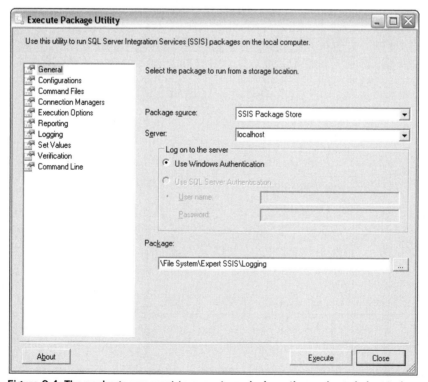

Figure 9-4: The package you want to execute and where the package is located

The next screen is the Configuration page. In this page, you can select additional configuration files that you want to use for this execution of the package. If you do not select an additional configuration file, any configuration files that are already on the server will be used. You will not be able to see existing configuration files that are being used in the package.

The Command Files page provides links to files that contain a series of additional switches you can use during execution. Remember, this tool wraps DTExec.exe, which is a command line utility. With a command file, you can place part of the standard DTExec.exe switches in a file and then reuse them again from every package.

The Connection Managers page shows the power of connection managers (see Figure 9-5). This page enables you to change the connection manager settings at runtime to a different setting than what the developer had originally intended. For example, perhaps you'd like to move the destination connection for a package to a production server instead of a QA server. Another typical example is when you do not have the same drive structure in production as in development, and you must move the connection manager to a different directory.

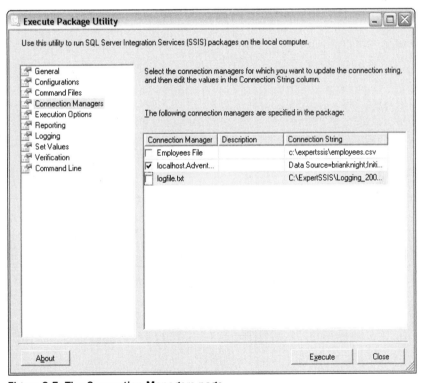

Figure 9-5: The Connection Managers page

The Execution Options page provides advanced settings for the package execution (see Figure 9-6). For example, you can force the package to fail upon the first package warning, which is normally ignored. You can also simply validate the package without executing the package. An especially powerful setting in this page is the Maximum concurrent executables option. This option simply controls how many concurrent tasks will run in parallel. Oftentimes, you may migrate the package to a different environment with fewer processors, which could cause performance issues until you lower this setting. A setting of –1 means that two tasks plus the number of CPUs will run concurrently. The last set of options on this page is the series of options to enable checkpoints on the package if they are not already enabled.

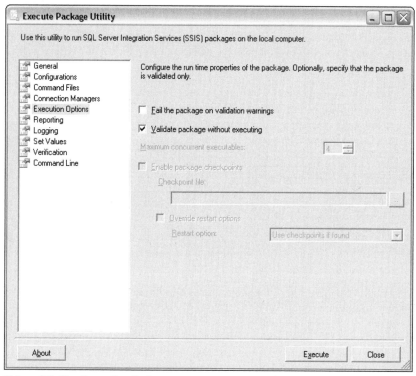

Figure 9-6: The Execution Options page

The Reporting page controls what type of detail will be shown in the console (see Figure 9-7). The default option is Verbose, which may be too detailed for you. You may decide that you'd rather only show Errors and Warnings, which would perform slightly better than the Verbose message. You can also control which columns will show in the console.

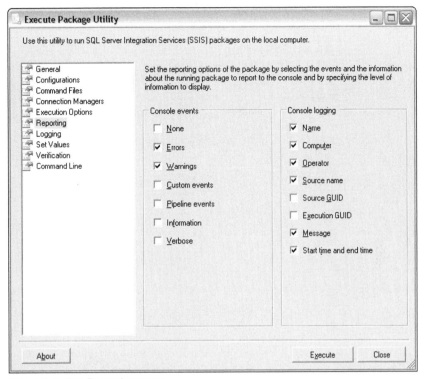

Figure 9-7: The Reporting page

Another powerful page is the Set Values page, shown in Figure 9-8. This page enables you to override nearly any property you want by typing the property path for the property. The most common use for this would be to set the value of a variable. To do this, you would use a property path such as \package .variables[myvariable].You would then type the value for the variable in the next column. This page is also a way to work around some properties that can't be set through expressions. With those properties, you generally can access them through the property path.

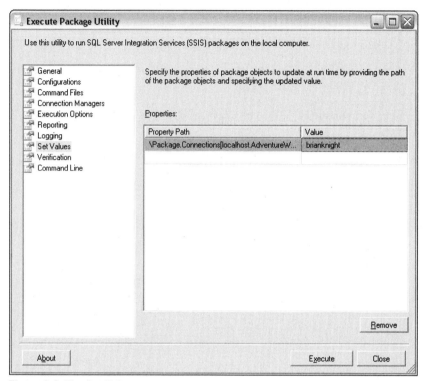

Figure 9-8: The Set Values page

The Verification page, shown in Figure 9-9, enables you to ensure that only packages that meet your criteria are executed. For example, you may want to ensure that you only execute signed packages or packages of a certain build number. This may be handy for Sarbanes-Oxley compliance, where you must guarantee that you don't execute a rogue package.

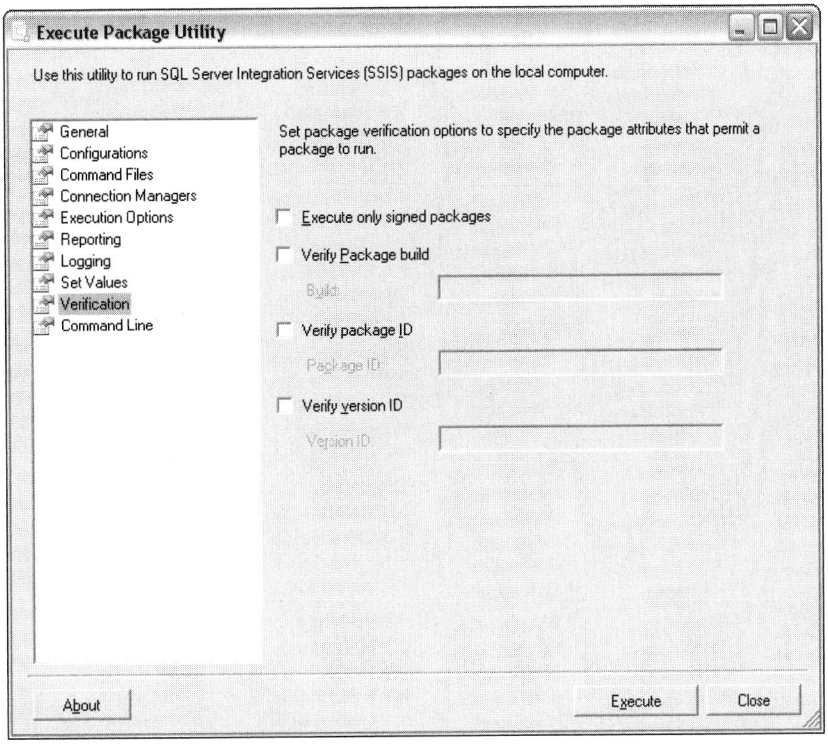

Figure 9-9: The Verification page

The Command Line page, shown in Figure 9-10, is one of the most important pages. This page shows you the exact DTExec.exe command that will be executing. You can also manually edit the command here as well. After the command appears the way you'd like it, you can copy and paste it in a command prompt after the command DTExec.exe. Later in this chapter, DTExec.exe will be examined in much more detail, but this can save you from having to learn how to use that utility. It is also sometimes the only way to execute the package in 64-bit mode.

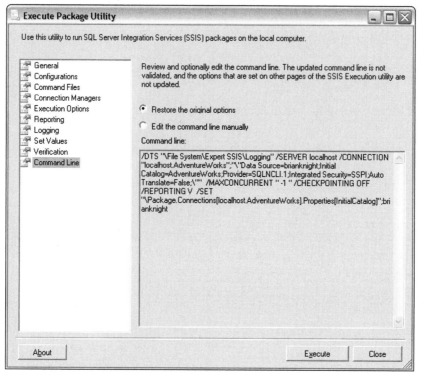

Figure 9-10: The Command Line page

You can also execute the package by clicking the Execute button at any time from any page. After you click the Execute button, you will see the Package Execution Progress window, which will show you any warnings, errors, and informational messages (as shown in Figure 9-11). You'll only see a fraction of the message in some cases, and you may hover over the message to see the full message in some cases.

Figure 9-11: The Package Execution Progress window

Security

The only login option you have to connect to the SSIS service is to use your Active Directory account. After you connect, you'll only see packages that you are allowed to see. This protection is accomplished based on *package roles*. Package roles are only available on packages stored in the msdb database. Packages stored on the file system must be protected with a password.

Package roles can be accessed by right-clicking a package that you want to protect and selecting Package Roles. The Package Roles dialog box, shown in Figure 9-12, enables you to choose the role that will be in the Writer Role and Reader Role. The Writer Role can perform administration-type functions (such as overwriting a package with a new version, deleting a package, managing security, and stopping the package from running). The Reader Role can execute and view the package. The role can also export the package from Management Studio.

Figure 9-12: The Package Roles dialog box

Package roles use database roles from the `msdb` database. By default, people who are in the `db_dtsadmin` and `db_dtsoperator` database roles, or the creator of the package, can be Readers. The Writer Role is held by members of the `db_dtsadmin` database role, or the creator of the package, by default. When you select the drop-down list box in the Package Roles dialog box, you can change the package role from the default one to another customized role from the `msdb` database.

You may want to customize a group of people who are the only ones who can execute the accounting set of packages. Let's do a quick example to secure a package to a role called `Accounting` for the Writer and Reader package roles.

First, open Management Studio and connect to your development or local database engine instance. Then, expand System Databases ⇨ msdb ⇨ Security, right-click Roles, and select New Role. This opens the Database Role - New dialog box, shown in Figure 9-13. You will, of course, need the appropriate security to create a new database role.

Name the role `AccountingExample` and make your own login a member of the role by clicking the Add button. Additionally, make your own user name an owner of the role. You may have to add your login as a user to the `msdb` database prior to adding the role if it's not there already.

You're now ready to tie this role to a package. In Management Studio, connect to Integration Services. Right-click any package stored in the `msdb` database and select Package Role to secure the package. For the Writer and Reader roles, select the newly created `AccountingExample` role and click OK. Now, only users in the `AccountingExample` role will be able to perform actions to the package. However, note that if you're a `sysadmin` role, you will still be able to perform all functions in SSIS such as executing and updating any package, and bypassing the package role.

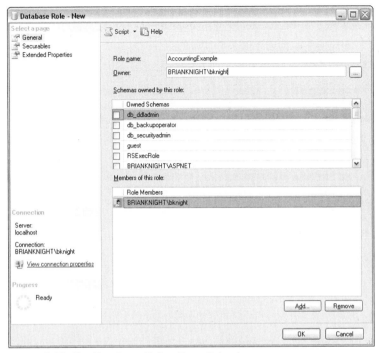

Figure 9-13: The Database Role - New dialog box

If your packages are stored on the file system, then you must set a package password on the package to truly secure the package. You can enforce security as well by protecting the directory with NTFS security on the file or folder where your packages are stored.

To set a package password in BIDS, you can set the ProtectionLevel property to EncryptSensitiveWithPassword and type a password for the PackagePassword property. You can also set a package password using a utility called DTUtil.exe, which is discussed later in this chapter.

Firewall Issues

To connect to a package store, the SSIS service must be started on the given server. Additionally, you must have TCP/IP port 135 open between your machine and the server. This port is a common port used for the Distributed Component Object Model (DCOM), and many network administrators will not have this open by default. You'll also need to have the SQL Server database engine port open (generally TCP/IP port 1433) to connect to the package store in the msdb database.

Command Line Utilities

Thus far, the discussion in this chapter has focused on the GUI tools you can use to administer SSIS. There are also a series of tools that you can use from a command line that act as a Swiss Army knife for an SSIS administrator. The two main tools that you'll use are DTExec.exe and DTUtil.exe.

DTExec.exe is a tool you'll use to execute your packages from a command line, and Dtutil.exe can help you migrate a package or change the security of a package, just to name a few of its functions.

DTExec.exe

You've already seen the power of DTExecUI.exe for executing your packages. That tool wraps the command line utility DTExec.exe. A shortcut here is to use DTExecUI.exe to create the command for you. You can see the full list of switches for this utility by typing the following:

```
dtexec.exe /?
```

For example, to execute a package that is stored in the msdb database on your localhost, you could use the following command:

```
DTExec.exe /DTS "\MSDB\DBSnapshots" /SERVER localhost /MAXCONCURRENT " -1 "
/CHECKPOINTING OFF  /REPORTING V
```

This command is more verbose than is required. In reality, you must only type the /DTS *and* /SERVER *switches to find and execute the package.*

DTUtil.exe

One of the best undiscovered command line tools in your administrator kit is DTUtil.exe. This is also a good tool for developers as well. The tool performs a number of functions, including moving packages, renumbering the PackageID, re-encrypting a package, and digitally signing a package. To see everything this tool can do, you can type the following command from a command prompt:

```
DTUtil.exe /?
```

Essentially, this tool can be used to do many of the things that you do in Management Studio and, to a lesser extent, BIDS. The next few sections show you a few creative ways to use DTUtil.exe.

Re-Encrypting All Packages in a Directory

By default, SSIS files in development are encrypted to prevent an unauthorized person from seeing your SSIS package. The type of encryption is seamless behind the scenes, and is at a workstation and user level. So, if you were to send a package that you're developing to another developer on your team, he or she would not be able to open it by default. The same would apply if you logged in with a different user name. You would receive the following error:

```
There were errors while the package was being loaded.
The package might be corrupted.
See the Error List for details.
```

The error is very misleading. In truth, you can't open the package because the originating user encrypted the package whether on purpose or not. To fix this, the owner of the package can open the package and, in the Properties pane, select a different option (such as a package password) for the ProtectionLevel option. The default option is EncryptSensitiveWithUserKey. To protect the entire package with a password, select the EncryptAllWithPassword option.

Another useful option is when an SSIS designer encrypts all packages with the default option, and when he or she is ready to send it to production, he or she develops a batch file to loop through a directory's .dtsx file and set a password. The batch file would use DTUtil.exe and look like the following:

```
for %%f in (*.dtsx) do Dtutil.exe /file %%f /encrypt file;%%f;3;newpassword
```

This would loop through each .dtsx file in your directory and assign the password of newpassword. The production support group could then use a similar batch file to first decrypt and then reset the password to a production password. If you run the preceding command directly from the command line and not via a batch file, then replace all the %%f tokens with %f, and the same goal is accomplished.

Handling a Corrupt Package

Occasionally, when you copy objects in and out of a container, you may corrupt a given task in the package. In that case, you can't delete the task, or move it outside the container, or link it in the container. This doesn't happen often, but when you suspect you have a corrupt package or object, you can use DTUtil.exe to re-generate the package's XML. To do this, you can use the -I switch to generate a new PackageID and regenerate the XML, as shown here:

```
DTUtil.exe -I -File dbsnapshots.dtsx
```

When you do this, the package may look different when you open it, since the XML has been regenerated. For example, some of your containers may be smaller than original, and placed in areas they weren't originally in. You can also use this command to regenerate the PackageID when the developer copies and pastes the command.

You can also create a batch file to loop through the directory and re-generate the ID for every package in the directory. The batch file will loop through every .dtsx file and execute DTUtil.exe. The batch file would look like this:

```
for %%f in (*.dtsx) do dtutil.exe /I /FILE "%%f"
```

Scheduling a Package

The primary way to schedule packages in SSIS is with SQL Server Agent, which ships with the SQL Server database engine. If you didn't have a database engine in your environment, then you must use something like Task Scheduler, which ships with Windows. Scheduling a package with SQL Server Agent is much simpler and gives you much more flexibility.

The first step to scheduling a package is to connect to the database engine. Ensure that the SQL Server Agent service is started. Right-click Jobs under the SQL Server Agent tree and select New Job. The New Job dialog box will open, where you can create a new job.

In the General page, type the name of your job such as **Execute Package**. In the Steps page, click New, which opens the New Job Step dialog box. Type **Execute Sample Package** for the Step name property in the General page, as shown in Figure 9-14. Then, select SQL Server Integration Services Package as the type of step. For the time being, use the default SQL Agent Service Account as the Run as account. This means that the account that starts SQL Server Agent will execute the package, and sources and destinations in your package will use Windows Authentication with that account if they're set up to use Windows Authentication.

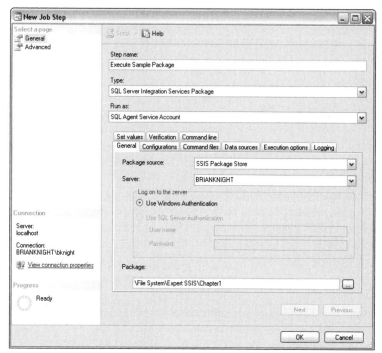

Figure 9-14: The General page

For the Package source, select the SSIS Package Store and point to a valid SSIS service. Pick any test package that won't have production impact by clicking the ellipsis button. When you click the ellipsis button, you'll see all the folders in the package store, whether in the `msdb` database or the file system.

The rest of the options resemble exactly what you saw earlier in `DTExecUI.exe`, with the exception of the Reporting tab, since there is no console to report to from a job. Optionally, you can also go to the Advanced page to set the Include step output in history option to get more information about the job when it succeeds or fails. Click OK to go back to the New Job Step dialog box. You can then go to the Schedules page to configure when you'd like the job to run. Click OK again to go back to the main Management Studio interface.

With the job now scheduled, right-click the newly created job and select Start job at step. You will then see a status box open that starts the job. After you see a success, it does not mean the job passed or failed. Instead, it simply means that the job was started successfully. You can right-click the job and select View history to see if it was successful.

This opens the Log File Viewer (shown in Figure 9-15), which shows you each execution of the package. You can drill into each execution to see more details about the step below. The information this step provides is adequate to help you diagnose a problem, but you may need package logs to truly diagnose a problem.

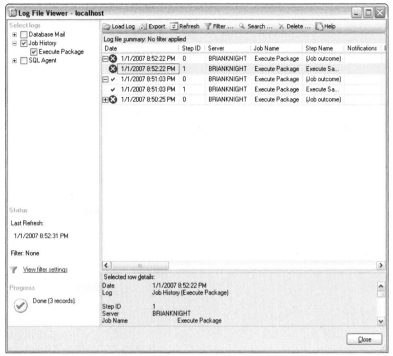

Figure 9-15: Log File Viewer

You can find a great article at `http://support.microsoft.com/kb/918760` that is updated on a regular basis and that will help you diagnose problems with scheduling packages.

Proxy Accounts

A classic problem in SSIS and DTS is that a package may work in the design environment, but not work once scheduled. Typically, this is because you have connections that use Windows Authentication. At design time, the package uses your credentials and, when you schedule the package, it uses the SQL Server Agent service account by default. This account may not have access to a file share or database server that is necessary to successfully run the package. *Proxy accounts* in SQL Server 2005 enable you to circumvent this problem.

With a proxy account, you can assign a job to use a different account than the SQL Server Agent account. Creating a proxy account is a two-step process. First, you must create a credential that will allow a user to use an Active Directory account that is not the user's own. Then, you specify how that account may be used.

To first create a credential, open Management Studio. Right-click Credentials (under the Security tree) and select New Credential to get to the screen shown in Figure 9-16. For this example, create a credential called Admin Access. The credential enables users to temporarily gain administrator access. For the Identity property, type the name of an administrator account or an account with higher rights. Lastly, type the password for the Windows account, confirm the password, and click OK.

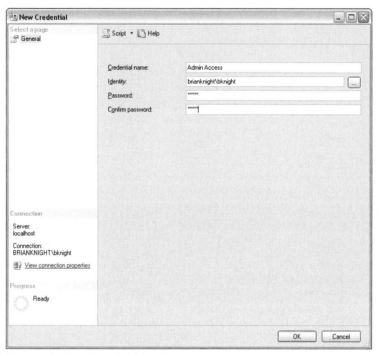

Figure 9-16: The New Credential page

The next step is to specify how the credential can be used. Under the SQL Server Agent tree, right-click Proxies and select New Proxy to open the New Proxy Account dialog box shown in Figure 9-17. Enter **Admin Access Proxy** for the Proxy name property and **Admin Access** as the Credential name. Select the SQL Server Integration Services Package subsystem type allowed to use this proxy.

Optionally, you can go to the Principals page in the New Proxy Account dialog box to state which roles or accounts can use your proxy from SSIS. As shown in Figure 9-18, you can explicitly grant server roles, specific logins, or members of given msdb roles rights to your proxy. Click Add to grant rights to the proxy one at a time.

You can now click OK to save the proxy. Now, if you were to create a new SSIS job step as was shown in Figure 9-14, you'll be able to use the new proxy by selecting Admin Access Proxy from the Run as drop-down list box. Any connections that use Windows Authentication will then use the proxy account instead of the standard account.

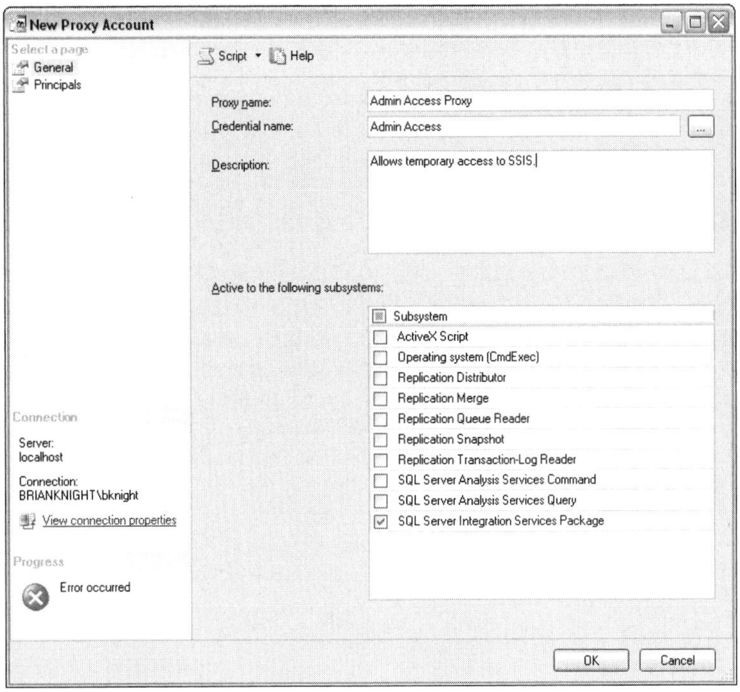

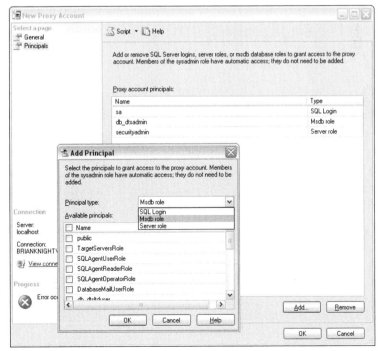

Figure 9-17: The New Proxy Account dialog box

Figure 9-18: Granting server roles, specific logins, or members of given
msdb roles rights to your proxy

64-Bit Issues

As mentioned earlier, `DTExecUI.exe` is a 32-bit application. Because of this, whenever you execute a package from `DTExecUI.exe`, it will execute in 32-bit mode even if you are running it on a 64-bit machine, which could potentially cause it to take longer to execute. Much of this is because data must be marshaled back and forth between 32-bit mode and 64-bit mode. To get around this problem, you can go to the Command Line page of this tool (shown earlier in Figure 9-10), copy the command out of the window, and paste it into a command prompt, prefixing `dtexec.exe` in front of it.

On a 64-bit machine, `DTExec.exe` comes in two flavors: 32-bit and 64-bit. The 32-bit version is stored in the `\Program Files (x86)` directory and the 64-bit version is stored in the main `\Program Files` directory. Occasionally, the environment variables may have issues and point to the wrong `C:\Program Files\Microsoft SQL Server\90\DTS\Binn\` directory. You can fix this by right-clicking My Computer on the desktop and selecting Properties. Go to the Advanced tab and select Environment Variables to produce the screen shown in Figure 9-19. From the System variables section in the lower portion of the window, select the Path variable and click Edit. In the next window, you will see several delimited paths to various folders on the system. Look for the path referring to the `Binn` directory mentioned earlier. Ensure here that this path is set to `\Program Files` and not `\Program Files (x86)` and click OK. After that, you can go to a command prompt, type **DTExec.exe**, and know that you're executing the 64-bit version (the version is of `DTExec.exe` shown in the first few lines of executing a package).

Figure 9-19: The Environment Variables dialog box

Another issue (up to and including Service Pack 2 of SQL Server 2005) is that Visual Studio .NET, and thus BIDS, does not work on Itanium 64-bit (IA64) machines. Because of this, you'll have to develop your packages on a 32-bit machine and then deploy them to your Itanium machine. Along with this Itanium issue, you may find that many IA64 connectivity drivers lag behind the release cycle of *x*86 and *x*64 architectures.

Another issue that you'll experience is with the Script Task or component inside of SSIS. If you use this task in a 64-bit environment, you must precompile your code. You can do this by opening each Script Task or component and setting the PrecompileScriptIntoBinaryCode to True, as shown in Figure 9-20. After you do this, you must click the Design Script button and close the script to actually precompile the script.

Figure 9-20: Setting the PrecompileScriptIntoBinaryCode to True

A particularly annoying quirk is that (as of this writing) there is no Microsoft Data Access Components (MDAC) driver for the 64-bit architecture. The impact of this is that you can't execute packages in 64-bit mode if they refer to anything that uses Jet in particular (Access and Excel). If you need to do this, you can execute the package using the 32-bit version of DTExec.exe. Another option in BIDS is to right-click on the project, select Properties, and set the Run64BitRuntime to False in the Debugging page (see Figure 9-21). This will set packages inside the project to run in 32-bit mode when debugging.

The good news is that the drivers are constantly changing and improving. A good wiki on 64-bit issues with connectivity (which is updated very frequently) can be read at http://ssis.wik.is. Just because your particular driver doesn't work today, that doesn't preclude it from working next month as vendors update your driver.

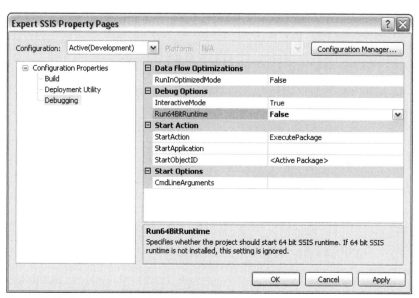

Figure 9-21: Setting the Run64BitRuntime to False

A few quirks of the 64-bit architecture and SSIS have been mentioned here, but the benefits are incredible. Keep in mind that SSIS is very memory-intensive. If you're able to scale up the memory on demand with a 64-bit architecture, there's a truly compelling reason to upgrade. Even though tools such as DTExecUI.exe are not 64-bit ready, packages that are scheduled will run under 64-bit mode. If you want a package to run under 32-bit mode, you'll have to schedule the step to run the 32-bit DTExec.exe from the scheduled job.

Performance Counters

There are a few key performance counters to watch when you're trying to monitor performance of your SSIS package. These counters will greatly help you to troubleshoot if you have memory contention, or if you need to tweak your SSIS settings. Inside the System Monitor (also known to old-school administrators as perfmon) is a Performance Object called SQLServer: SSIS Pipeline. There is another object as well, but it's not useful enough to describe here.

If you're trying to benchmark how many rows are being read and written, you can use the Rows Read and Rows Written counters. These counters show you the number of rows since you started monitoring the packages. It sums all rows in total across all packages, and does not allow you to narrow down to a single package.

The most important counters are the buffer counters. The Buffer Memory counter shows you the total amount of memory being used by all the packages. The Buffers In Use counter shows you how many buffers are actually in use. The critical counter here, though, is Buffers Spooled. This shows you how many buffers have been written from memory to disk. This is critical for the performance of your system.

If you have buffers being spooled, you have a potential memory contention, and you may want to consider increasing the memory, or changing your buffer settings in your package. This will be discussed more in Chapter 12, but for the time being, know that you should never see this number creep above a 5 (if not 0).

Summary

In this chapter, you've been shown how to administer SSIS. The discussion showed you how to run and schedule your packages from Management Studio, as well as how to use some of the more advanced command line tools to perform the same functions. Lastly, you were shown some of the key performance counters in SSIS to watch for performance issues.

In Chapter 10, you will see how to get around some common awkward data issues that you may experience with less-than-perfect databases. You'll also see how to manage connecting to data sources such as DB2 and Oracle, as well as to other sources.

10

Handling Heterogeneous and Unusual Data

Because of its price-point (out of the box with SQL Server 2005), SSIS is not only being used to push data into SQL Server, but also to heterogeneous sources. On the other side of the coin, you will often receive data that's not anywhere close to perfect that you must transform with SSIS. This chapter walks you through some of the scenarios witnessed in the field, that kept us up late at night. These examples should cover most scenarios that you'll see in your company, and will hopefully keep you from having to have the same sleepless nights that we had while creating these solutions!

Unusual Data Flow Scenarios

It never fails. Just when you think you've seen the worst possible extract, someone tops it. We've been consulting for years and we have competitions to see what the worst extract is. The examples you're about to see talk about how you can clean these horrible extracts. Oftentimes, you may have purchased a third-party product where you're not allowed to have direct access to the data. Instead, you must generate reports or access the data through web services and make this your data source. Painful as it may seem, there is a solution for solving almost any strange data feed in SSIS. In most cases, you won't even have to break out the Script Component. This chapter has many examples that explain how to handle this bad data, but the examples won't walk you through step-by-step on how to do the basics such as how to create a proper connection manager.

Creating Rows from Columns

As you know, mainframe screens rarely conform to any normalized form. For example, a screen may show `Bill to Name`, `Ship To Customer`, and `Dedicated To Name` fields. Typically, the data source would store these three fields as three columns in a file (such as VSAM). So, when you receive an extract from the mainframe, you may have three columns, as shown in Figure 10-1.

OrderID	BillToName	ShipToName	DedicatedToName
1	Jason Quest	Margie Quest	
2	Bayer White	Robin White	Sarah White
3	Brian Knight	Jennifer Knight	Scott Knight
4	Erik Veerman	Susie Veerman	
5	David Page	Susan Page	Alex Page

Figure 10-1: Extract from the mainframe

Your goal is to load this file into a `Customer` table in SQL Server. You want a row for each customer in each column, for a total of 13 rows in the `Customer` table, as shown in the `CustomerName` and `OrderID` columns in Figure 10-2.

Original Column	CustomerName	OrderID
BillToName	Jason Quest	1
ShipToName	Margie Quest	1
BillToName	Bayer White	2
DedicatedToName	Sarah White	2
ShipToName	Robin White	2
BillToName	Brian Knight	3
DedicatedToName	Scott Knight	3
ShipToName	Jennifer Knight	3
BillToName	Erik Veerman	4
ShipToName	Susie Veerman	4
BillToName	David Page	5
DedicatedToName	Alex Page	5
ShipToName	Susan Page	5

Figure 10-2: CustomerName and OrderID columns

The Unpivot transform and the Script Component Source are both mechanisms to accomplish this task. This example demonstrates how to use the Unpivot transform to create rows in the data flow from columns. Although it is possible to use a Script source to accomplish the task, it is much more complex, and should only be used if there are much more complex business rules than the stock Unpivot transform can accomplish.

The first step is to create a new package, `PivotExample.dtsx`. Drag a new Data Flow Task onto the control flow and go into the Data Flow tab to configure the task. For this example, create a Flat File connection manager that points to `PivotExample.csv`. The file can be downloaded from the Wrox web site (`www.wrox.com`); the Connection Manager properties should resemble Figure 10-3. Name the connection manager `Pivot Source`. The first row should be a header row. The file is comma-delimited, so you will want to specify the delimiter on the Columns page.

After creating the connection manager, add a new Flat File Source and rename it to **Mainframe Data**. Point the connection to the Pivot Source connection manager. Ensure that all the columns are selected in the Columns page on the source and then click OK to return to the data flow.

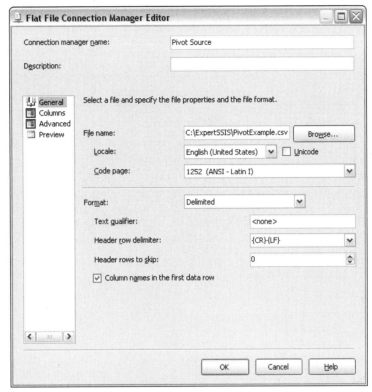

Figure 10-3: The Flat File Connection Manager Editor

The next step is the most important step. Now, you must unpivot the data and turn each column into a row in the data flow. You can do this by dragging an Unpivot transform onto the data flow and connecting it to the source. In this example, you want to unpivot the `BillToName`, `ShiptToName`, and `DedicatedToName` columns, and the `OrderID` column will just be passed through for each row. To do this, select each column you want to unpivot, as shown in Figure 10-4, and select Pass Through for the `OrderID` column.

As you select each column that you want to unpivot, the column will be added to the grid below, as shown in Figure 10-4. You'll then need to type **CustomerName** for the Destination Column property for each row in the grid. This will write the data from each of the three columns into a single column called `CustomerName`. Optionally, you can also type **Original Column** for the Pivot Key Column Name property. By doing this, each row that's written by the transform will have an additional column called `Original Column`. This new column will state where the data came from.

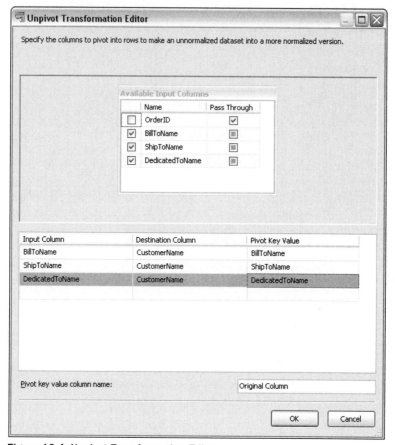

Figure 10-4: Unpivot Transformation Editor

The Pivot transform will take care of columns that have NULL values. For example, if your DedicatedtoName column for OrderID 1 has a NULL value as shown in Figure 10-1, that column will not be written as a row. However, you may want to handle empty string values, which will create blank rows in the data flow. To throw these records out, you can use a Conditional Split transform, as shown in Figure 10-5. In this transform, you can use the following code to create one condition for your good data that you want to keep, which only brings in rows with actual data:

```
ISNULL(CustomerName) ==  FALSE  && TRIM(CustomerName) != ""
```

The else condition handles empty strings and NULL customers, and, in this example, the relevant Conditional Split output is called NULL Customer. After this, you're ready to send the data to the destination of your choice. The simplest example is to send the data to a new SQL Server table in the AdventureWorks database.

Figure 10-5: The Conditional Split Transformation Editor

The final package should look something like Figure 10-6. The Valid Customer output goes to the customer table and the NULL data condition just gets thrown out. You're now finished and you can execute the package.

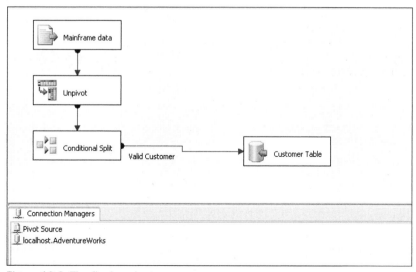

Figure 10-6: The final package

Multiple Record Types in a Single File

Oftentimes, mainframe developers may send you a single file that contains information about multiple tables inside the single file, as shown in Figure 10-7. In this figure, you can see two record types: record type 1 is the order header and record type 2 represents the individual line items for the order. The first column in this csv file (CH10_OrderRecordExtract.csv, which you can download from the Wrox web site) contains the record type.

1	43659		0	SO43659	PO522145787	
2	43659	4911-403C-98	1	776	2024.994	2024.994
2	43659	4911-403C-98	3	777	2024.994	6074.982
2	43659	4911-403C-98	1	778	2024.994	2024.994
2	43659	4911-403C-98	1	771	2039.994	2039.994
2	43659	4911-403C-98	1	772	2039.994	2039.994
2	43659	4911-403C-98	2	773	2039.994	4079.988
2	43659	4911-403C-98	1	774	2039.994	2039.994
2	43659	4911-403C-98	3	714	28.8404	86.5212
2	43659	4911-403C-98	1	716	28.8404	28.8404
2	43659	4911-403C-98	6	709	5.7	34.2
2	43659	4911-403C-98	2	712	5.1865	10.373
2	43659	4911-403C-98	4	711	20.1865	80.746
1	43660		1	SO43660	PO18850127500	
2	43660	6431-4D57-83	1	762	419.4589	419.4589
2	43660	6431-4D57-83	1	758	874.794	874.794

Figure 10-7: File containing information about multiple tables

This section discusses this common example often seen with mainframe extracts, and explains how to parse the file into multiple tables. This example has been simplified dramatically to fit into a chapter, so many of the performance considerations are being ignored in an effort to just show the functionality of how to master this problem. As you can see in Figure 10-7 (the file being used in this example), there are two orders which are indicated by the first column being set to 1. Under those two orders, there are many line items.

There are several ways to solve this parsing issue. In this case, you will make a pass at the file to load it into multiple raw files. The second pass of the raw files will load those files into SQL Server tables. Prior to starting this example, run Chapter10_OrderTables.sql, which will create the necessary tables in SQL Server. You could indeed load the data directly to the target tables in one pass, but there are certain advantages to a two-step process, depending on the business and technical requirements.

One advantage of not making this a two-step process is that you would only have to load the data into the server's memory buffers a single time. On the contrary, if you were to make two passes at the data, you will ultimately slow down your processing. The advantage of making the two passes at the data is for both the restartability and availability of the data. If the loading of the data into the production tables were to fail, you would still have the data massaged and in easy-to-access intermediate files. If this first process took three hours and the second pass failed, then all you must do then is execute the second pass, or place checkpoint files on the process to control that execution logic.

Another advantage is availability. In some cases, you will not be able to load the data into the production tables during operational hours. If you had a two-step process, you could stage the data into raw files, and perform all the transformations during operational hours. Then, during your load window, you could take the final step.

In some cases, you will have to stage the data in a table or a raw or text file. Those scenarios usually consist of very complex fixed-width or ragged-right data where the number and length of the columns are variable. The main problem is the length of each column. If that is variable and there are multiple record types in the file, then you must stage each record type into its own file, and then use a Derived Column transform and the SUBSTRING() function to break up the data.

This example assumes that you must break the data into two stages; however, as you can see, this depends on your business requirements. Start by creating a new package called RawFile.dtsx and add a new Data Flow Task onto the control flow. Name the Data Flow Task **Break up File**.

Next, create a Flat File connection manager that points to CH10_OrderRecordExtract.csv. This is the comma-delimited file that contains multiple record types and has no header row. As you can see in the Columns page (shown in Figure 10-8), Columns 5 and 6 have no data for record type 1. The first column (Column 0) contains the record type.

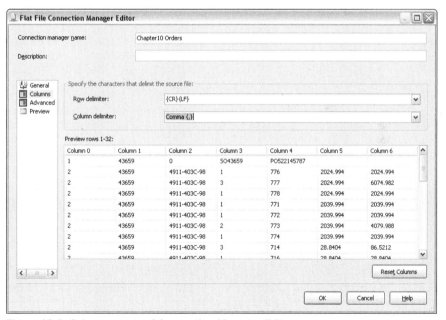

Figure 10-8: Columns page of Connection Manager Editor

Although most of the data is not shared between the various record types, there is a key that pairs the records together. In this case, it's the `Order Number` column, which is in Column 1. Before exiting the Connection Manager screen, let's update the common columns to the proper column names and data types.

Change the name of the first column to `RecordType` and the second column to `OrderNumber` in the Advanced page for the Name property. Each column will be a signed integer (`DT_I4`), as shown in Figure 10-9. The last two columns (Columns 5 and 6) should be named `UnitPrice` and `LineItemPrice`, respectively, and should both be set to Currency (`DT_CY`) as the data type. Leave the other column names and data types alone.

Figure 10-9: Column 4 properties in Connection Manager Editor

Inside the Data Flow Task you created earlier, you're ready to begin using the Flat File Connection Manager by creating a Flat File source in the data flow. Point the source to the Flat File Connection Manager you just created. Name the source **Initial Extract**.

Create a new Conditional Split transform and name it **Split By Record Type**. You will create three conditions, including the default output. The first condition is called `Orders` and will contain all the records that have a `RecordType` of 1. The expression `RecordType == 1` will suffice to grab only the orders. To get the Order Details case, you can use the expression `RecordType == 2`. The default condition should be called `Unhandled` and will catch any potential NULL record types or bad data that doesn't meet your requirements. Figure 10-10 shows the final configuration of the transform.

Figure 10-10: Final configuration of the transform

Next, create a Data Conversion transform and name it **Data Conversion – Order**. Drag the Order output from the Conditional Split onto the newly created transform. Inside the Data Conversion transform, select Columns 2, 3, and 4 from the Available Input Columns. Change the Output Alias to `InternetOrderFG` for Column 2, `SalesOrderNumber` for Column 3, and `PurchaseOrderNumber` for Column 4. The data type for `InternetOrderFG` should be set to Boolean, and the other two columns should be set to a 15-character string, as shown in Figure 10-11.

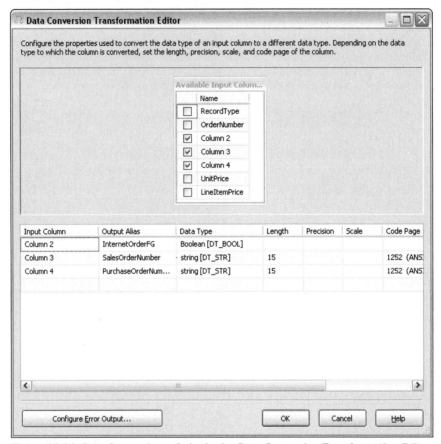

Figure 10-11: Data Conversion – Order in the Data Conversion Transformation Editor

Drag over a second Data Conversion transform and name it **Data Conversion – Order Details**. Connect it to the Order Details output from the Conditional Split transform. Inside the Data Conversion transform, select Columns 2, 3, and 4, as shown in Figure 10-12. Set the Output Alias to CarrierTrackingID for Column 2, OrderQuantity for Column 3, and ProductID for Column 4. The data type should be a 20-character string (DT_STR) for CarrierTrackingID and Integer (DT_I4) for the other two columns. It's important to have a Data Conversion Transformation here, not after the source, since the data types will be different for each record type.

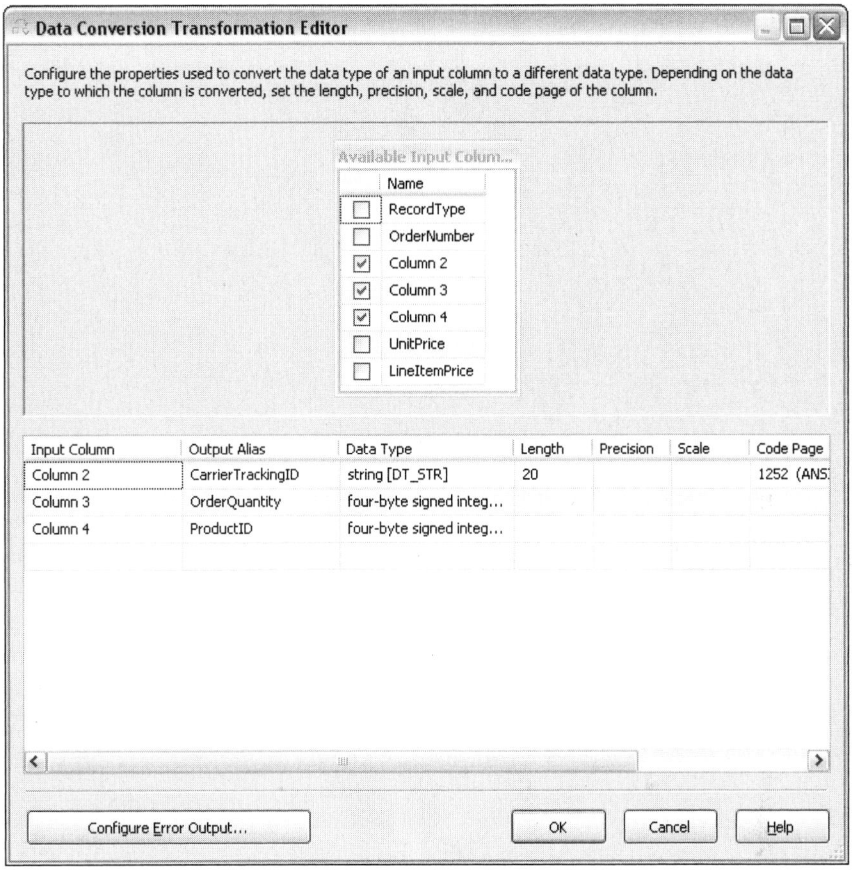

Figure 10-12: Data Conversion – Order Details in the Data Conversion Transformation Editor

With the columns now converted, you're ready to write the data to your raw files. Drag over the first Raw File destination and connect it to the Data Conversion – Order Data Conversion transform. Name the Raw File destination **Order Extract** and double-click it to configure it.

In the Component Properties tab of the Raw File destination, ensure that the Access Mode property is set to File Name. Type **C:\ExpertSSIS\OrderData.raw** for the FileName property and change the WriteOption property to Create Always. These options will create the .raw file each time the package runs, and you will create a process later to remove the file upon successful completion of the package. In the Input Columns tab, check the OrderNumber, InternetOrderFG, SalesOrderNumber, and PurchaseOrderNumber columns, as shown in Figure 10-13.

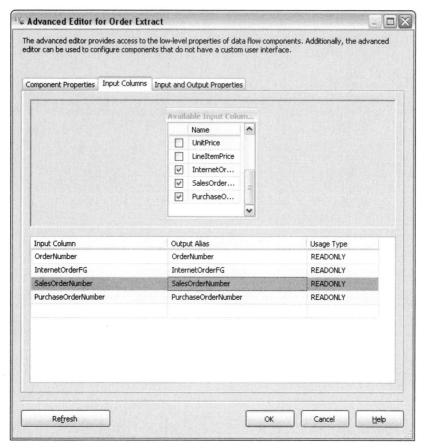

Figure 10-13: Configuring the Order Extract destination

Drag over another Raw File destination and name it **Order Details Extract**. Connect it to the Data Conversion – Order Details transform. In the destination, configure it just like you did the last Raw File destination, except have the destination create the `C:\ExpertSSIS\OrderDetailsData.raw` file. This time, in the Input Columns tab, select the `OrderNumber`, `UnitPrice`, `LineItemPrice`, `CarrierTrackingID`, `OrderQuantity`, and `ProductID` columns, as shown in Figure 10-14.

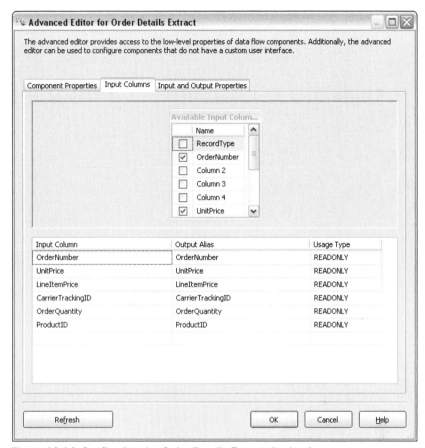

Figure 10-14: Configuring the Order Details Extract destination

Using the Raw File

Now that you've transformed the data and written two raw files with the first pass, you're ready to consume the raw files. The first process could have been accomplished during a non-maintenance window, and the second process could now be un-tethered from this package and executed independently during maintenance.

First, create another Data Flow Task in the same package and drag a Success (green) precedence constraint from the first Break Up File Data Flow Task to it. Name the newly created Data Flow Task **Orders** and double-click it to configure it. Inside the Data Flow tab, create a new Raw File source and name it **Order Extract**. Inside the source, set the `AccessMode` option to File Name and type **C:\ExpertSSIS\ OrderData.raw** for the `FileName` property.

The last step in this data flow is to drag over an OLE DB Destination and name it **Order Table**. In this destination's Connection Manager page, select the `Order` table in the `AdventureWorks` database from the table drop-down box. You will have to create this table by running `Chapter10_OrderTables.sql` from the Wrox web site. Of course, you will also have to create a connection manager to the `AdventureWorks` database. In the Mappings page, the columns will not line up exactly, so you may have to connect them manually. Your final configuration should look like Figure 10-15.

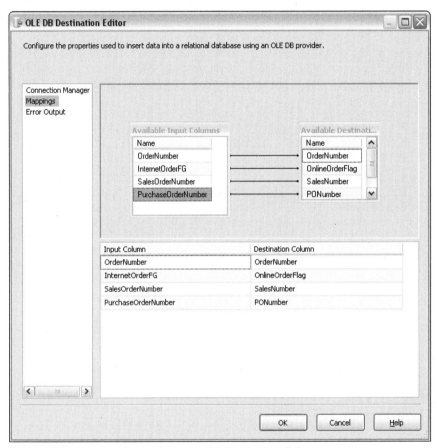

Figure 10-15: Final configuration in the DB Destination Editor

In the control flow, create a last Data Flow Task and name the task `OrderDetails`. Connect the `Orders` task to the `OrderDetails` task with a Success precedence constraint. In the `OrderDetails` Data Flow Task, add a Raw File source. This time, the Raw File source should have the `FileName` property set to `C:\ExpertSSIS\OrderDetailsData.raw` in the Component Properties page.

Connect the Raw File source to a new OLE DB destination named **OrderDetail Table**. This time, point the destination to the `OrderDetail` table in the `AdventureWorks` connection manager. The Mappings page should align perfectly, and only the `OrderLineNumber` column should be ignored, as shown in Figure 10-16, since it's an auto-incrementing identity column.

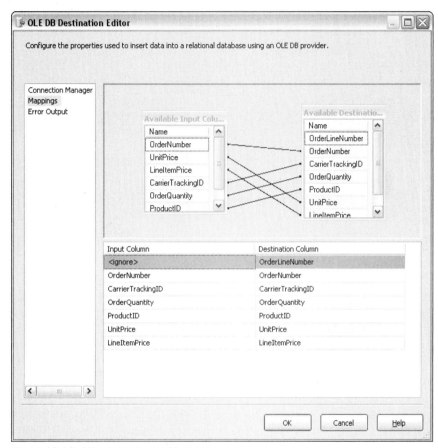

Figure 10-16: Alignment in the Mappings page

You're now ready to execute the package. The Break Up File Data Flow Task should look like Figure 10-17. As you can see, there are three order records and 29 line items for those orders. In the Control Flow tab, you should have three total tasks, but you may choose to add a File System Task to remove the raw files after they've been consumed. Doing this will use the space on the drive only during the execution of the package. This is not mandatory, though, if you have ample space, since you specified that you wanted the raw file to always be created. One additional thing to consider is that if later on you choose to select data out of the `Order` table, you will need to encapsulate this table in quotation marks or square brackets, since `Order` is a reserved word in T-SQL.

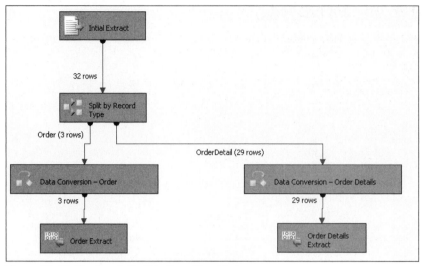

Figure 10-17: The Break Up File Data Flow Task

Oracle

Since SSIS made its appearance, some people who would never consider using a Microsoft database are purchasing SQL Server licenses just for the SSIS functionality. Many Oracle IT customers have indicated that they want to continue to use Oracle as their source or target data, and use SSIS just as an integration platform. SSIS can help Oracle users in three ways: help migrate from Oracle, help load data into Oracle, and help synchronize data between database systems, no matter the type.

Before using SSIS to connect to Oracle, you must first install the Oracle client network components on the machine running SSIS, which can be found on your Oracle CD or online at www.oracle.com. After these components are installed, you will need to edit the tnsnames.ora file, which is typically in the c:\oracle\ora92\network\admin directory in a default installation. This file will have a set of lines for each server you want to connect to. For example, if you had a server called FullyQualifiedServerName, your entry may look like this:

```
MyServer =
(DESCRIPTION =
(ADDRESS_LIST =
(ADDRESS = (PROTOCOL = TCP)(HOST = 10.10.10.10)(PORT = 1521))
)
(CONNECT_DATA =
(SERVICE_NAME = MyServer)
)
)
```

In SSIS, you would then use MyServer property for your server name, much like an alias in SQL Server. This file can be edited in any editing tool like Notepad, and it adds a slightly new layer of complexity for someone who's more familiar with SQL Server. Don't forget to also install the Oracle tools on any server that will be running the package (such as your QA or production server).

Reading from Oracle

You have many different options when you choose to read data out of Oracle. Each has its pros and cons. First, it comes down to a choice between connection providers: the Oracle OLE DB Provider for Oracle, the Microsoft OLE DB Provider for Oracle, or the ADO.NET Provider for Oracle (from Microsoft). There's no silver bullet, though, that says to always use one driver over another. Really, this will depend on the type of problem you're trying to solve.

The first question is what adapter you should use to pull data out of Oracle in the data flow. You have the option to use the Microsoft or Oracle provider. In the data flow, you can use the OLE DB Source or a Data Reader Destination. If you choose to use the Microsoft OLE DB Provider for Oracle, an issue with numeric data types may come up occasionally in older releases of Oracle. This issue was resolved when Oracle began using the `Integer` data type. This issue is where sometimes the provider guesses the precision and scale incorrectly. In this case, you can open the Advanced Editor to fix the issue.

To use the Advanced Editor, right-click the source component in the data flow and select Show Advanced Editor. Next, go to the Input and Output Properties pane and drill into the OLE DB Source Output ➪ Output Columns. Select the column you want to correct and change the Data Type, Precision, and Scale as necessary (see Figure 10-18). Oftentimes, the Precision and Scale properties will be set to 18 and 0, respectively, which will not hold numbers to the right of the decimal.

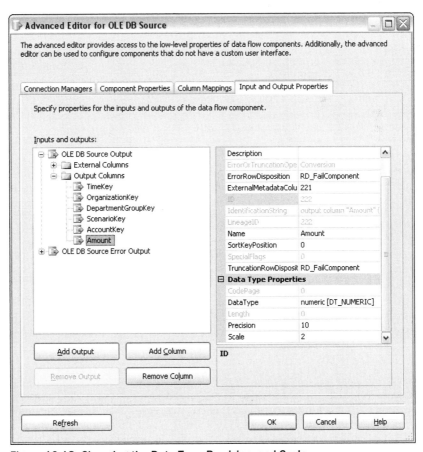

Figure 10-18: Changing the Data Type, Precision, and Scale

The Microsoft provider for Oracle also does not read CLOB, BLOB, BFILE, and UROWID data types. If you need to read from a table that uses one of those data types, you must use the Oracle OLE DB Provider for Oracle. From a speed perspective, it is recommended that you use the Oracle OLE DB Provider for Oracle.

There are other providers that you can use to read data out of Oracle. It's a constantly expanding list, but as of this writing, the following table shows you a list of providers that can be used to read data from Oracle. Only some of these providers can be used from within SSIS, although many of the ones that can't are planning to add compatibility.

Vendor	API	Version	SSIS Natively Compatible
Microsoft	OLE DB	7.3.4 and later	Yes
Microsoft	ADO.NET	8.0 and later	Yes
Oracle Corp	OLE DB	8i and later	Yes
Oracle Corp	ADO.NET	8i and later	Yes
Oracle Corp	ODBC	8i and later	No
Microsoft	ODBC	8i and later	No
Attunity	OLE DB	9i and later	Yes
DataDirect	OLE DB	8i and later	No
DataDirect	ADO.NET	8i and later	No
ETI	Bulk Load	9.0 and later	Yes

Code Page Issues

When you create a new OLE DB Source in the data flow that doesn't use SQL Server, you may receive a warning that won't go away. This warning would show the following warning message when you hover over the OLE DB Source and in the logs at execution time:

```
Cannot retrieve the column code page info from the OLE DB Provider. If the component
supports the "DefaultCodePage" property, the code page from that property will be
used. Change the value of the property if the current string code page values are
incorrect. If the component does not support the property, the code page from the
component's locale ID will be used.
```

This message is displayed because SSIS is not able to get an answer from the data provider on what code page to use. You can fix this warning by selecting the OLE DB Source and changing the AlwaysUseDefaultCodePage property to True. The warning will immediately go away.

Parameterized Queries

Another issue with pulling data out of Oracle is that it does not handle parameterized queries in the OLE DB Source or in the Execute SQL Task. The workaround for this is to use expressions. At runtime, the expression will either set a variable that contains a query, or the query text, depending on the usage.

For the Execute SQL Task, you must use an expression on the SQLStatementSource property in the task. When using the expression with variables, keep in mind that you will have to cast variables of data types that don't match to a string to match the SQL statement. This can be seen in Figure 10-19. In this example, the goal was to parameterize a query to pass in a variable that was a datetime. To do that, you must use the (DT_STR) casting function and pass the length and code page of the target value. After doing that, a variable of any data type will concatenate into a string as shown in the following query:

```
"SELECT * FROM TableName
WHERE StartTime > " +(DT_STR, 30, 1252) @[User::Query_StartTime]+""
```

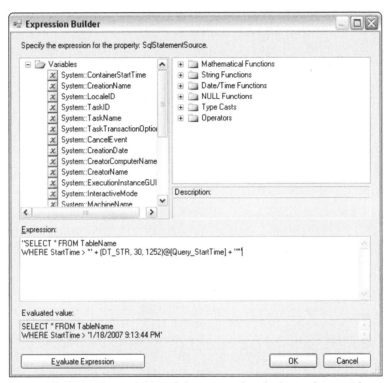

Figure 10-19: Casting variables of data types that don't match to a string to match the SQL statement

For an OLE DB source in the data flow to be dynamic, you must use a variable and set an expression on the variable. To do this, first create a string variable to store the query. Next, select the variable. In the Properties window, change the EvaluateAsExpression property to True. Above that property, set the Expression property to a dynamic query, as you did in the Execute SQL example (see Figure 10-19).

The final step is to configure the OLE DB source in the data flow. In the source, change the Data access mode to SQL command from variable. Then, specify the variable that had the expression on it for the Variable name property, as shown in Figure 10-20.

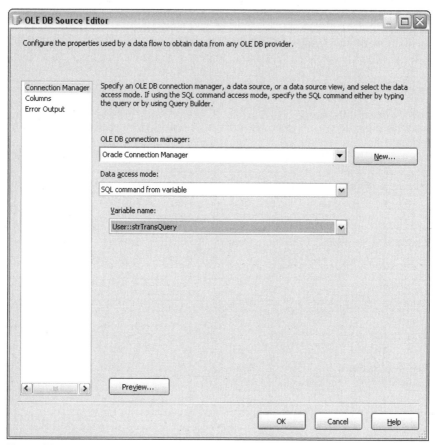

Figure 10-20: Specifying the variable that had the expression on it

Writing Data to Oracle

Writing data into Oracle is a tough situation. The predicament that you're in is that Microsoft has not written a provider that will bulk load data quickly into Oracle (such as the Fast Load option in SQL Server). This is not an investment that you should expect Microsoft to make, since it would be very resource-intensive to test and improve every third-party vendor's connectivity components, and they may see it as prolonging Oracle's life span in your environment. To give you an idea on the poor performance, a 50 MB file with one million rows took approximately 50 minutes to load into Oracle using the OLE DB Destination in the data flow on a dual-core laptop. Of course, pulling data out of Oracle was much, much faster.

However, there are some workarounds to this performance problem. One solution is to stage the data into a text file and use sqlldr (Oracle's Bulk Loader) to load the data. You would call the sqlldr command in the Execute Process Task. Although it is a clunky solution, it does allow for a great restartability opportunity with checkpoints.

The best solution (if the budget allows) at this point is to build an interface into sqlldr using a Script destination or a canned component. One canned component is from Persistent Systems (www.persistentsys.com/products/ssisoracleconn/ssisoracleconn.htm) and they have built an out-of-the-box, optimized Oracle destination. In one test, that same 50-minute load dropped to under a minute with their destination or the `sqlldr` command line tool.

Other Data Sources

Each data source will have its own intricacies based on how much effort the provider themselves invested in making it efficient. With data sources such as DB2, you have many options, just like in Oracle. Many customers have legacy data sources that lack OLE DB providers to assist you. In these cases, you can use ODBC and the Script source to read data, or the Script destination to write data into the database. This section covers a few other common data sources that we have found in the field, and some interesting alternatives you may not have known about. You may be interested in a fantastic site by the connectivity team that may help you connect to a data source that's not listed in this section: `http://ssis.wik.is`.

DB2

If you are a consumer of DB2, there are several options you have. One of the easiest options you have is to use the Microsoft OLE DB Provider for DB2. This can be downloaded for free as part of the SQL Server 2005 Feature Pack if you have an Enterprise Edition license of SQL Server. To find the Feature Pack, search for "SQL Server 2005 Feature Pack" in your favorite search engine. You can also use drivers such as DB2 Connect from IBM and StarSQL (by StarQuest). Each of these providers has its own benefits and problems.

With any of these providers, it's best to use the OLE DB source in the data flow instead of the Datareader (which is actually Ado.Net) source. The Microsoft Provider has an incredibly fast provider option that speeds up reading out of the data source tremendously. This option is an advanced option called Rowset Cache Size and, when set to a number such as 30, it will multithread the reads from the SSIS machine. The problem with the provider (as of this writing) is that it does not support large data types such as LOB, CLOB, BLOB, or their `varchar` and `vargraphic` equivalents. This support is coming, but providers such as StarSQL support it today. There are also options in the providers to turn `datetime` data types into `varchar` data types.

Writing data to DB2 can be extremely slow with the Microsoft provider. The fact is, Microsoft won't be investing much R&D in efficiently writing data to a competing database platform. If this is important to you, then you should test other providers like StarSQL or the IBM driver. Persistent is also making a driver that will hook right into the data flow and will be very fast for writing data to DB2. The following table shows a list of some other drivers to consider.

Vendor	API	Version of DB2	SSIS Natively Compatible
Microsoft	OLE DB	All DRDA compliant	Yes
IBM	OLE DB	z/OS and UDB 7.0 and later, AIX 5.0 and later, AS400 4.5 and later	Yes
IBM	ADO.NET	DB2 UDB 9.0	No

Table continued on following page

Vendor	API	Version of DB2	SSIS Natively Compatible
IBM	ODBC	z/OS and UDB 7.0 and later	No
		AIX 5.0 and later, AS400 4.5 and later	
Attunity	OLE DB	6.1, 7.x, 8.0 on z/OS	Yes
		7.x, 8.0 on UNIX	
		7.x, 8.0 on Windows	
Attunity	OLE DB	On AS/400 5.1 and later	Yes
DataDirect	OLE DB	z/OS and UDB 7.0 and later	No
		AIX 5.x	
		AS400 4.5 and later	
HIT	OLE DB	z/OS and UDB 8.0 and later	No
		AIX 5.x, AS400 4.5 and later	
DataDirect	ADO.NET	z/OS and UDB 7.0 and later	
		AIX 5.x, AS400 4.5 and later	
ETI	Bulk Load	8.0 and later	Yes

VSAM

VSAM is a particularly nasty data format to deal with. There are two main providers that you can use for this format: OLE DB Provider for VSAM and a similar middleware provider that is made by Attunity. Each can be challenging to install and configure, but after they are configured, they will perform fairly fast for reading data out of VSAM.

In several clients' performance tests that we performed, the Attunity provider far exceeded the performance of the Microsoft driver, and provided easy support of change data capture (CDC). This provides a great way to build a bridge to the mainframe to gradually remove your applications from it. The disadvantage to the Attunity provider is that it has a heavier footprint on the mainframe. With either provider, it's important that you have very good indexes on the VSAM files so that you can retrieve data quickly. This especially applies to any time you want to retrieve data out of the VSAM file with a predicate (where clause).

For most people, however, the best option is to retrieve an extract from VSAM. If you choose this as a source, ensure that you allot enough time in your project plan for the mainframe group to produce these programs. It's easy to take that group for granted, and before you know it, they want an additional month in your project plan.

Summary

In this chapter, you've learned how to deal with a variety of data issues such as how to unpivot data and deal with multiple tables in the same extract file. Unfortunately, these awkward files are prevalent, and with a little creative package engineering, you can get around the issues. You also learned how to deal with various Oracle, DB2, and VSAM provider issues. Each of the providers that Microsoft and other vendors offer has its own benefits and problems that can be worked through with simple workarounds like parameterizing queries through expressions.

In Chapter 11, you'll learn how to convert legacy DTS packages to SSIS. This process may be more challenging than you anticipated.

Migrating from DTS to SSIS

The SQL Server perfect storm is about to approach. SQL Server 2005 does still support Data Transformation Services (DTS) from a runtime perspective, but the next release of SQL Server may not. This gives you a small window of opportunity to upgrade your packages from DTS to SSIS using SQL Server 2005. This chapter discusses first how to run DTS from within a SQL Server 2005 environment, and then how to upgrade your DTS packages to SSIS. The first part of this process can be done through a wizard, but the conversion doesn't stop when the package is migrated.

SQL Server 2005 DTS Backward Compatibility

Although SSIS is a completely new architecture that doesn't resemble DTS at all, SQL Server 2005 still does ship with the DTS runtime engine. As you'll see in this section, the DTS tools in 2005 are just good enough to run packages and perhaps tweak them, but not for full DTS package development. It becomes increasingly obvious that Microsoft wanted to provide people with a disincentive to using DTS going forward, by not providing the typically amazing management and design tools.

Administering and Editing a DTS Package

The good news is that even though the interface may not be superb, you can still edit, run, and schedule packages inside SQL Server 2005. You can do this through Management Studio. Assuming you upgrade an existing SQL Server 2000 instance to SQL Server 2005, your DTS packages will be imported into the new SQL Server 2005 instance as DTS packages as well. They would appear in Management Studio when connected to the Database Engine under Management ➪ Legacy ➪ Data Transformation Services (shown in Figure 11-1). Any package would remain intact, except for those stored in the Metadata Repository.

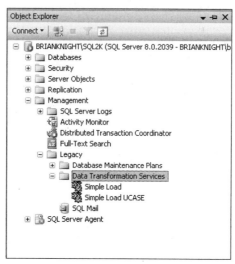

Figure 11-1: Data Transformation Services shown in Object Explorer

You can open any package by right-clicking the package and selecting Open. However, in order to perform this task, you must have Microsoft SQL Server 2000 DTS Designer Components installed, which is part of the feature pack. To download this component, search for the SQL Server 2005 Feature Pack with your favorite search engine. The feature pack includes many additional tools that didn't make the installation DVD for SQL Server (such as the designer components, the DTS runtime, and some additional drivers for SSIS like DB2).

When you open the package, you'll be able to edit the package just like you would in SQL Server 2000. Unfortunately, the screen is modal, so you won't be able to do anything else until you close the designer. You can also right-click the Data Transformation Services folder and select Open Package File to open a .DTS file that's on the file system.

Another important item that you can do is import a package from a .DTS file. To do this, right-click the Data Transformation Services folder and select Import Package File. You'll then point to the package file and it will be imported into the Data Transformation Services folder. To execute a package, simply open it and click the Run button. Features like DTS package logs have not been implemented in SQL Server 2005. You also cannot create a new package unless you modify an existing package and click Save As to save it with a new name.

To schedule a DTS package in SQL Server 2005, the normal simple tactic of right-clicking the package and selecting Schedule no longer works. You will instead have to schedule it manually or employ a little trick to schedule the package. Your goal is to have the scheduler execute the package by using DTSRun.exe from a SQL Server Agent CMDExec job step.

You can either type this DTSRun.exe command manually, or you can open the DTSRun.exe wrapper, which is called DTSRunUI.exe. This wrapper program is hidden in the SSIS bin directory and can be accessed from a Run command in Windows.

In DTSRunUI.exe, point to a package on your SQL Server 2005 machine and the rest of the options will become available, as shown in Figure 11-2. For example, in this screen, you can run a package by clicking the Run button. You can also schedule the package in SQL Server 2005 by clicking Schedule. The package will be scheduled and the full DTSRun.exe command will be encrypted.

Figure 11-2: DTSRun.exe wrapper

You can click the Advanced button to see much more detail about your DTS package and to see advanced options. For example, you can set the global variables of the package as shown in Figure 11-3. Most importantly, you have the ability to click the Generate button to generate the exact DTSRun.exe command to execute for a SQL Agent job. You can also encrypt the command by selecting the Encrypt the command option.

If you choose to generate a command from DTSRunUI.exe manually, enter the DTSRun.exe command, and the steps for scheduling the package look much the same. To schedule the package, create a new job in SQL Server Agent. When you create a new step, specify that the type of step is an Operating System (CmdExec) command. After you specify the type, paste in the command from DTSRunUI.exe and you're ready to go (see Figure 11-4).

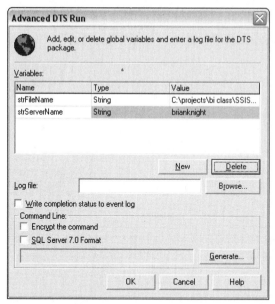

Figure 11-3: Detail about your DTS package and advanced options

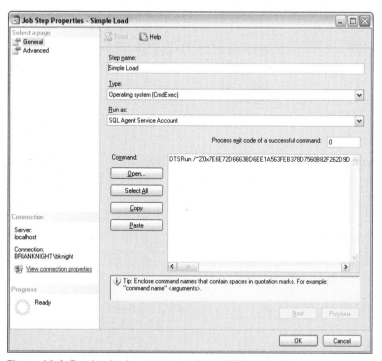

Figure 11-4: Pasting in the command from DTSRunUI.exe

Following is a simple command unencrypted. This command runs the Simple Load package on the `brianknight` server. The `/G` switch is optional and specifies the package GUID. The `/A` commands specify the input global variables that you may want to set.

```
DTSRun /S "brianknight" /N "Simple Load" /G "{8742BBB1-B6C5-4778-
A734-50A1E5BEFDD2}" /A "strFileName":"8"="C:\ExpertSSIS\ZipCodeExtract.csv" /A
"strServerName":"8"="brianknight" /W "0" /E
```

Upgrading from DTS

As you can see, Microsoft is giving you every incentive to migrate your packages from DTS to SSIS, since there are very few tools to help you manage the packages in DTS. To migrate a DTS package, you can use the DTS Migration Wizard. The wizard is good at migrating packages, but you may be unhappy with the outcome of the package it creates. The success rate for the package migration is generally less than a coin toss for most solutions. This section shows how to use this migration wizard, and then how to handle the package it creates.

The following table shows what we have seen in several migration projects that we've been a part of. The table shows the probability of successfully migrating some of the core tasks. Your results may vary, based on the type of work you're doing inside of DTS.

Task	Maps to IS Task	Success Probability
ActiveX Script	ActiveX Script	20 percent
Analysis Services	Analysis Services Processing	0 percent
Bulk Insert	Bulk Insert	80 percent
Data Driven Query	Execute DTS 2000 Package	50 percent
Dynamic Properties	Script Task	0 percent
Execute Package	Execute DTS 2000 Package	90 percent
Execute Process	Execute Process	95 percent
Execute SQL	Execute SQL	95 percent
Send Mail	Send Mail (with SMTP)	90 percent
Transform Data	Data Flow	50 percent
Global Variables	Variables	100 percent

Even though the tasks may migrate, they may not actually work after they are migrated. For example, as you can see in the preceding table, the ActiveX Script Task's migration success is 30 percent. This is not because it doesn't migrate. Everything in the preceding table migrates to SSIS. The question is whether the object model works in SSIS. If you're using anything that refers to the DTS object model, then its execution will fail.

For example, in DTS there was some complex coding you could have written to loop through a directory and execute a package for every file found in the directory. Each time you would execute the package, you would set the connection string dynamically. Because the object model has changed, all of this code will no longer work in SSIS. Instead, you would now use the ForEach Loop with a ForEach File enumerator, and in seconds, you can achieve the same result.

You must also consider what you're missing out on by migrating. This platform is so different that you're going to be missing out on some of the restartability features, event handlers, logging, and many other very nice features. Because of this, many people decide to use the upgraded package as a starting point, and then complete the migration by re-architecting the package.

The Upgrade Advisor

The first step of any migration is determining how much work you have in store. The best methodology for doing this is the SQL Server Upgrade Advisor (see Figure 11-5). You can download this tool for free off of the Microsoft web site. Its job is to tell you how much of an effort you have to migrate to the new platform.

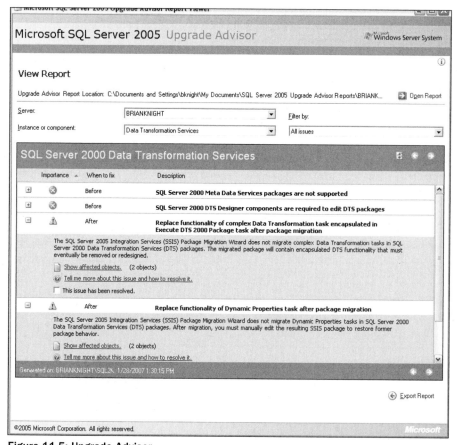

Figure 11-5: Upgrade Advisor

You can use the Upgrade Advisor to point to any folder on the operating systems of packages or a SQL Server. It will then scan through all the packages on the server or folder and tell you which issues you're likely to experience. Anyone pointing to a SQL Server will get very standard errors about the Metadata Repository not being supported, or the DTS Designer components not being installed in SQL Server 2005.

The other messages will be conditional, based on the packages on the instance or folder. You will then be presented with a report that you can reference again with the issues in each package, when you need to resolve them, and how. For example, in Figure 11-5 you can see that the Dynamic Properties Task needs to be replaced after the upgrade of the package.

This tool may need to be updated occasionally. You can do this when you first open the Upgrade Advisor. There, you'll see an option to check for updates. Updates don't occur often, however.

The Migration Wizard

To migrate DTS packages quickly to SSIS, you can use the Package Migration Wizard. The wizard is about 40 percent to 50 percent effective, based on your individual situation, as referred to before. If you're using lots of ActiveX Script Tasks or Dynamic Properties Tasks, for example, it will not be a straightforward conversion. The packages will migrate over, but not be ready to use until you adjust them after the migration. The 40 percent to 50 percent of the packages that it does migrate easily can be used immediately without any re-engineering.

The wizard can be launched either in BIDS or in Management Studio. It will be much simpler in the long run, however, if you always use BIDS as your launching point for the wizard. Doing so will automatically import the package or set of packages into the project that you launched the wizard from. Launching the wizard from Management Studio forces you to immediately deploy your package prior to inspection.

To step through the wizard, you can download two packages from the Wrox web site (www.wrox.com) that are very basic, but demonstrate some functionality issues. The packages are named Simple Load.dts and Simple Load (UCASE).dts. Both packages look like Figure 11-6, with some slight variations to their internal operations. The second package has an ActiveX script on the Transform Data Task to uppercase data as it flows through.

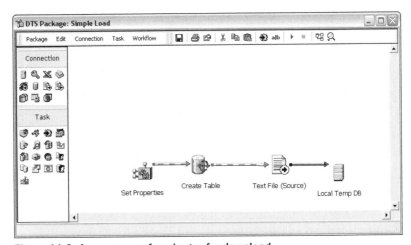

Figure 11-6: Appearance of packages for download

The packages have two variables that make the package somewhat dynamic. The `strFileName` variable sets the source file name and `strServerName` sets the target server name. The properties are set to these variables by using the Dynamic Properties Task. After the properties are set with this task, a table is created in the `TempDB` using the Execute SQL Task, and then finally data is loaded into that table. These packages represent most of the scenarios that we see in the industry, and should encapsulate most of the issues you're going to experience.

To open the wizard in BIDS, right-click the SSIS Packages tree in the Solution Explorer window and select Migrate DTS 200 Package. You will first be asked which packages you'd like to migrate. You can migrate packages that are stored on a SQL Server instance, or an individual DTS package file. If your packages are stored on the file system, you'll have to migrate packages one at a time (see Figure 11-7). If you want to pull from a SQL Server instance, specify the instance name. If you want to migrate a package file, simply point the File Name option to the `.DTS` package file.

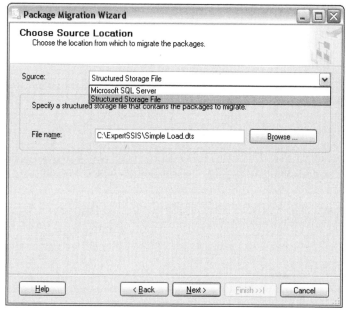

Figure 11-7: Migrating packages one at a time in the Package Migration Wizard

When you click Next, you'll be taken to the Choose Destination Location screen. In this screen, you type in the folder name that you want the newly converted packages to be written to. They'll also be added to your project, and the files will be physically located in this directory.

After clicking Next, you'll see a list of DTS packages you're about to convert (Figure 11-8). If you have multiple packages, check each package you'd like to migrate. You can also select the version that you'd like to migrate for each package from the Creation Date drop-down list box. For the Destination Package option, you can change the name of the SSIS package. In some cases, your DTS package will be using a reserved special character, and you may have to change the name of the package here to enable it to convert.

Figure 11-8: List of DTS packages you're about to convert

The next screen prompts you to type the name of the log file that you'd like to output the success or failure of each package conversion. The package conversions can take a lot of time to complete. For the small package illustrated here, the conversion should take about 30 seconds, but with larger, more complex packages, the migration could take up to 5 minutes or more. If you're migrating dozens of packages, it sometimes is very useful to output the status to a log, start the migration at night, and let it migrate all night long.

The next screen shows the migration in progress (see Figure 11-9). If there are any problems, you'll sometimes see pop-up error messages. At other times, you'll see the status turn to `Failure`, and you'll see the error in the Message column. After you click Close, you're taken back to the project to see the new SSIS package and clean up the problems.

If you're following this example, perform the tasks mentioned in the previous section for `Simple Load.dts` and `Simple Load (UCASE).dts`. Each of these packages will have its own issues that you'll resolve later in this chapter. Since you're migrating two packages, you'll need to run through the wizard twice.

Figure 11-9: Packages migrating

Handling Exceptions

With the packages now migrated, the real work begins. As you can see in Figure 11-10, when you open the converted package, there are a number of errors that will need to be addressed. The specific errors in this case are that the target table that you're trying to load doesn't exist. You can fix this error in one of two ways. You can either run the Create Table Execute SQL Task manually, or change the DelayValidation property to True for the Data Flow Task. This validation error is because the table that the later step refers to doesn't exist until the Execute SQL Task has been run.

When using the wizard to convert your DTS packages, you may experience quite a few exceptions. The remaining sections in this chapter speak to some of those exceptions.

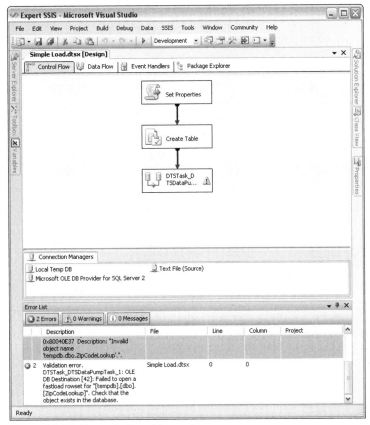

Figure 11-10: Errors to be addressed

Dynamic Properties Task

The first problem to solve with both of the example downloaded DTS packages is what to do with the Dynamic Properties Task that didn't convert over. As you know, there is no such thing as a Dynamic Properties Task in SSIS, so the wizard converts the task to a Script Task with stub code. The following stub code does nothing at all, other than to offer you a scope document on how to finish the conversion of your package:

```
Public Class ScriptMain

    ' DTS Execution Engine will call this method when your task is executed.
    ' You can access DTS object model through Dts identifier. Connections,
Variables,
    ' Events and Logging features are available as static members of Dts class.
```

```
' Before returning, set Dts.TaskResult to indicate success or failure.
'
' Use F1 key to open help system and Ctrl-Alt-J to open Object Browser.

Public Sub Main()
'
' Add your code here
' Source Type = 2
' Global variable = strServerName
' Destination = 'Connections';'Local Temp DB';'OLEDBProperties';'Data
Source';'Properties';'Value'
' ****************************************************
' Source Type = 2
' Global variable = strFileName
' Destination = 'Connections';'Text File (Source)';'Properties';'DataSource'
' ****************************************************
'

    Dts.TaskResult = Dts.Results.Success
End Sub

End Class
```

In this code, you can see that the Source Type is equal to 2, which means that the following variable is mapping to some property in the package. In this case, the `strServerName` variable maps to the `Data Source` property in the Local Temp DB Connection Manager. Additionally, the `strFileName` property maps to the `DataSource` property in the Text File (Source) Connection Manager.

This stub code is essentially useless to you since it serves no purpose other than to show you what to change. At this point, you can delete the Script Task after you see the scope of the change.

The first step is to select the Local Temp DB Connection Manager in the Connection Managers pane of the package. In the Properties window, click the ellipsis button next to the Expressions option to open the Property Expressions Editor. Select `ServerName` from the property drop-down list box. For the Expression column, click the ellipsis button to open the Expression Builder. In the builder, drag the `User::strServerName` variable into the Expression box, as shown in Figure 11-11.

When you click OK, you'll be taken back to the Property Expressions Editor screen, where the screen will now be filled out as shown in Figure 11-12. You will now want to repeat the same steps for the Text File (Source) Connection Manager. For that connection manager, you'll want to set the `ConnectionString` property to the `strFileName` variable, just as you did for the other Connection Manager.

The package is now dynamic again and the Script Task that was once the Dynamic Properties Task can now be removed. The `Simple Load.dts` package should now be fully migrated and is production-ready.

To tidy up the package, the last thing you may want to do is remove the duplicate SQL Server Connection Manager, which is called Microsoft OLE DB Provider for SQL Server 2. DTS often keeps orphaned connections that are no longer being used. Those all migrate as orphaned connection managers. Removing those should cause no harm to your package.

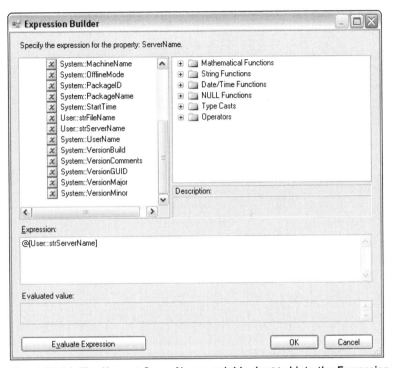

Figure 11-11: The User::strServerName variable dragged into the Expression box

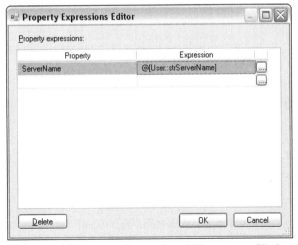

Figure 11-12: Property Expressions Editor screen filled out

Complex Transform Data Tasks

Complex Transform Data Tasks are not handled properly by the migration wizard. By *complex*, we mean a Transform Data Task that contains any business logic inside of it. For example, say that you were to encapsulate business logic in an ActiveX Script inside the Transform Data Task, as shown in Figure 11-13. In this example (`Simple Load (UCASE).dts`), the transformation between the `StateAbbr` columns has an ActiveX Script Task on it to uppercase the data as it flows in. This simple transformation causes the task to not migrate properly to a Data Pump Task.

Figure 11-13: Encapsulated business logic in an ActiveX Script inside the Transform Data Task

The task will instead migrate into an Execute DTS 2000 Package Task. Inside this task, the part of the package that could not be migrated will be embedded into the task, as shown in Figure 11-14. This now creates an interesting usability issue with the SSIS package. When the package is running, it will jump out of the package and load and run the DTS package. Although this is functional, it may not be feasible to go to production with pieces of the DTS package still in the SSIS package. It makes it much harder to support, since you'll have pieces in two different architectures.

The segment of the DTS package that could not be migrated can be viewed inside the task by clicking Edit Package. An example of this view is shown in Figure 11-15. To edit or view the package, you must have the DTS Designer Components installed. You can locate this component by searching for the SQL Server 2005 Feature Pack with your favorite search engine.

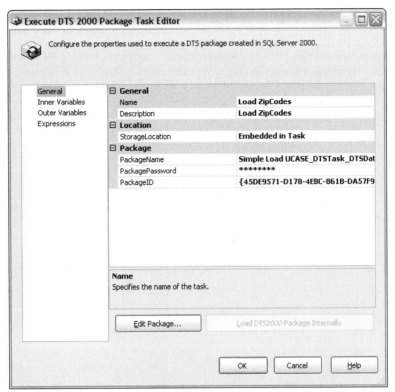

Figure 11-14: Part of the package that could not be migrated over

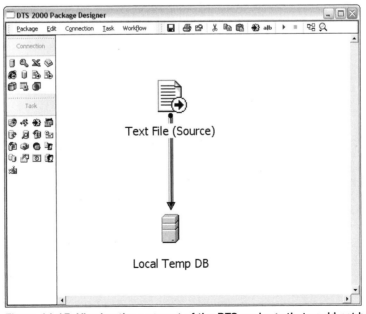

Figure 11-15: Viewing the segment of the DTS package that could not be migrated

The only way to truly migrate this task is to start this one component from scratch. First, document the business logic functionality being performed inside the Transform Data Task. Then, delete the Execute DTS 2000 Package Task and replace it with a Data Flow Task. In the Data Flow Task, you create a Flat File Source that connects to a Character Map transform. The Character Map transform will uppercase the data in place. Finally, the Character Map transform connects to the SQL Server destination, which loads the ZipCodeLookup table. The final data flow resembles Figure 11-16.

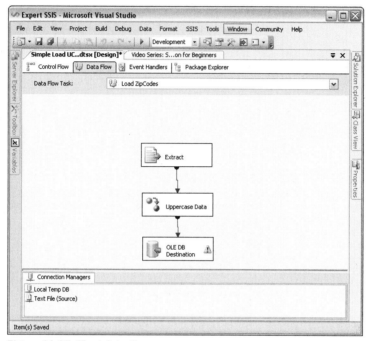

Figure 11-16: Final data flow

After this, you're ready to execute the package. There may be issues with the Flat File Connection Manager, but those will be discussed in the next section. The warning you see on the OLE DB Destination in Figure 11-16 is a truncation warning, where the metadata is incorrect in the Flat File Connection Manager.

If the ActiveX Script business logic is not important, you can use a free tool called DTStoSSIS-Prepare to remove the logic from a command line. You can also remove it inside the DTS designer, but the DTStoSSIS-Prepare tool (which can be downloaded from www.sqlbi.eu/) can be automated for you. DTS Xchange is another tool, which will perform a much more complex migration easily (www.pragmaticworks.com).

Flat File Connection Managers

Quite often, you will see issues when you migrate a flat file connection in DTS to a Flat File Connection Manager. If your DTS package uses a flat file, you will want to be sure that, prior to deploying your package to production, you open the converted connection manager and configure the metadata in the

Advanced page. By default, the columns will all be set up as 50-character string data types, and will need to be set up to the appropriate data type.

Sometimes, when you first open the connection manager, you'll see an error as shown in Figure 11-17, where the columns need to be defined. In this situation, you must only go to the Columns page for the columns to be detected automatically. Then, go to the Advanced page to set up the metadata for each column.

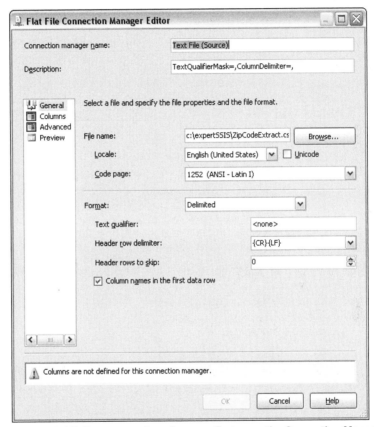

Figure 11-17: Error appearing when you first open the Connection Manager

ActiveX Script Task

ActiveX Script Tasks are more likely than not going to migrate over to SSIS. They will, of course, migrate to an ActiveX Script Task in SSIS, but the task will probably have bad code in it for SSIS. This is mainly because most DTS programmers used this task to set variables or to interface with the DTS object model. This object model has changed completely now, and anywhere you interfaced with the DTS object model, it will no longer be able to run.

For setting variables, you can quickly do this with the expression language. Simply select the variable and change the `EvaluateAsExpression` option to `True`. Then, write an expression to set the variable to your desired value at runtime. This works for simple business logic on variables. You can also use the Script Task to set your variables if the business logic is too complex for an expression. To do this, you'd use the `Dts.Variables` object inside the Script Task.

Another common usage for the ActiveX Script Task is to interface with the file system. In these cases, you can quickly and easily replace the functionality with the File System Task. A common use for this task was to archive a file or move a file. All of this is now done through a GUI File System Task, and will be much easier to read and maintain for future developers looking at your SSIS package.

Previously, the most common example for using the ActiveX Script Task in DTS was to loop through a directory of files, dynamically load the file into a destination, and change the connections based on the file name. That is now replaced easily with the ForEach Loop and the For Each File enumerator. Again, this is out-of-the-box and requires no coding; making it much easier for your successors to read your work.

Just because you can migrate your DTS ActiveX Script Tasks to SSIS, it doesn't mean you want to. So, many of the reasons for which you would use this task have now been ported to simple out-of-the-box tasks in SSIS. If you choose to keep the script, be sure to migrate the logic to SSIS Script Tasks and not ActiveX Script Tasks, since the task has been deprecated and will most likely not survive the next release of SQL Server.

Summary

In this chapter, you've learned some of the good, the bad, and the ugly of migrating DTS packages to SSIS. The DTS Migration Wizard does a good job of migrating the core package, but leaves out many issues that need to be addressed. That's where most of the work occurs, and you'll sometimes find yourself throwing away the migrated package and starting again from scratch.

Chapter 12 discusses how to scale and performance tune SSIS.

12

Scaling SSIS

As a fitting conclusion to this book, considering how to scale SSIS will help tie several concepts together. The topic is not new, as ways to achieve scalability have been presented throughout the book (such as how to efficiently work with transactions and snapshots, and how to scale your dimension processing). This chapter hones the discussion of scalability to several key areas, including data flow tuning, destination adapter optimization, SSIS execution architectures, and effective use of SQL.

This chapter is grouped into three sections:

❑ The first section, "SSIS Scalability Foundations," looks at the low-hanging fruit. In other words, you may be reading this chapter because your packages are not performing to the level you would like. In this section, you'll find out what you should consider when trying to identify and improve performance. Additionally, one of the main areas of concern when architecting a package is when to use database scripts versus leveraging the data flow. Therefore, this section will provide guidelines to identifying when to use each of these valuable tools.

❑ The second section, "Data Flow Optimization," deals with scalability of the data flow. When it comes to tuning SSIS performance, a majority of the resource impact (directly from SSIS) will come from the data flow itself, since the control flow simply is coordinating the execution of other services and programs. Among other topics, this optimization review of the data flow will examine destination optimizations.

❑ The final section, "Package Execution Principles," discusses package architecture and execution location. Identifying where packages should run impacts scalability. Included in this section is a discussion of distributed package execution.

SSIS Scalability Foundations

When it comes to identifying bottlenecks in packages, over time, you will develop that innate ability to know where to look. Similarly, you will also start designing your packages with scalability in mind, which will come out of knowing what works best for different challenges.

Some of the basics when you want to take your packages to the next level of scalability include knowing where your performance hits are, and choosing the right task to handle your data processing. When it comes to evaluating performance, the primary areas are identifying the control flow task durations and checking memory utilization. However, before diving into these areas, the first thing to look at is your SSIS service.

SSIS Service Status

The first thing you should check when encountering a performance problem is whether the SSIS service is started and set up to auto-start. The service provides some core functionality, such as enumerating and caching the component. By doing this, packages load faster and start up faster. The service name is SQL Server Integration Services, which uses the executable MsDTSSrvr.exe. To check the status of the SSIS service, open the SQL Server Configuration Manager and browse the SQL Server 2005 Services container, as Figure 12-1 shows.

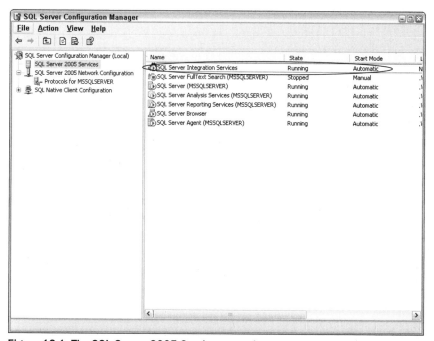

Figure 12-1: The SQL Server 2005 Services container

The service State should be Running, and the Start Mode should be set to Automatic to ensure that when the server reboots, the service is restarted.

Identifying Task Durations

When you have a package that is taking a long time to run, the natural first step is to identify which tasks are taking the longest. If you are running a package in BIDS, you can pretty much see how long each task is taking. However, if your package is running via a command line script, then identifying the long-running tasks will be more difficult than it sounds.

Even if you've turned on package logging, the events that are sent do not provide the task-duration information in a single line. Instead, the log events are sent out as the events happen. For example, the OnPreExecute event is sent out with a timestamp of its occurrence. Later, when the task finishes, the OnPostExecute is sent out. Therefore, to display the duration of tasks, you will need to associate the OnPreExecute and OnPostExecute, and compare the times.

The following TSQL statement can be run against the dbo.sysdtslog90 table. It will display each execution of a package and the tasks contained within that execution, as well as their execution times.

```
    WITH Task_Details_CTE (Source,SourceID,ExecutionID,StartTime,EndTime)
     AS                                  --provides the task exec. detail
(
SELECT sys1.Source, sys1.SourceID, sys1.ExecutionID
     , sys1.StartTime, sys2.EndTime
  FROM dbo.sysdtslog90 sys1
 INNER JOIN dbo.sysdtslog90 sys2
     ON sys1.Event = 'OnPreExecute'      --gets only the start time
    AND sys2.Event = 'OnPostExecute'     --gets only the completed time
    AND sys1.ExecutionID = sys2.ExecutionID --groups package execution
    AND sys2.SourceID = sys1.SourceID    --associates identical tasks
)

 SELECT                                  --identifies the "package" tasks
   CASE WHEN sys.SourceID = CTE.SourceID THEN CTE.Source
        ELSE '    TASK: ' + CTE.Source
     END AS [Package|Task]               --indents tasks to package execs
     , CTE.StartTime
     , CTE.EndTime
     , RIGHT('00' + CAST(DATEDIFF(SECOND,CTE.StartTime, CTE.EndTime)/60
              AS VARCHAR(20)),3) + ' min.' +
       RIGHT('0'  + CAST(DATEDIFF(SECOND,CTE.StartTime, CTE.EndTime)%60
              AS VARCHAR(20)),2) + ' sec.' AS TaskDuration
  FROM dbo.sysdtslog90 sys
 INNER JOIN Task_Details_CTE CTE
    ON sys.Event = 'PackageStart'        --lists single row pkg exec.
   AND sys.ExecutionID = CTE.ExecutionID
 ORDER BY CTE.ExecutionID, CTE.StartTime--orders by package, task
```

This query uses a *common table expression (CTE)* to perform the task associations. It joins the CTE with the task details to the package executions themselves, and performs some simple datediffs to create a duration in minutes and seconds. This, of course, can be written in several different ways, or extended to include error details. The following table shows the query output.

Package	Start Time	End Time	Duration
Processes_Daily_Orders	12/4/2006 14:20:52	12/4/2006 14:45:02	022 min.10 sec.
TASK: Delete stage	12/4/2006 14:20:52	12/4/2006 14:21:01	000 min.09 sec.
TASK: Filter detail	12/4/2006 14:21:01	12/4/2006 14:29:35	008 min.34 sec.
TASK: Main data load	12/4/2006 14:29:35	12/4/2006 14:40:40	011 min.05 sec.
TASK: Cleanup tasks	12/4/2006 14:40:40	12/4/2006 14:45:02	004 min.22 sec.

Although simplistic in its output, it is able to show the durations of each control flow task, the first step in identifying areas that need attention for performance tuning.

In addition, Microsoft has released a report pack that includes a SQL Server 2005 Reporting Service (SSRS) report that runs against the `dbo.sysdtslog90` table. It can be downloaded from `www.microsoft.com/downloads/details.aspx?FamilyID=526e1fce-7ad5-4a54-b62c-13ffcd114a73&DisplayLang=en`. Figure 12-2 shows a sample SSIS log report from the report pack download.

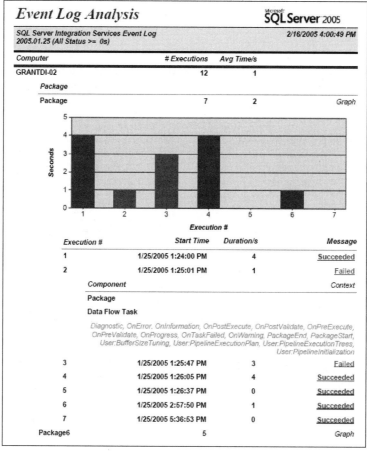

Figure 12-2: Sample SSIS log report

Memory Utilization

In many cases, as you are looking to identify areas for improvement, you will see that the Data Flow Tasks are taking the most time. And this is expected, since the data flow itself is the core processing mechanism in a package. Furthermore, when it comes to the data flow, the most important thing to be aware of is your system memory. Therefore, one big area of focus for SSIS scalability is memory management—identifying when you exceed thresholds and when you have more memory to leverage for performance.

> When it comes to identifying the bottleneck of a system, the standard Performance Monitor counters can be used, such as memory usage and paging, disk throughput and queue lengths, and processor utilization. Although out of the scope of this discussion, they are the foundation to identifying which server resource is constraining the processes.

With SSIS, often you will see bottlenecks in the area of memory and disk input/output (I/O). If you are seeing both, and the only application running on your server is SSIS (and your destinations are on a different server), chances are that the disk I/O is being caused by the limited memory. Low memory will cause the operating system to start using virtual memory and swapping files between the physical disk and the physical memory. Low memory will also cause SSIS to start using temporary space on a drive to manage the size of the memory request. This is called buffer spooling, and it can quickly escalate to very poor SSIS package performance.

To demonstrate, Figure 12-3 shows a package that is importing three identical flat files (each contain approximately four million records). They are first brought together through a Union All transformation and then sent into a Sort transformation, which applies an order across the five columns in the file. They are being landed into a Row Count transformation for demonstration purposes.

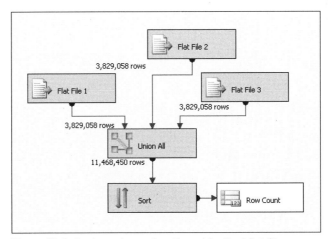

Figure 12-3: Package importing three identical flat files

On a single processor machine with 750 MB of memory (with about 400 MB of memory free), the package ran into performance problems when the memory reached the 750 MB limit of physical RAM. This package completed in 16 minutes and 25 seconds. Visually, through the debugger, when the package reached about 10 million rows read, the package significantly slowed. Figure 12-4 shows Performance Monitor counters (of this execution), including Memory: Available MBytes, Physical Disk: Average Disk Queue Length, SSIS Pipeline: Rows read, and SSIS Pipeline: Buffers spooled.

As you can see, as soon as the Memory: Available MBytes reached 0, the server started experiencing disk I/O issues. The Physical Disk: Disk Queue Length began spiking over 6 (which is 3–4 times over what this single disk subsystem can efficiently handle). Second, the Sort transformation started to use temporary disk space to complete its operation, and you can see this because the SSIS Pipeline: Buffers spooled shows that SSIS needed to temporarily store more than 500 buffers to disk during this execution. With approximately 10,000 records per buffer, that is about five million rows temporarily stored to disk. Clearly, this package was unable to run efficiently on this system.

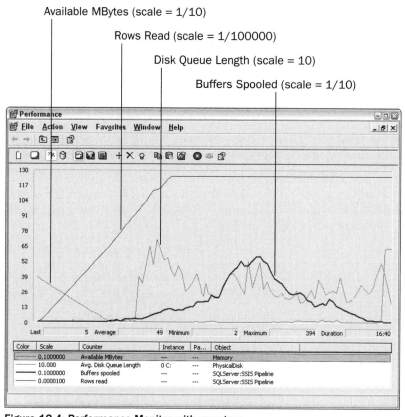

Figure 12-4: Performance Monitor with counters

When the same machine is upgraded to 1.5 GB of RAM, and the package run again, this time it completes in 9 minutes 45 seconds. Figure 12-5 shows the Performance Monitor counters during execution.

As you can see, during this execution, the Memory: Available MBytes never reached 0, showing the amount of physical RAM was sufficient; the Physical Disk: Disk Queue Length rarely increased over 0, showing the disk was sufficiently handling the I/O needs; and the SSIS Pipeline: Buffers spooled counter showed that SSIS never needed to spool buffers to disk.

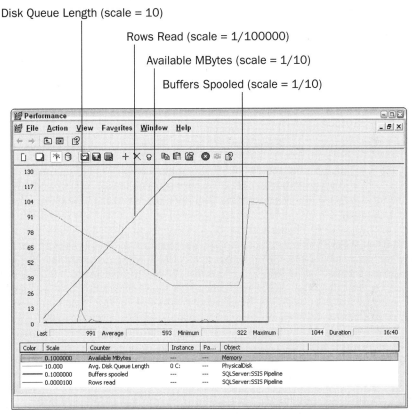

Figure 12-5: Performance Monitor counters during execution

The second execution ran almost twice as fast as the first test. By looking at the Available MBytes captured during the second execution, you can see that this simple package needed approximately 700 MB of memory for efficient execution. Since the first execution started out at about 400 MB of available memory, this means that the machine had a memory deficiency of approximately 300 MB, which translated to a heavy performance hit. This overall comparison demonstrates that a sufficient amount of system memory will keep your data flows leveraging the memory and eliminating the need to use temporary storage.

Furthermore, when the data flow started spooling buffers to disk, it caused a disk bottleneck on the system, and the disk queue length jumped up well over 2, indicating that the disk I/O could not keep up with the I/O requests. Although not shown, when this test was done with 500 MB of physical RAM and 150 MB available memory when the package started, the package ran for approximately one hour before being prematurely stopped without completing.

Memory management is key when it comes to SSIS performance, and several of the data flow optimization techniques will show ways to manage the amount of memory that is needed in order to optimize the buffers and package execution.

Balancing SQL Operations with the Data Flow

This section provides the framework for knowing when to apply SQL functionality (leveraging the underlying database) versus the SSIS data flow. This, indeed, is a matter of scalability because the appropriate use of SQL scripting and the data flow will enable your solutions to scale. In essence, this is about choosing the right tool for the job.

Data Flow Advantages as Compared with SQL

To be sure, the point of this discussion is not to downplay the value of SQL scripting, or of the data flow. Rather, it's to set the stage for making a determination of when to use each technology in your ETL process. As you will see in the ensuing pages, the data flow also has some limitations when compared with using SQL statements.

❑ From a core data transformation architecture standpoint, *the data flow can perform true in-line transformation processing*, meaning that while data is being extracted into the data flow pipeline, business transformation logic can be performed on the data before it is loaded to the destination. On the other hand, SQL-based processing has a limited ELT-type architecture, meaning Extraction, Loading, and then Transforming. When using SQL code to process data, the data must first be moved from one location to another, and then transformed. In-line transformations are not possible with Transact-SQL. For example, with a bulk insert or when BCP imports data, SQL transformation logic cannot be applied to the data. This has implications related to sequential operations, I/O impacts, and error handling, which are addressed later in this chapter.

❑ *The data flow has the capability to perform transformations asynchronously* or in parallel on the same data stream being brought into the pipeline. This provides greater scalability by reducing the steps needed to transform your data. Contrastingly, SQL scripts are inherently synchronous processes, meaning that Step 1 must be fully complete before Step 2, and Step 2 before Step 3. If you have a source flat file that must be brought into your database, first the BCP step must finish loading data to a staging table, then the update or transformation process must complete before the data is ready to be loaded, and then, finally, the data can be inserted into the destination. The SSIS data flow can be extracting the same data, transforming the data in-memory, and loading the data, potentially while it is still being extracted from the file. To be sure, SQL can be executed in parallel through the SSIS control flow, but this does not alleviate the synchronous requirement that SQL has to finish each ETL step before the data can be loaded to the destination.

❑ The SSIS pipeline engine *leverages system memory to scale its operations*, which can perform exponentially better than disk operations. Memory I/O operations are much faster than disk I/O operations. Therefore, when your server has enough memory to handle the data flow process, your packages will perform tremendously well. SQL inherently causes disk I/O, which, for large operations, is very intensive and often the bottleneck for an ETL process. The disk I/O overhead comes from the underlying relational database dependency that any RDBMS has by the obligation of consistency and durability (which is what the second and fourth letters in the distinctive ACID acronym of relational databases stand for). This database dependence can also affect end-user querying or transactional system performance (depending on where the code is run), because the SQL operations use the database engine resources to operate.

❑ Included with SSIS is *the ability to handle data flow errors without affecting the entire data set*. For example, when a row is being processed through the data flow and a conversion error happens on a particular value, that row can be redirected and handled separately and the row can either be brought back into the same pipeline or sent out to an error row table. On the other hand, SQL code is an all-or-nothing proposition when it comes to processing data. For sure, SQL has error handling, but the error handling is at the batch level, not the row level. If one row being converted fails, the entire batch statement fails.

❑ Within a single SSIS data flow, the *source-to-destination transformation can involve many-to-many mappings*. This means that you are able to bring data together from many sources, perform transformations, do data correlation, multicast or conditionally split the data, and then land the data in multiple destinations simultaneously. A SQL INSERT statement, on the other hand, is fixed with one-to-one, source-to-destination mapping.

❑ The SSIS data flow contains *data cleansing, text mining, and data mining capabilities*, which provide advanced data transformation logic beyond the standard capabilities that SQL scripting can perform. With a host of out-of-the-box basic and advanced transformations (including the Fuzzy Grouping, Fuzzy Lookup, Term Extraction, Term Lookup, and Data Mining Query transformations), the SSIS data flow can handle many unique and complicated scenarios not easily handled by SQL functionality.

❑ When dealing with large data insert operations, *the data flow can handle large data sets by batching inserts* through the destination adapter's advanced properties. A review of these features appears later in this chapter. SQL can also perform batching when doing bulk insert operations. For normal insert statements, the entire data set being loaded must be handled in one transaction, which often comes with long commit times.

In all, the data flow provides some nice benefits and features over and above what a SQL-based process can perform for many operations that are very common for ETL.

SQL Advantages when Compared with the Data Flow

When it comes to the advantages that SQL has when compared with data flow, there are several. SQL contains some significant value over and above the data flow for some ETL operations.

❑ The most notable advantage that SQL brings to the table is its *ability to perform set-based updates*. This concept has been discussed in several places in this book, but is important to highlight here because, when compared with how the data flow performs updates, SQL is able to significantly scale beyond the data flow. To perform an update natively in the data flow requires the use of the OLE DB Command transformation, which runs the update statement one row at a time. SQL can handle the update in a single operation by joining a temporary table with the table to be updated.

❑ *Relational database engines can perform sorting operations efficiently* with appropriate indexing. With large tables where scans are necessary, even though sorting with the ORDER BY statement may require inefficient query plans, the sort can often complete faster than leveraging the SSIS data flow Sort transformation. This will be true in cases where the SSIS server does not have enough memory to fit the sort set into the private buffer cache. When this happens, SSIS is forced to write temporary information to disk, severely impacting the performance of the transformation and other packages and data flows being executed.

❑ One advantage of SQL coding is its *native relationship to the database engine*. Because of this integration, code written in SQL has less conversion operations and, therefore, less chance for conversion failures with implicit conversions. The data flow requires data conversions into the pipeline engine and conversions out of the pipeline into the destination. The data flow also relies on data access providers to connect and import or export, whereas data coming from a SQL table into another SQL table is much more integrated with the database engine.

❑ Finally, *SQL (specifically TSQL) excels in performing advanced queries* such as recursive self-joins, correlated sub queries, multi-table joins, and more. Although the data flow can perform various data correlation operations in the data flow, some queries are too difficult to model with the available out-of-the-box transformations.

As you can see, SQL-based operations provide some valuable functionality that, when leveraged, can assist in providing scalability to your packages. Relative to the areas reviewed previously, SQL should be applied to the following key areas:

❑ Where updates (as opposed to inserts) are required, and the number of records that need to be updated is more than several thousand, then leveraging SQL code for a set-based update will scale your operation. If your current set-based operations are merely transformation logic not affecting existing destination rows, then look to integrate that transformation logic into the data flow.

❑ Storing auditing and logging information in a database will enable easy querying and reporting. Therefore, SQL can provide the mechanism to integrate between a relational database and SSIS, through the Execute SQL Task. This use of SQL and the database applies to auditing tables for capturing performance and status information; management tables for tracking metadata administration information (such as persisting incremental extraction information); and procedures and functions that drive the auditing and lineage.

❑ Even within the data flow itself, custom SQL can enable faster performance and better scalability such as for source query filtering, ordering, and shaping.

Data Flow Optimization

Integration Services is a platform, meaning that its purpose is to support applications built on its features. The data flow, for example, has no value in and of itself; the value is gained when it is applied to a data-processing purpose (such as warehouse ETL, system integration processes, or DBA data management operations). What this means when it comes to optimization techniques for the data flow is that there are no guaranteed formulas that yield performance gains, because every data flow design has a unique scenario. This section includes principles and common areas for you to evaluate against your data flows to determine applicability.

Pipeline Architecture Review

The SSIS data flow engine uses data buffers to manage data as it flows through the pipeline. As data is extracted form the sources, it is consumed into reserved memory spaces, called *buffers*. These buffers are acted upon by the various transformations as the data flows through the data flow to the destination. A complete review of the SSIS pipeline engine is found in Chapter 10 of the *Professional SQL Server 2005 Integration Services* book (Indianapolis: Wiley, 2006). Here are key points to remember:

- ❑ When data is loaded into a buffer, the transformation logic is applied to the data in place (where possible). In a sense, the transformations pass over the buffers, giving SSIS the capability to stream data through the pipeline. These inline buffer changes are cheap as compared to when the pipeline needs to copy data to new buffers. In some cases, the source data can be in the process of extraction while at the same time, data is being landed to a destination.

- ❑ Transformations can be categorized as blocking transformations, partially blocking, or streaming transformations (streaming transformations are sometimes called *row transformations*). *Blocking transformations*, like the Aggregate or Sort transformations, hold all the rows up in the pipeline before they are allowed downstream. *Partially blocking transformations* hold up a portion of the data, and *streaming transformations* allow the data to be available to the next transformation immediately.

- ❑ Partially blocking and blocking transformations have asynchronous outputs, meaning that the output of the transformation is not synchronously connected to the inputs of the next transformation. The effect is that the data in the buffers is copied to a new buffer from the upstream transformation to the downstream transformation. This has obvious resource overhead.

- ❑ The Conditional Split and Multicast are examples of streaming components, even though they appear to copy data. Their outputs are synchronous and, therefore, their operations perform logical multicasting and splitting, not physical. This helps optimize the data flow by limiting the places that require data copies, which are expensive. The Union All transformation has an asynchronous output and is, therefore, a semi-blocking transformation, even though it appears to be streaming.

- ❑ Each data flow has *execution trees*, which are groupings of sources, transformations, and destinations based on whether data is copied to new buffers (asynchronous outputs). A single execution tree only has one process thread that can work on the transformations contained in it.

- ❑ Sources also get their own *process threads* (or *engine threads*). Therefore, in SQL Server 2005 Integration Services, the total number of threads that can perform work on a data flow is the number of sources plus the number of execution trees. However, this can be throttled by the EngineThreads property at the data flow level (which is more of a hint to the thread scheduler than a rule). Sources always get their own thread, so this setting only applies to execution trees. If a data flow has seven execution trees but the EngineThreads property is set to 5, then two of the execution trees will share a process thread.

    Note that in the next release of SQL Server, the SSIS thread mapping model will be more free-threaded and, therefore, these direct thread mappings to sources and execution trees will not apply.

- ❑ Execution trees and engine thread mappings are viewable by logging the PipelineExecutionTrees and PipelineExecutionPlan events, which are available in the SSIS Logging at the data flow level.

To demonstrate, the following two packages are significantly different in how many threads the engine can apply. In the first example, Figure 12-6 shows the data flow containing seven execution trees.

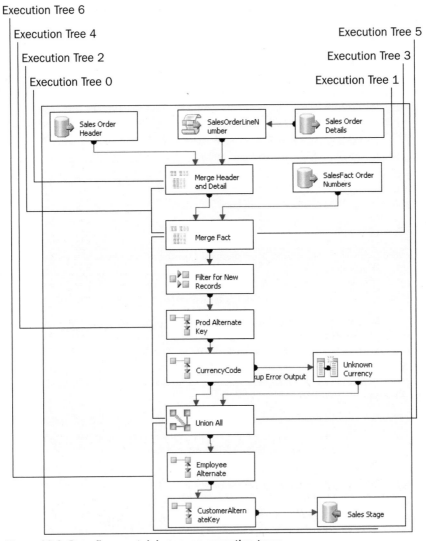

Execution Tree 6

Execution Tree 4

Execution Tree 2

Execution Tree 0

Execution Tree 5

Execution Tree 3

Execution Tree 1

Figure 12-6: Data flow containing seven execution trees

In this example, since the Merge Join and Union All are both examples of semi-blocking transformations with asynchronous outputs, each use causes a new execution tree.

In contrast, the example shown in Figure 12-7 only has one execution tree for the entire data flow.

In this example, the Lookup transformation, Derived Column, and Conditional Split are examples of streaming transformations (or transformations with synchronous outputs). Therefore, this second data flow only contains a single execution tree.

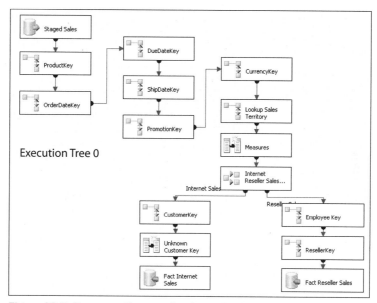

Figure 12-7: One execution tree for the entire data flow

General Pipeline Optimization

This first data flow optimization section covers general design practices to be mindful of when building or optimizing a data flow. The ensuing sections will look at the data flow settings and the OLE DB destination.

Look for Data Flow Backpressure

Backpressure is the situation when a transformation or destination is causing enough impact that the upstream data feed has to slow down because the transformation or destination cannot keep up. This is caused by resource bottlenecks. For example, if an Aggregate transformation is being used, and there is either not enough RAM to handle all the buffers in memory, or not enough processor utilization to handle the aggregate calculations, then the upstream source extraction or transformation will be slowed down. If you are trying to extract data from a source as quickly as possible, then you must resolve the backpressure.

Use Blocking Transformations Sparingly

Blocking transformations (such as Sort, Aggregate, and Fuzzy Grouping) can impact performance when dealing with large data sets in the pipeline. If you do not have enough memory to handle these operations, then SSIS will use temporary disk space to store data, which increases I/O and processor impact.

Pre-sort Sources as an Alternate to the Sort Transformation

You can tell a source adapter that the data is pre-sorted, and, therefore, limit the Sort transformation use. As already mentioned, a relational database can effectively apply an ORDER BY statement to reduce or eliminate the need to use the Sort transformation. However, flat files may also be created in a physical sort order. Therefore, these and any source adapters can be set up to know that the data entering the pipeline is sorted. Other transformations such as Merge and Merge Join require that the inputs be sorted. Memory can be preserved and performance enhanced by eliminating the Sort. Pre-sorting requires the input source and column properties to be modified. Details are discussed in Chapter 4.

Limit Row-by-Row Operations

A row-by-row (or *row-based*) operation requires that independent actions be taken, one at a time, for each row going through the particular transformation. The worst offender is the OLE DB Command transformation, because it calls an OLE DB command (such as an UPDATE statement or stored procedure) for every row that is sent through it. The non-cached Lookup, Fuzzy Lookup, Import and Export Column, and Slowly Changing Dimension transformations all exhibit similar characteristics. To be sure, these transformations provide valuable functionality in moderate to low volumes, or where expected package execution time is flexible.

Optimizing the Lookup and Managing the Cache Size

When you have a large table required for a Lookup reference table, there are a few methods to optimize its performance. First of all, a non-cached lookup is a row-based operation, and when your input row count is large, then the cost of every source row causing a separate database query is expensive. Therefore, it is better to use a partial cache or full cache Lookup. A *partial cache* builds the cache as the Lookup is executing, and, therefore, also comes with high transaction impact. A partial cache approach is a viable solution if you have a large number of input rows, but the unique count of distinct values is low for the lookup key columns. However, the best option is to use the *full cache* feature of the Lookup and filter the reference table.

Following are two approaches that can filter the reference table cache:

1. Apply an 80/20 rule and load one Lookup transformation with 20 percent (or some smaller percentage) of the most common matching records, which will allow at least 80 percent matches in the full cache. Then, for any row that does not match, redirect the row to a non-cached lookup, which will catch the rest of non-matched rows. This approach would look like the data flow in Figure 12-8, and greatly reduce the memory requirement.

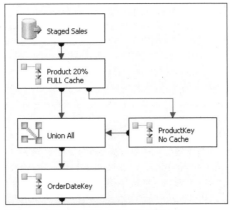

Figure 12-8: Applying an 80/20 rule

2. A second approach to filter the Lookup is to use a view or hard-coded SQL statement that only loads the rows that are needed in the Lookup cache. This assumes, however, that you know which rows need to be available in the Lookup cache. To do this, you must have the matching key columns from the source in a staging table on the same server. If you already have a staging table, then you can simply perform an INNER JOIN with the primary Lookup reference table (hard-coding the SQL statement or using a SQL view). If you don't already have a staging table, then you must add a new data flow to your package (before the data flow that contains the Lookup cache) that creates a staging table with only the matching key columns. You may be surprised, but this approach often produces a package that will run faster than not filtering the Lookup, even though there is an added data flow. And, in many cases, this approach will allow the use of the full-cache Lookup, where before it was not possible.

However, when all else fails and you need to use a non-cached lookup, then you should at least be sure that the underlying reference table has an index with the matching key columns as the first column in the index, followed by the Lookup return columns.

Removing Unused Columns from the Data Flow

An often unheeded warning in the execution results is that there are columns in the data flow that are not being used downstream in the pipeline. Sometimes this is seen as an annoyance, but in reality it is a very important warning. What is happening is that the pipeline engine is reserving space in the buffers when columns are not being used downstream, and that can cause significant memory overhead. With the extra columns, your data flow buffers will take up more space than necessary. By removing the columns, you are making more memory available for other operations. To be sure, you can only remove columns between execution trees. So, for the Union All, Aggregate, Sort, Merge Join, and other transformations with asynchronous outputs, be sure to edit the transformations and only let the columns through if they are being used! This is similar to the DBA tenet of never using SELECT * and instead always naming only the columns needed in a SQL SELECT statement so that the SQL engine can optimize the query.

Use the Union All to Break Up Execution Tree

Sometimes you will have a data flow with a very large execution tree due to the transformations that are used. The potential bottleneck here is that any single execution tree can only use one process thread. Therefore, if you have a lot of Lookup or Data Convert transformations that don't create new execution trees, but have higher processing requirements, then you may run into a process thread bottleneck with a single engine thread trying to handle all the operations.

The solution is to add a dummy Union All transformation in the middle to break up the execution tree. The Union All would only have one input and output, but allow multiple threads to perform the operations. Figure 12-9 shows a modified version of the previous example shown in Figure 12-7. Previously, this data flow had a single execution tree, and now a second has been added.

You might think that the data copied to new buffers would negate the value of forcing a new execution tree. However, another value of this approach is that it enables you to remove the columns not needed in the downstream transformations, thus also reducing the buffer size below the Union All. For example, if you have a Lookup transformation before the Union All that uses a set of business keys to look up a primary key reference, once the Lookup is complete, those business keys are often not needed later in the data flow, and, therefore, they can be removed at the Union All.

Note that the SSIS threading will change in the next release of SQL Server, therefore, this optimization will only apply to SQL Server 2005 SSIS.

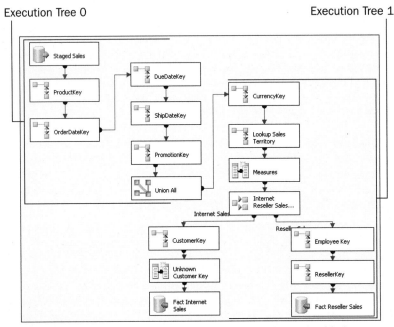

Figure 12-9: Example data flow with a second execution tree added

Stage Data with a Multicast

As mentioned in Chapter 3, another data flow optimization technique is to leverage the Multicast transformation when you need to stage data, instead of using two separate data flows. This approach is further worked out in Chapter 3, but the advantage comes in the reduced disk I/O and the parallel or asynchronous nature of this approach.

Be Mindful of the SSIS Logging Impact

SSIS logging certainly provides a valuable tool for monitoring and troubleshooting packages, but be aware that if you are logging every event and have a moderately complicated to complicated package, this will produce a lot of overhead activity for the package, as well as the underlying connection that the logging is configured to use, especially if the connection is a database (as opposed to a file). By limiting the logging to only the `OnPreExecute`, `OnPostExecute`, `OnWarning`, `OnError`, and `OnTaskFailed` events, you will reduce the possibility of your logging significantly impacting your package performance.

Transactions

You should be careful of the impact of transactions on your data flow. When you set the `Transaction Option` property of a package or task to required, SSIS uses the Distributed Transaction Coordinator (DTC, a system service) to allow transaction association with various technologies. However, this comes with overhead and it may be better (depending on your situation) to use native transactions in the database with which you are working. For example, for SQL Server, coordinating Execute SQL Tasks before and after your data flow with BEGIN TRAN and COMMIT TRAN will allow you to use native transactions.

The bigger impact of transactions is rollback time. If you have large volumes in your data flow and get an error near the end of the large transaction, it may take just as much time (if not more) to roll back your transaction as it did to process the data flow before the error! And, if you set a transaction on the entire package or parent package, this is exasperated. Review the Chapter 7 discussion on leveraging Database Snapshots as a transaction mechanism if you are working with SQL Server, which can greatly ease the rollback time and requirements for large volumes.

Data Flow Properties

Each Data Flow Task has a series of properties and settings that are important to know and understand so that you can tune your data flows. Figure 12-10 highlights a simple data flow with the Properties window showing.

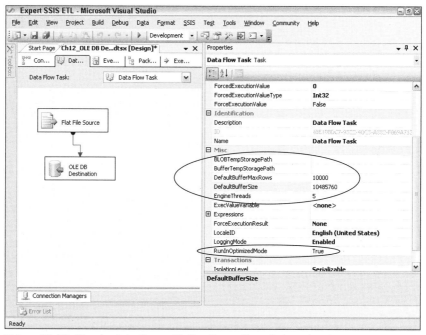

Figure 12-10: Simple data flow with the Properties window showing

Highlighted in Figure 12-10 are six properties that each Data Flow Task has that can affect performance. Take the following into consideration when you are working with these properties.

Up the EngineThreads Value

Be sure to set the `EngineThreads` property on your data flow to at least the number of execution trees that the data flow contains. In fact, it may be easier to just jump up the value of the `EngineThreads` property to 20 or 30, just to ensure that each execution tree has its own thread. Even if your server only has two or four processors, many process threads can be running efficiently in parallel, because each may not be working with the same level of intensity, or require code execution for every processor cycle. However, remember that this property is just a hint to the scheduler; there is no danger of creating a set of unused threads by setting this value too high.

Optimize the Temporary Storage Locations

The `BufferTempStoragePath` and `BLOBTempStoragePath` properties tell the data flow where to store temporary data to disk if needed. By leaving these blank, SSIS will use the system-defined `temp` path in the server's system properties. If the data flow ever needs to use temporary space, be sure that it is pointing to a system volume or mount point that has higher I/O throughput. Setting this is especially important when dealing with large object binary data (either flowing through your data flow or through the use of the Import or Export Column transformations) because BLOB data takes up considerably more space than standard number or character data types.

Leave RunInOptimizedMode as True

`RunInOptimizedMode` will help performance by removing columns from execution trees with leaf components (such as destinations or other transformations that terminate a pipeline) where a column is not used in the leaf component. This does *not* mean that columns are removed from other execution trees if a column is no longer needed after already being used in an earlier transformation. This does mean that you should still apply the principle mentioned earlier of removing columns from components that have asynchronous outputs not used downstream in a data flow.

Tuning Buffers

Two advanced properties of the data flow enable you to tune the size and number of rows that are in the allocated buffers. These settings, the `DefaultBufferMaxRows` and `DefaultBufferSize`, apply to all of the different buffers in a data flow, not just a single buffer type for one of the execution trees.

Essentially, the `DefaultBufferMaxRows` is defaulted to 10,000, which means that no single buffer can have more than 10,000 rows. However, this may not be optimal if your average row width is very small, because the buffers will be small, and in total there will be many more buffers for the execution trees to manage. So, in these cases, you should consider revising this number upward and testing performance.

The `DefaultBufferSize` is also a threshold setting specifying the number of bytes that a single buffer cannot exceed. If the max row setting multiplied by the width of a single row is greater than this value, then the number of rows used in the buffer will be reduced to be under this limitation. For example, if the `DefaultBufferMaxRows` is set to 10,000 and the `DefaultBufferSize` is set to 10,485,760 and a single row is 1,200 bytes, then the calculation of max rows (10,000) times row width (1,200) equates 12,000,000, which is greater than the `DefaultBufferSize` (10,485,760). So, the pipeline engine would scale back the count of rows in the buffers so that this threshold would not be exceeded.

An excellent treatment on this topic is the Microsoft white paper titled "Integration Services: Performance Tuning Techniques" (`www.microsoft.com/technet/prodtechnol/sql/2005/ssisperf.mspx`). Note that there is no magical formula that determines how to set and balance these properties. It is a matter of testing, because each transformation that is used in a data flow is affected differently by the size and row count in the buffers. Buffer size and row counts do have an effect on batching rows into a destination, which is discussed in the next section.

Optimizing Destinations

To optimize a destination, the first thing you should attempt to understand is the destination's impact on the package performance. It is not always the case that your data flow is slow because the destination cannot consume the rows fast enough to keep up. At times, it may just be that the data flow cannot pass the rows fast enough to the destination. To understand which case you have, perform the following test:

1. Run your data flow and capture the execution time.

2. Remove the destinations and replace them with Row Count transformations. Then, re-run your data flow and capture the execution time.

If the execution times of these two tests are identical (or very close), then your data flow cannot send rows fast enough to the destinations. If the second run of the data flow is a lot faster, then your destinations are impacting your data flow performance, and you should look at optimizing those destinations. Some optimizations for the OLE DB Destination adapter are discussed later in this chapter.

Here are a few other generalities when considering scaling your data flow destinations.

Database Growth

With SQL Server, when the underlying files reach a certain saturation point, the server will pause operations and grow the files. This is a problem if you or your DBA are not performing file-management operations to ensure that the file growth does not happen during peak hours or during ETL operations. Since ETL and other data processing operations perform bulk data inserting, it makes database growth more possible during these times. If you see your destinations chugging along and all of a sudden they pause for a long period of time, then it may be caused by a database growth process (or a locking/blocking condition).

For SQL Server, be sure to set your destination database `Auto Shrink` setting to `False`; otherwise, the files will shrink, and then more space will have to be re-allocated, which takes time.

Consider Dropping and Re-creating Indexes on Destination Tables

When records are inserted into a relational table (or updated) and the table has indexes, the engine has to reorganize the underlying indexes before the commit process is complete. This can add significant overhead to your data flow destinations.

To understand the overall impact of the indexes, in your test environment, drop all the indexes on the destination table and rerun the data flow, which will show you the delta of change and impact of the indexes.

A very common optimization technique for bulk operations is to first drop the indexes on the destination, run the data load, and then re-create the indexes. It is more often than not faster to drop and re-create the indexes, rather than to insert the records with the indexes in place and force the relational engine to manage the changes.

SQL Server 2005 Partition Tables

Although it is possible to insert partitioned tables directly into SQL Server 2005, this does come with relational engine overhead. A good approach to deal with partitioned tables is to have your destinations insert into a separate table, and then have the partitioned table consume the secondary table. You could also first separate out a partition from the partitioned table, drop the index, load the table, re-create the indexes, and then include the table back into the partitioned table as a partition. This is the approach that the Project REAL solution takes. The code is available and this approach is written up in the paper titled "Project REAL: Business Intelligence ETL Design Practices," which is available at `www.microsoft.com/technet/prodtechnol/sql/2005/realetldp.mspx`.

OLE DB Destination Optimization

The most common destination adapter used to insert data into a relational database is the OLE DB Destination adapter. This is because an ADO.NET destination adapter does not exist out-of-the-box. This destination adapter has several features that control what tables to insert the data into, and how that data is being inserted. Figure 12-11 shows the OLE DB Destination Editor.

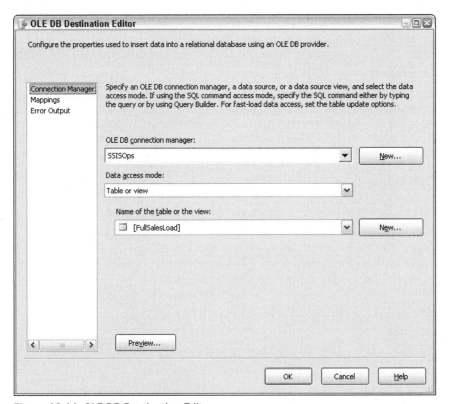

Figure 12-11: OLE DB Destination Editor

The OLE DB Destination settings shown in Figure 12-11 are the default settings when configured to insert into a table. The Data access mode is set to the Table or view option and a table is selected. For the purpose of demonstration, this destination is used in the sample data flow shown in Figure 12-12.

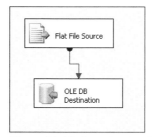

Figure 12-12: Sample data flow

This adapter is configured to land data into a table called `FullSalesLoad` in a database called `SSISOps`. The data flow in this example contains a single source file with two million rows, which is directly connected to the OLE DB Destination adapter referenced earlier. The problem with this destination in its default configuration is that each row is inserted separately into the table. Figure 12-13 shows a SQL Server Profile trace on the database while this destination is being landed.

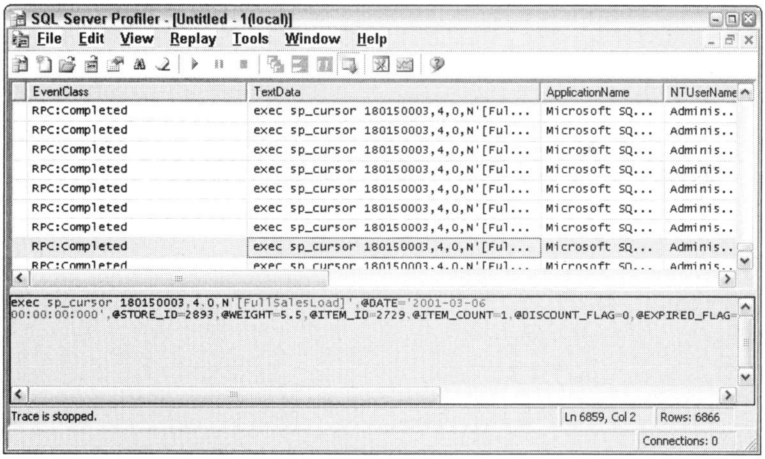

Figure 12-13: SQL Server Profile trace

This profiler session reveals that the insert statement would have run two million individual times and taken a couple hours if the package had not been stopped prematurely. Therefore, when dealing with large volumes and scalability, using the Table or view option for the Data access mode is not the right approach to take with the OLE DB Destination.

If you are using SQL Server as a destination, a better approach when configuring the OLE DB Destination adapter is to use the Table or view – fast load option of the Data access mode. This will allow the rows to be bulk inserted into a single batch or multiple batches. Figure 12-14 shows the options available when using the fast load feature.

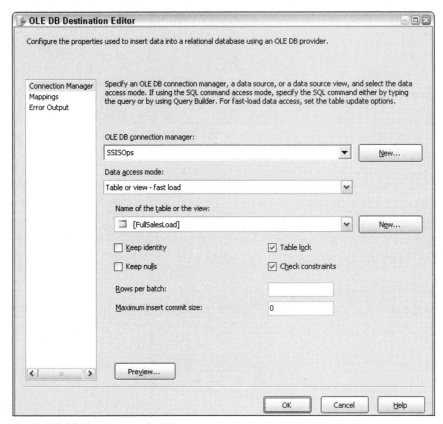

Figure 12-14: Fast load options

By choosing the fast load support, you are given several more advanced features to configure for the destination. These options align directly with the BULK INSERT statement in SQL Server, the mechanism actually used for the inserts. Following is a summary of the options:

❑ **Keep identity** — By selecting this option, you are able to insert explicit values into an IDENTITY column. This is identical to the IDENTITY INSERT function within TSQL.

❑ **Keep nulls** — Checking this option will ignore DEFAULT assignments in the destination table if a NULL value is inserted, which has the effect of helping performance, although negligible. However, this setting may adversely affect data integrity if default values were meant to avoid NULL values being present in certain columns.

❑ **Table lock** — Enabling this will put an exclusive lock on the destination table so that the insert process can optimize the inserts. However, this could cause locking or blocking problems if other processes are trying to update the same table simultaneously.

❑ **Check constraints** — With check constraints enabled, the insert will still go through the process of checking the constraints on the destination table. De-selecting this will increase performance if you are handling the value checks in the data flow. However, the constraints will be marked as not-trusted.

❑ **Rows per batch** — This entry simply provides an estimated source row count to help the bulk insert optimize the insert.

❑ **Maximum insert commit size** — The insert commit size drives the size of the batches that are inserted. When set to 0, the entire batch will be inserted; otherwise, this will dictate how many rows should be committed to a destination at one time. More details are provided later in this chapter, as this can help to optimize your destination insert by committing rows in smaller batches than the entire statement.

The bottom-line impact of these settings must be tested in your environment with your data and destination table. However, if you are looking to achieve the best scalability, begin by selecting the Keep nulls and Table lock options, and clearing the Check constraints option. Of course, these must be evaluated with the business rules behind you process. If at all possible, handle the constraints and NULL values in your data flow and allow the table to have an exclusive lock. The Maximum insert commit size setting can also have a profound impact on your inserts, and is discussed next.

Maximum Insert Commit Size

With large data volume processing in the multi-millions of records, you will be able to control the insert transaction batch sizes with the Maximum insert commit size entry setting (referenced in the prior section). Here are some considerations to make when setting this and testing various values for optimization:

❑ Any insert failures within a batch commit group will cause that entire batch to be unsuccessfully inserted.

❑ Leaving the max commit size at 0 will require the entire data set to be batched in one commit. This has a couple drawbacks. First of all, *if there is a failure, the entire data set will be rolled back* and no rows will be committed. Secondly, if you have indexes and foreign key relationships, the commit time can be very lengthy in a single large volume insert because the database must reorganize the indexes and check the foreign keys.

❑ A setting greater than 0 will not necessarily mean that the engine will batch that exact number of rows. *The commit size will be the lesser of the number of rows in this setting or the number of rows in the data flow being inserted.* For example, if you set the max commit size to 50,000 but your pipeline buffers only contain 9,000 rows, then only 9,000 rows will be committed at a time. Similarly, if you set the commit size to 7,000 and you have 9,000 rows in your buffers, the first batch for every buffer will be 7,000 rows and the second will only be 2,000 rows.

❑ For every commit batch, the database engine will perform the index reorganization and check any foreign keys, therefore reducing the overall performance impact if this all happened at once.

❑ If your destination table doesn't have indexes, foreign keys, or constraints, the commit time will be very rapid and negligible no matter what you set the commit size to be. The only difference is that a 0 setting will be an all-or-nothing insert.

Consider these two situations when evaluating this setting.

1. If you set the max commit size, but do not want to lose all the rows in the batch for one row that fails, you can redirect the batch, and then do a second OLE DB Destination that inserts the data one row at a time. Figure 12-15 shows how this would look.

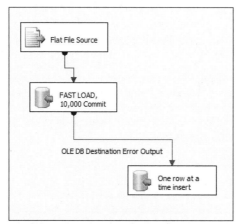

Figure 12-15: Redirecting the batch and then doing a second OLE DB Destination

2. To achieve much larger commit batches, you will need to modify the DefaultBufferMaxRows and DefaultBufferSize settings. A high-level review explained these settings earlier. Simple data flows that have limited row widths can greatly benefit by increasing the number of rows in a data flow buffer, which will allow you to set the insert commit size higher.

Package Execution Principles

Scalability is also a matter of designing a package execution strategy that minimizes resource impact (memory, processor, and I/O capabilities) on the servers that need resources for other purposes or have little resources, and leveraging the servers that have resource availability or that can handle the impact load from package execution. When it comes to where a package should be executed, there is no absolute answer. However, there are general principles that can direct one architecture design over another.

Package Storage Location versus Execution Location

First of all, when it comes to running a package, there is a difference between where a package is run and where that package is stored. A package can be stored as a file and put in a file system folder, or a package can be loaded into the MSDB system database in SQL Server 2005. Either way, when the package is executed, the storage location is merely where the metadata of that package lives. The package is loaded from that source location through an execution method and run on the machine where the execution is kicked off. In other words, if you are running a package through the command line DTExec, the package will run on the machine where DTExec is called, not the place where the SSIS package is stored.

Figure 12-16 shows the storage location server on the left and the execution server on the right. The package is executed on the server on the right, where the resources are available.

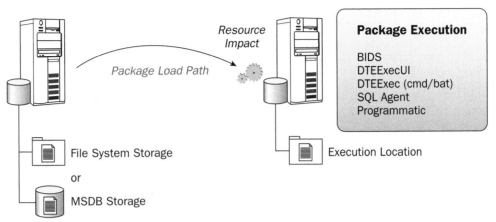

Figure 12-16: Package storage and execution location

When it comes to knowing on which servers to install the Integration Services service, it's simply a matter of identifying the servers that will be running the packages, not necessarily the servers that are storing the packages, unless they will also be running packages.

SSIS packages can be executed in several ways, the most common being the command line executable DTExec or through SQL Agent. Wherever the command line is executed or the SQL Agent job is started, that is where the package will be loaded and run. The same principle applies to executing a package through the debugger in BIDS, or running a package with DTExecUI. When you run the package through these UI mechanisms, the local resources on the machine (perhaps a development machine or laptop) will be used to handle the execution. The following sections look at the impact of a package that contains at least one data flow on the source, destination, and execution machines.

Execute SQL Task and Bulk Insert Task Execution

Although a package may be run on any machine with the SSIS service (or really, that has the SSIS executables and DLLs), this isn't necessarily the place where all the work is being done in the package. For example, if you run an Execute SQL Task in a package and kick the package off on a different server than where the Execute SQL Task connection is defined, then the SQL statement is run where the connection is configured, not on the SSIS execution machine. To be sure, the workflow coordination will still be handled on your SSIS execution machine, but the actual SQL code would be run on a different machine.

For the Execute SQL Task and Bulk Insert Task, the SQL code or BCP command is executed on the machine that the connection specifies. This is different from the Data Flow Task, which runs on the machine where the package is executed.

Package Execution and the Data Flow

For your packages that have data flows (which is probably most of your packages), you should understand what happens to the data based on where you execute that package (with the embedded data flow). Additionally, understanding where the data flow execution impact will be dictates where you decide to run your packages.

The data flow impact on the package execution server involves the resources needed to manage the data buffers, the data conversion requirements as data is imported from sources, the memory involved in the lookup cache, the temporary memory and processor utilization required for the Sort and Aggregate transformations, and so on. Essentially, any transformation logic contained in the data flows will be handled on the server where the package is executed.

The following examples are common configurations for where data is sourced, the destination location, and where packages are executed. Obviously, data flows can be varied and complex with multiple sources and destinations each, so this simplification provides the framework with single-source locations and single-destination locations.

Packages Executed on the Source or Destination Servers

The most common example is when a package (that contains a data flow) is executed on either the source or destination server, assuming they are separate.

Source Server Package Execution

Figure 12-17 shows the data path and impact on the environment when the package is executed on the machine where the source data is located.

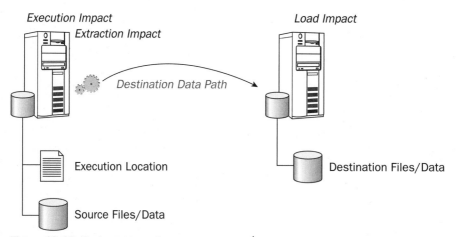

Figure 12-17: Package execution on source server

The source server will both provide the extracted data and handle the data flow transformation logic, and the destination server will require any data load overhead such as disk I/O for files or database inserts or index reorganization.

The benefits of this approach include the following:

❏ There is decreased impact on the destination server, where potential users are querying.

❏ Data flow buffers are loaded rapidly, given that the location of the source files and package execution is local and involves no network I/O.

❏ The impact on the destination server is limited, which is useful for destination servers that have 24/7 use or the SSIS process runs often.

Following are the drawbacks of this approach:

❏ The impact on the source server's resources, which may affect applications and users on the source server

❏ Potential reduced performance of the data flow destination adapter and the inability to use the SQL Destination adapter, which requires the package be executed on the same server as the package

Destination Server Package Execution

Similar to the impact when a package is run on a source server, running a package on the destination server, as Figure 12-18 demonstrates, will have similar benefits and drawbacks, just reversed.

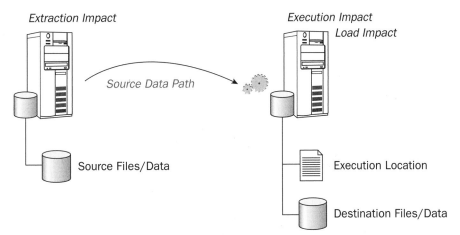

Figure 12-18: Package execution on destination server

Following are benefits of executing a package on a destination server:

❏ Limited impact on your source server if it is running other critical tasks

❏ Potential performance benefits for data inserts, especially since the SQL Destination component can now be used

❏ Licensing consolidation if your destination server is also running SQL Server 2005

One drawback of this approach is that it has a heavy impact on the destination server, which may affect users querying the server.

This approach is very useful if you have users querying and using the destination during the day, and your SSIS processing requirements can be handled through nightly processes.

Stand-alone SSIS Servers

An alternate execution option is to run your SSIS packages on a second or third server.

In Figure 12-19, an SSIS package is executed on a second server, and in this diagram, both the source and destination are on the same machine.

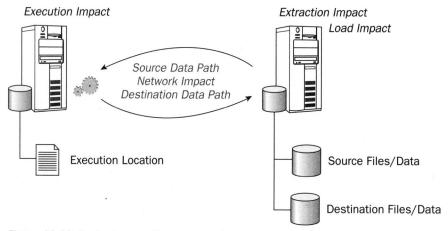

Figure 12-19: Package execution on secondary server

As you can see, this is not the ideal scenario, since the data would need to travel over the network to the second server, be processed, and then travel back to the same original machine, creating potentially high network utilization, depending on the volume. However, it would reduce the resource impact on the data source and destination server.

It makes more sense to use a stand-alone SSIS server if your sources and destinations are not on the same physical machines. Figure 12-20 highlights this architecture.

In this case, the impact on both the source and destination machines is reduced because the SSIS server would handle the data flow transformation logic. This architecture also provides a viable SSIS application server approach, where the machine can handle all the SSIS processing packages no matter where the data is coming from and going to. The drawbacks to this approach are in the ability to optimize the source extraction and destination import, increased network I/O (since the data has to travel over the wire two times), as well as licensing.

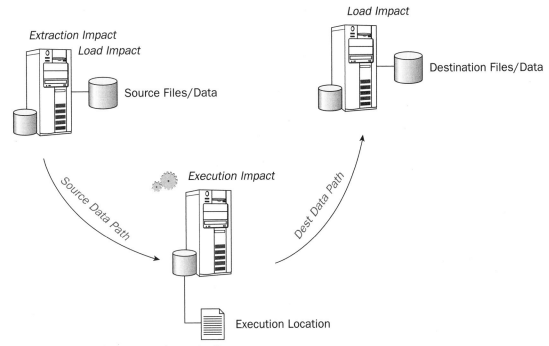

Figure 12-20: Package execution on tertiary server

Distributed Package Execution

No matter where a package is stored, it is loaded and run on the server that invokes the execution. This means that if you need to achieve distributed execution for your packages, you must have a mechanism for kicking off the packages on different servers. Distributed execution just means that you are implementing a scale-out approach to your SSIS architecture. This can be very valuable for achieving large scalability that can expand. It can also reduce hardware costs, considering that scale-up servers are very expensive.

A distributed execution needs a central server that houses the packages and has the application that coordinates the execution on the remote machines. Each remote server that will be performing the executions needs a scheduling agent that runs the packages. Figure 12-21 shows what this server architecture would look like.

This scheduling server can use a variety of mechanisms that actually kick off packages on other servers with associated applications, often called *agents*. Here are a few of the application and agent possibilities:

❑ **SQL Server Agent** — The most common approach to distributed execution is using SQL Agent and either leveraging the master-child SQL Agent capabilities, or just calling jobs to kick off on remote servers with the sp_start_job stored procedure. SQL Agent jobs are asynchronous, so you would lose the ability to know when the remote job is complete, but it makes for an easy-to-implement solution.

❑ **SQL Procedures with the Execute SQL Task** — When you run the system extended procedure, xp_cmdshell, you are able to kick off an executable on the server where the stored procedure is run. By using this procedure to call a command line with DTExec, you could have a master SSIS package on the central server that is running several Execute SQL Tasks with connections to remote SQL Servers. Each Execute SQL Task could run the xp_cmdshell, and the package would actually run on the remote server. The xp_cmdshell is synchronous, so the Execute SQL Task would wait until the child package was finished executing on the remote server before completing. This would enable control flow constraints to be used. Security must be evaluated with this choice.

❑ **Application Programming** — Packages can be run programmatically by using the load and execute methods in the object model. Therefore, it is possible to create applications on the central server and remote server that communicate and coordinate package execution, such as leveraging .NET remoting technologies.

❑ **Queuing Technologies** — MSMQ or SQL Server 2005 Service Broker can also be a mechanism to execute packages on remote servers. Capturing both messages that define the package to execute and the execution details can inform agents that run the packages.

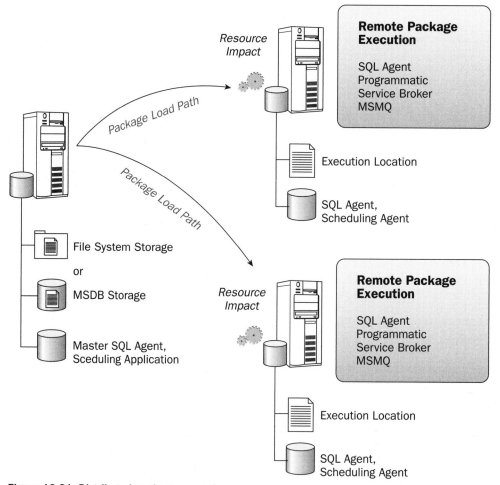

Figure 12-21: Distributed package execution

Summary

When it comes to SSIS scalability, there is no silver bullet. However, there are several ways to isolate performance limitations and identify impacting tasks. Furthermore, since SSIS is a platform, there can be many ways to design the same process. This makes package design important in achieving scalability. Know when and where to use SQL code, and when to employ the data flow.

The critical aspect of SSIS when it comes to scalability is optimizing the data flow, which boils down to memory management and destination optimization. Ensure that your designs are leveraging the features and functionality of SSIS in the right creative ways that limit common bottlenecks such as blocking transformations and large Lookup caches.

Finally, choose a package architecture that considers your source and destination servers and the impact that the data flow will have on those, and, if needed, create a distributed or scaled-out execution architecture. Applying these principles and the others found in this book will take you on the way to designing and implementing stable and scalable SSIS solutions that meet the demanding business requirements for your data processing.

Index

P